INJUSTICE

GODS AMONG US: YEAR THREE
VOLUME 2

INJU
GODS AMON

Brian Buccellato Ray Fawkes
Writers

Bruno Redondo Mike S. Miller
Sergio Davila Xermanico Juan Albarran Pete Woods
Artists

J. Nanjan Rex Lokus Alejandro Sanchez
Colorists

Wes Abbott
Letterer

Aaron Lopresti and Rex Lokus
Cover Artists

STICE

U S : YEAR THREE
VOLUME 2

SUPERMAN Created by JERRY SIEGEL and JOE SHUSTER.
By Special Arrangement with the Jerry Siegel Family.

BASED ON THE VIDEO GAME INJUSTICE: GODS AMONG US

Jim Chadwick Editor – Original Series
Jeb Woodard Group Editor – Collected Editions
Paul Santos Editor – Collected Edition
Steve Cook Design Director-Books
Louis Prandi Publication Design

Bob Harras Senior VP – Editor-in-Chief, DC Comics

Diane Nelson President
Dan DiDio and Jim Lee Co-Publishers
Geoff Johns Chief Creative Officer
Amit Desai Senior VP – Marketing & Global Franchise Management
Nairi Gardiner Senior VP – Finance
Sam Ades VP – Digital Marketing
Bobbie Chase VP – Talent Development
Mark Chiarello Senior VP – Art, Design & Collected Editions
John Cunningham VP – Content Strategy
Anne DePies VP – Strategy Planning & Reporting
Don Falletti VP – Manufacturing Operations
Lawrence Ganem VP – Editorial Administration & Talent Relations
Alison Gill Senior VP – Manufacturing & Operations
Hank Kanalz Senior VP – Editorial Strategy & Administration
Jay Kogan VP – Legal Affairs
Derek Maddalena Senior VP – Sales & Business Development
Jack Mahan VP – Business Affairs
Dan Miron VP – Sales Planning & Trade Development
Nick Napolitano VP – Manufacturing Administration
Carol Roeder VP – Marketing
Eddie Scannell VP – Mass Account & Digital Sales
Courtney Simmons Senior VP – Publicity & Communications
Jim (Ski) Sokolowski VP – Comic Book Specialty & Newsstand Sales
Sandy Yi Senior VP – Global Franchise Management

INJUSTICE: GODS AMONG US: YEAR THREE VOLUME 2

Published by DC Comics.Compilation and all new material Copyright
© 2016 DC Comics. All Rights Reserved.

Originally published in single magazine form in INJUSTICE: GODS
AMONG US: YEAR THREE 8-12, INJUSTICE: GODS AMONG US: YEAR
THREE ANNUAL 1. Copyright © 2015 DC Comics. All Rights Reserved.
All characters, their distinctive likenesses and related elements
featured in this publication are trademarks of DC Comics. The stories,
characters and incidents featured in this publication are entirely
fictional. DC Comics does not read or accept unsolicited ideas, stories
or artwork.

DC Comics, 2900 W. Alameda Ave, Burbank, CA. 91505
Printed by RR Donnelley, Salem, VA, USA. 3/25/16. First Printing.
ISBN: 978-1-4012-6129-0

Library of Congress Cataloging-in-Publication Data is Available.

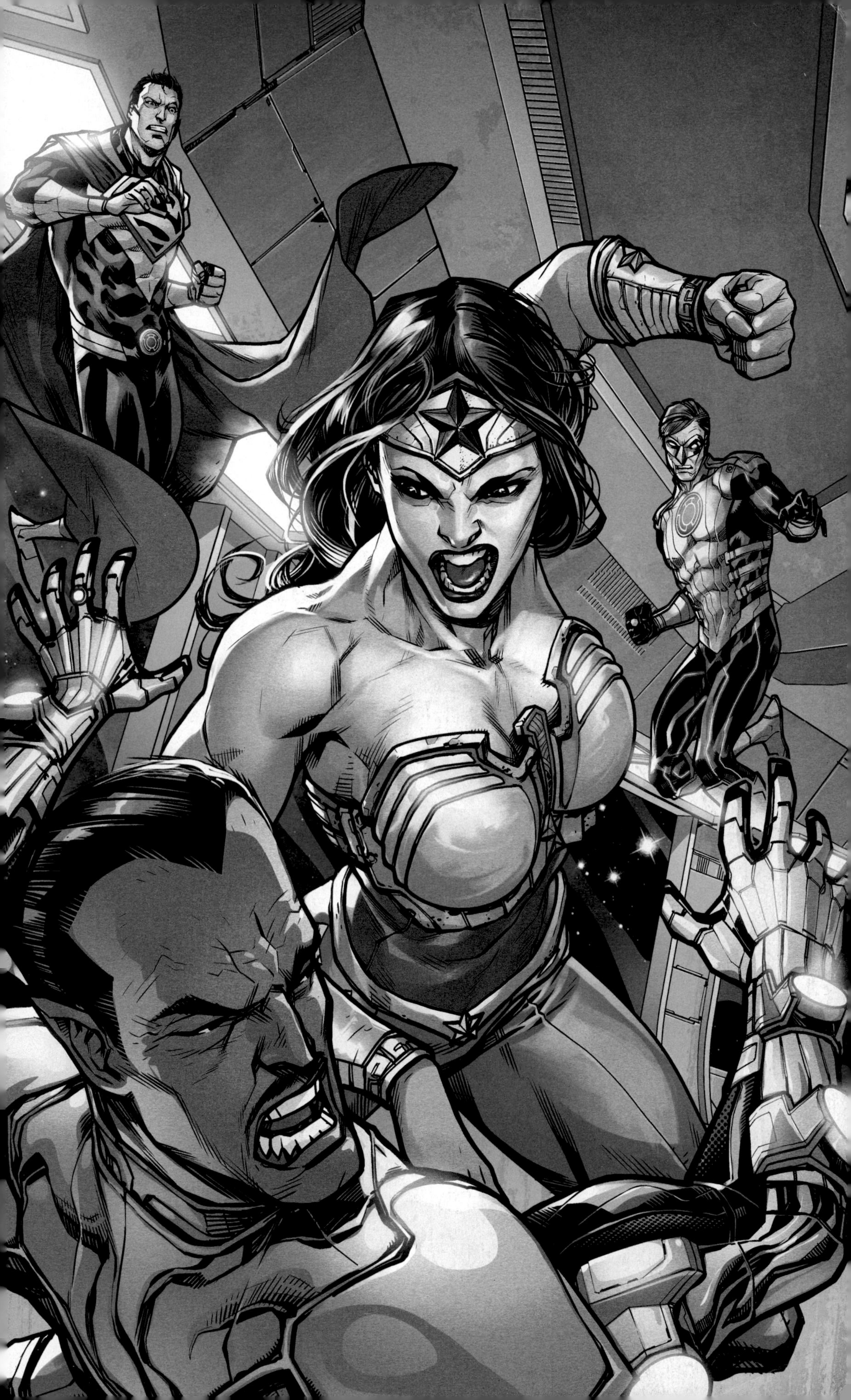

"Awakenings" Mike S. Miller, Sergio Davila, Juan Albarran - Artists
J. Nanjan and Rex Lokus - Colorists
Cover Art by Neil Googe & J. Nanjan

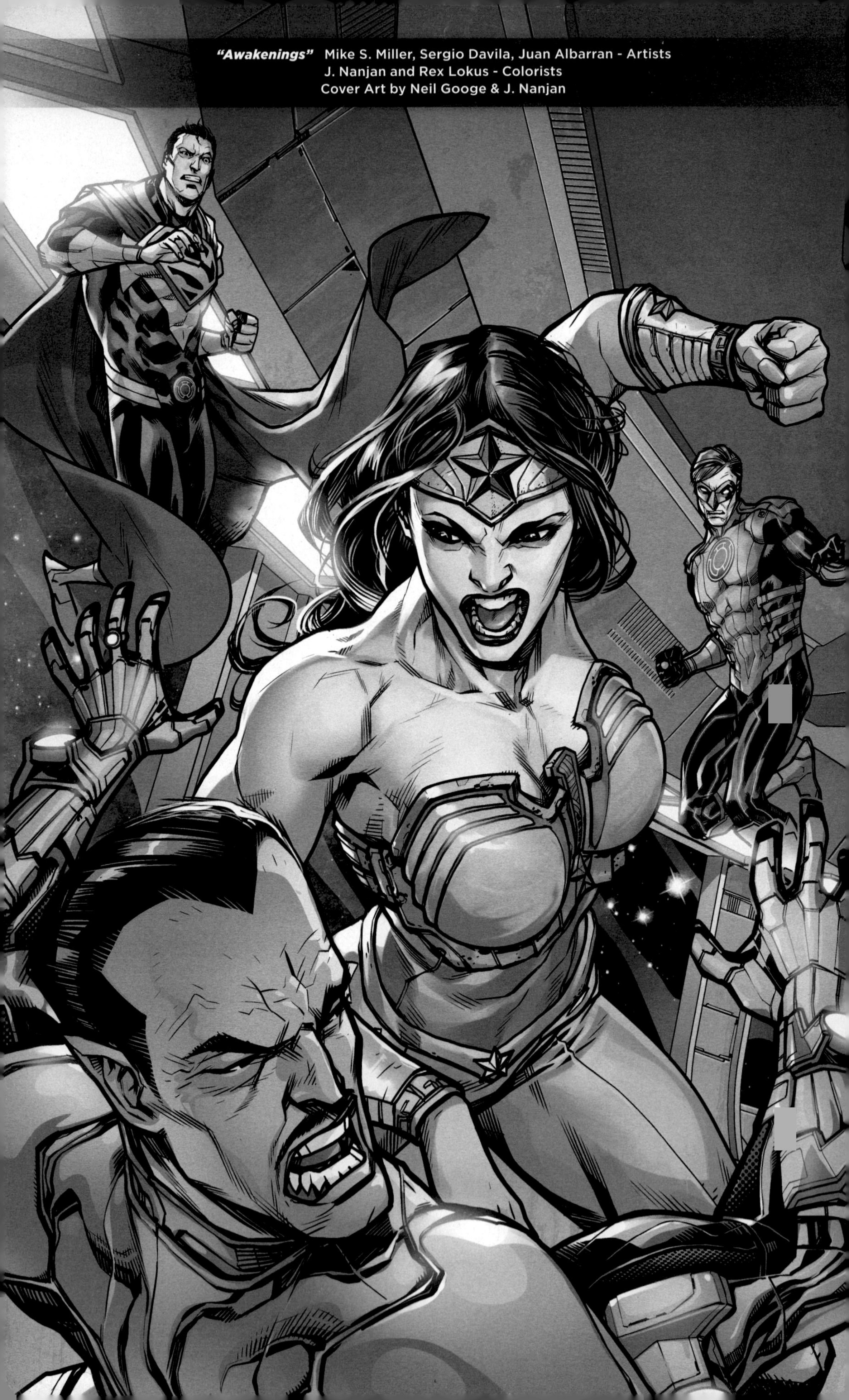

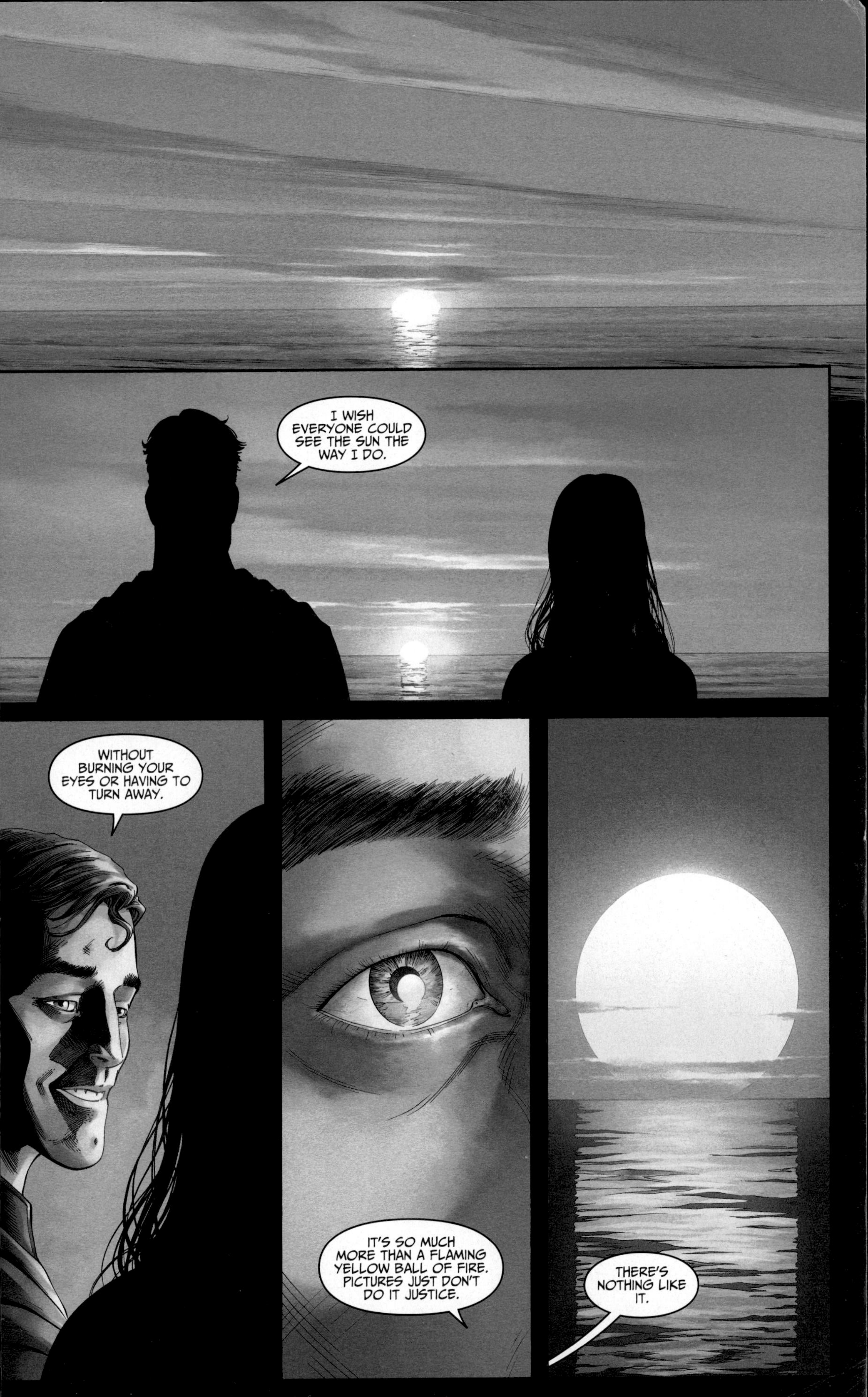
I WISH EVERYONE COULD SEE THE SUN THE WAY I DO.
WITHOUT BURNING YOUR EYES OR HAVING TO TURN AWAY.
IT'S SO MUCH MORE THAN A FLAMING YELLOW BALL OF FIRE. PICTURES JUST DON'T DO IT JUSTICE.
THERE'S NOTHING LIKE IT.

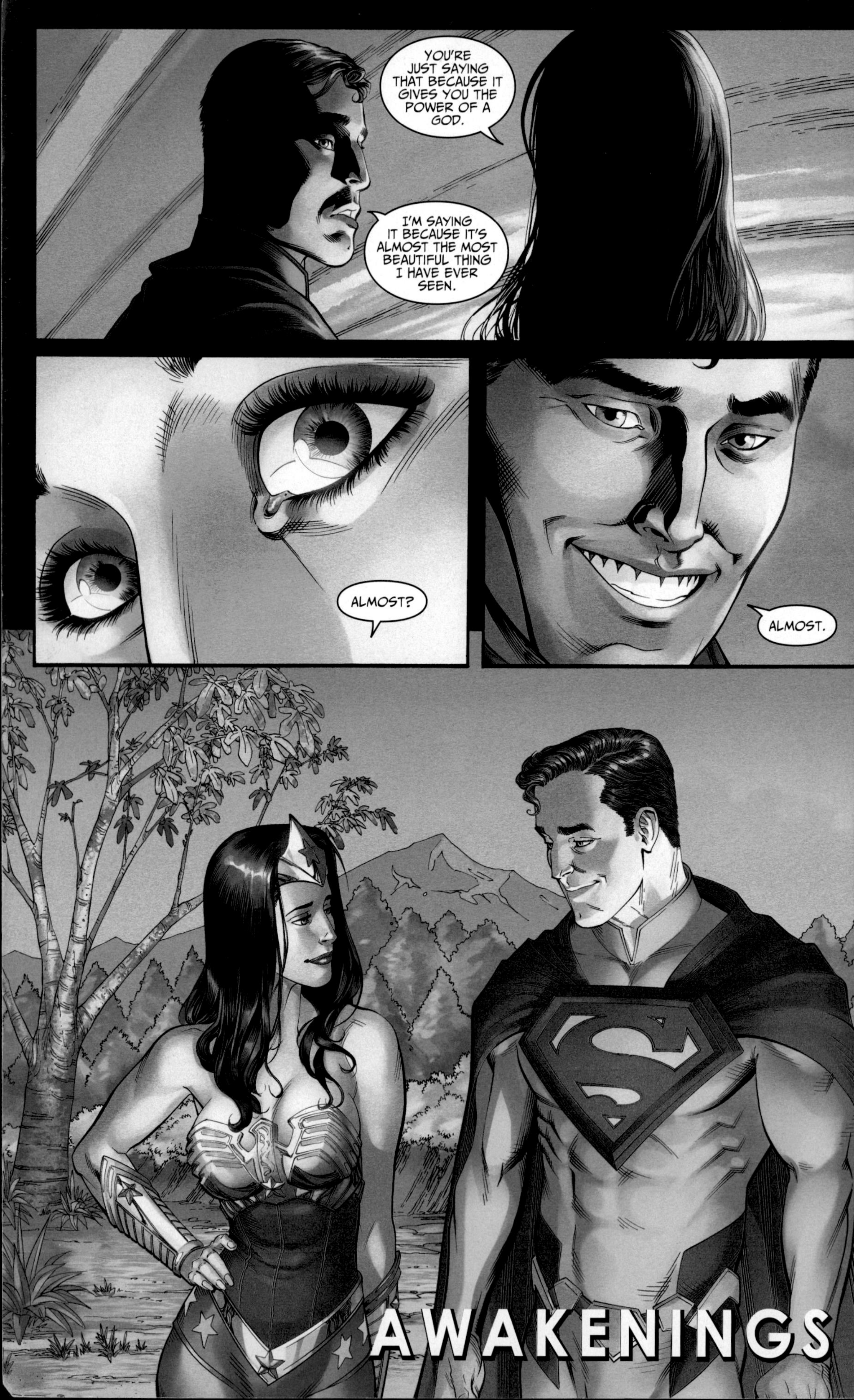
YOU'RE JUST SAYING THAT BECAUSE IT GIVES YOU THE POWER OF A GOD.
I'M SAYING IT BECAUSE IT'S ALMOST THE MOST BEAUTIFUL THING I HAVE EVER SEEN.
ALMOST?
ALMOST.
AWAKENINGS

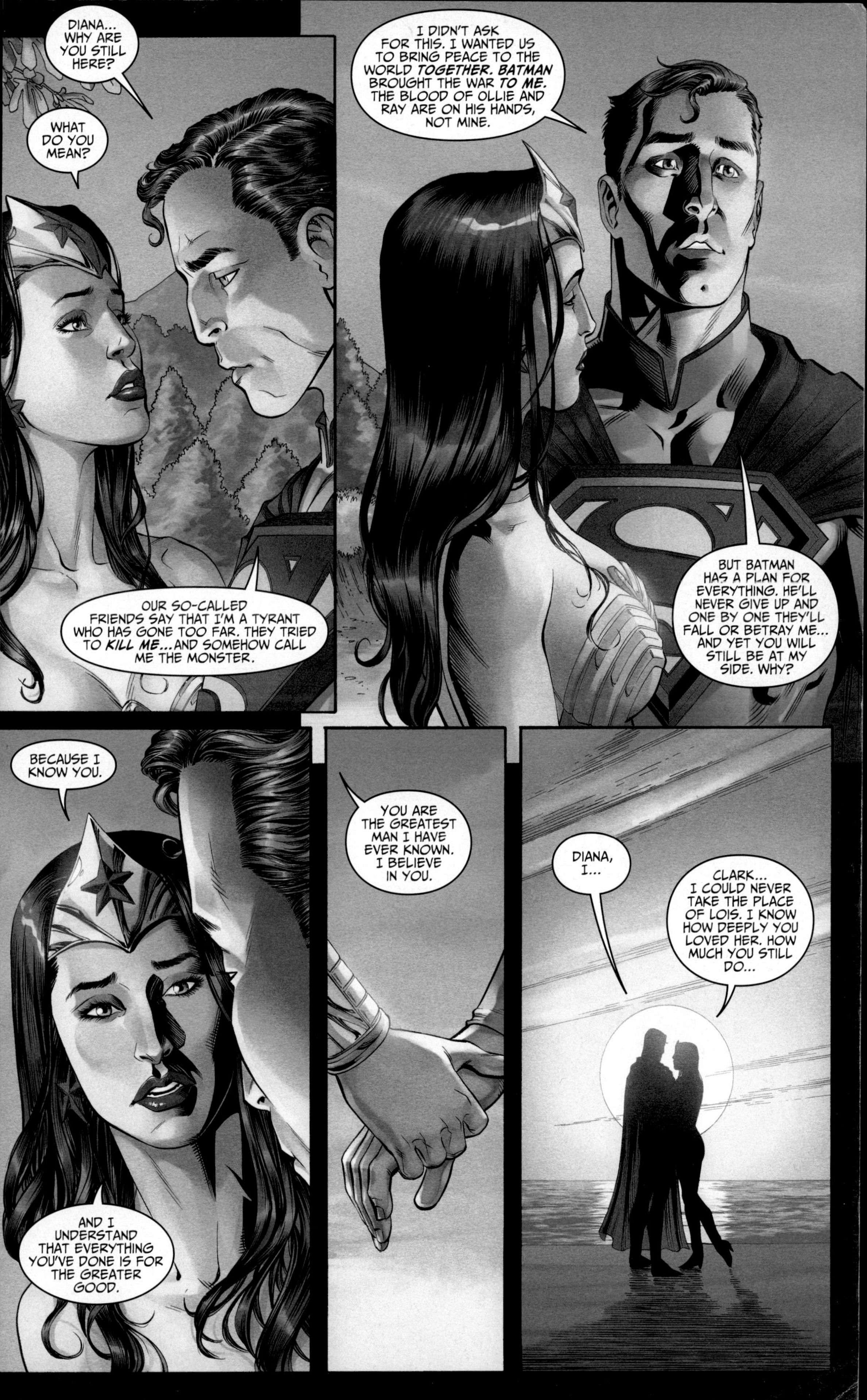
DIANA... WHY ARE YOU STILL HERE?
WHAT DO YOU MEAN?
OUR SO-CALLED FRIENDS SAY THAT I'M A TYRANT WHO HAS GONE TOO FAR. THEY TRIED TO KILL ME... AND SOMEHOW CALL ME THE MONSTER.
I DIDN'T ASK FOR THIS. I WANTED US TO BRING PEACE TO THE WORLD TOGETHER. BATMAN BROUGHT THE WAR TO ME. THE BLOOD OF OLLIE AND RAY ARE ON HIS HANDS, NOT MINE.
BUT BATMAN HAS A PLAN FOR EVERYTHING. HE'LL NEVER GIVE UP AND ONE BY ONE THEY'LL FALL OR BETRAY ME... AND YET YOU WILL STILL BE AT MY SIDE. WHY?
BECAUSE I KNOW YOU.
AND I UNDERSTAND THAT EVERYTHING YOU'VE DONE IS FOR THE GREATER GOOD.
YOU ARE THE GREATEST MAN I HAVE EVER KNOWN. I BELIEVE IN YOU.
DIANA, I...
CLARK... I COULD NEVER TAKE THE PLACE OF LOIS. I KNOW HOW DEEPLY YOU LOVED HER. HOW MUCH YOU STILL DO...

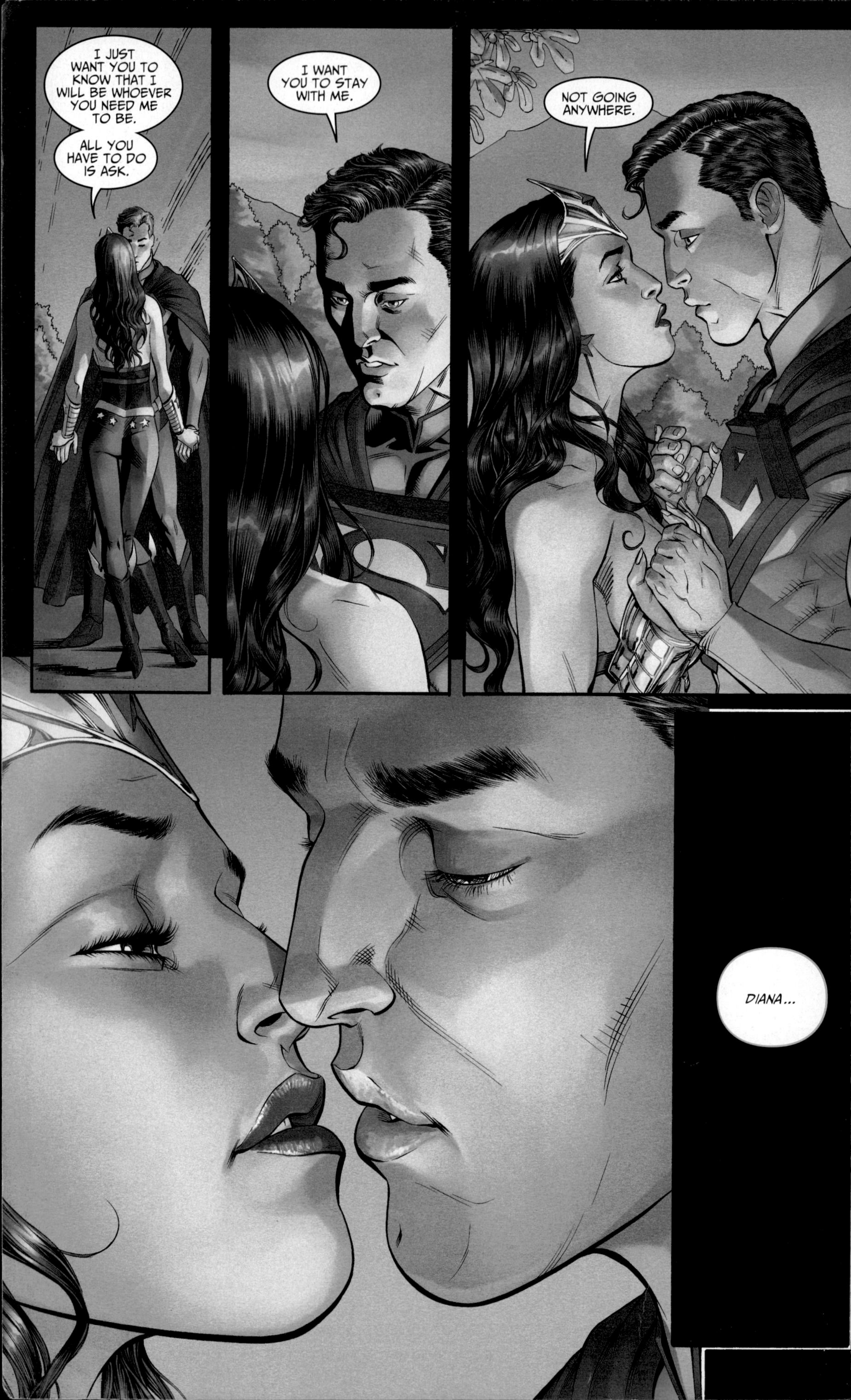
I JUST WANT YOU TO KNOW THAT I WILL BE WHOEVER YOU NEED ME TO BE.
ALL YOU HAVE TO DO IS ASK.
I WANT YOU TO STAY WITH ME.
NOT GOING ANYWHERE.
DIANA...

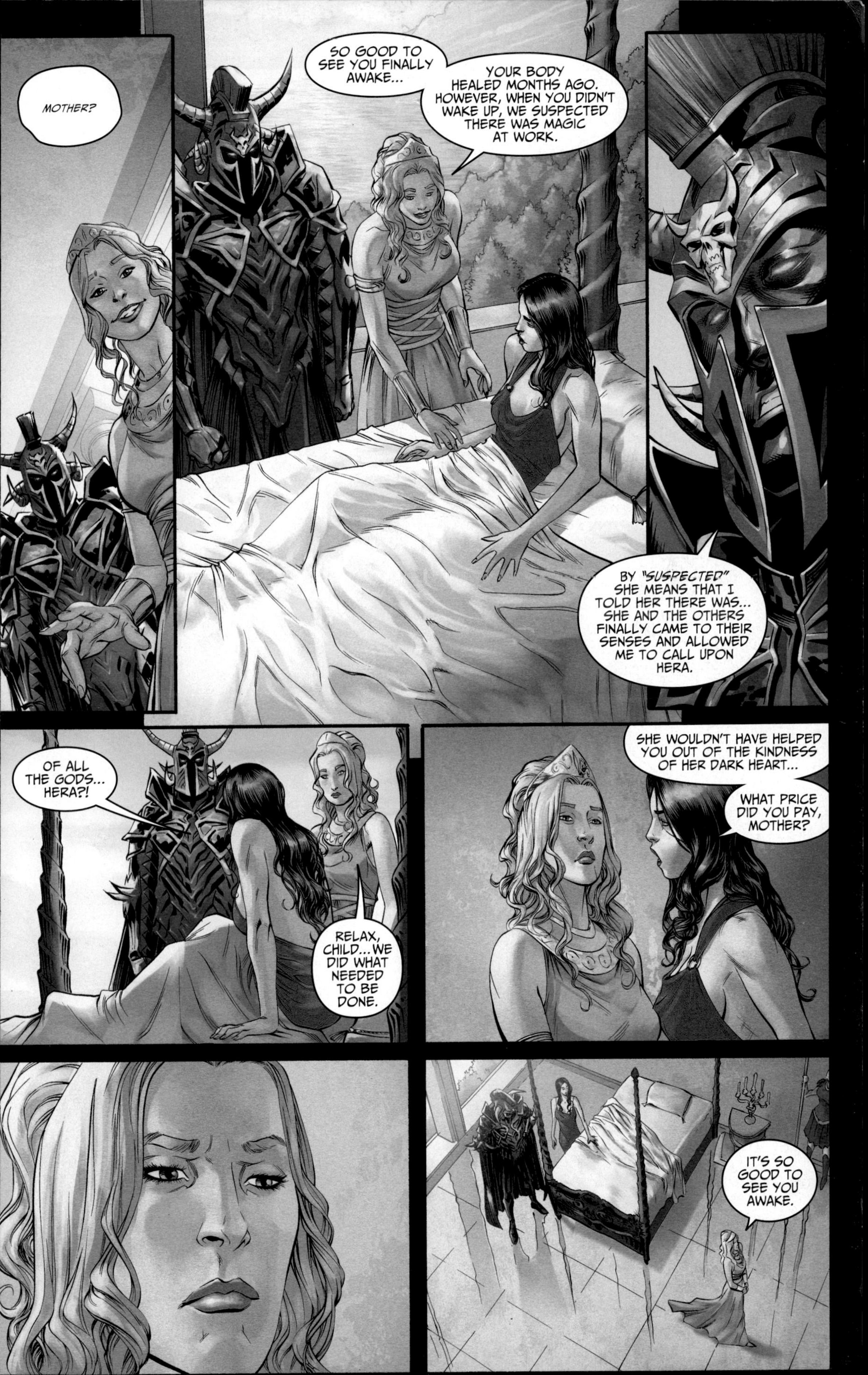
MOTHER?
SO GOOD TO SEE YOU FINALLY AWAKE...
YOUR BODY HEALED MONTHS AGO. HOWEVER, WHEN YOU DIDN'T WAKE UP, WE SUSPECTED THERE WAS MAGIC AT WORK.
BY "SUSPECTED" SHE MEANS THAT I TOLD HER THERE WAS... SHE AND THE OTHERS FINALLY CAME TO THEIR SENSES AND ALLOWED ME TO CALL UPON HERA.
OF ALL THE GODS... HERA?!
RELAX, CHILD...WE DID WHAT NEEDED TO BE DONE.
SHE WOULDN'T HAVE HELPED YOU OUT OF THE KINDNESS OF HER DARK HEART...
WHAT PRICE DID YOU PAY, MOTHER?
IT'S SO GOOD TO SEE YOU AWAKE.

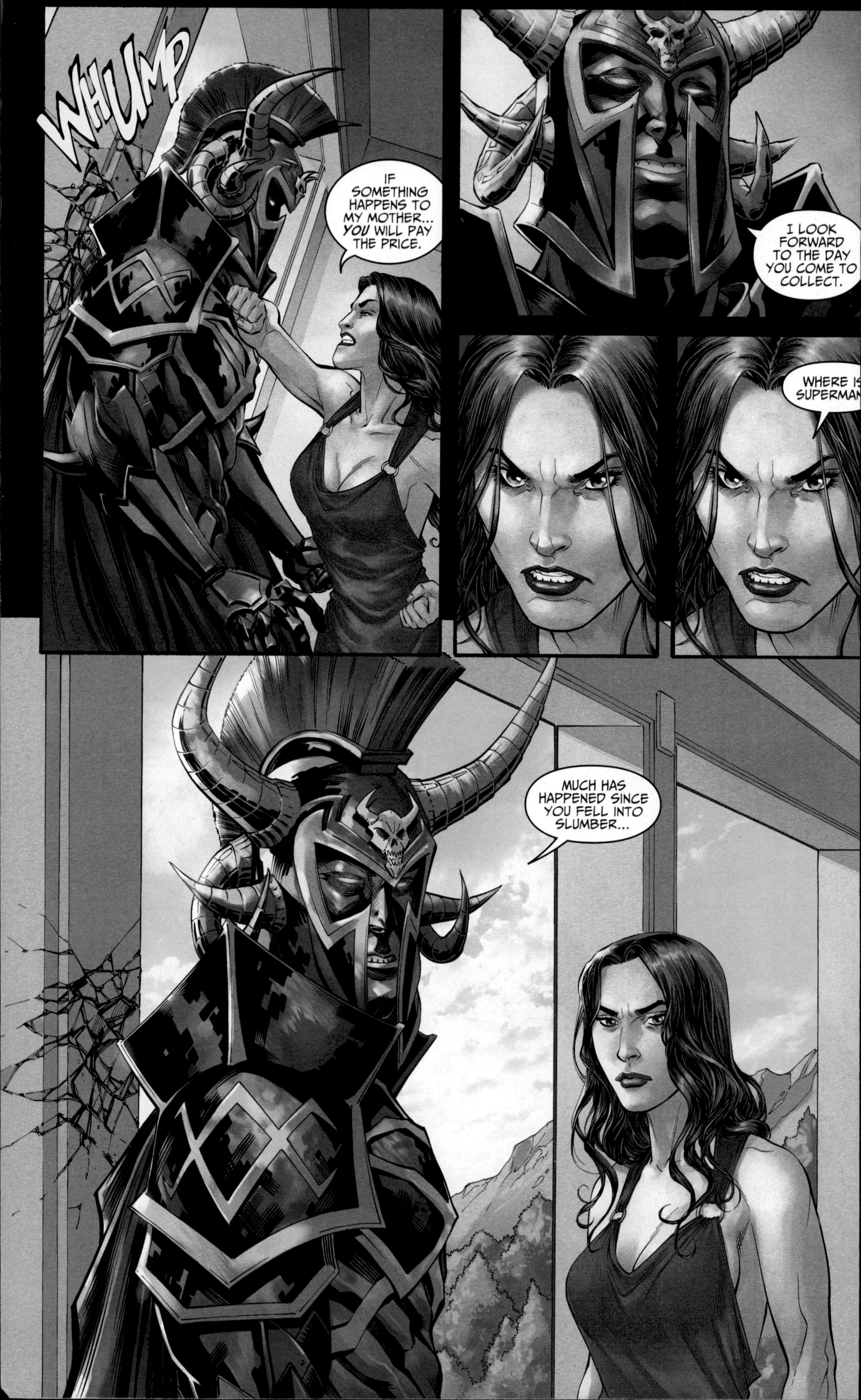
WHUMP
IF SOMETHING HAPPENS TO MY MOTHER... YOU WILL PAY THE PRICE.
I LOOK FORWARD TO THE DAY YOU COME TO COLLECT.
MUCH HAS HAPPENED SINCE YOU FELL INTO SLUMBER...

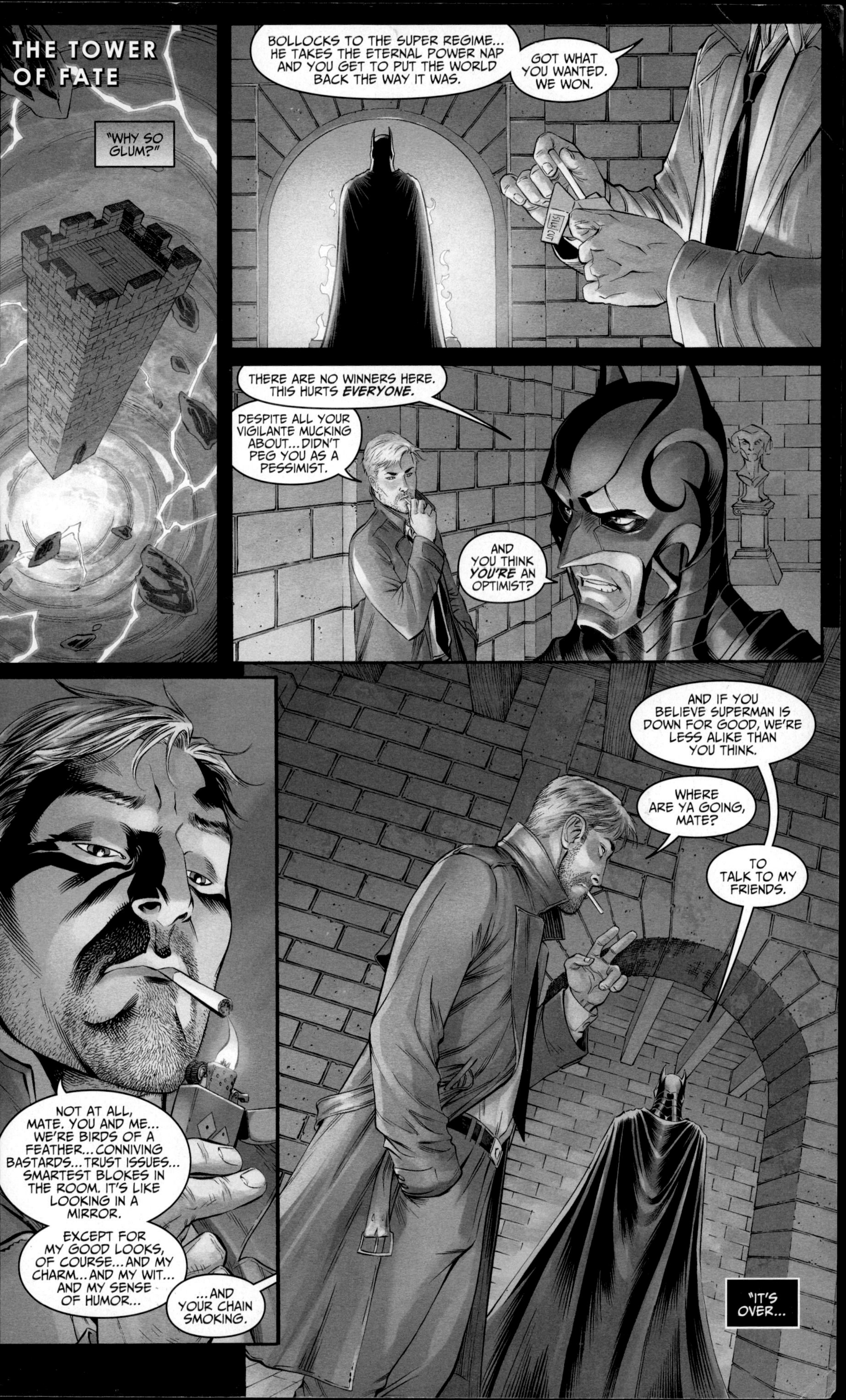
THE TOWER OF FATE
"WHY SO GLUM?"
BOLLOCKS TO THE SUPER REGIME... HE TAKES THE ETERNAL POWER NAP AND YOU GET TO PUT THE WORLD BACK THE WAY IT WAS.
GOT WHAT YOU WANTED. WE WON.
THERE ARE NO WINNERS HERE. THIS HURTS EVERYONE.
DESPITE ALL YOUR VIGILANTE MUCKING ABOUT...DIDN'T PEG YOU AS A PESSIMIST.
AND YOU THINK YOU'RE AN OPTIMIST?
NOT AT ALL, MATE. YOU AND ME... WE'RE BIRDS OF A FEATHER...CONNIVING BASTARDS...TRUST ISSUES... SMARTEST BLOKES IN THE ROOM. IT'S LIKE LOOKING IN A MIRROR.
EXCEPT FOR MY GOOD LOOKS, OF COURSE...AND MY CHARM...AND MY WIT... AND MY SENSE OF HUMOR...
...AND YOUR CHAIN SMOKING.
AND IF YOU BELIEVE SUPERMAN IS DOWN FOR GOOD, WE'RE LESS ALIKE THAN YOU THINK.
WHERE ARE YA GOING, MATE?
TO TALK TO MY FRIENDS.
"IT'S OVER...

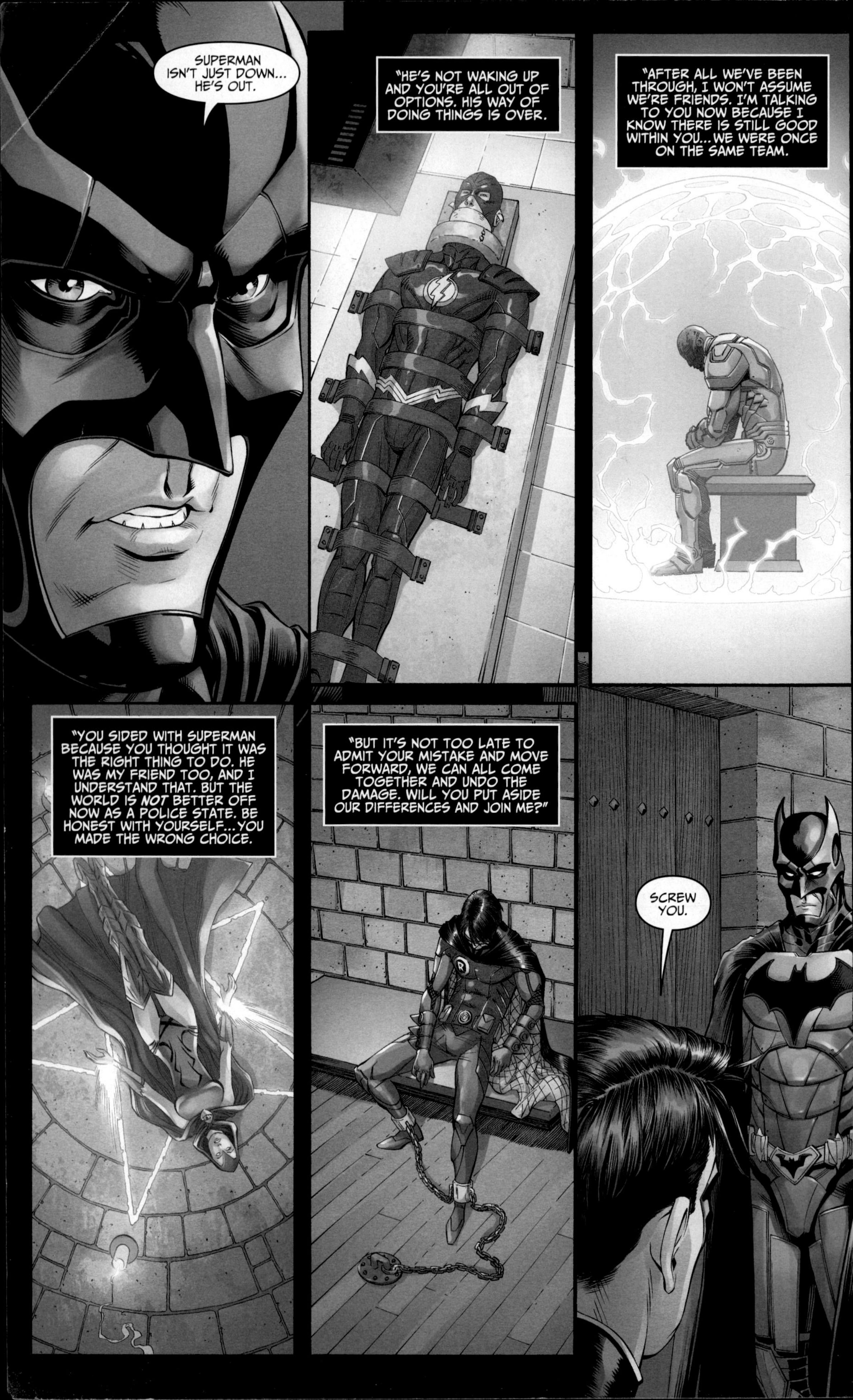
SUPERMAN ISN'T JUST DOWN... HE'S OUT.
"HE'S NOT WAKING UP AND YOU'RE ALL OUT OF OPTIONS. HIS WAY OF DOING THINGS IS OVER.
"AFTER ALL WE'VE BEEN THROUGH, I WON'T ASSUME WE'RE FRIENDS. I'M TALKING TO YOU NOW BECAUSE I KNOW THERE IS STILL GOOD WITHIN YOU...WE WERE ONCE ON THE SAME TEAM.
"YOU SIDED WITH SUPERMAN BECAUSE YOU THOUGHT IT WAS THE RIGHT THING TO DO. HE WAS MY FRIEND TOO, AND I UNDERSTAND THAT. BUT THE WORLD IS *NOT* BETTER OFF NOW AS A POLICE STATE. BE HONEST WITH YOURSELF...YOU MADE THE WRONG CHOICE.
"BUT IT'S NOT TOO LATE TO ADMIT YOUR MISTAKE AND MOVE FORWARD, WE CAN ALL COME TOGETHER AND UNDO THE DAMAGE. WILL YOU PUT ASIDE OUR DIFFERENCES AND JOIN ME?"
SCREW YOU.

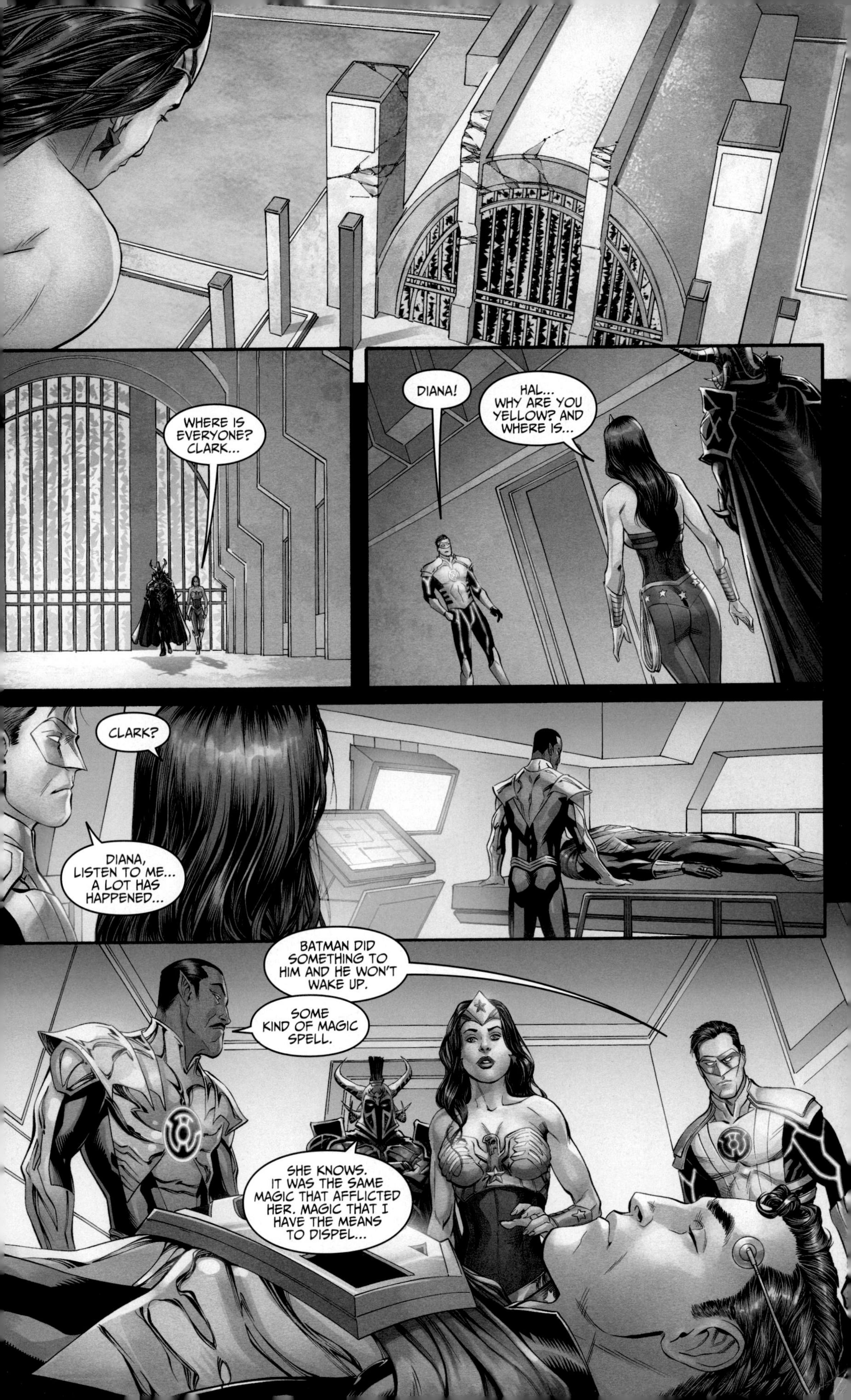
WHERE IS EVERYONE? CLARK...
DIANA!
HAL... WHY ARE YOU YELLOW? AND WHERE IS...
CLARK?
DIANA, LISTEN TO ME... A LOT HAS HAPPENED...
BATMAN DID SOMETHING TO HIM AND HE WON'T WAKE UP.
SOME KIND OF MAGIC SPELL.
SHE KNOWS. IT WAS THE SAME MAGIC THAT AFFLICTED HER. MAGIC THAT I HAVE THE MEANS TO DISPEL...

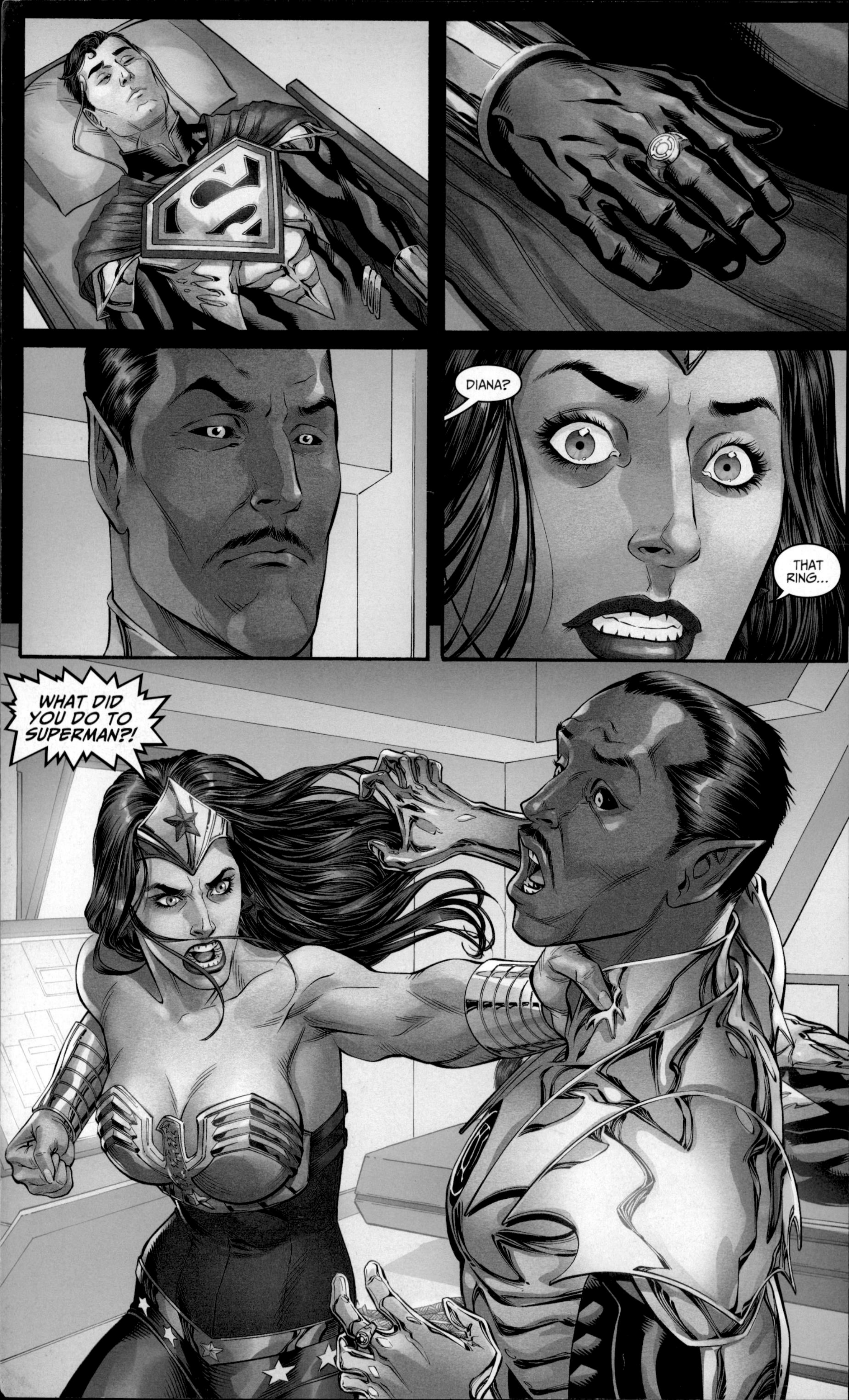
DIANA?
THAT RING...
WHAT DID YOU DO TO SUPERMAN?!

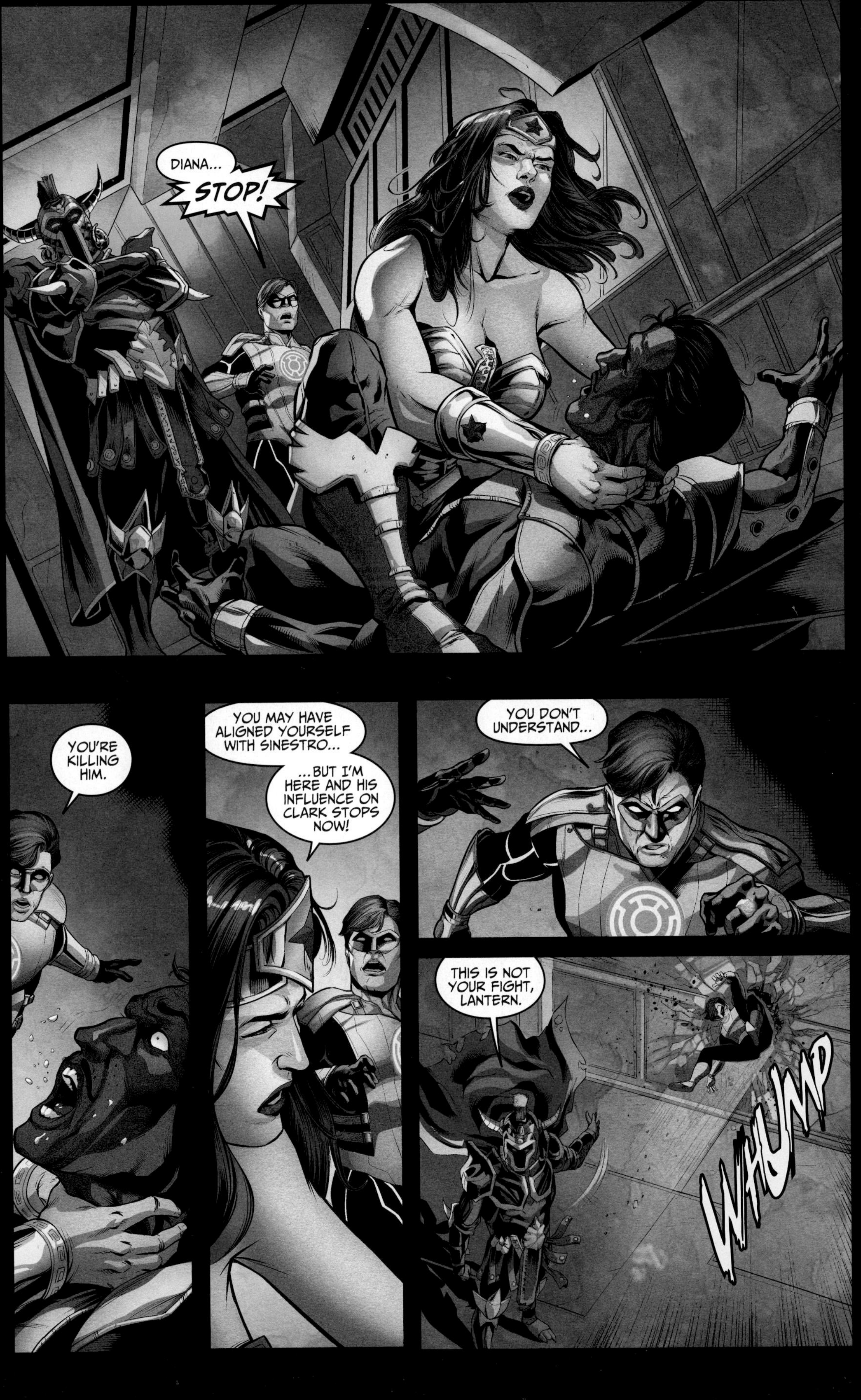
DIANA... STOP!
YOU'RE KILLING HIM.
YOU MAY HAVE ALIGNED YOURSELF WITH SINESTRO...
...BUT I'M HERE AND HIS INFLUENCE ON CLARK STOPS NOW!
YOU DON'T UNDERSTAND...
THIS IS NOT YOUR FIGHT, LANTERN.
WHUMP

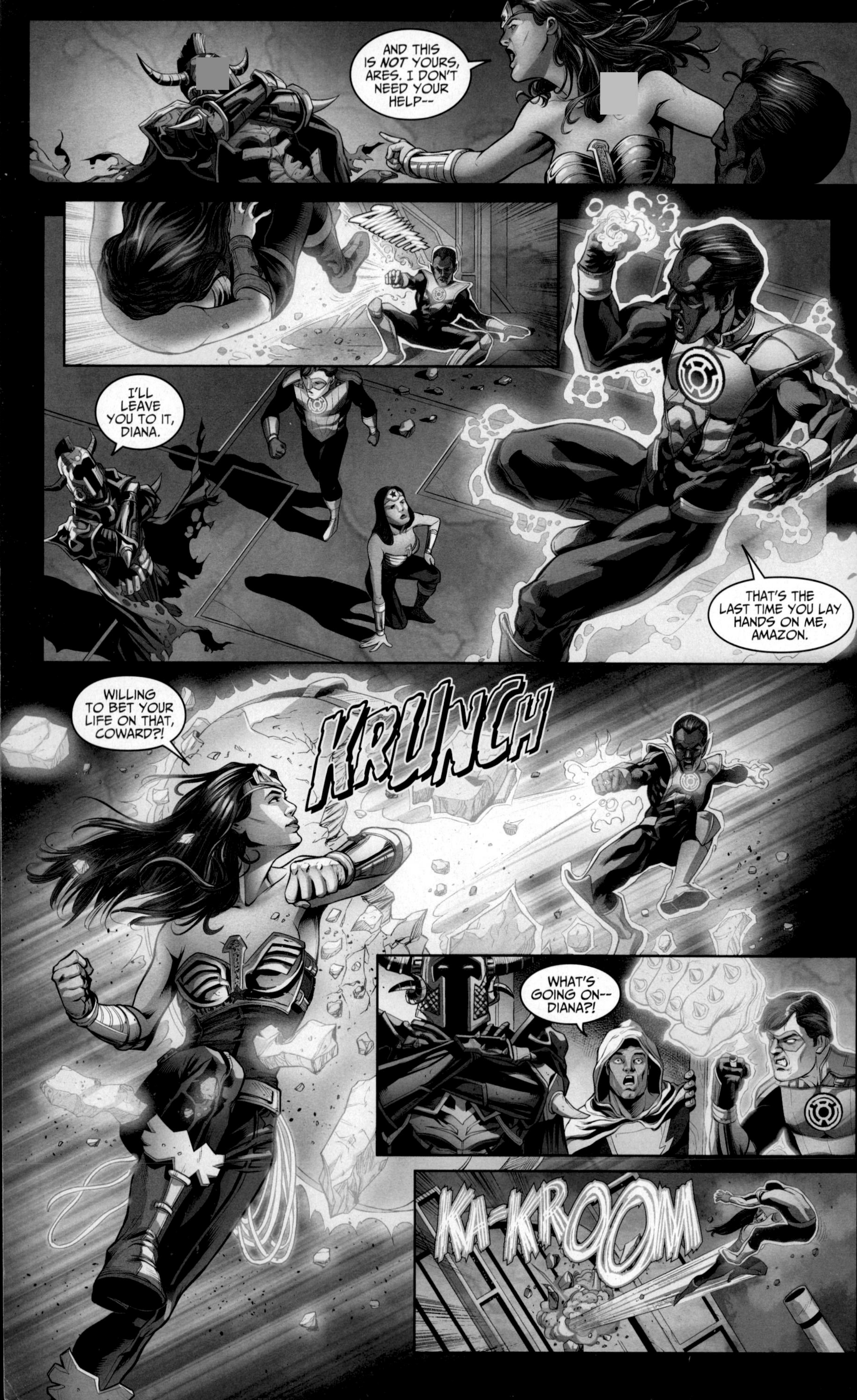
AND THIS IS *NOT* YOURS, ARES. I DON'T NEED YOUR HELP--
I'LL LEAVE YOU TO IT, DIANA.
THAT'S THE LAST TIME YOU LAY HANDS ON ME, AMAZON.
WILLING TO BET YOUR LIFE ON THAT, COWARD?!
KRUNCH
WHAT'S GOING ON-- DIANA?!
KA-KROOM

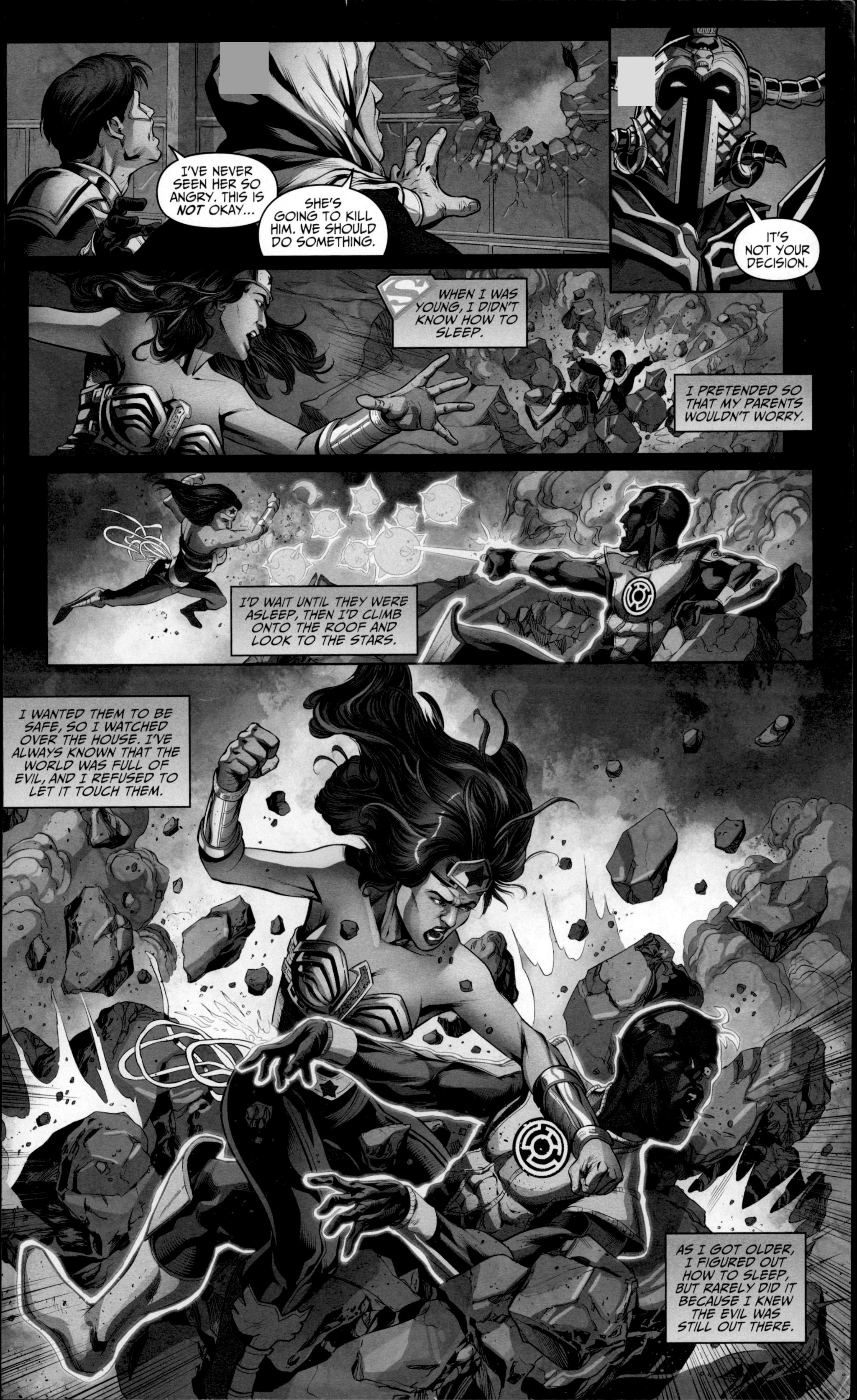
I'VE NEVER SEEN HER SO ANGRY. THIS IS NOT OKAY...
SHE'S GOING TO KILL HIM. WE SHOULD DO SOMETHING.
IT'S NOT YOUR DECISION.
WHEN I WAS YOUNG, I DIDN'T KNOW HOW TO SLEEP.
I PRETENDED SO THAT MY PARENTS WOULDN'T WORRY.
I'D WAIT UNTIL THEY WERE ASLEEP, THEN I'D CLIMB ONTO THE ROOF AND LOOK TO THE STARS.
I WANTED THEM TO BE SAFE, SO I WATCHED OVER THE HOUSE. I'VE ALWAYS KNOWN THAT THE WORLD WAS FULL OF EVIL, AND I REFUSED TO LET IT TOUCH THEM.
AS I GOT OLDER, I FIGURED OUT HOW TO SLEEP, BUT RARELY DID IT BECAUSE I KNEW THE EVIL WAS STILL OUT THERE.

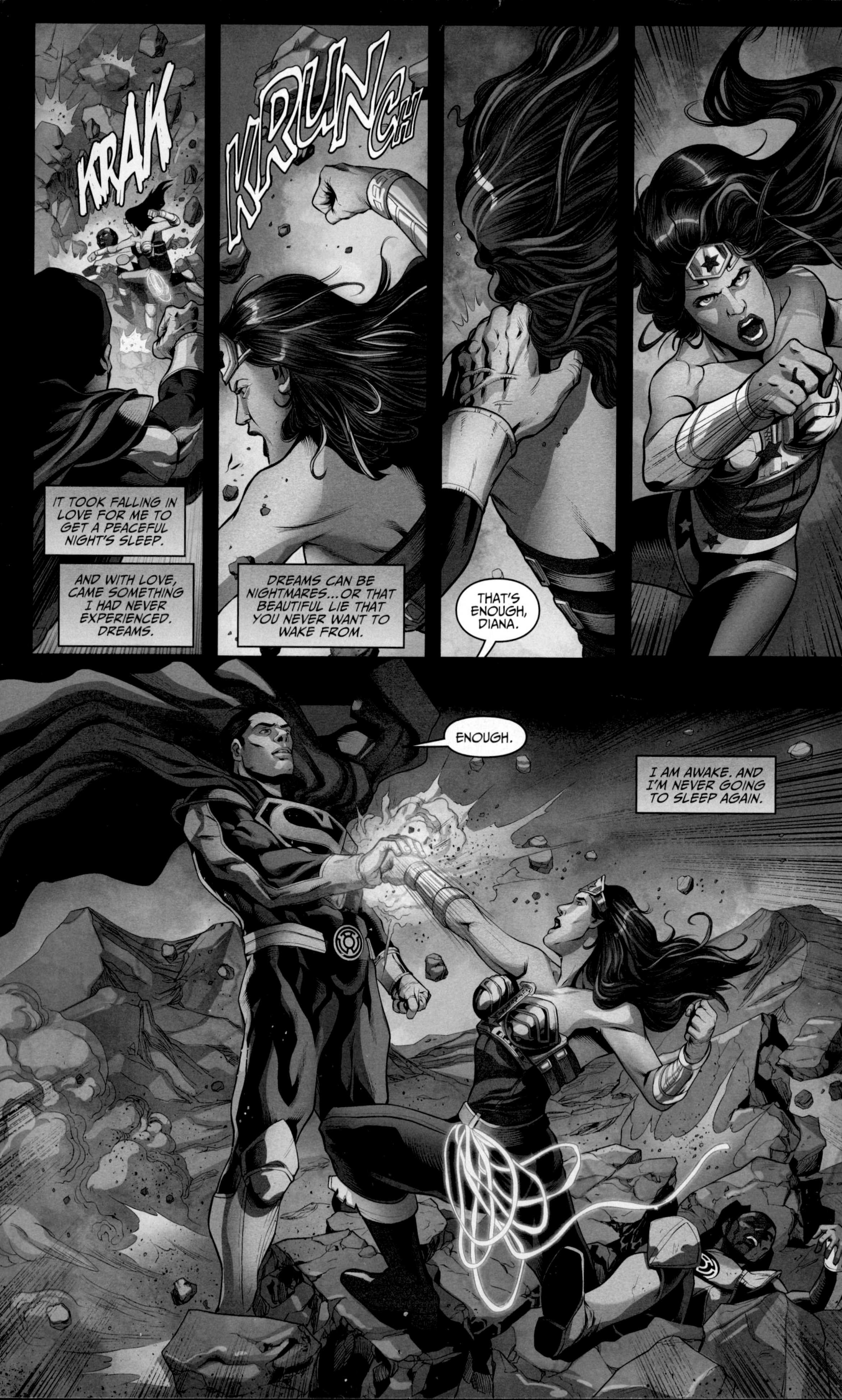
KRAK
IT TOOK FALLING IN LOVE FOR ME TO GET A PEACEFUL NIGHT'S SLEEP.
AND WITH LOVE, CAME SOMETHING I HAD NEVER EXPERIENCED. DREAMS.
KRUNCH
DREAMS CAN BE NIGHTMARES...OR THAT BEAUTIFUL LIE THAT YOU NEVER WANT TO WAKE FROM.
THAT'S ENOUGH, DIANA.
ENOUGH.
I AM AWAKE. AND I'M NEVER GOING TO SLEEP AGAIN.

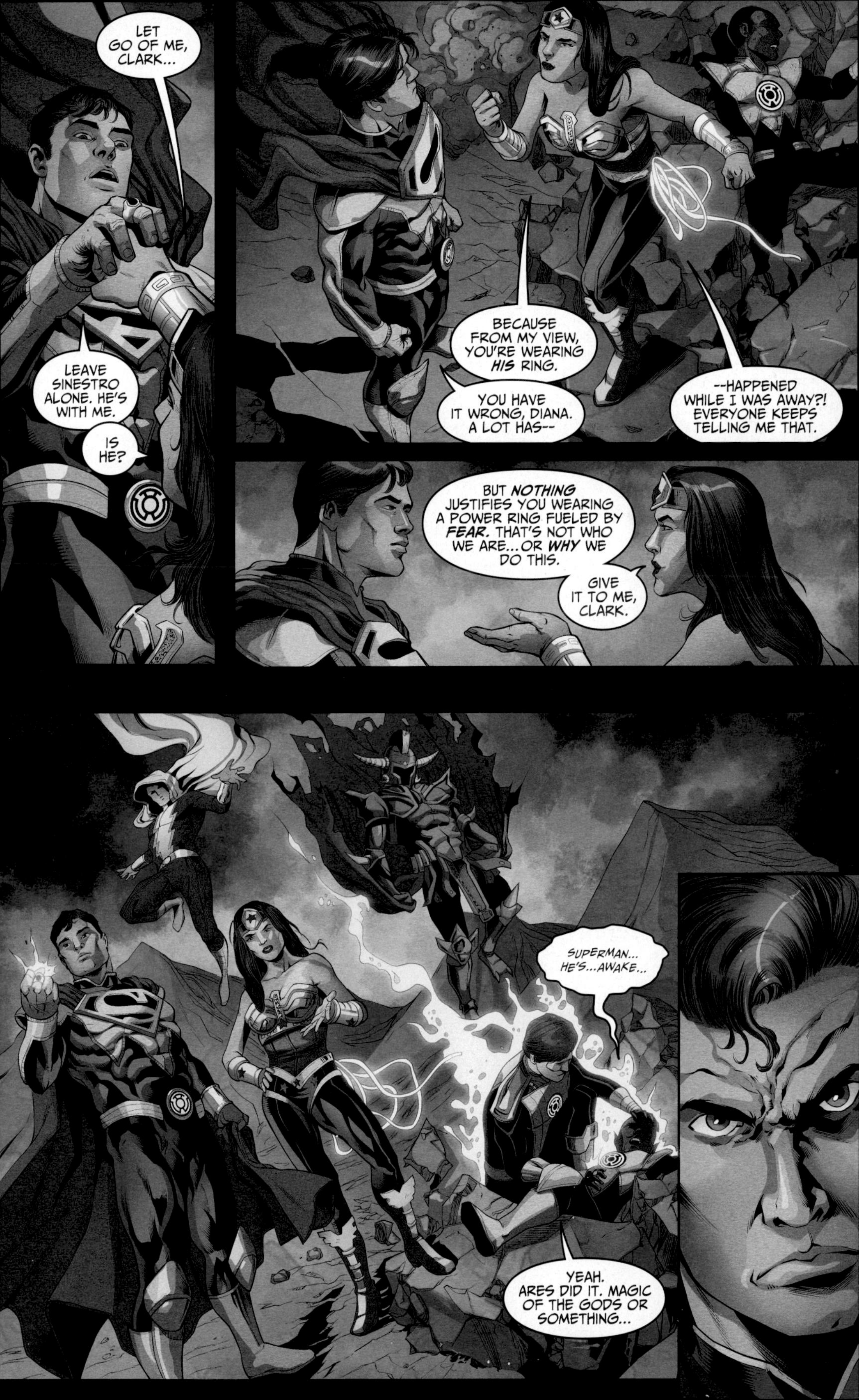
LET GO OF ME, CLARK...
LEAVE SINESTRO ALONE. HE'S WITH ME.
IS HE?
BECAUSE FROM MY VIEW, YOU'RE WEARING HIS RING.
YOU HAVE IT WRONG, DIANA. A LOT HAS--
--HAPPENED WHILE I WAS AWAY?! EVERYONE KEEPS TELLING ME THAT.
BUT NOTHING JUSTIFIES YOU WEARING A POWER RING FUELED BY FEAR. THAT'S NOT WHO WE ARE...OR WHY WE DO THIS.
GIVE IT TO ME, CLARK.
SUPERMAN... HE'S...AWAKE...
YEAH. ARES DID IT. MAGIC OF THE GODS OR SOMETHING...

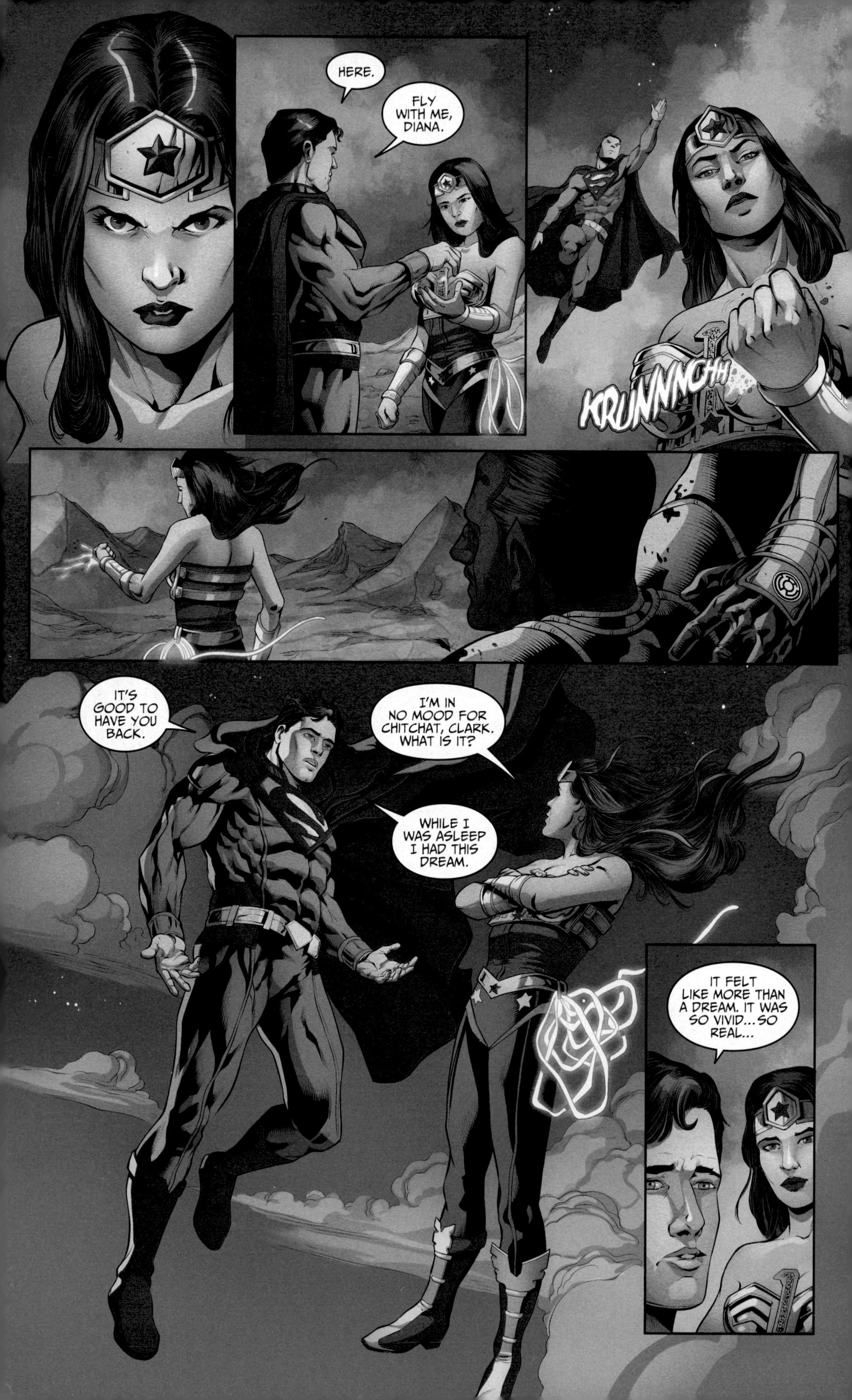
HERE.
FLY WITH ME, DIANA.
KRUNNNCHH
IT'S GOOD TO HAVE YOU BACK.
I'M IN NO MOOD FOR CHITCHAT, CLARK. WHAT IS IT?
WHILE I WAS ASLEEP I HAD THIS DREAM.
IT FELT LIKE MORE THAN A DREAM. IT WAS SO VIVID... SO REAL...

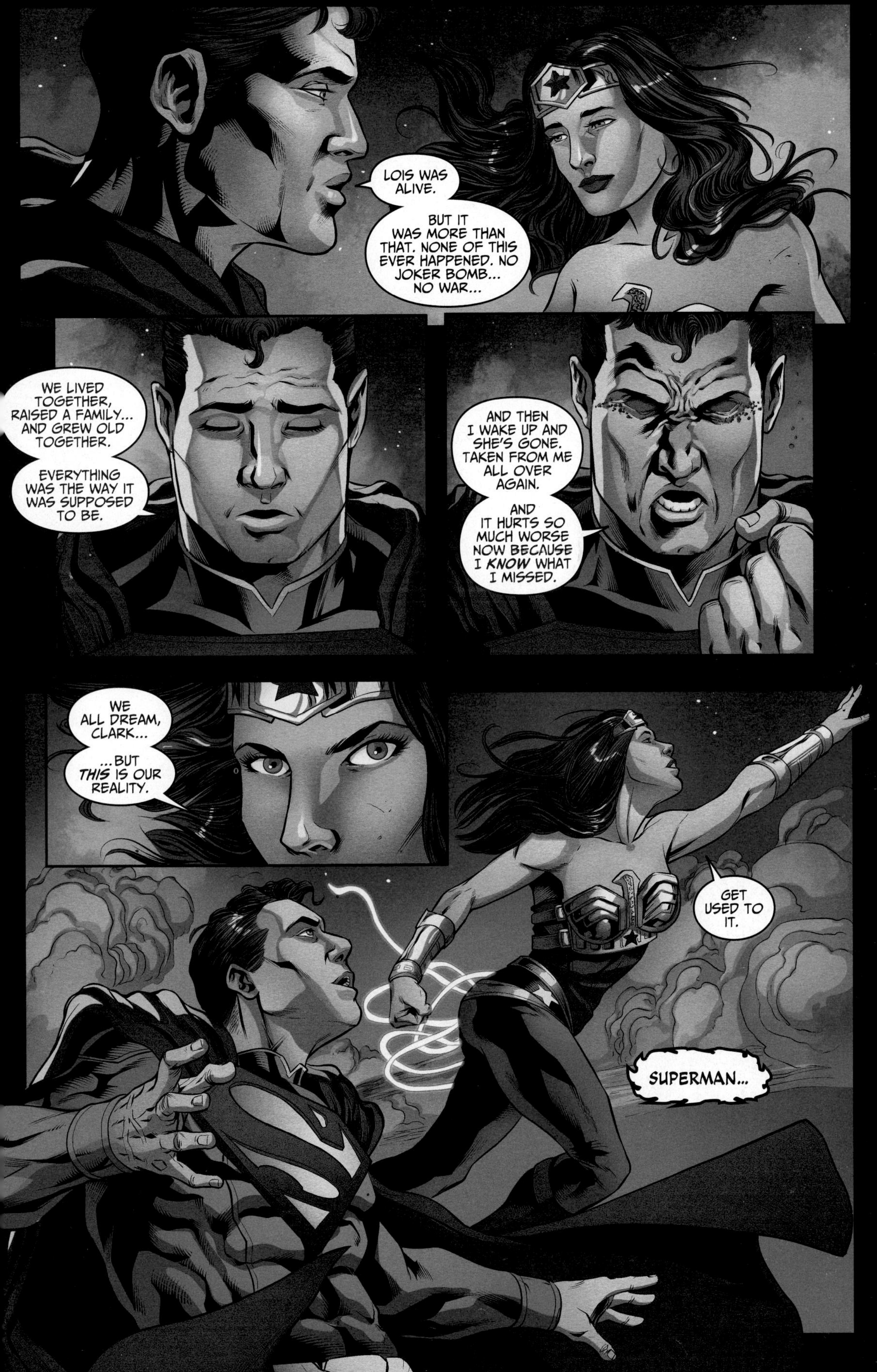
LOIS WAS ALIVE.
BUT IT WAS MORE THAN THAT. NONE OF THIS EVER HAPPENED. NO JOKER BOMB... NO WAR...
WE LIVED TOGETHER, RAISED A FAMILY... AND GREW OLD TOGETHER.
EVERYTHING WAS THE WAY IT WAS SUPPOSED TO BE.
AND THEN I WAKE UP AND SHE'S GONE. TAKEN FROM ME ALL OVER AGAIN.
AND IT HURTS SO MUCH WORSE NOW BECAUSE I *KNOW* WHAT I MISSED.
WE ALL DREAM, CLARK...
...BUT *THIS* IS OUR REALITY.
GET USED TO IT.
SUPERMAN...

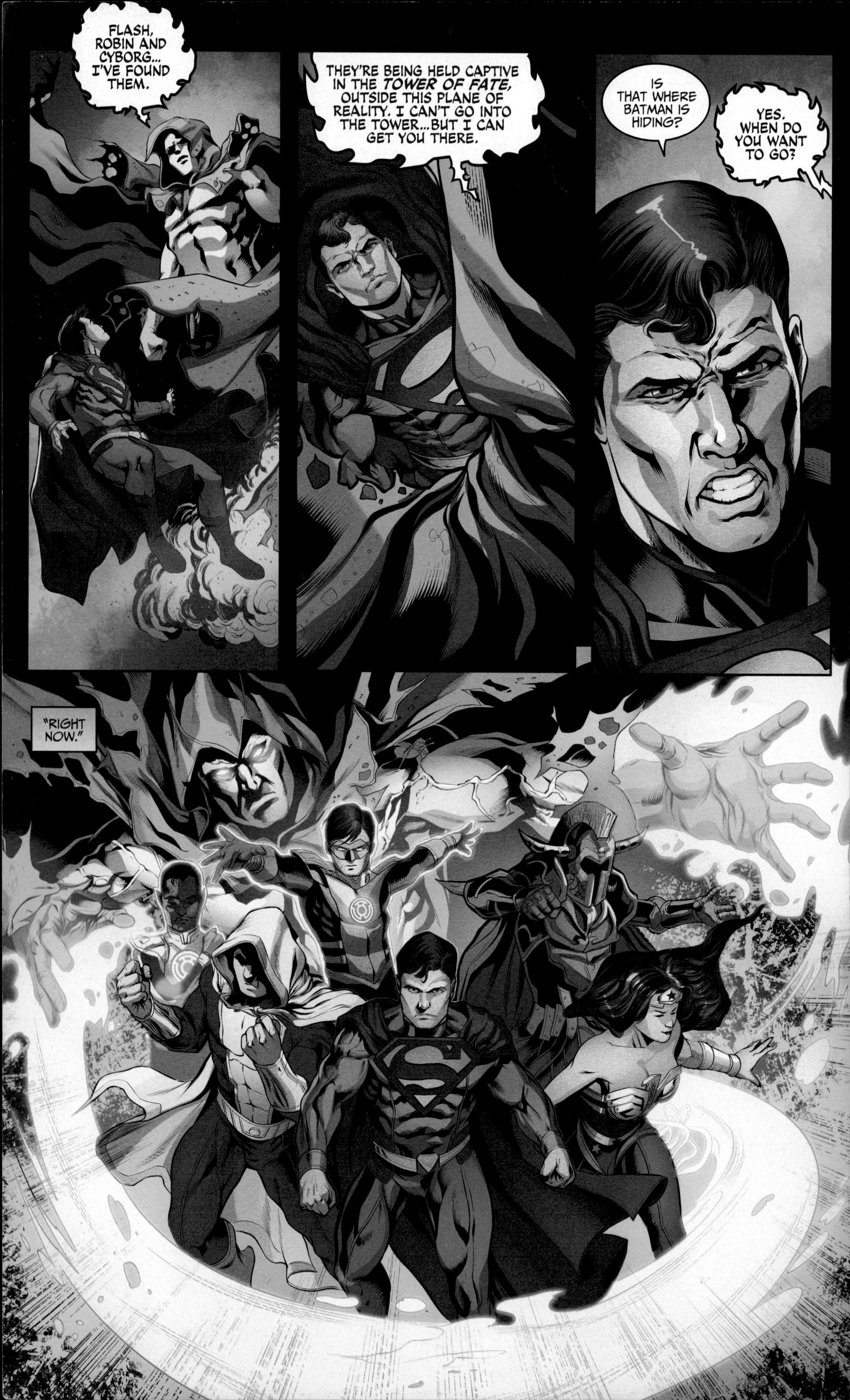
FLASH, ROBIN AND CYBORG... I'VE FOUND THEM.
THEY'RE BEING HELD CAPTIVE IN THE *TOWER OF FATE,* OUTSIDE THIS PLANE OF REALITY. I CAN'T GO INTO THE TOWER...BUT I CAN GET YOU THERE.
IS THAT WHERE BATMAN IS HIDING?
YES. WHEN DO YOU WANT TO GO?
"RIGHT NOW."

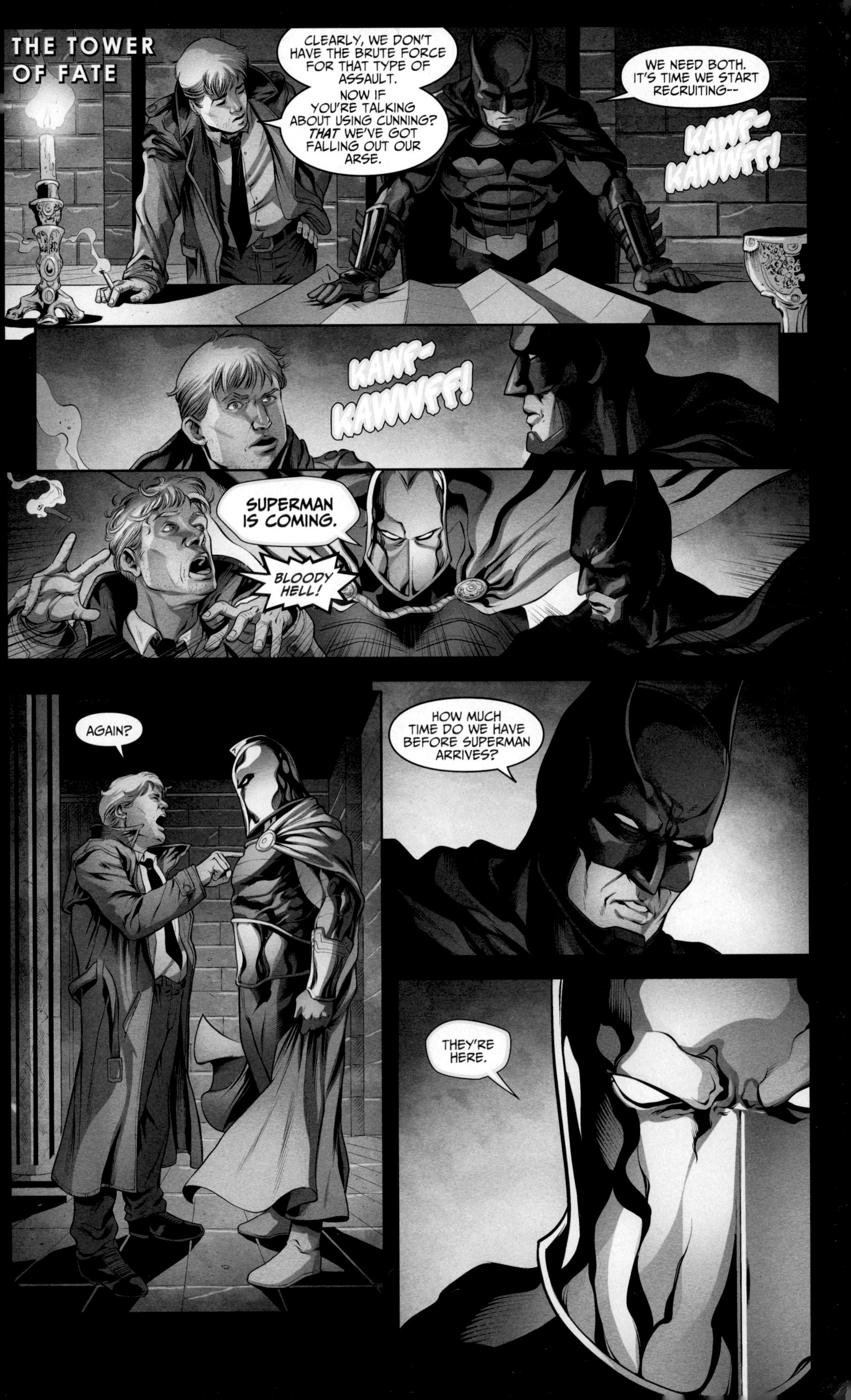
THE TOWER OF FATE
CLEARLY, WE DON'T HAVE THE BRUTE FORCE FOR THAT TYPE OF ASSAULT.
NOW IF YOU'RE TALKING ABOUT USING CUNNING? THAT WE'VE GOT FALLING OUT OUR ARSE.
WE NEED BOTH. IT'S TIME WE START RECRUITING--
KAWF-KAWWFF!
KAWF-KAWWFF!
SUPERMAN IS COMING.
BLOODY HELL!
AGAIN?
HOW MUCH TIME DO WE HAVE BEFORE SUPERMAN ARRIVES?
THEY'RE HERE.

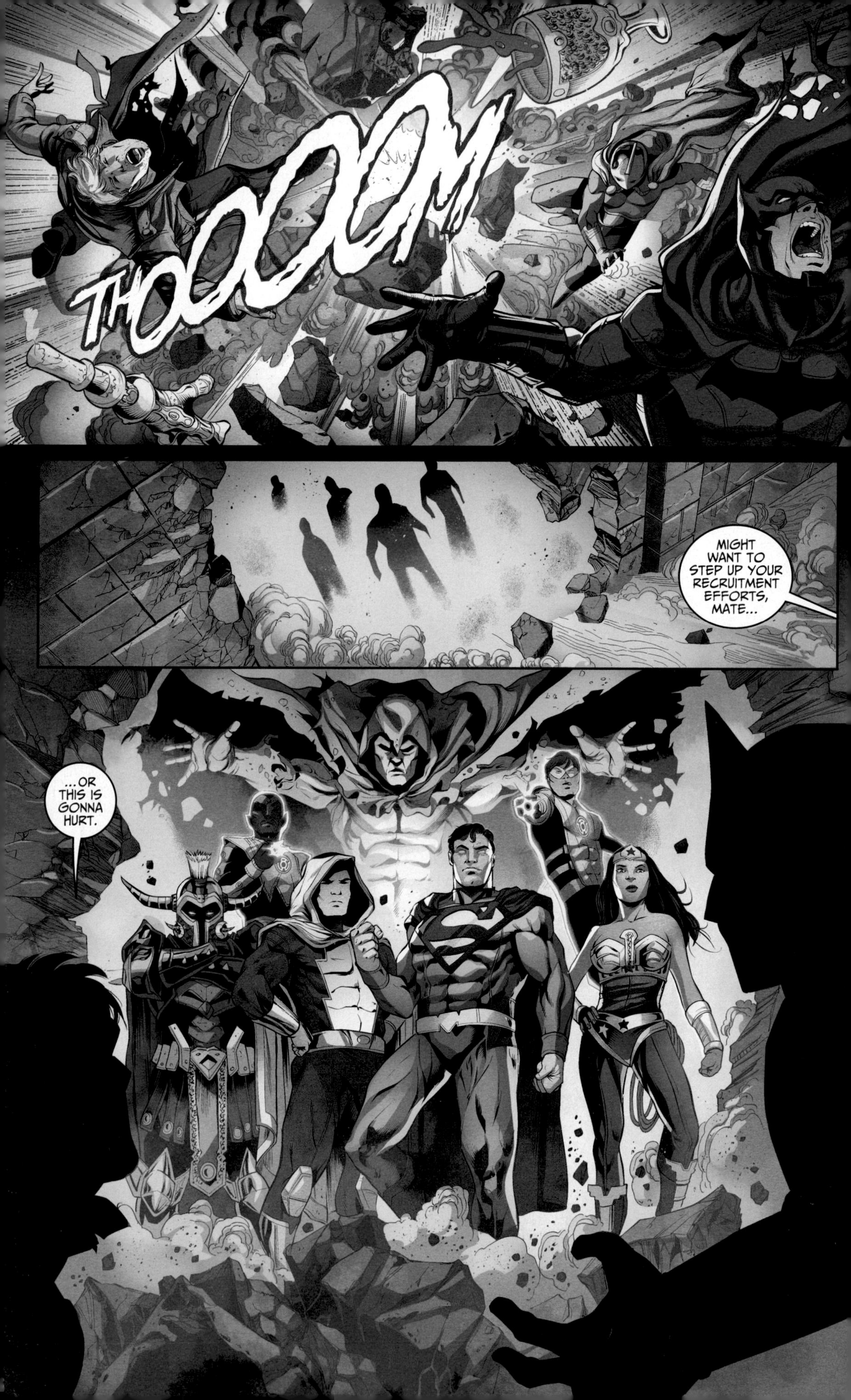
THOOOM
MIGHT WANT TO STEP UP YOUR RECRUITMENT EFFORTS, MATE...
...OR THIS IS GONNA HURT.

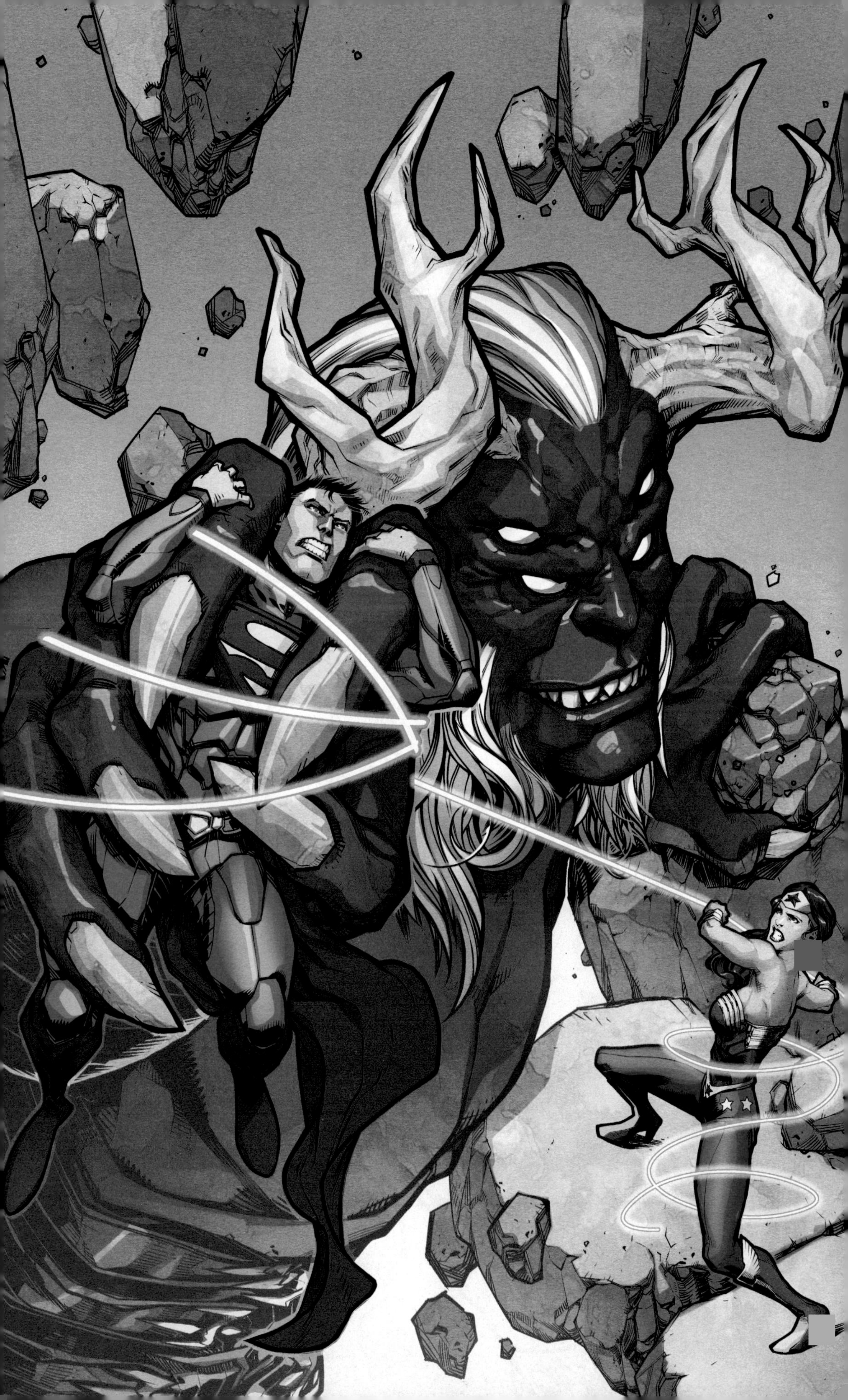

"Assault on the Tower" Xermanico, Bruno Redondo, Juan Albarran - Artists Rex Lokus - Colorist
"Fight or Flight" Bruno Redondo and Juan Albarran - Artists Rex Lokus - Colorist
Cover Art by Neil Googe and J. Nanjan

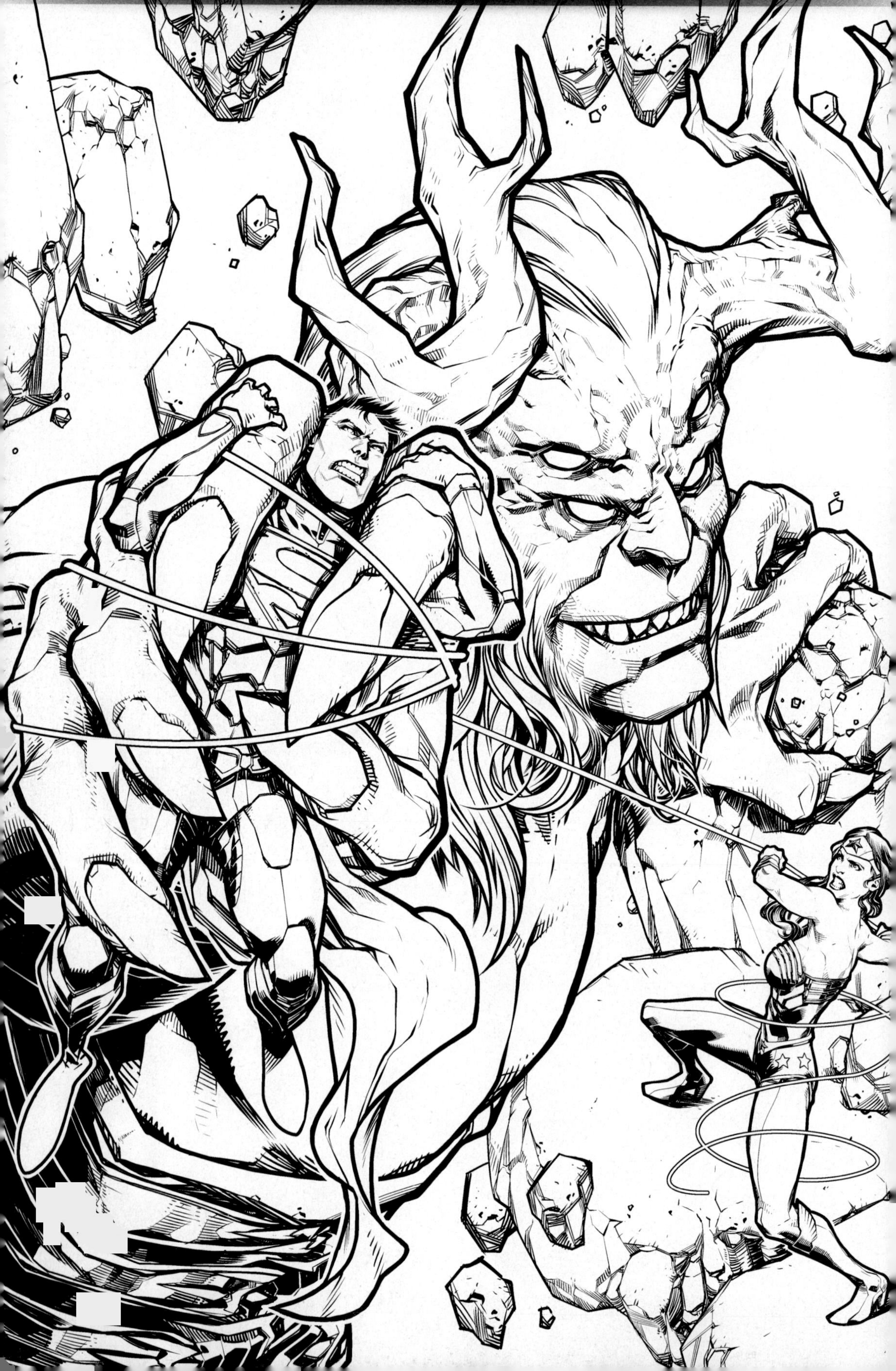

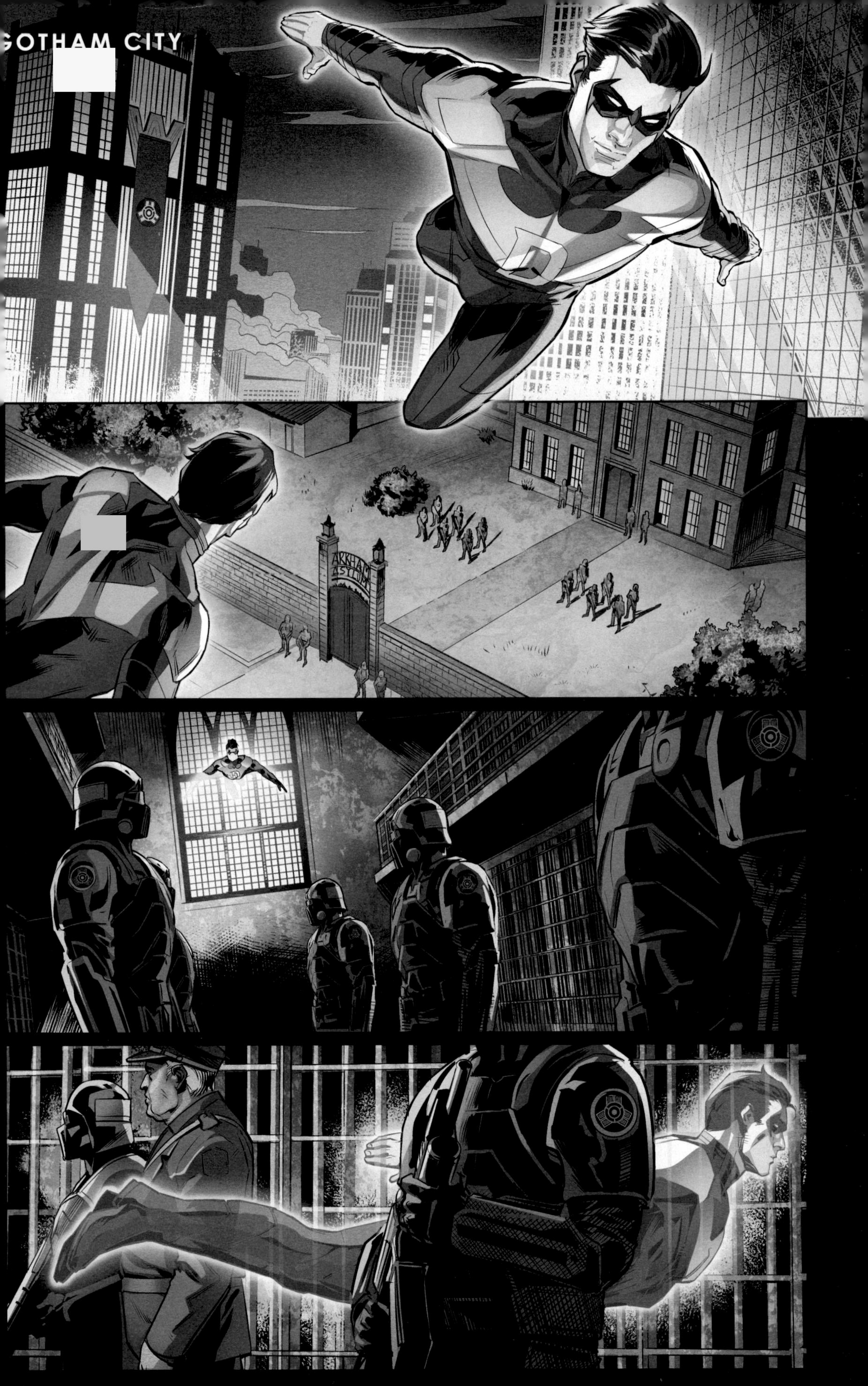
GOTHAM CITY
ARKHAM ASYLUM

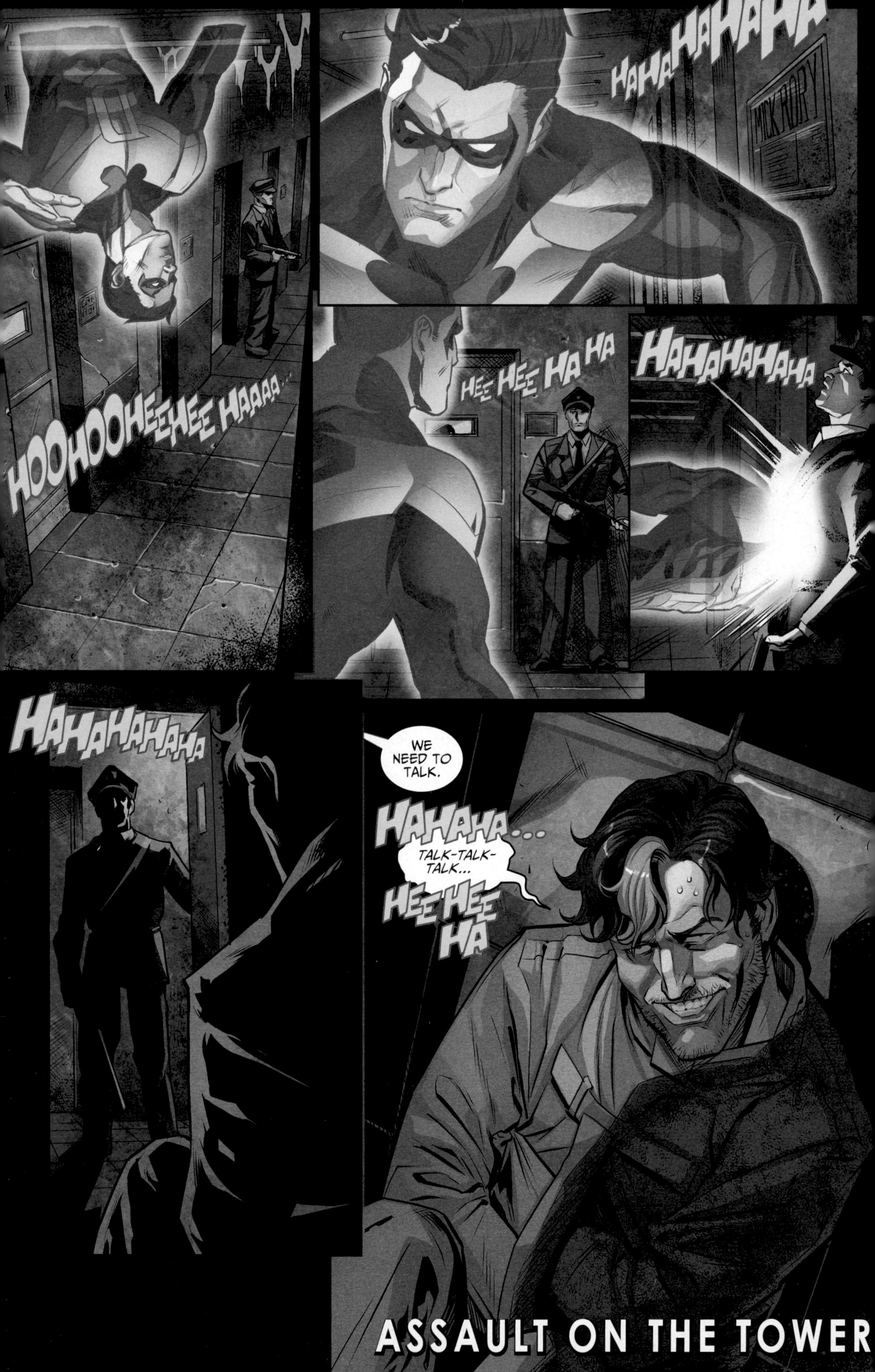
HOOHOOHEEHEE HAAAA...
HAHAHAHAHAHA
MICK RORY
HEE HEE HA HA
HAHAHAHAHAHA
HAHAHAHAHAHA
WE NEED TO TALK.
HAHAHA...
TALK-TALK-TALK...
HEE HEE HA
ASSAULT ON THE TOWER

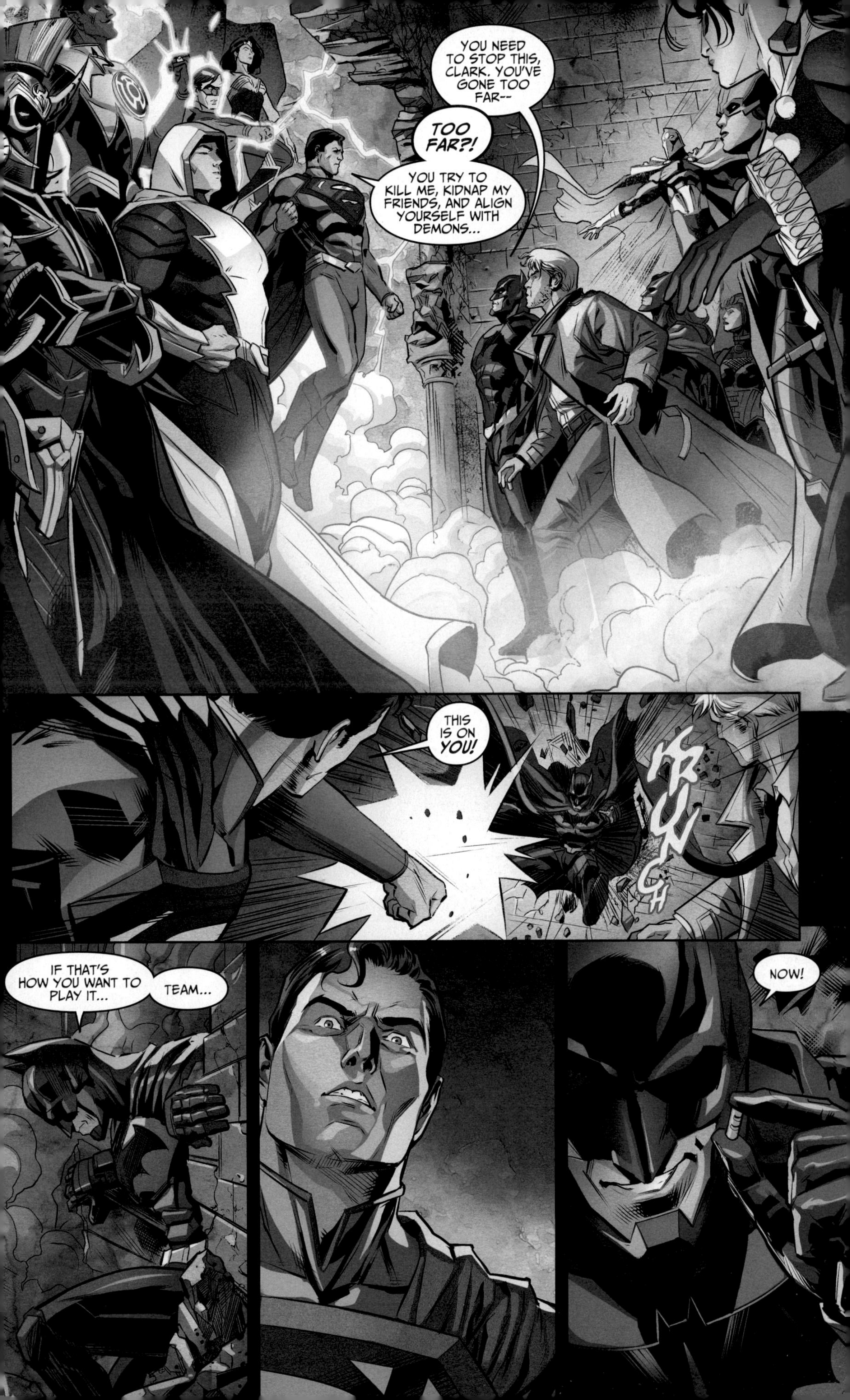

YOU NEED TO STOP THIS, CLARK. YOU'VE GONE TOO FAR--
TOO FAR?!
YOU TRY TO KILL ME, KIDNAP MY FRIENDS, AND ALIGN YOURSELF WITH DEMONS...
THIS IS ON YOU!
KRUNCH
IF THAT'S HOW YOU WANT TO PLAY IT...
TEAM...
NOW!

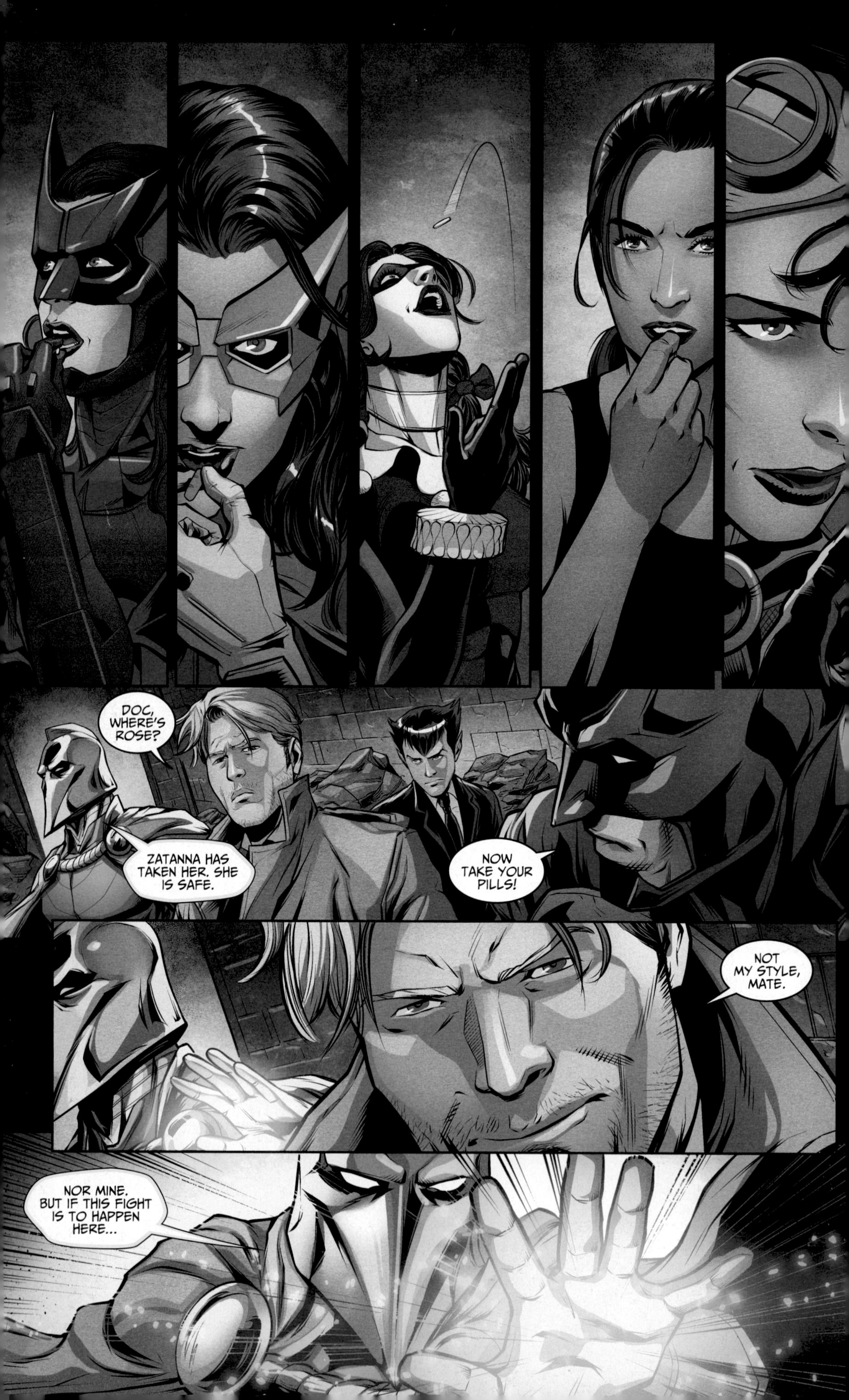
DOC, WHERE'S ROSE?
ZATANNA HAS TAKEN HER. SHE IS SAFE.
NOW TAKE YOUR PILLS!
NOT MY STYLE, MATE.
NOR MINE. BUT IF THIS FIGHT IS TO HAPPEN HERE...

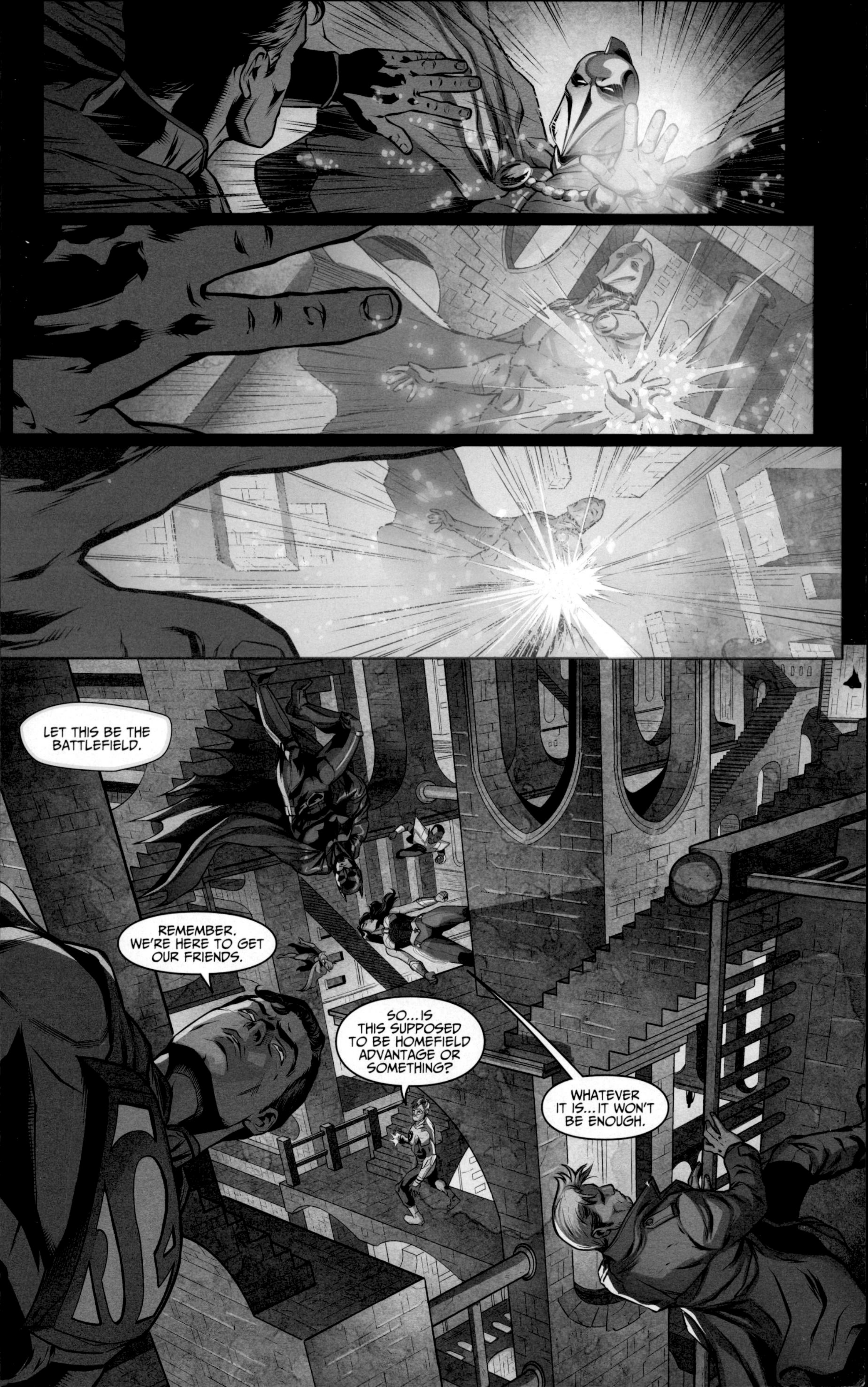
LET THIS BE THE BATTLEFIELD.
REMEMBER. WE'RE HERE TO GET OUR FRIENDS.
SO...IS THIS SUPPOSED TO BE HOMEFIELD ADVANTAGE OR SOMETHING?
WHATEVER IT IS...IT WON'T BE ENOUGH.

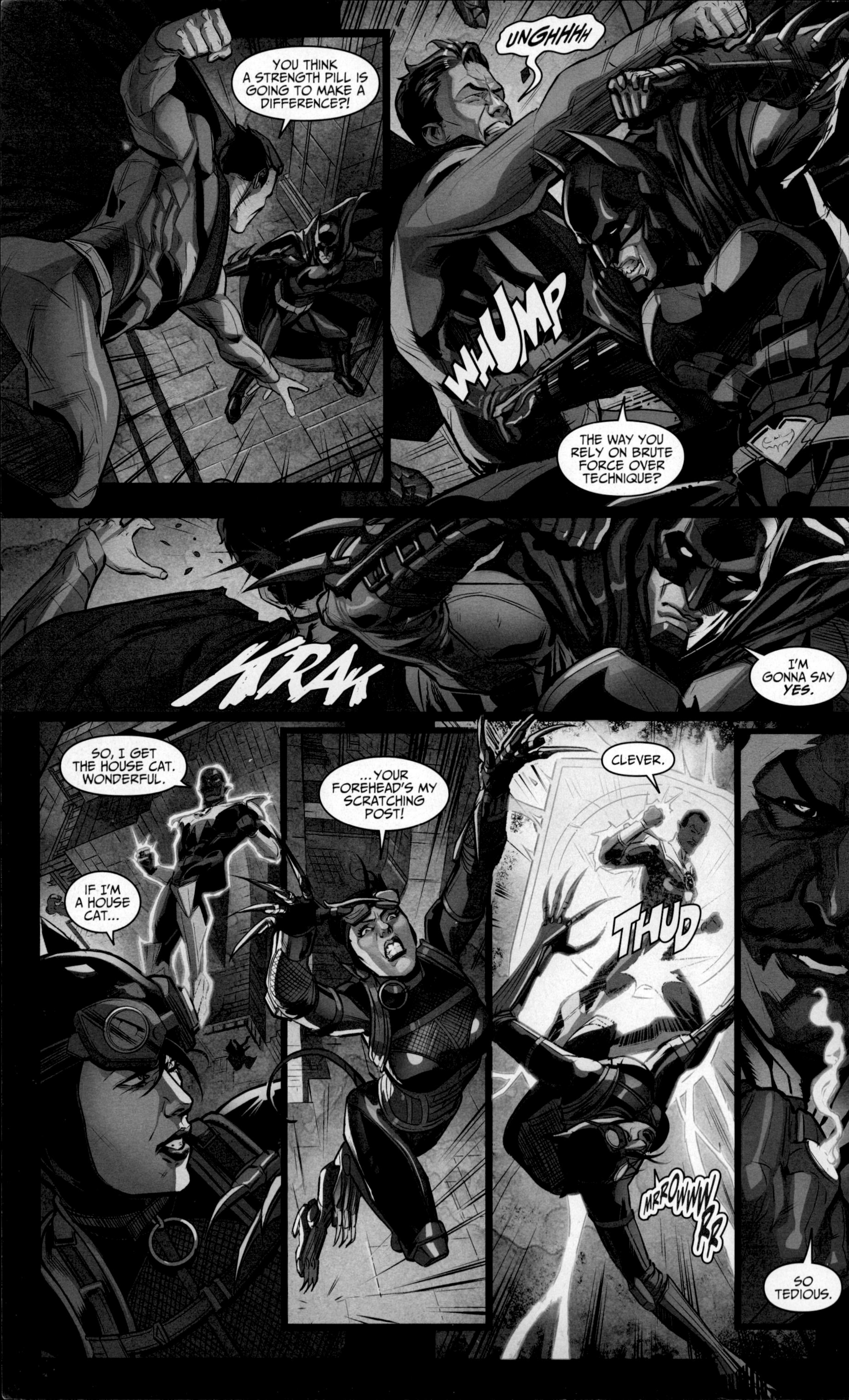
YOU THINK A STRENGTH PILL IS GOING TO MAKE A DIFFERENCE?!
UNGHHHH
WHUMP
THE WAY YOU RELY ON BRUTE FORCE OVER TECHNIQUE?
KRAK
I'M GONNA SAY YES.
SO, I GET THE HOUSE CAT. WONDERFUL.
IF I'M A HOUSE CAT...
...YOUR FOREHEAD'S MY SCRATCHING POST!
CLEVER.
THUD
MRROWWWRR
SO TEDIOUS.

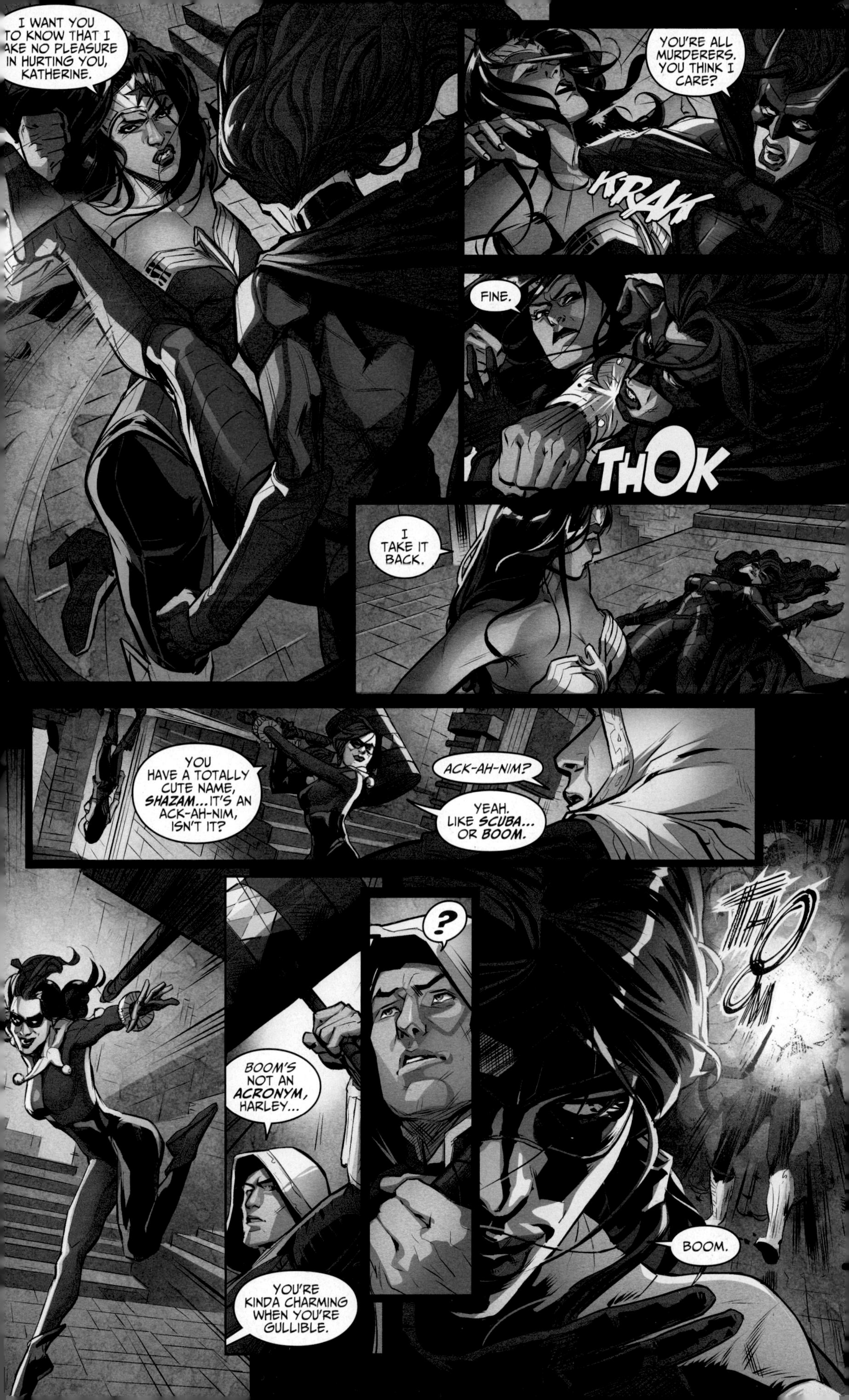
I WANT YOU TO KNOW THAT I TAKE NO PLEASURE IN HURTING YOU, KATHERINE.
YOU'RE ALL MURDERERS. YOU THINK I CARE?
KRAK
FINE.
THOK
I TAKE IT BACK.
YOU HAVE A TOTALLY CUTE NAME, SHAZAM...IT'S AN ACK-AH-NIM, ISN'T IT?
ACK-AH-NIM?
YEAH. LIKE SCUBA... OR BOOM.
?
BOOM'S NOT AN ACRONYM, HARLEY...
YOU'RE KINDA CHARMING WHEN YOU'RE GULLIBLE.
THOOM
BOOM.

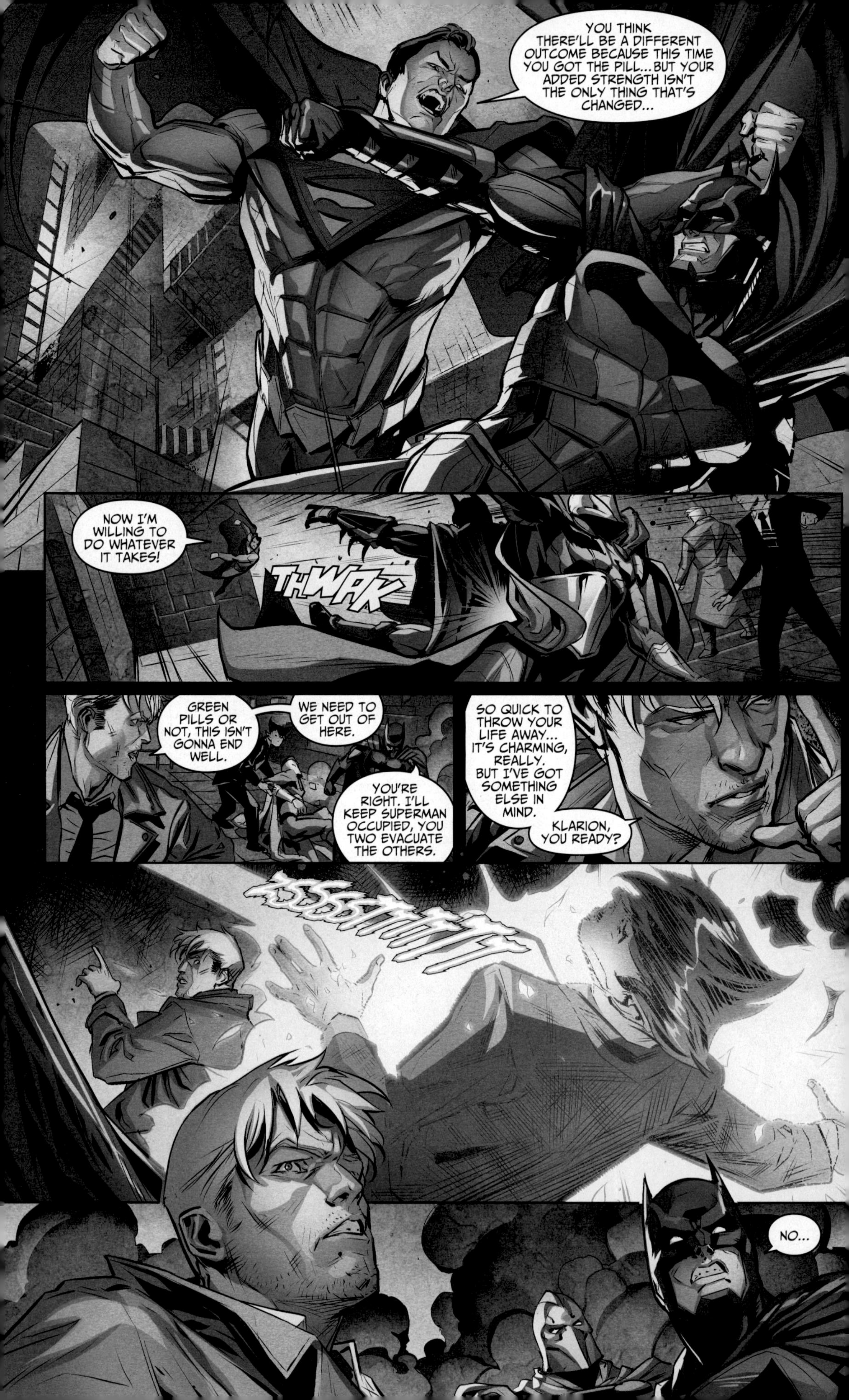
YOU THINK THERE'LL BE A DIFFERENT OUTCOME BECAUSE THIS TIME YOU GOT THE PILL...BUT YOUR ADDED STRENGTH ISN'T THE ONLY THING THAT'S CHANGED...
NOW I'M WILLING TO DO WHATEVER IT TAKES!
THWAK
GREEN PILLS OR NOT, THIS ISN'T GONNA END WELL.
WE NEED TO GET OUT OF HERE.
YOU'RE RIGHT. I'LL KEEP SUPERMAN OCCUPIED, YOU TWO EVACUATE THE OTHERS.
SO QUICK TO THROW YOUR LIFE AWAY... IT'S CHARMING, REALLY. BUT I'VE GOT SOMETHING ELSE IN MIND.
KLARION, YOU READY?
NO...

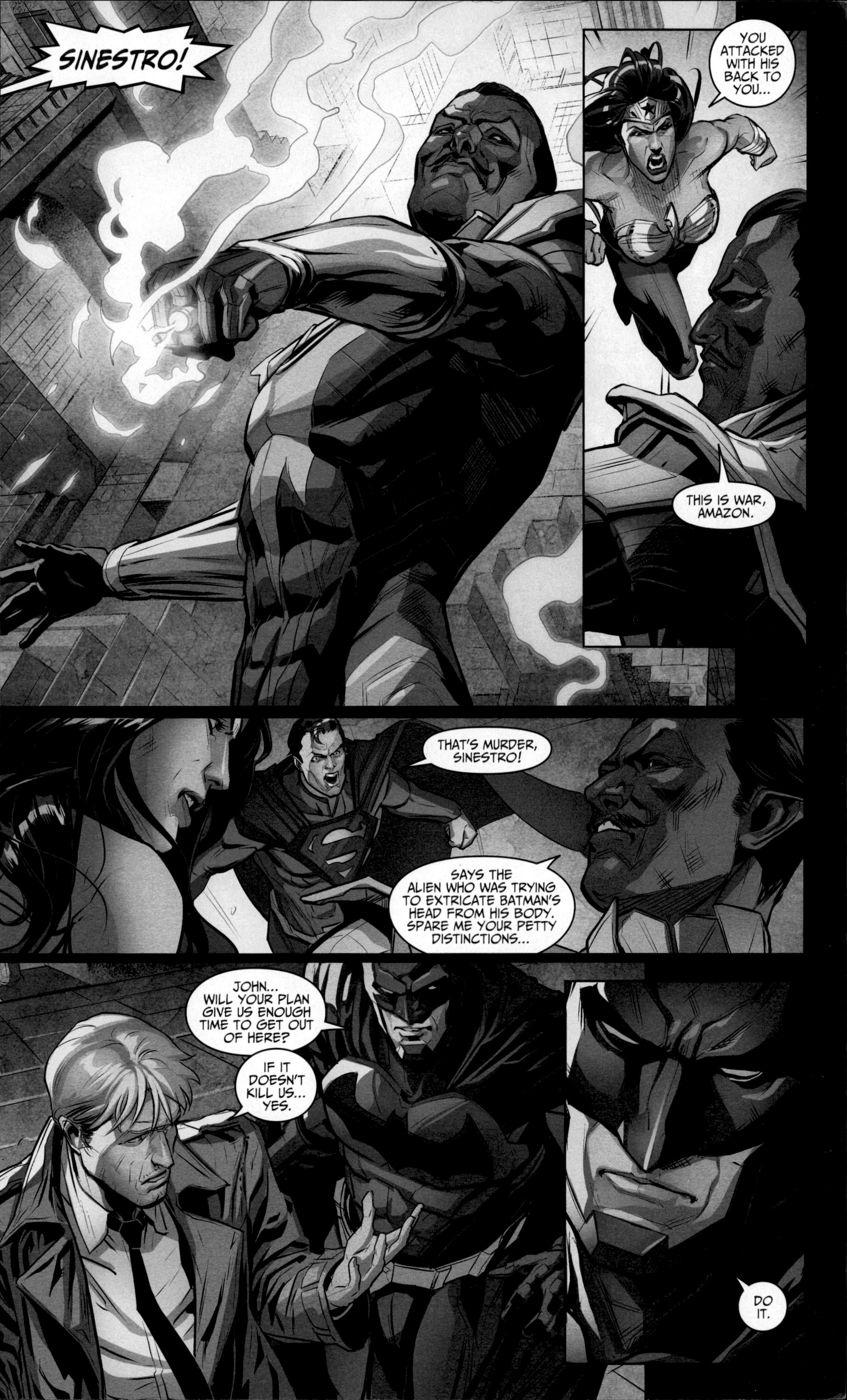
SINESTRO!
YOU ATTACKED WITH HIS BACK TO YOU...
THIS IS WAR, AMAZON.
THAT'S MURDER, SINESTRO!
SAYS THE ALIEN WHO WAS TRYING TO EXTRICATE BATMAN'S HEAD FROM HIS BODY. SPARE ME YOUR PETTY DISTINCTIONS...
JOHN... WILL YOUR PLAN GIVE US ENOUGH TIME TO GET OUT OF HERE?
IF IT DOESN'T KILL US... YES.
DO IT.

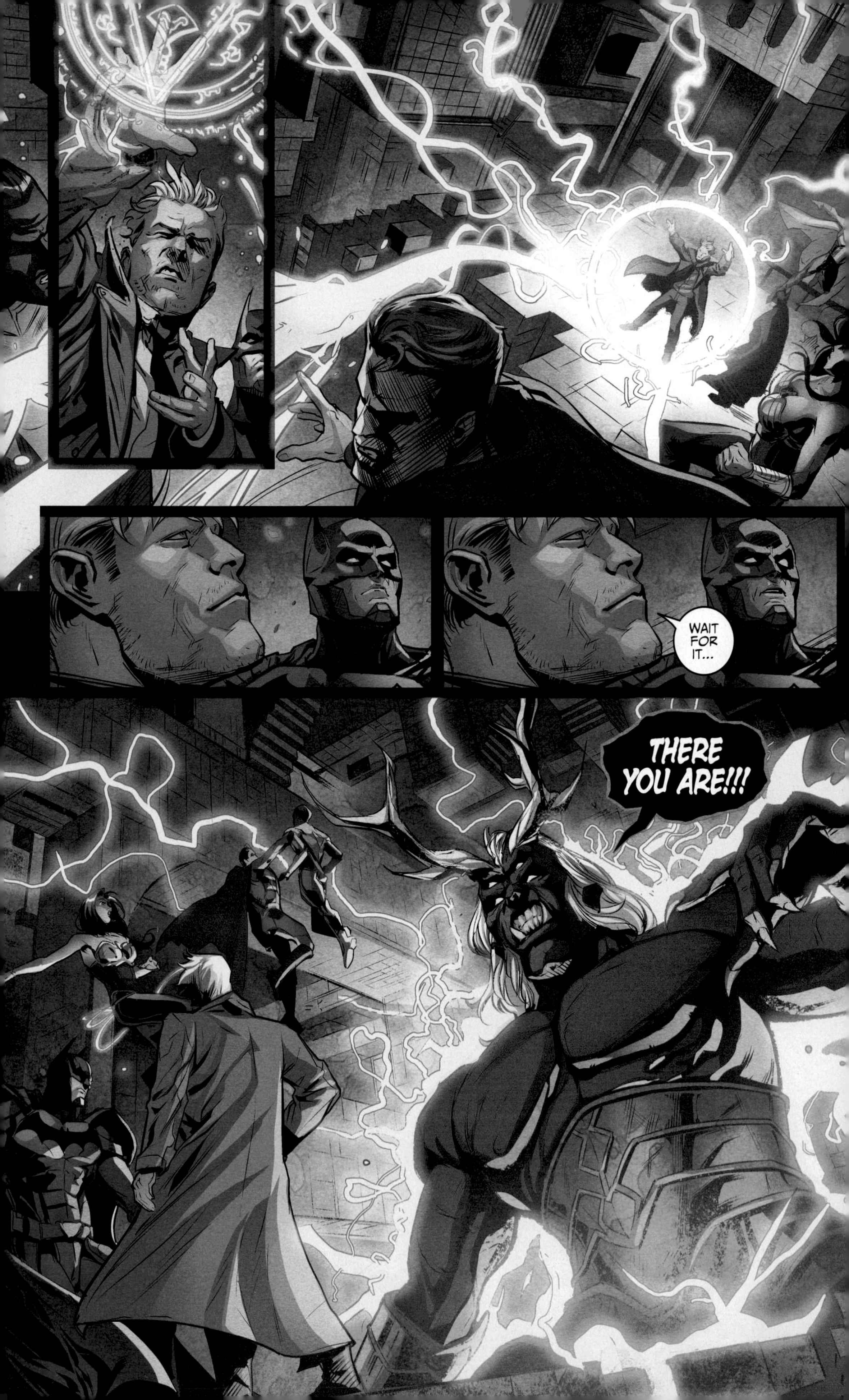
WAIT FOR IT...
THERE YOU ARE!!!

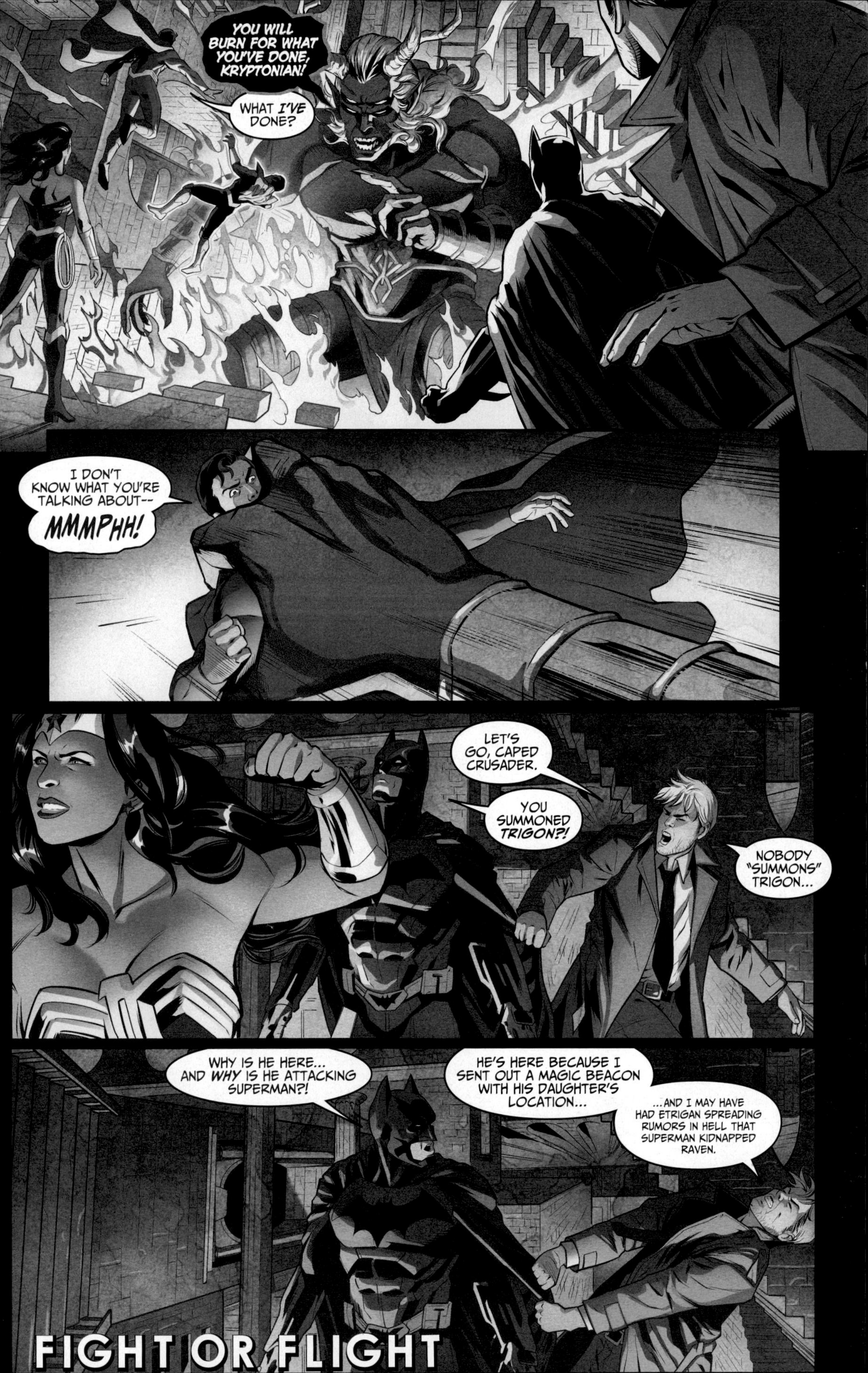
YOU WILL BURN FOR WHAT YOU'VE DONE, KRYPTONIAN!
WHAT *I'VE* DONE?
I DON'T KNOW WHAT YOU'RE TALKING ABOUT--
MMMPHH!
LET'S GO, CAPED CRUSADER.
YOU SUMMONED *TRIGON?!*
NOBODY "SUMMONS" TRIGON...
WHY IS HE HERE... AND *WHY* IS HE ATTACKING SUPERMAN?!
HE'S HERE BECAUSE I SENT OUT A MAGIC BEACON WITH HIS DAUGHTER'S LOCATION...
...AND I MAY HAVE HAD ETRIGAN SPREADING RUMORS IN HELL THAT SUPERMAN KIDNAPPED RAVEN.
FIGHT OR FLIGHT

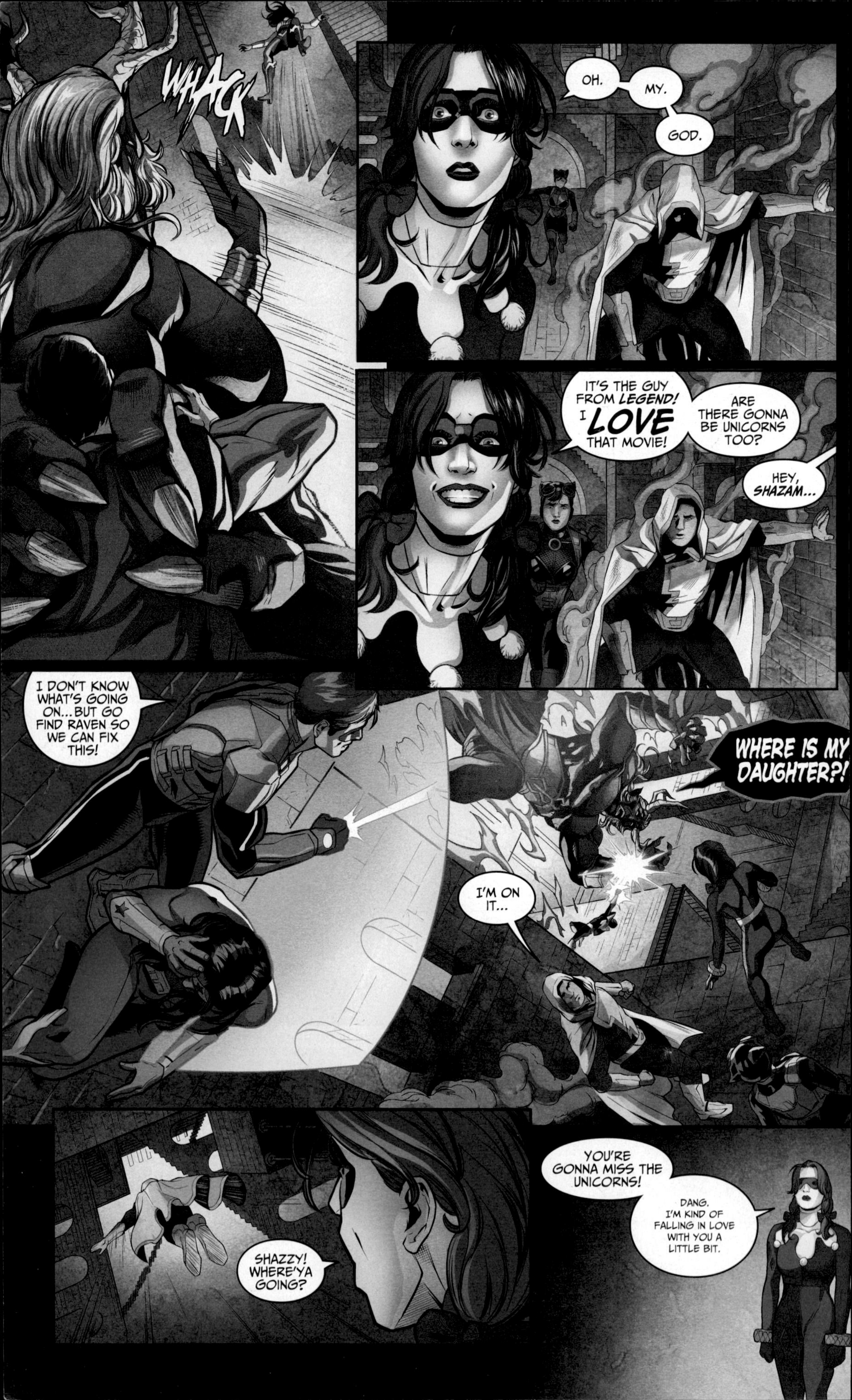
WHACK
OH.
MY.
GOD.
IT'S THE GUY FROM LEGEND! I LOVE THAT MOVIE!
ARE THERE GONNA BE UNICORNS TOO?
HEY, SHAZAM...
I DON'T KNOW WHAT'S GOING ON...BUT GO FIND RAVEN SO WE CAN FIX THIS!
WHERE IS MY DAUGHTER?!
I'M ON IT...
SHAZZY! WHERE'YA GOING?
YOU'RE GONNA MISS THE UNICORNS!
DANG. I'M KIND OF FALLING IN LOVE WITH YOU A LITTLE BIT.

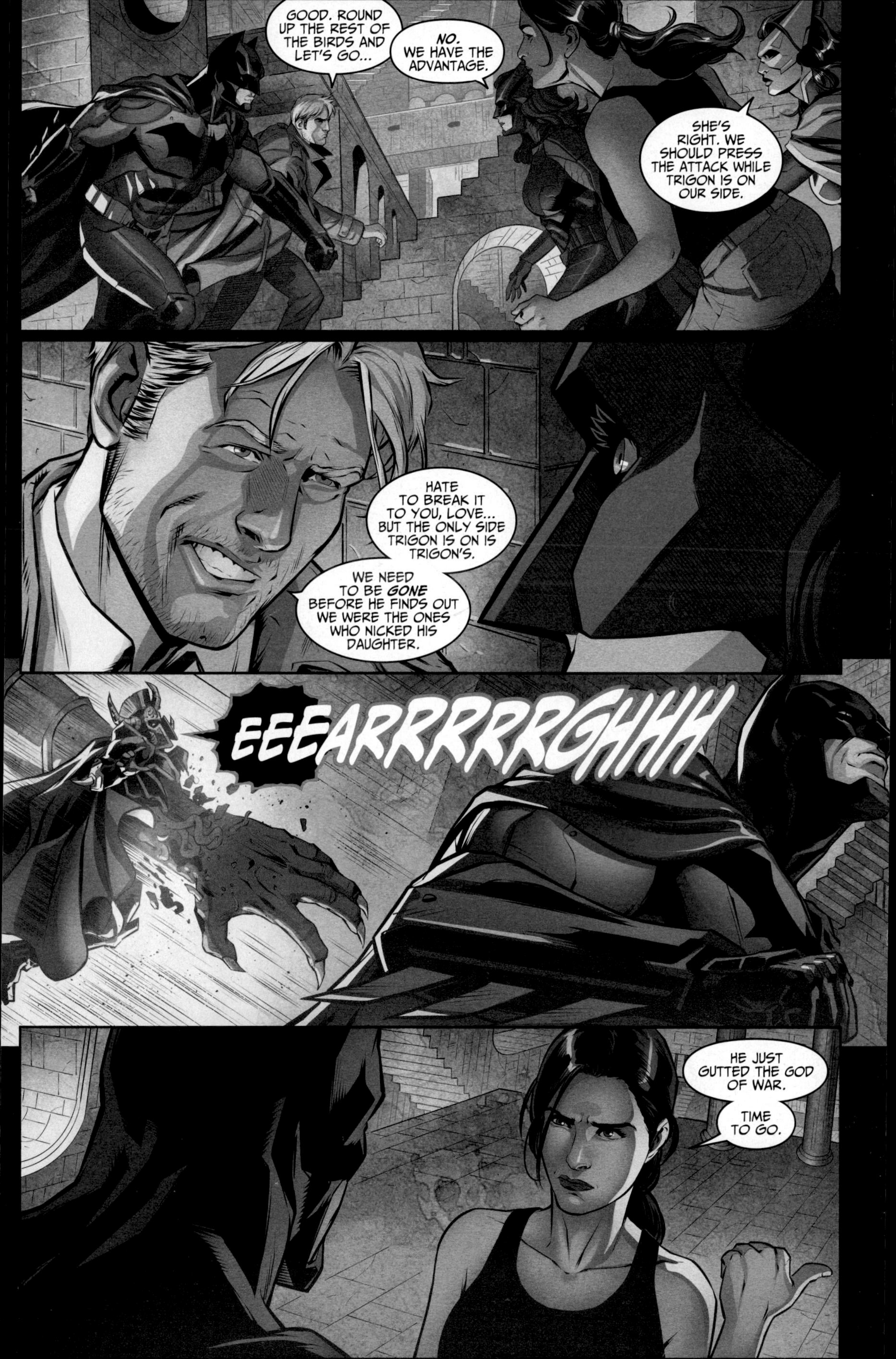
GOOD. ROUND UP THE REST OF THE BIRDS AND LET'S GO...
NO. WE HAVE THE ADVANTAGE.
SHE'S RIGHT. WE SHOULD PRESS THE ATTACK WHILE TRIGON IS ON OUR SIDE.
HATE TO BREAK IT TO YOU, LOVE... BUT THE ONLY SIDE TRIGON IS ON IS TRIGON'S.
WE NEED TO BE GONE BEFORE HE FINDS OUT WE WERE THE ONES WHO NICKED HIS DAUGHTER.
EEEARRRRRRGHHH
HE JUST GUTTED THE GOD OF WAR.
TIME TO GO.

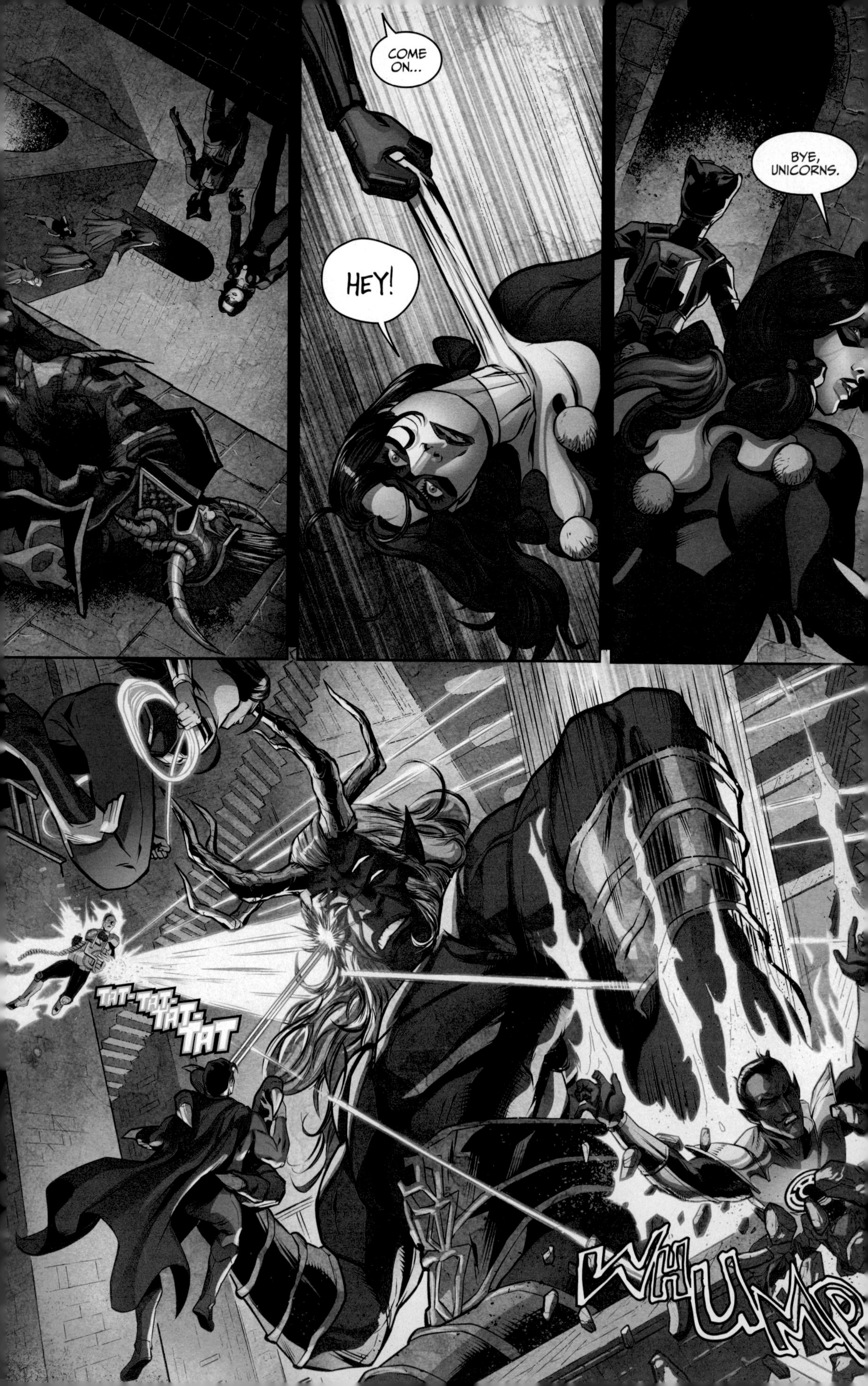
COME ON...
HEY!
BYE, UNICORNS.
TAT-TAT-TAT-TAT
WHUMP

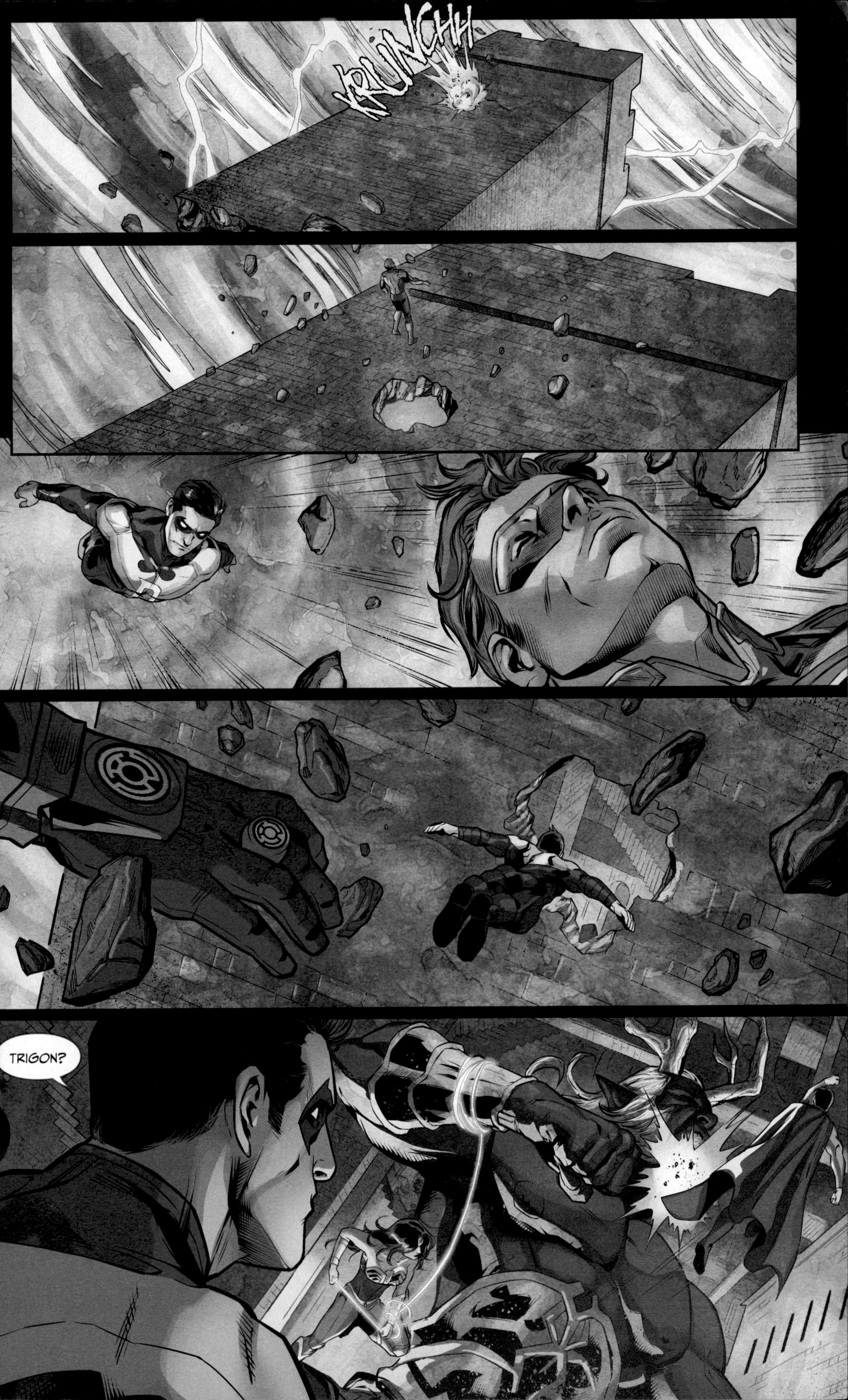
KRUNCHH
TRIGON?

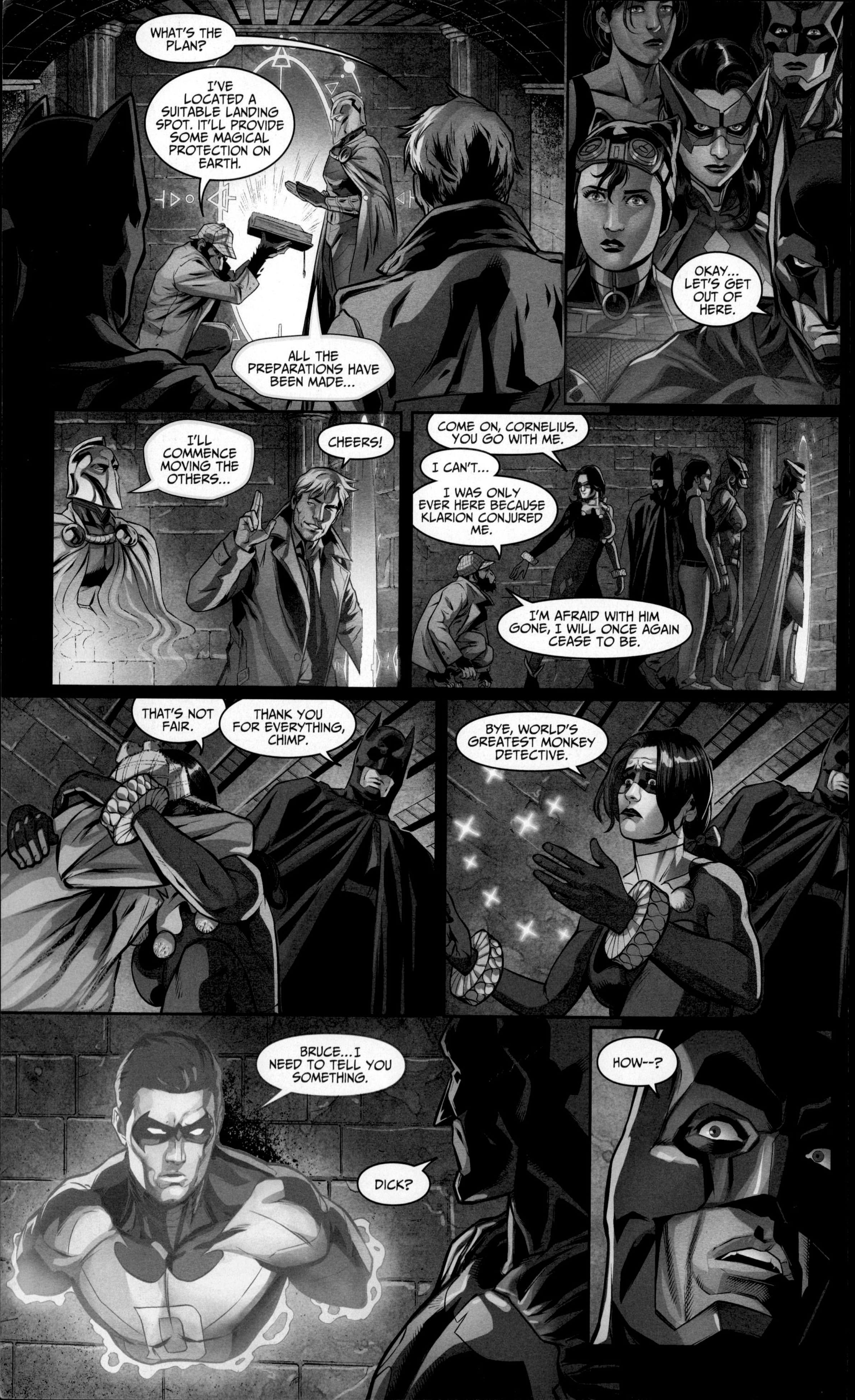
WHAT'S THE PLAN?
I'VE LOCATED A SUITABLE LANDING SPOT. IT'LL PROVIDE SOME MAGICAL PROTECTION ON EARTH.
ALL THE PREPARATIONS HAVE BEEN MADE...
OKAY... LET'S GET OUT OF HERE.
I'LL COMMENCE MOVING THE OTHERS...
CHEERS!
COME ON, CORNELIUS. YOU GO WITH ME.
I CAN'T...
I WAS ONLY EVER HERE BECAUSE KLARION CONJURED ME.
I'M AFRAID WITH HIM GONE, I WILL ONCE AGAIN CEASE TO BE.
THAT'S NOT FAIR.
THANK YOU FOR EVERYTHING, CHIMP.
BYE, WORLD'S GREATEST MONKEY DETECTIVE.
BRUCE...I NEED TO TELL YOU SOMETHING.
DICK?
HOW--?

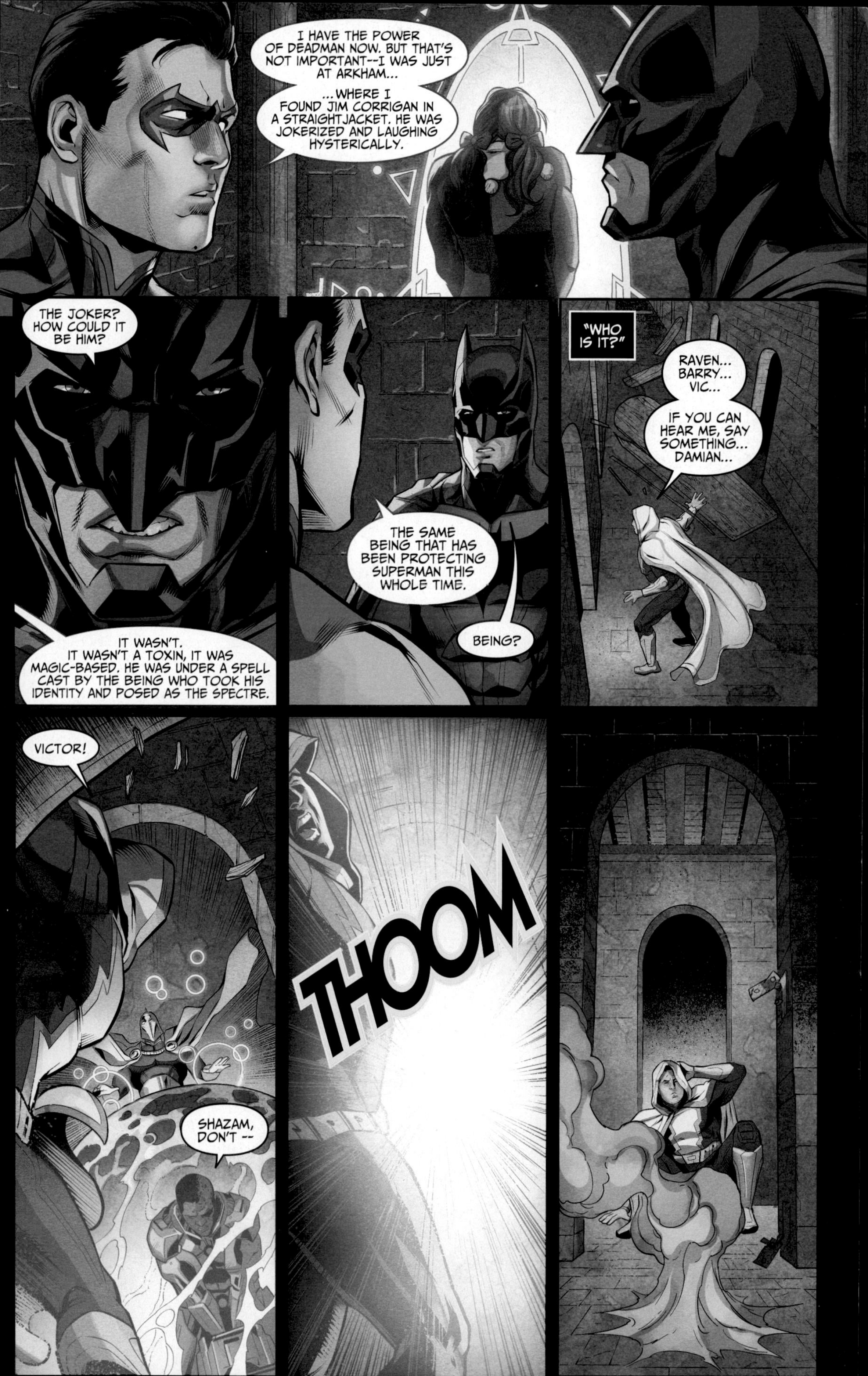
I HAVE THE POWER OF DEADMAN NOW. BUT THAT'S NOT IMPORTANT--I WAS JUST AT ARKHAM...
...WHERE I FOUND JIM CORRIGAN IN A STRAIGHTJACKET. HE WAS JOKERIZED AND LAUGHING HYSTERICALLY.
THE JOKER? HOW COULD IT BE HIM?
IT WASN'T. IT WASN'T A TOXIN, IT WAS MAGIC-BASED. HE WAS UNDER A SPELL CAST BY THE BEING WHO TOOK HIS IDENTITY AND POSED AS THE SPECTRE.
THE SAME BEING THAT HAS BEEN PROTECTING SUPERMAN THIS WHOLE TIME.
BEING?
"WHO IS IT?"
RAVEN... BARRY... VIC...
IF YOU CAN HEAR ME, SAY SOMETHING... DAMIAN...
VICTOR!
SHAZAM, DON'T --
THOOM

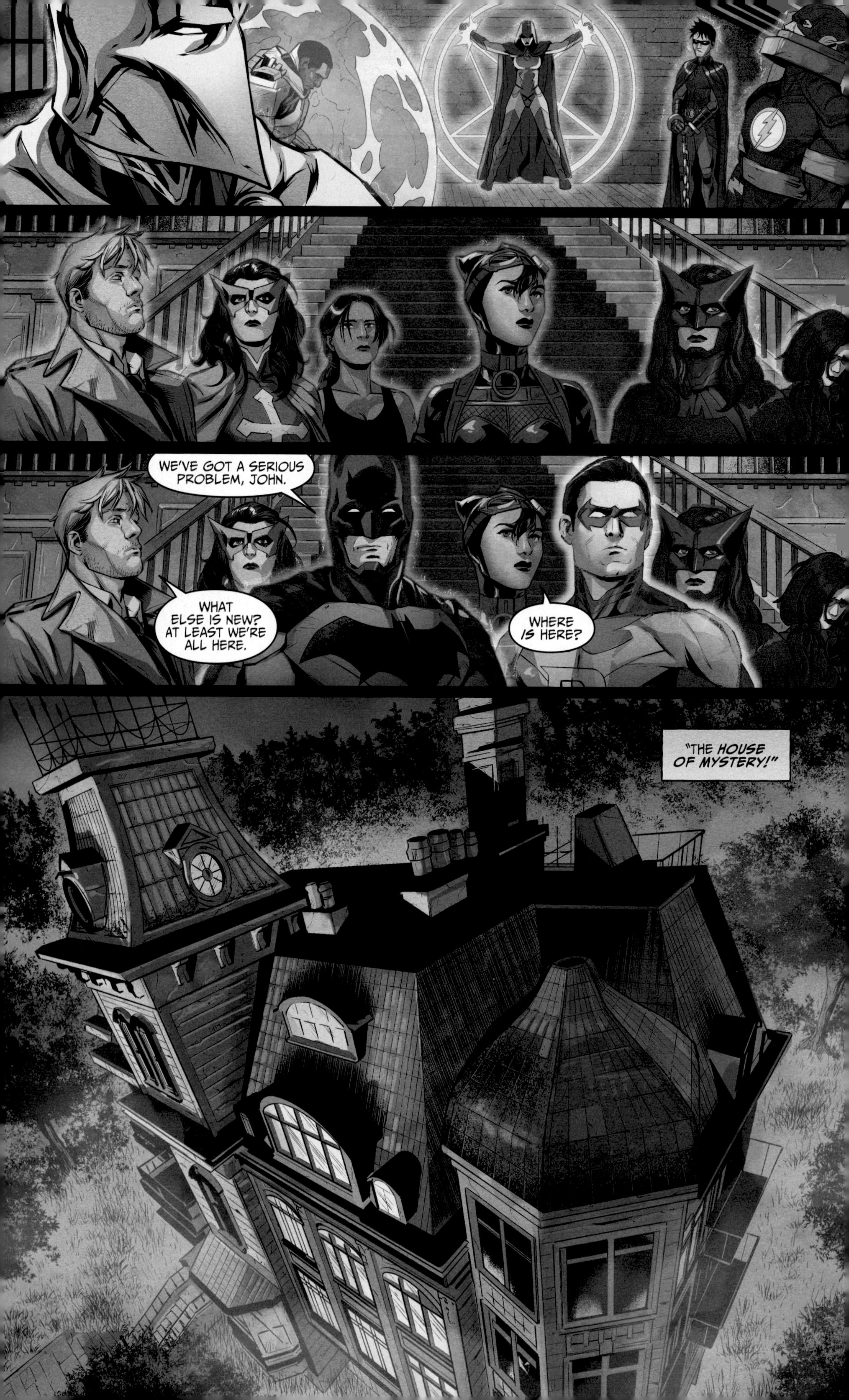
WE'VE GOT A SERIOUS PROBLEM, JOHN.
WHAT ELSE IS NEW? AT LEAST WE'RE ALL HERE.
WHERE IS HERE?
"THE HOUSE OF MYSTERY!"

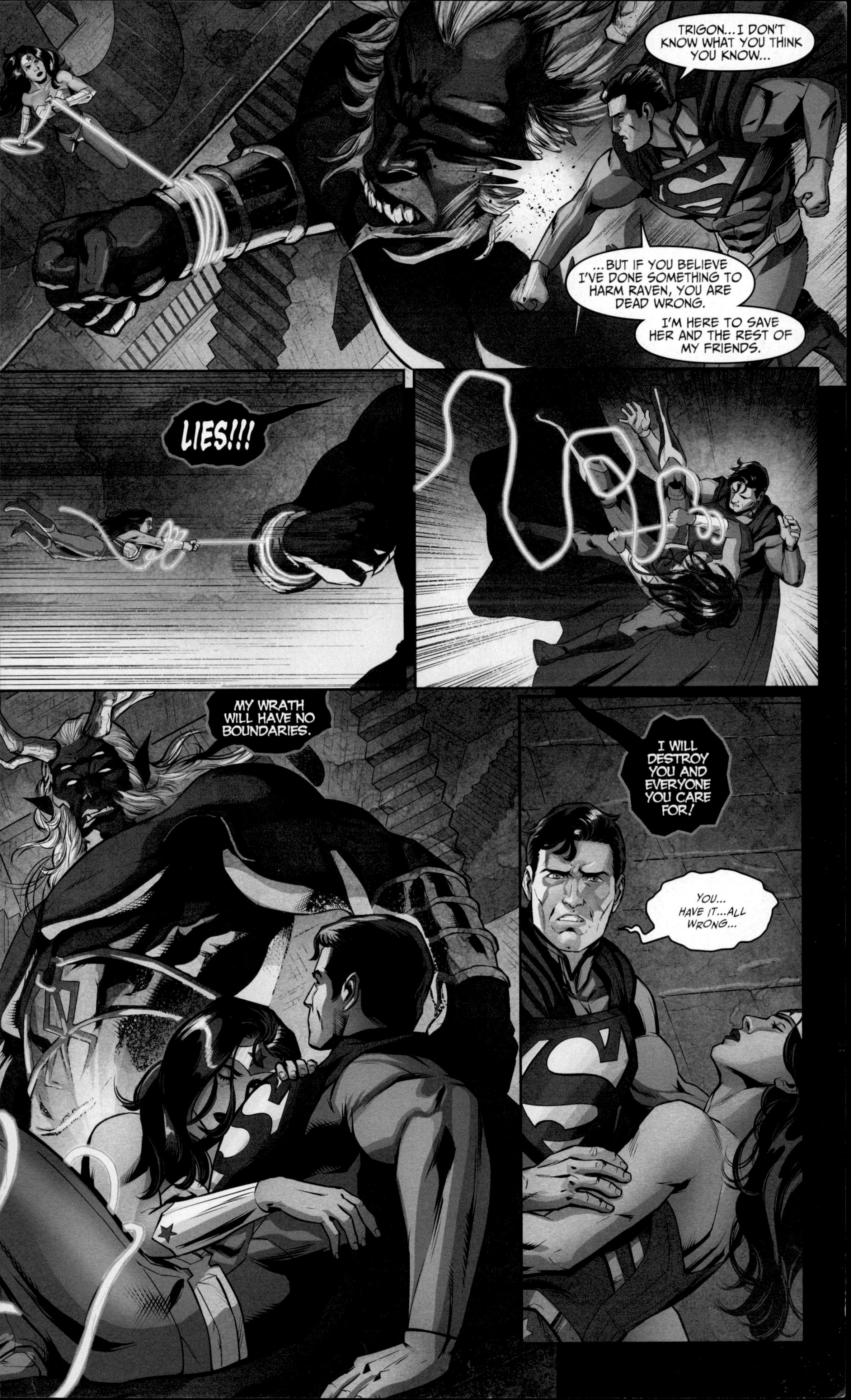
TRIGON...I DON'T KNOW WHAT YOU THINK YOU KNOW...
...BUT IF YOU BELIEVE I'VE DONE SOMETHING TO HARM RAVEN, YOU ARE DEAD WRONG.
I'M HERE TO SAVE HER AND THE REST OF MY FRIENDS.
LIES!!!
MY WRATH WILL HAVE NO BOUNDARIES.
I WILL DESTROY YOU AND EVERYONE YOU CARE FOR!
YOU... HAVE IT...ALL WRONG...

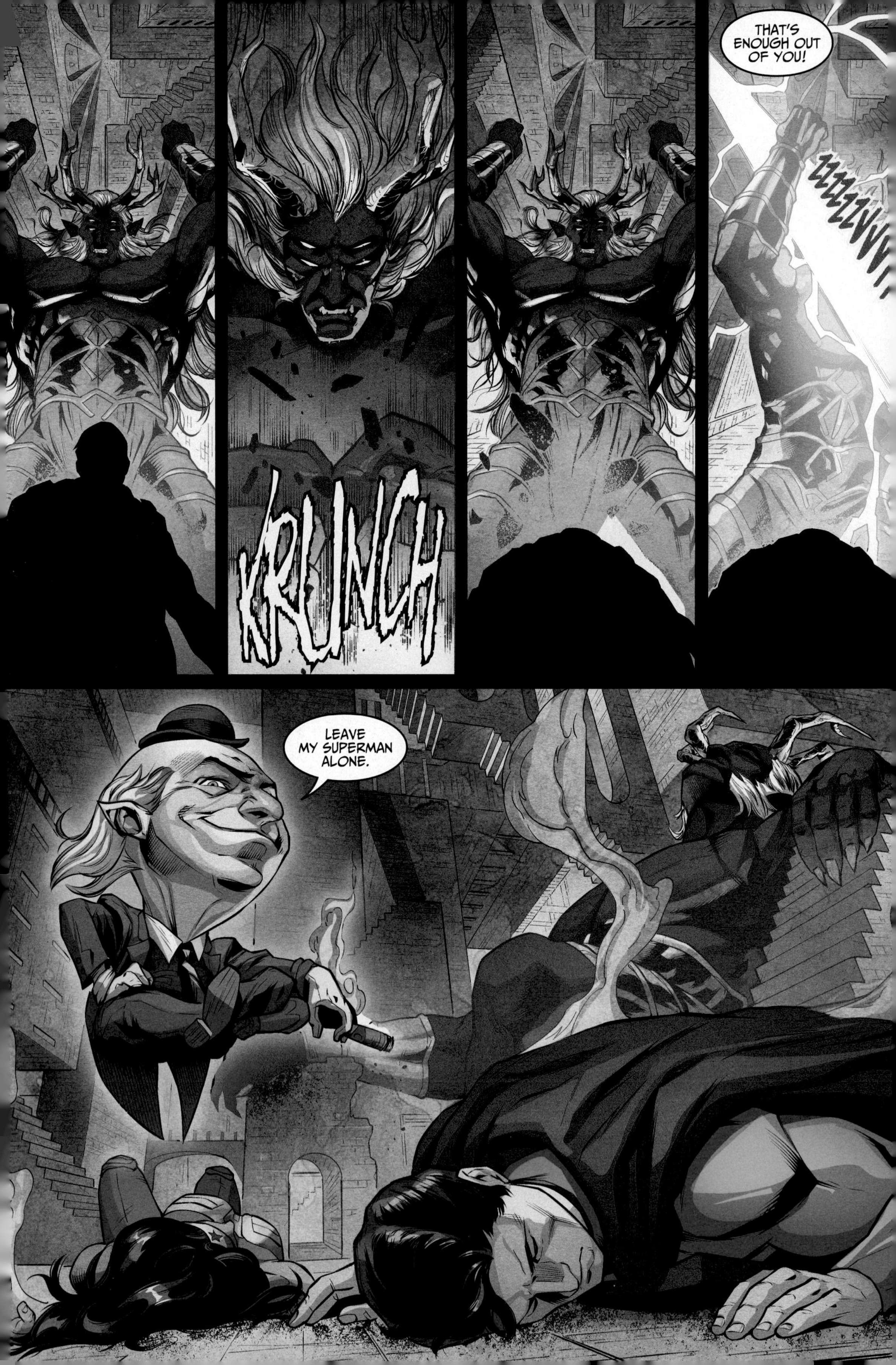
KRUNCH
THAT'S ENOUGH OUT OF YOU!
ZZZZZZVVV
LEAVE MY SUPERMAN ALONE.

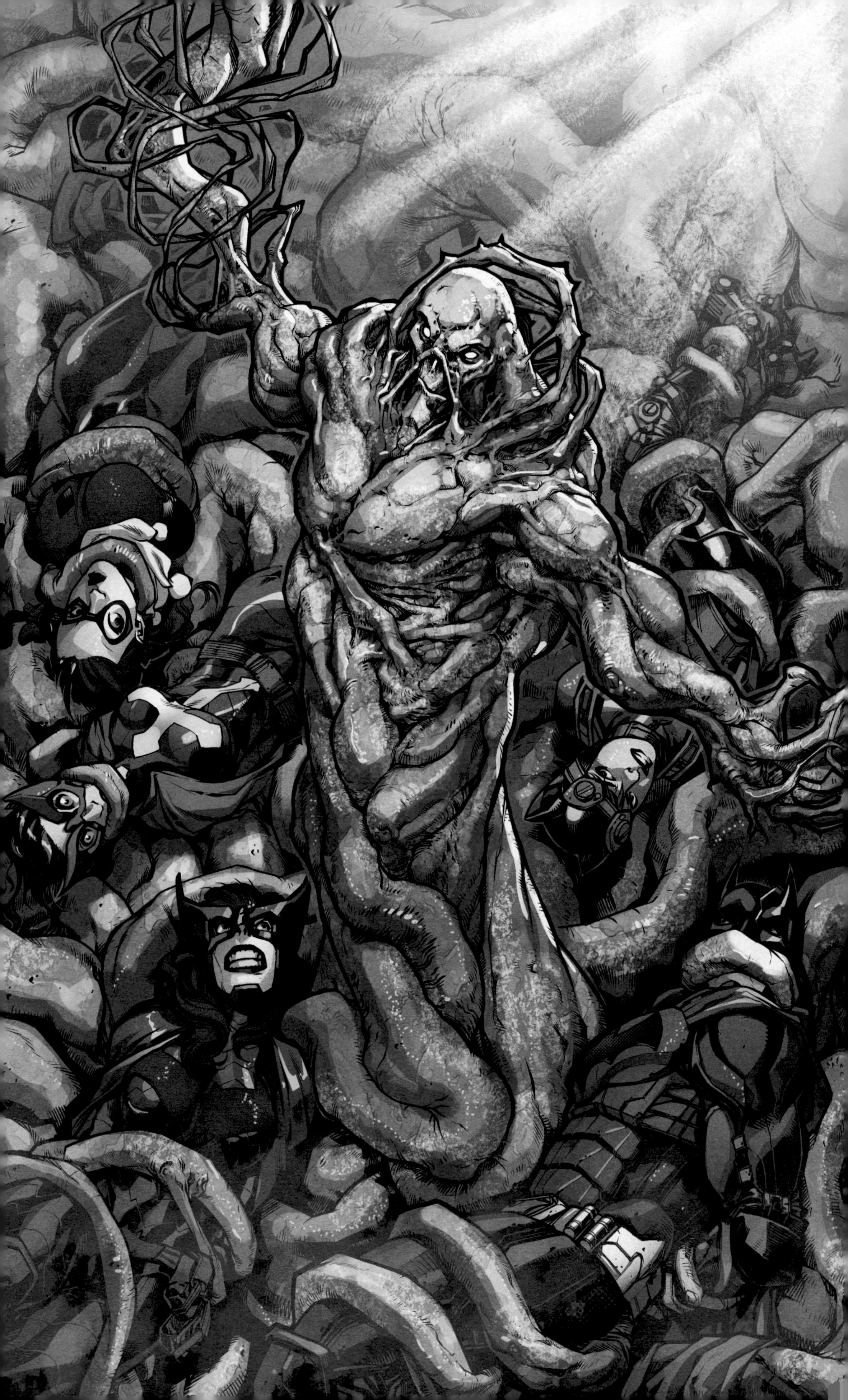

"House of Mystery" Mike S. Miller - Artist J. Nanjan - Colorist
"House of Secrets" Pete Woods - Artist J. Nanjan - Colorist
Cover Art by Neil Googe and Rex Lokus

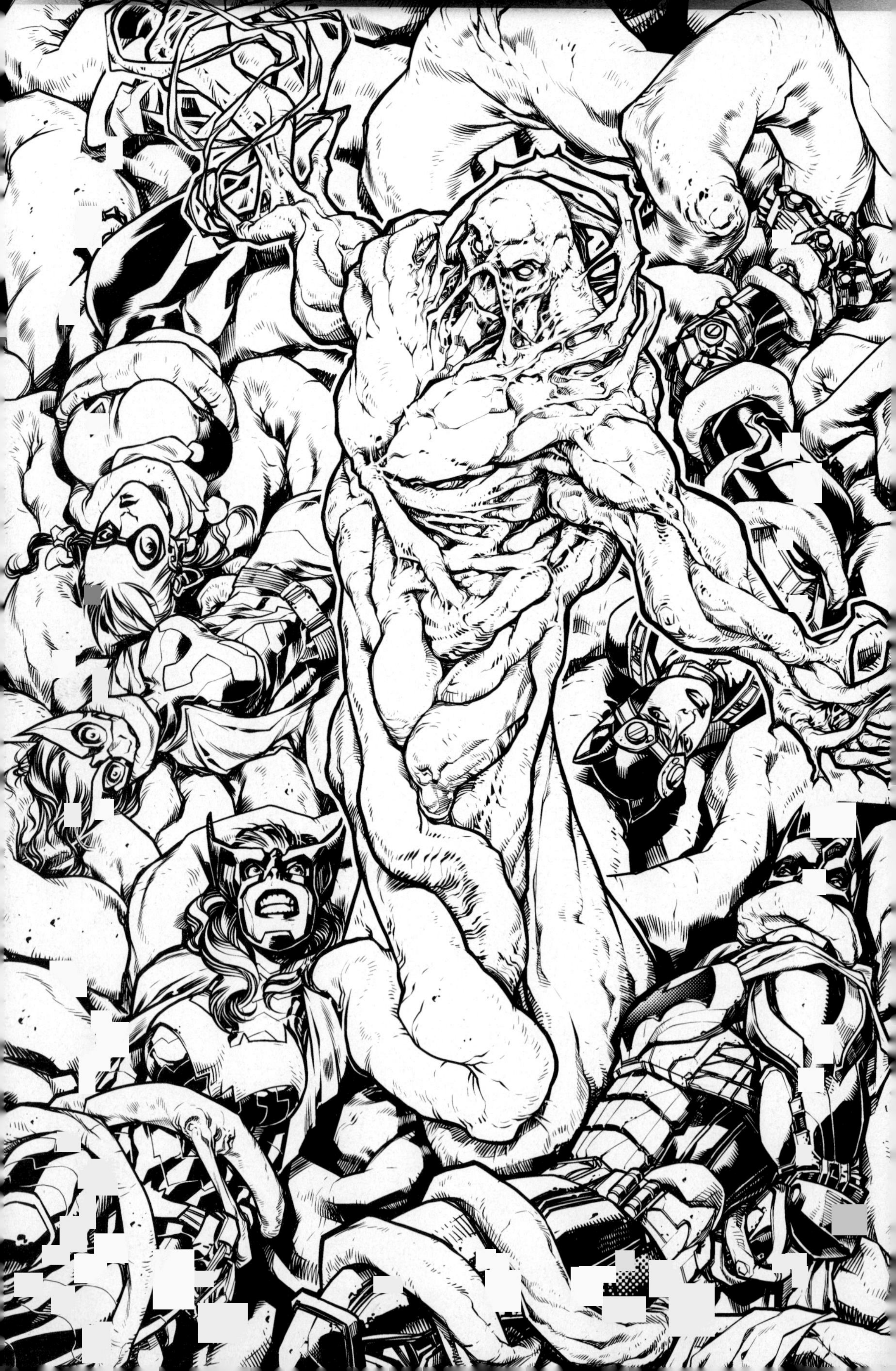

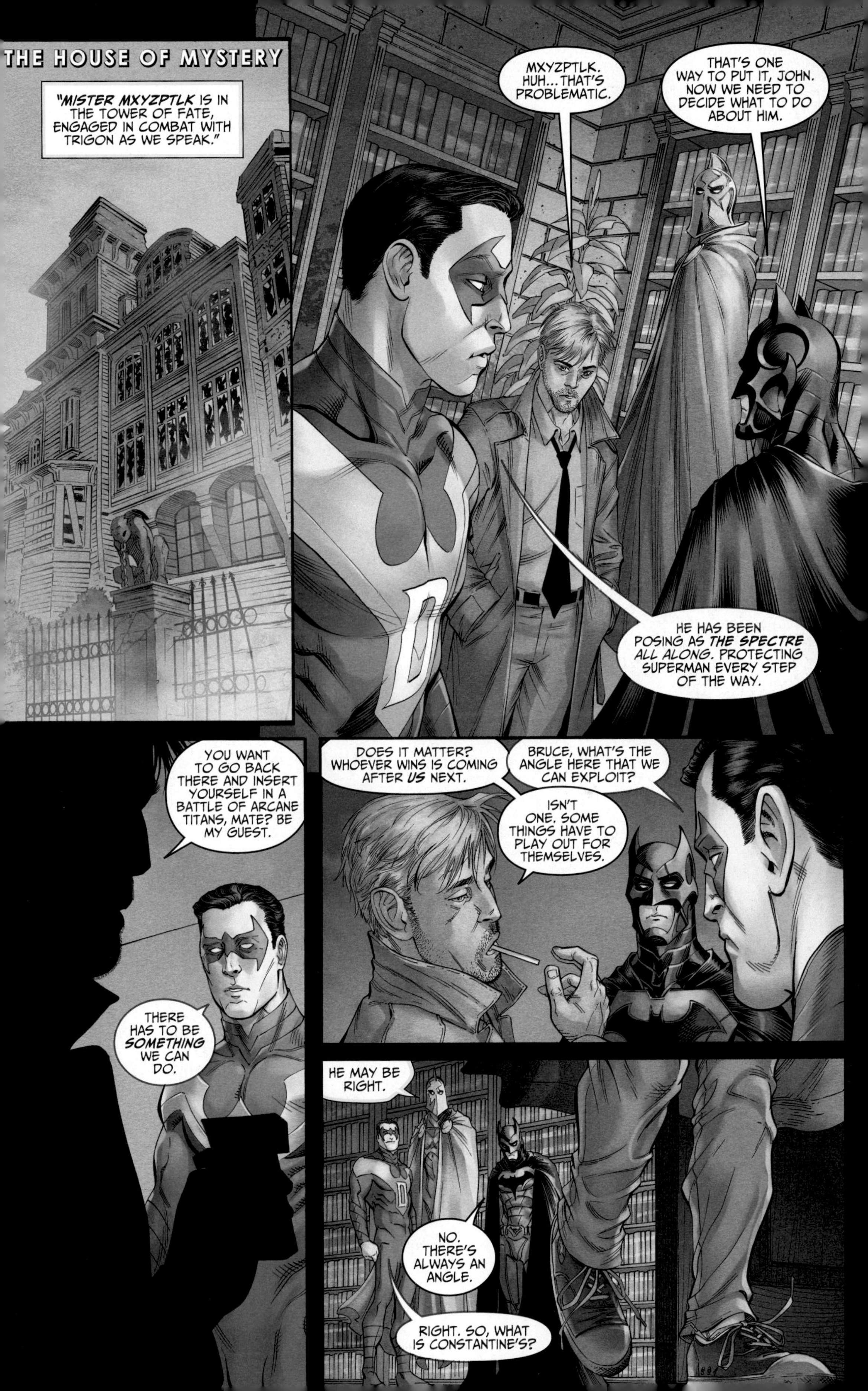
THE HOUSE OF MYSTERY
"MISTER MXYZPTLK IS IN THE TOWER OF FATE, ENGAGED IN COMBAT WITH TRIGON AS WE SPEAK."
MXYZPTLK. HUH... THAT'S PROBLEMATIC.
THAT'S ONE WAY TO PUT IT, JOHN. NOW WE NEED TO DECIDE WHAT TO DO ABOUT HIM.
HE HAS BEEN POSING AS THE SPECTRE ALL ALONG. PROTECTING SUPERMAN EVERY STEP OF THE WAY.
YOU WANT TO GO BACK THERE AND INSERT YOURSELF IN A BATTLE OF ARCANE TITANS, MATE? BE MY GUEST.
THERE HAS TO BE SOMETHING WE CAN DO.
DOES IT MATTER? WHOEVER WINS IS COMING AFTER US NEXT.
BRUCE, WHAT'S THE ANGLE HERE THAT WE CAN EXPLOIT?
ISN'T ONE. SOME THINGS HAVE TO PLAY OUT FOR THEMSELVES.
HE MAY BE RIGHT.
NO. THERE'S ALWAYS AN ANGLE.
RIGHT. SO, WHAT IS CONSTANTINE'S?

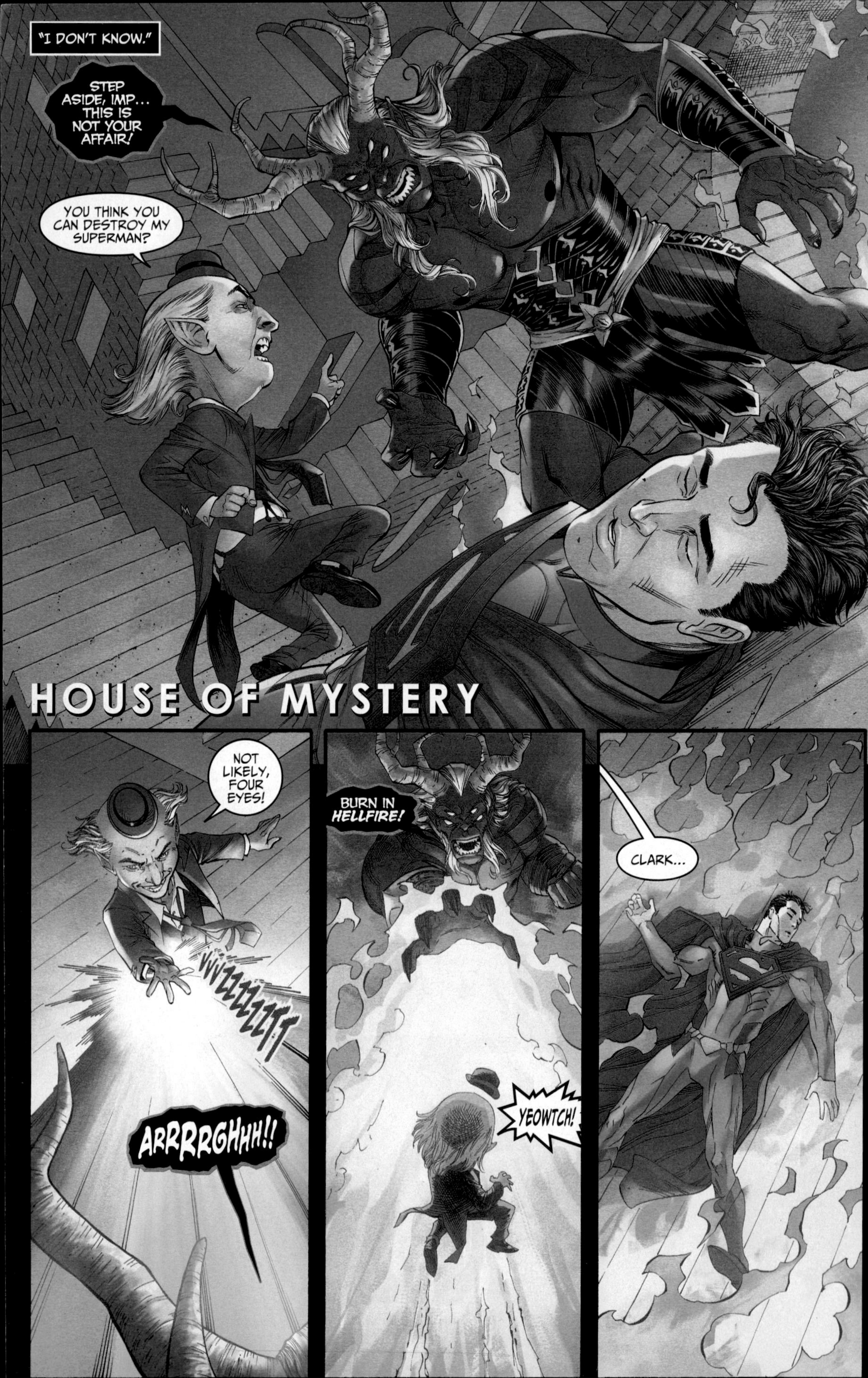
"I DON'T KNOW."
STEP ASIDE, IMP... THIS IS NOT YOUR AFFAIR!
YOU THINK YOU CAN DESTROY MY SUPERMAN?
HOUSE OF MYSTERY
NOT LIKELY, FOUR EYES!
VVVZZZZZZTT
ARRRRGHHH!!
BURN IN HELLFIRE!
YEOWTCH!
CLARK...

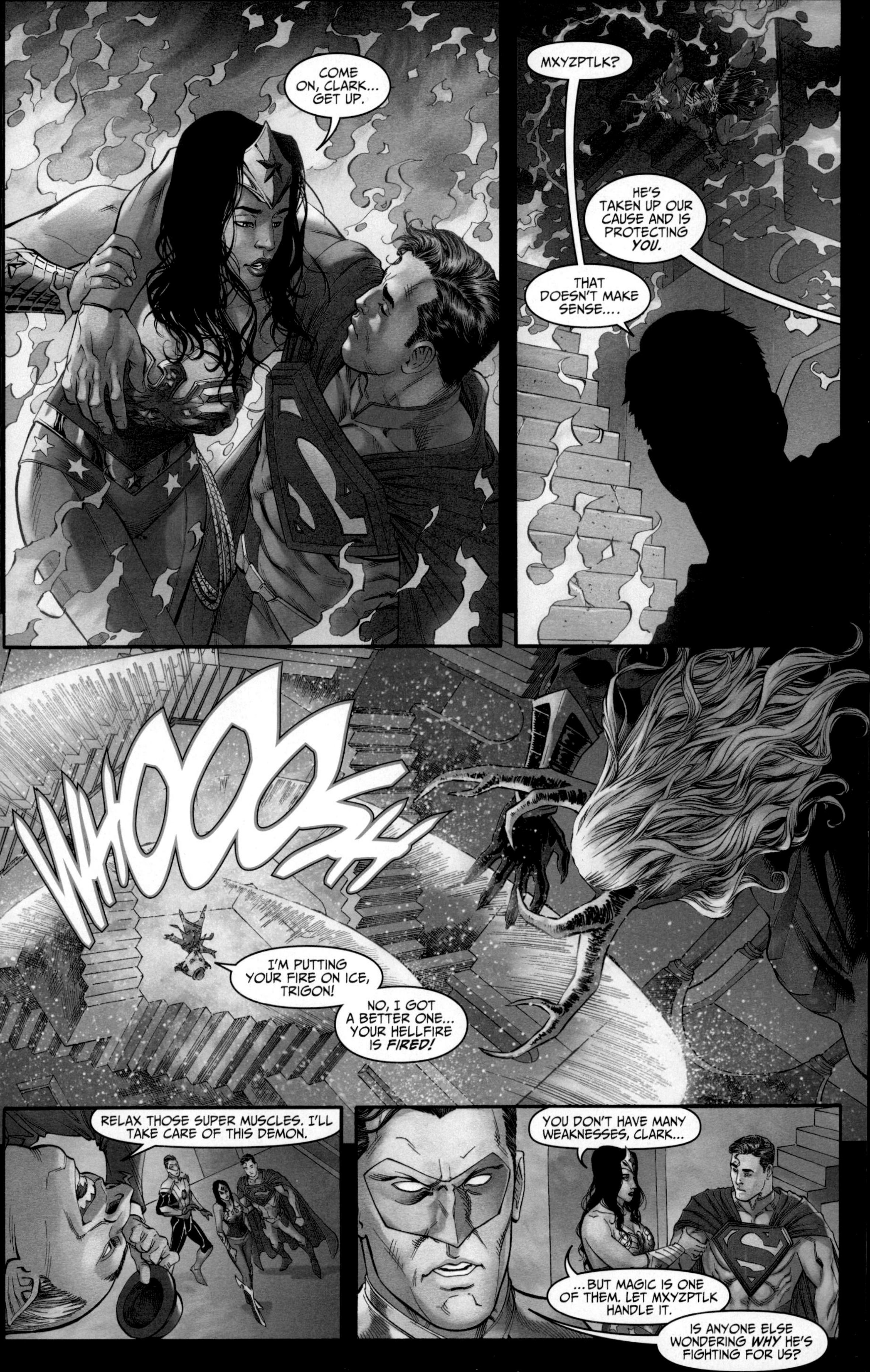
COME ON, CLARK... GET UP.
MXYZPTLK?
HE'S TAKEN UP OUR CAUSE AND IS PROTECTING *YOU.*
THAT DOESN'T MAKE SENSE....
WHOOOSH
I'M PUTTING YOUR FIRE ON ICE, TRIGON!
NO, I GOT A BETTER ONE... YOUR HELLFIRE IS *FIRED!*
RELAX THOSE SUPER MUSCLES. I'LL TAKE CARE OF THIS DEMON.
YOU DON'T HAVE MANY WEAKNESSES, CLARK...
...BUT MAGIC IS ONE OF THEM. LET MXYZPTLK HANDLE IT.
IS ANYONE ELSE WONDERING *WHY* HE'S FIGHTING FOR US?

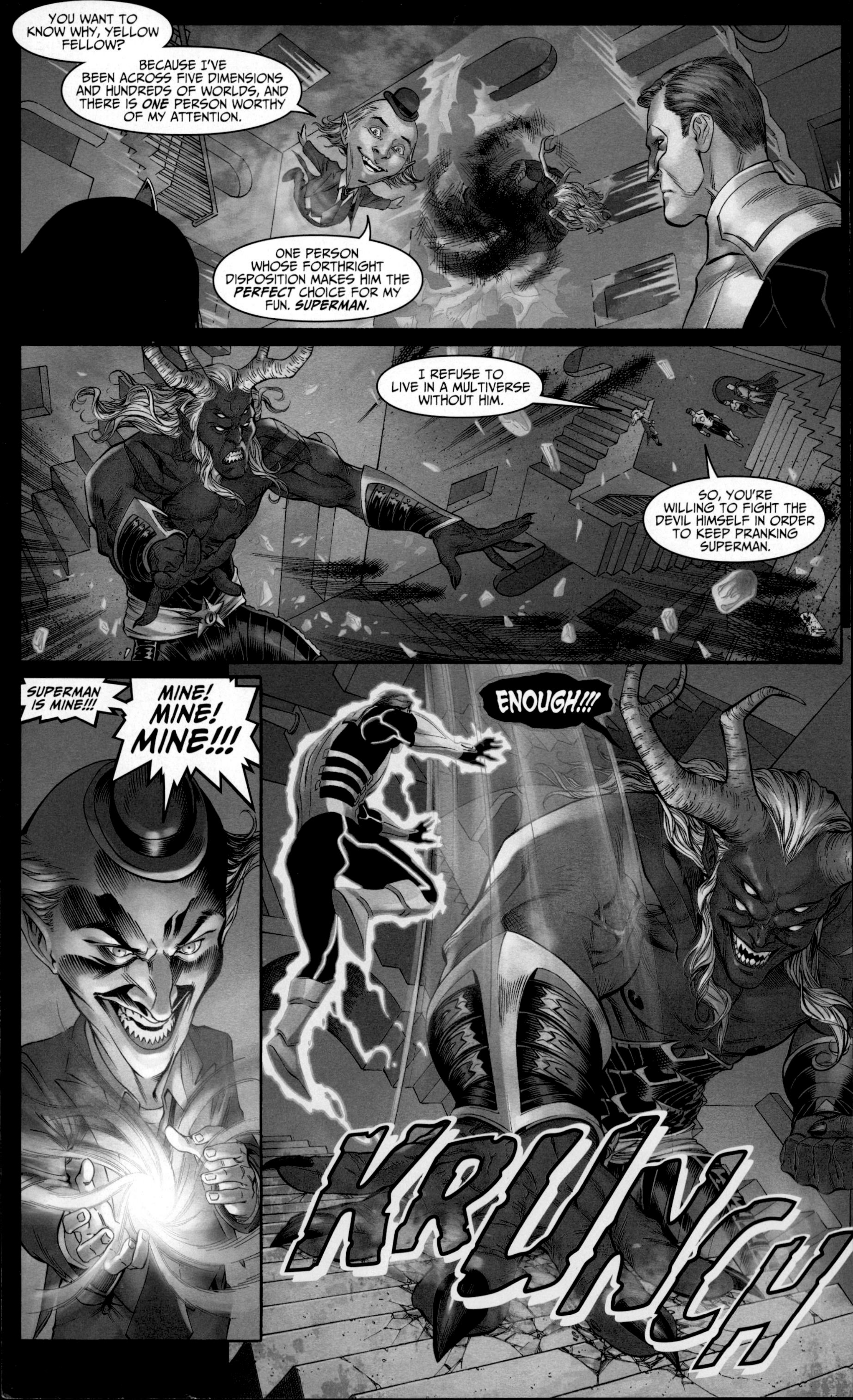
YOU WANT TO KNOW WHY, YELLOW FELLOW?
BECAUSE I'VE BEEN ACROSS FIVE DIMENSIONS AND HUNDREDS OF WORLDS, AND THERE IS ONE PERSON WORTHY OF MY ATTENTION.
ONE PERSON WHOSE FORTHRIGHT DISPOSITION MAKES HIM THE PERFECT CHOICE FOR MY FUN. SUPERMAN.
I REFUSE TO LIVE IN A MULTIVERSE WITHOUT HIM.
SO, YOU'RE WILLING TO FIGHT THE DEVIL HIMSELF IN ORDER TO KEEP PRANKING SUPERMAN.
SUPERMAN IS MINE!!!
MINE! MINE! MINE!!!
ENOUGH!!!
KRUNCH

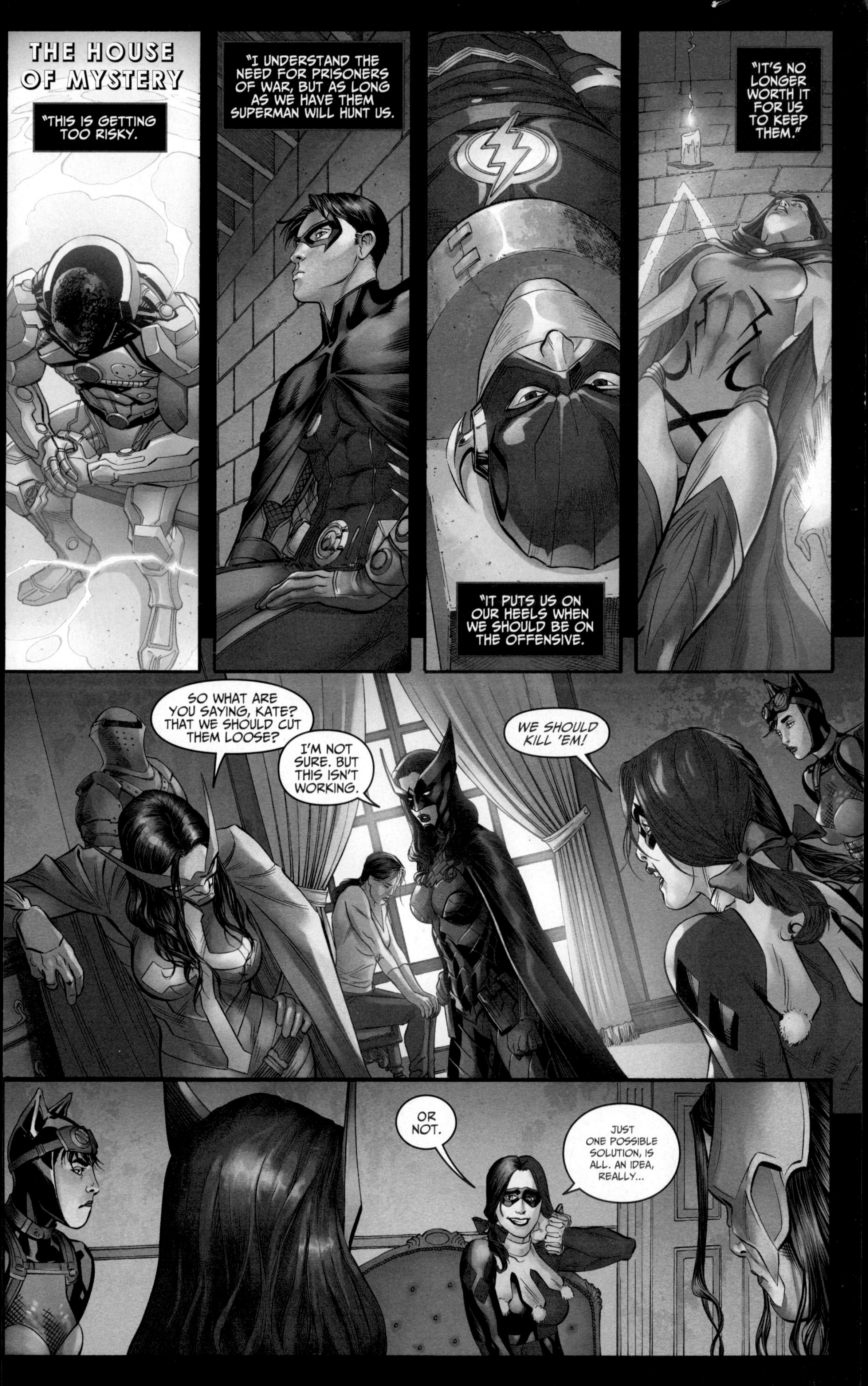
THE HOUSE OF MYSTERY
"THIS IS GETTING TOO RISKY.
"I UNDERSTAND THE NEED FOR PRISONERS OF WAR, BUT AS LONG AS WE HAVE THEM SUPERMAN WILL HUNT US.
"IT PUTS US ON OUR HEELS WHEN WE SHOULD BE ON THE OFFENSIVE.
"IT'S NO LONGER WORTH IT FOR US TO KEEP THEM."
SO WHAT ARE YOU SAYING, KATE? THAT WE SHOULD CUT THEM LOOSE?
I'M NOT SURE. BUT THIS ISN'T WORKING.
WE SHOULD KILL 'EM!
OR NOT.
JUST ONE POSSIBLE SOLUTION, IS ALL. AN IDEA, REALLY...

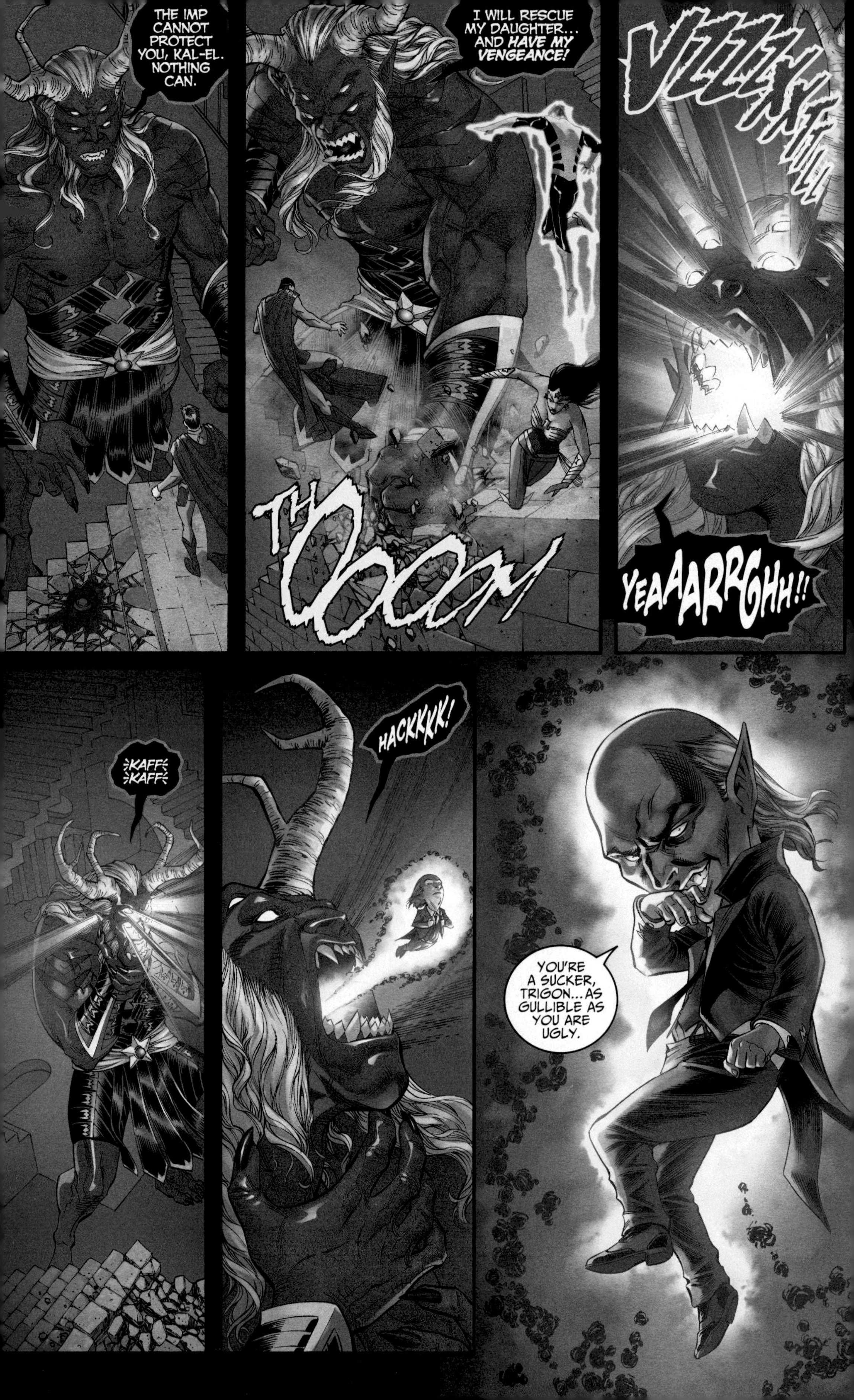
THE IMP CANNOT PROTECT YOU, KAL-EL. NOTHING CAN.
I WILL RESCUE MY DAUGHTER... AND HAVE MY VENGEANCE!
THOOOM
YEAAARRGHH!!
KAFF KAFF
HACKKKK!
YOU'RE A SUCKER, TRIGON... AS GULLIBLE AS YOU ARE UGLY.

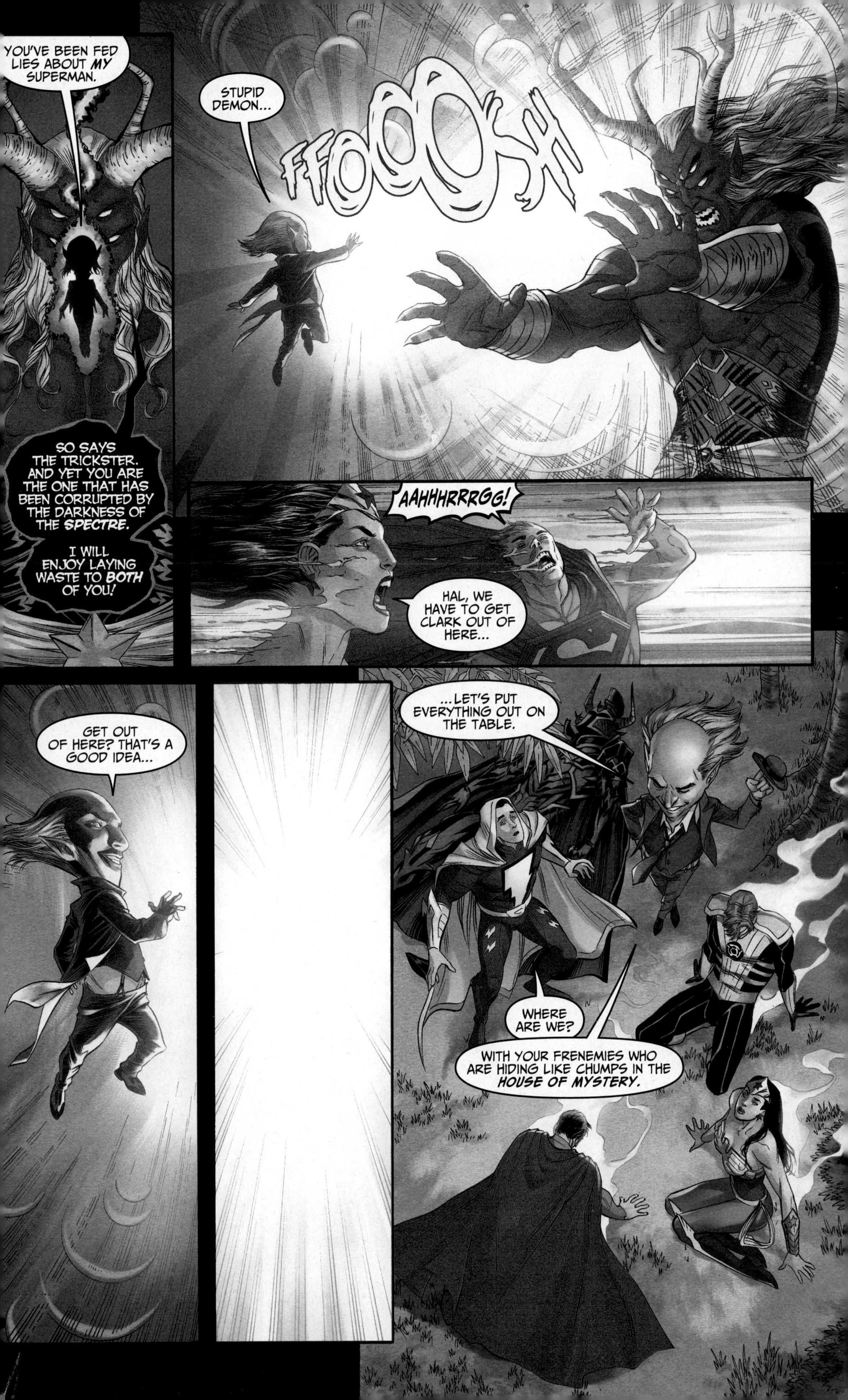
YOU'VE BEEN FED LIES ABOUT *MY* SUPERMAN.
STUPID DEMON...
FFOOOOSH
SO SAYS THE TRICKSTER. AND YET YOU ARE THE ONE THAT HAS BEEN CORRUPTED BY THE DARKNESS OF THE *SPECTRE*.
I WILL ENJOY LAYING WASTE TO *BOTH* OF YOU!
AAHHHRRRGG!
HAL, WE HAVE TO GET CLARK OUT OF HERE...
GET OUT OF HERE? THAT'S A GOOD IDEA...
...LET'S PUT EVERYTHING OUT ON THE TABLE.
WHERE ARE WE?
WITH YOUR FRENEMIES WHO ARE HIDING LIKE CHUMPS IN THE *HOUSE OF MYSTERY*.

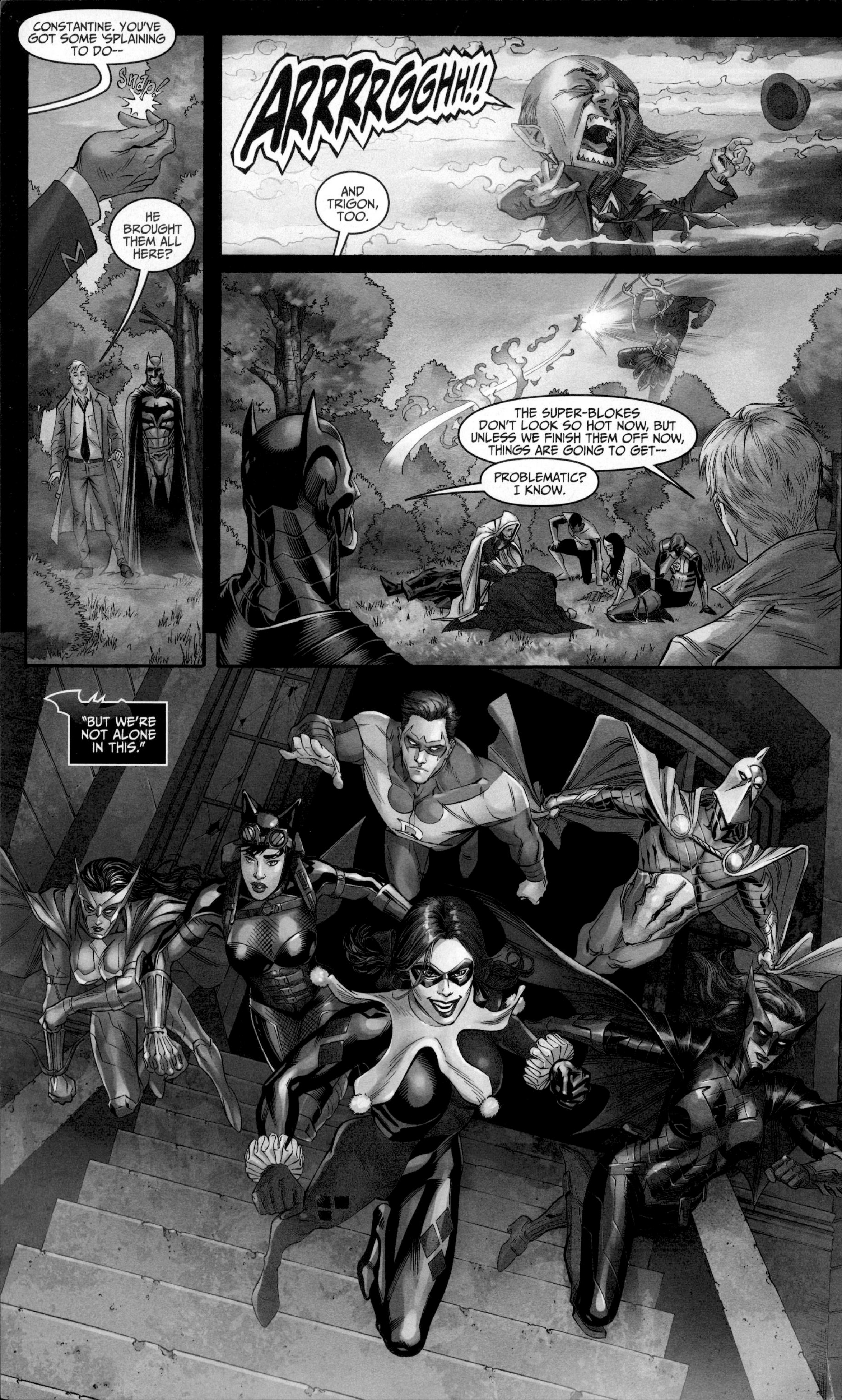

CONSTANTINE. YOU'VE GOT SOME 'SPLAINING TO DO--
Snap!
HE BROUGHT THEM ALL HERE?
ARRRRGGHH!!!
AND TRIGON, TOO.
THE SUPER-BLOKES DON'T LOOK SO HOT NOW, BUT UNLESS WE FINISH THEM OFF NOW, THINGS ARE GOING TO GET--
PROBLEMATIC? I KNOW.
"BUT WE'RE NOT ALONE IN THIS."

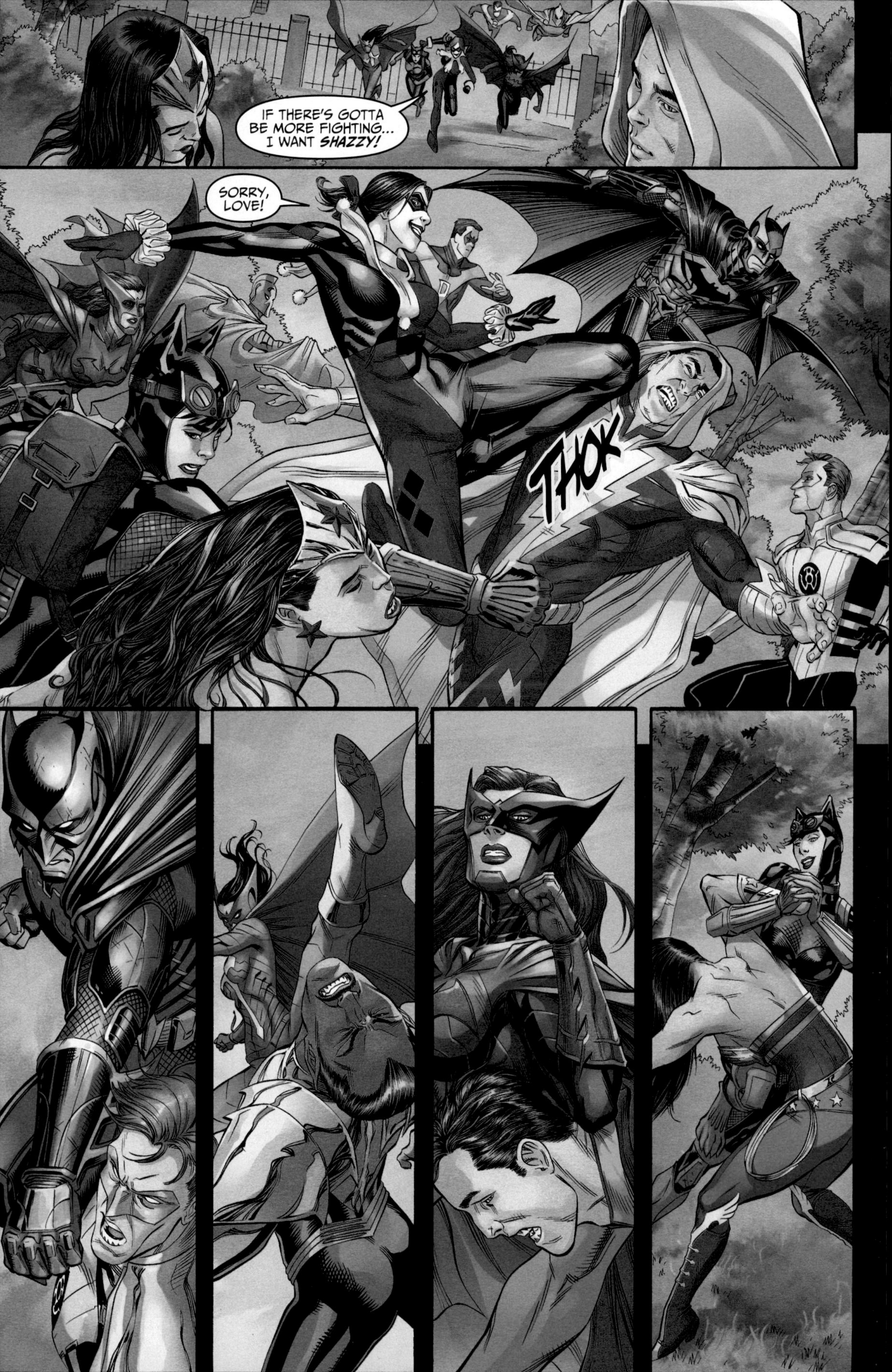
IF THERE'S GOTTA BE MORE FIGHTING... I WANT SHAZZY!
SORRY, LOVE!
THOK

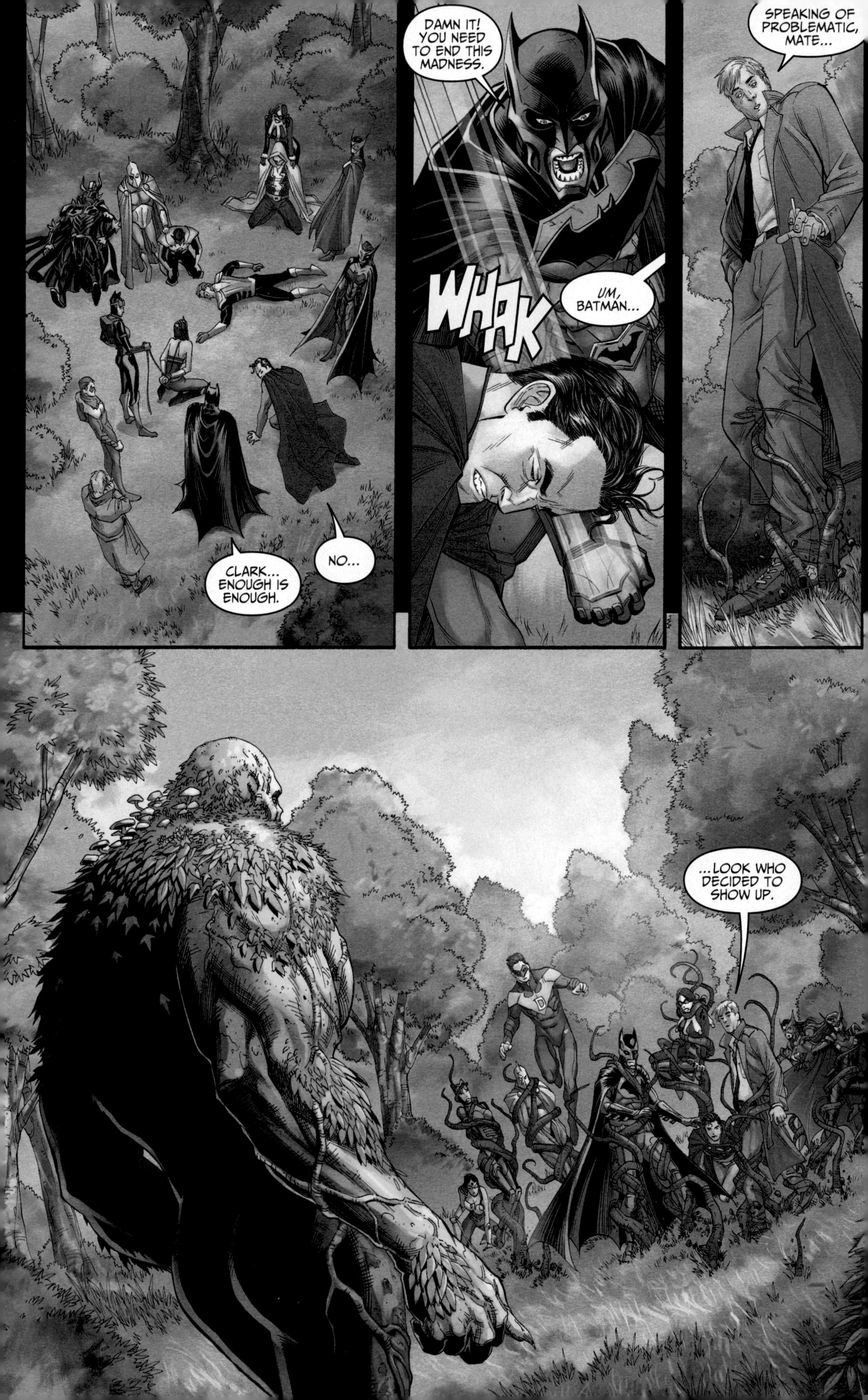
CLARK... ENOUGH IS ENOUGH.
NO...
DAMN IT! YOU NEED TO END THIS MADNESS.
WHAK
UM, BATMAN...
SPEAKING OF PROBLEMATIC, MATE...
...LOOK WHO DECIDED TO SHOW UP.

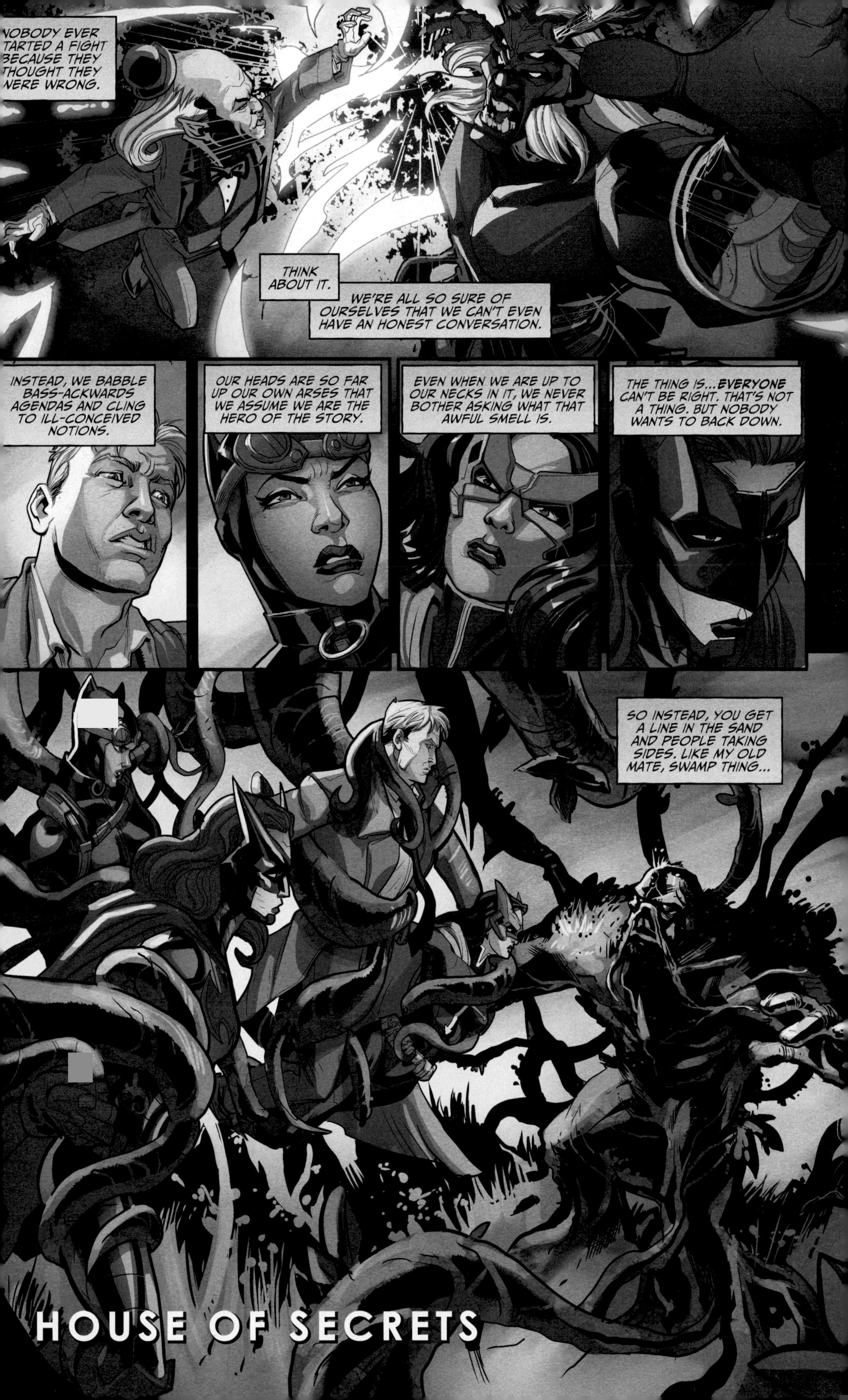
NOBODY EVER TARTED A FIGHT BECAUSE THEY THOUGHT THEY NERE WRONG.
THINK ABOUT IT.
WE'RE ALL SO SURE OF OURSELVES THAT WE CAN'T EVEN HAVE AN HONEST CONVERSATION.
INSTEAD, WE BABBLE BASS-ACKWARDS AGENDAS AND CLING TO ILL-CONCEIVED NOTIONS.
OUR HEADS ARE SO FAR UP OUR OWN ARSES THAT WE ASSUME WE ARE THE HERO OF THE STORY.
EVEN WHEN WE ARE UP TO OUR NECKS IN IT, WE NEVER BOTHER ASKING WHAT THAT AWFUL SMELL IS.
THE THING IS...**EVERYONE** CAN'T BE RIGHT. THAT'S NOT A THING. BUT NOBODY WANTS TO BACK DOWN.
SO INSTEAD, YOU GET A LINE IN THE SAND AND PEOPLE TAKING SIDES. LIKE MY OLD MATE, SWAMP THING...
HOUSE OF SECRETS

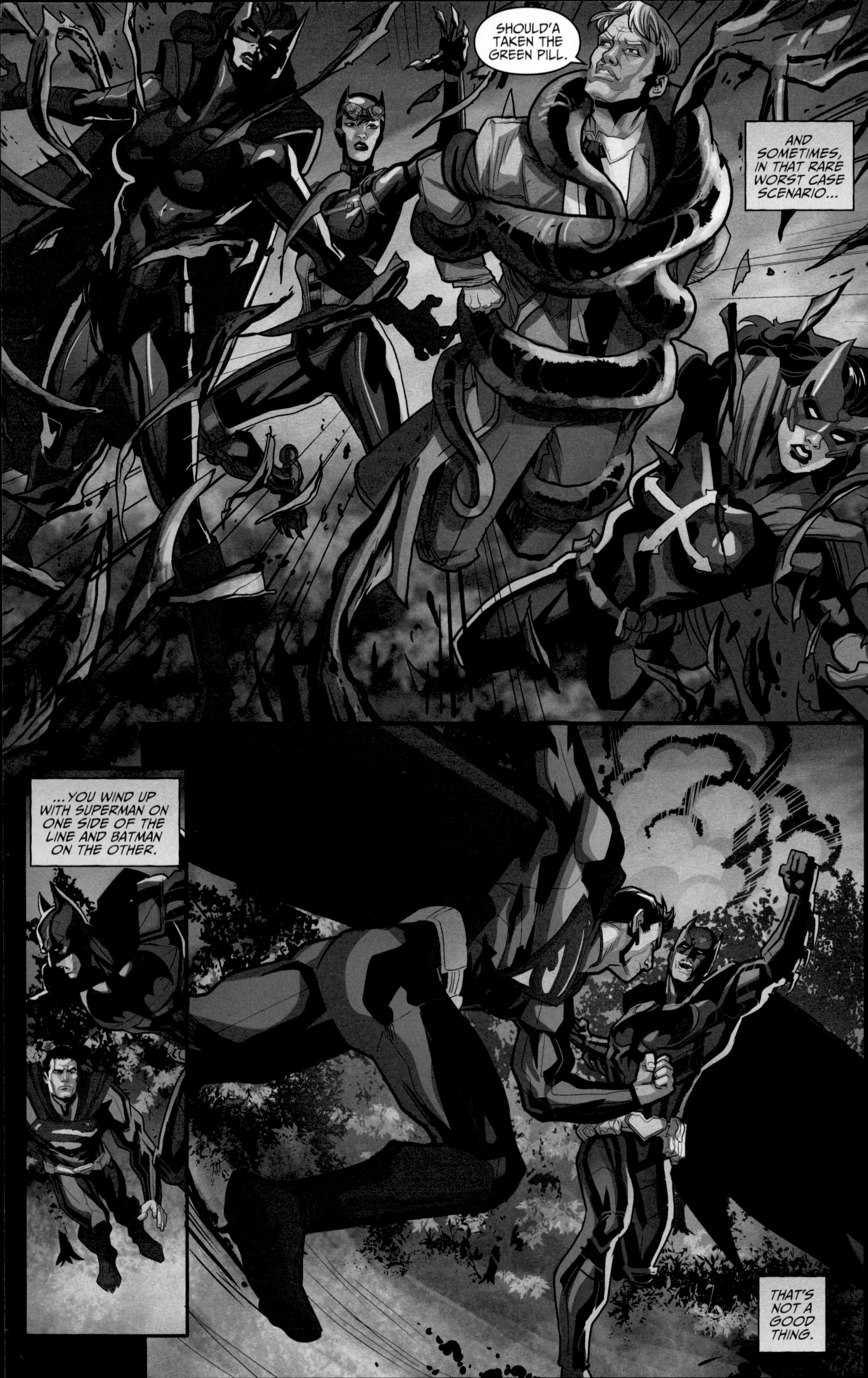
SHOULD'A TAKEN THE GREEN PILL.
AND SOMETIMES, IN THAT RARE WORST CASE SCENARIO...
...YOU WIND UP WITH SUPERMAN ON ONE SIDE OF THE LINE AND BATMAN ON THE OTHER.
THAT'S NOT A GOOD THING.

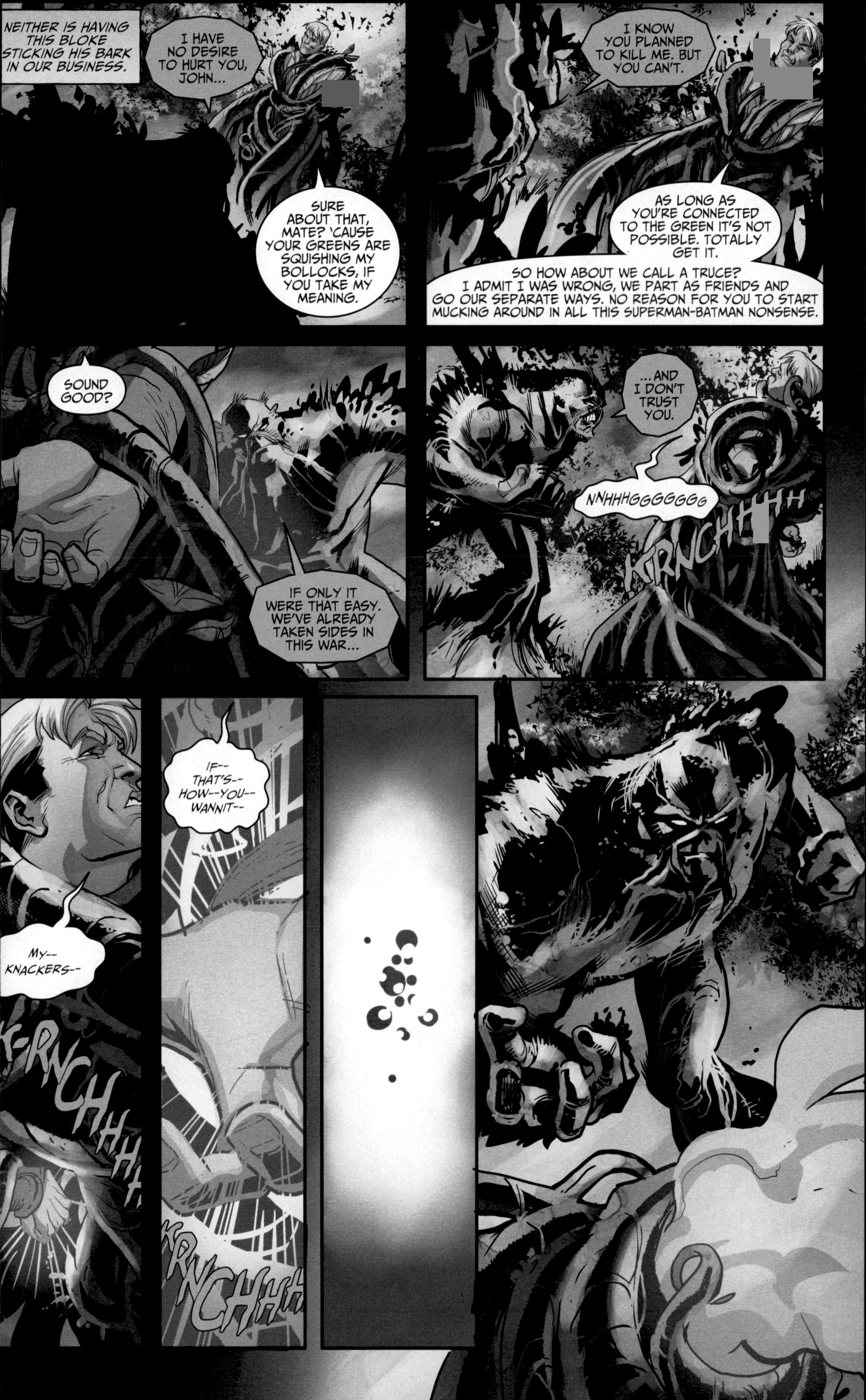
NEITHER IS HAVING THIS BLOKE STICKING HIS BARK IN OUR BUSINESS.
I HAVE NO DESIRE TO HURT YOU, JOHN...
SURE ABOUT THAT, MATE? 'CAUSE YOUR GREENS ARE SQUISHING MY BOLLOCKS, IF YOU TAKE MY MEANING.
I KNOW YOU PLANNED TO KILL ME. BUT YOU CAN'T.
AS LONG AS YOU'RE CONNECTED TO THE GREEN IT'S NOT POSSIBLE. TOTALLY GET IT.
SO HOW ABOUT WE CALL A TRUCE? I ADMIT I WAS WRONG, WE PART AS FRIENDS AND GO OUR SEPARATE WAYS. NO REASON FOR YOU TO START MUCKING AROUND IN ALL THIS SUPERMAN-BATMAN NONSENSE.
SOUND GOOD?
IF ONLY IT WERE THAT EASY. WE'VE ALREADY TAKEN SIDES IN THIS WAR...
...AND I DON'T TRUST YOU.
NNHHHGGGGGGG
KRNCHHHHH
MY-- KNACKERS--
KRNCHHHHH
IF-- THAT'S-- HOW--YOU-- WANNIT--
KRNCHHHH

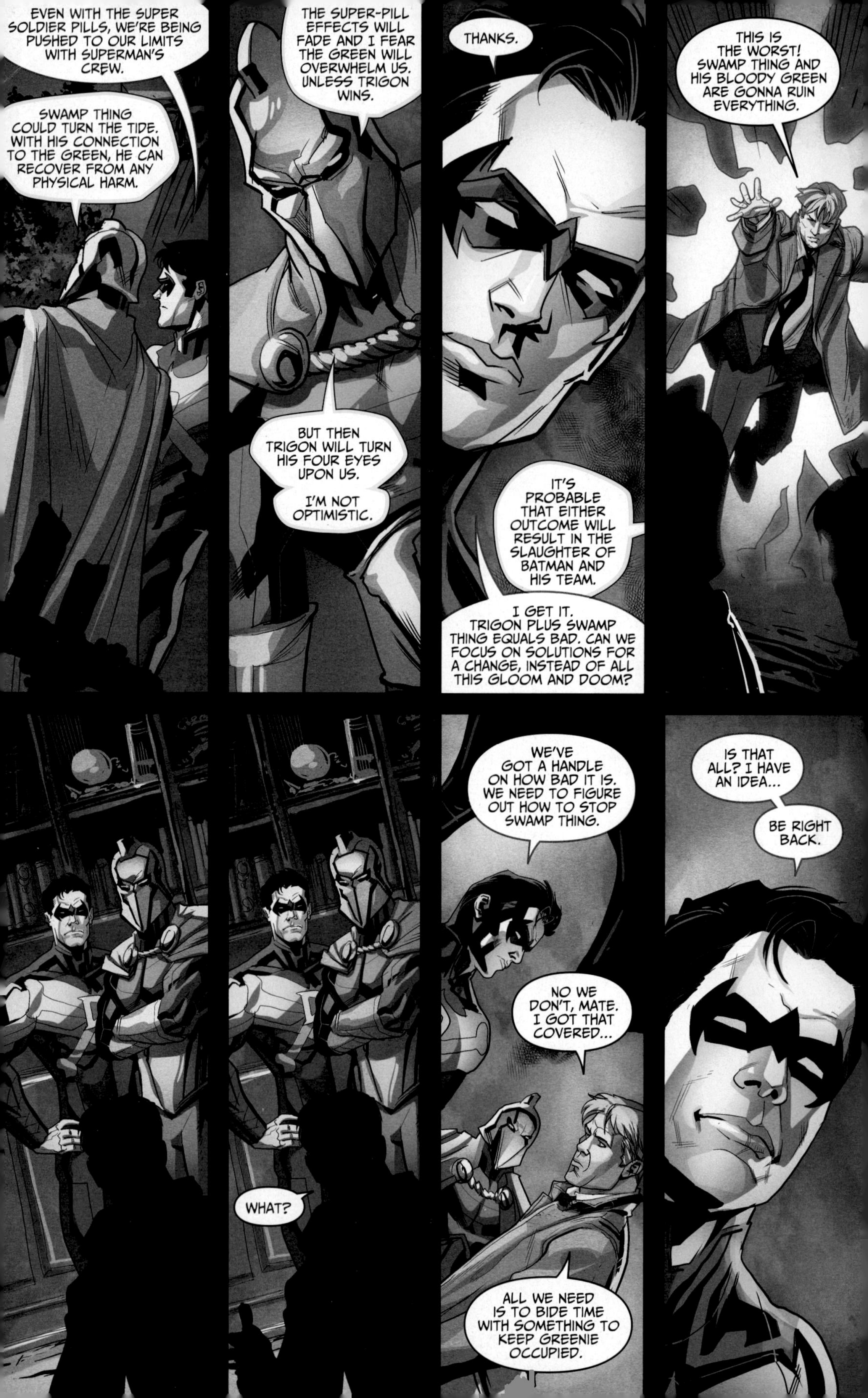
EVEN WITH THE SUPER SOLDIER PILLS, WE'RE BEING PUSHED TO OUR LIMITS WITH SUPERMAN'S CREW.
SWAMP THING COULD TURN THE TIDE. WITH HIS CONNECTION TO THE GREEN, HE CAN RECOVER FROM ANY PHYSICAL HARM.
THE SUPER-PILL EFFECTS WILL FADE AND I FEAR THE GREEN WILL OVERWHELM US. UNLESS TRIGON WINS.
BUT THEN TRIGON WILL TURN HIS FOUR EYES UPON US.
I'M NOT OPTIMISTIC.
THANKS.
IT'S PROBABLE THAT EITHER OUTCOME WILL RESULT IN THE SLAUGHTER OF BATMAN AND HIS TEAM.
I GET IT. TRIGON PLUS SWAMP THING EQUALS BAD. CAN WE FOCUS ON SOLUTIONS FOR A CHANGE, INSTEAD OF ALL THIS GLOOM AND DOOM?
THIS IS THE WORST! SWAMP THING AND HIS BLOODY GREEN ARE GONNA RUIN EVERYTHING.
WHAT?
WE'VE GOT A HANDLE ON HOW BAD IT IS. WE NEED TO FIGURE OUT HOW TO STOP SWAMP THING.
NO WE DON'T, MATE. I GOT THAT COVERED...
ALL WE NEED IS TO BIDE TIME WITH SOMETHING TO KEEP GREENIE OCCUPIED.
IS THAT ALL? I HAVE AN IDEA...
BE RIGHT BACK.

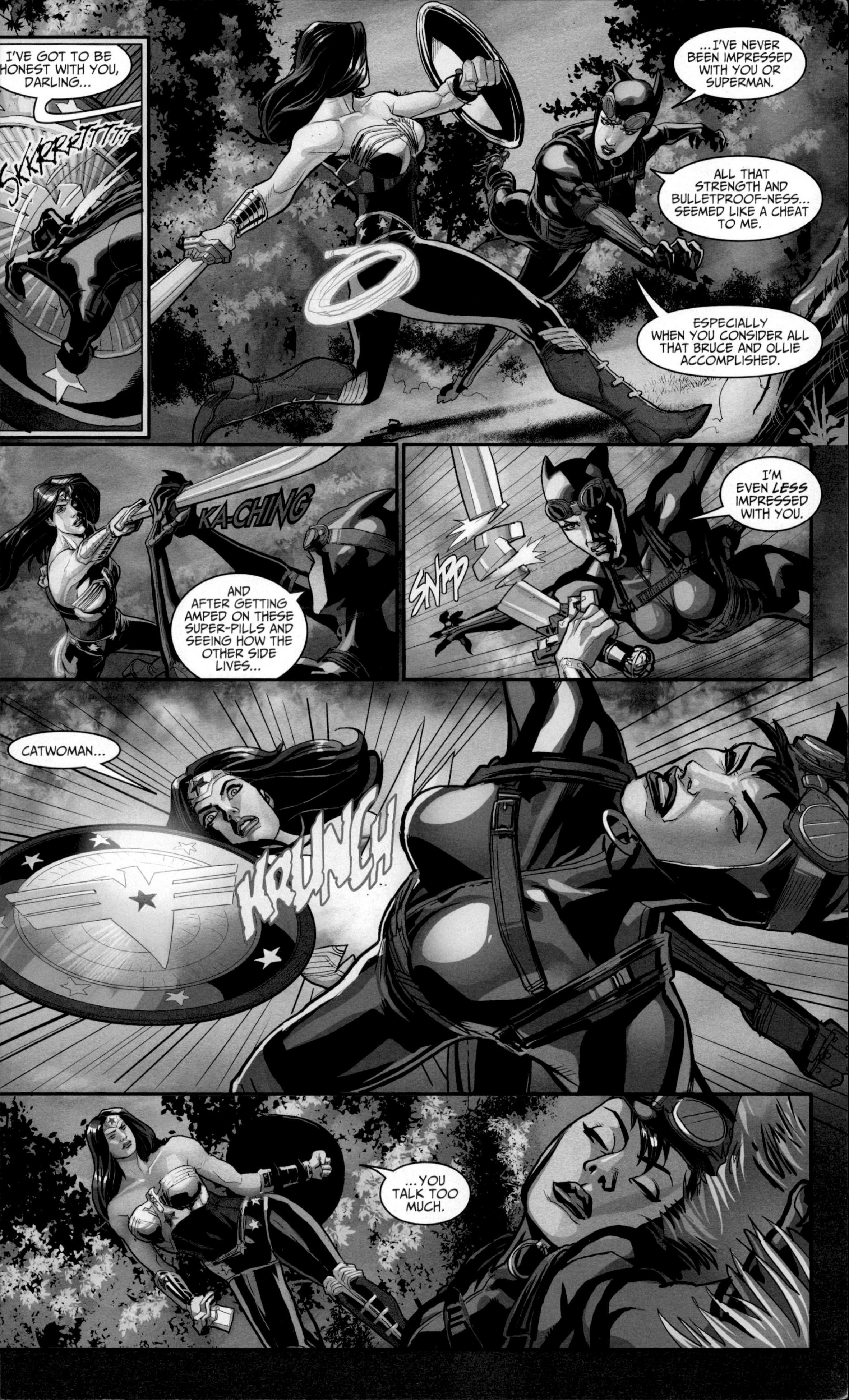
I'VE GOT TO BE HONEST WITH YOU, DARLING...
SKKRRRTTTTTT
...I'VE NEVER BEEN IMPRESSED WITH YOU OR SUPERMAN.
ALL THAT STRENGTH AND BULLETPROOF-NESS... SEEMED LIKE A CHEAT TO ME.
ESPECIALLY WHEN YOU CONSIDER ALL THAT BRUCE AND OLLIE ACCOMPLISHED.
KA-CHING
AND AFTER GETTING AMPED ON THESE SUPER-PILLS AND SEEING HOW THE OTHER SIDE LIVES...
I'M EVEN LESS IMPRESSED WITH YOU.
SNPP
CATWOMAN...
KRUNCH
...YOU TALK TOO MUCH.

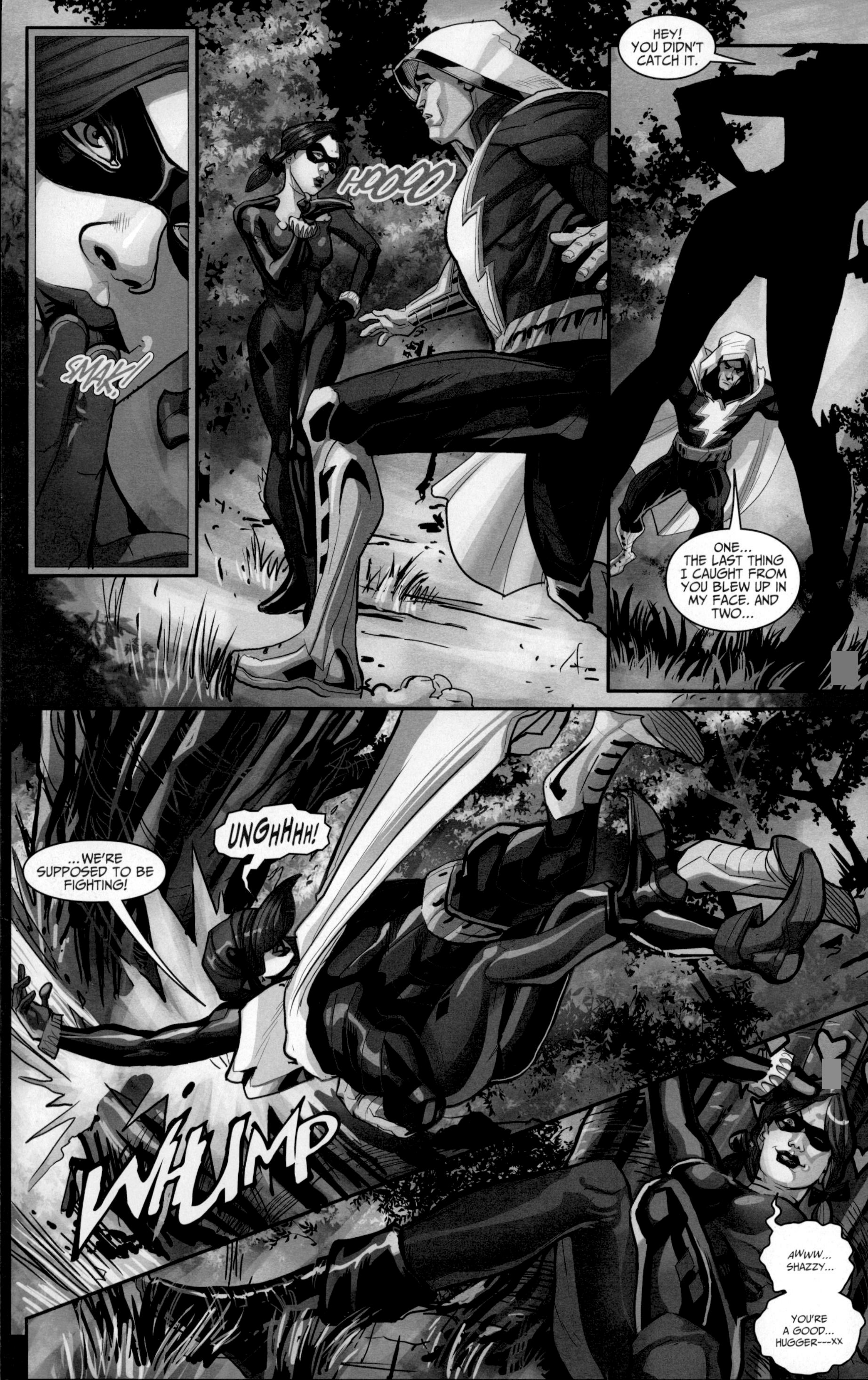
SMAK!
HOOOO
HEY! YOU DIDN'T CATCH IT.
ONE... THE LAST THING I CAUGHT FROM YOU BLEW UP IN MY FACE. AND TWO...
...WE'RE SUPPOSED TO BE FIGHTING!
UNGHHHH!
WHUMP
AWWW... SHAZZY...
YOU'RE A GOOD... HUGGER---XX

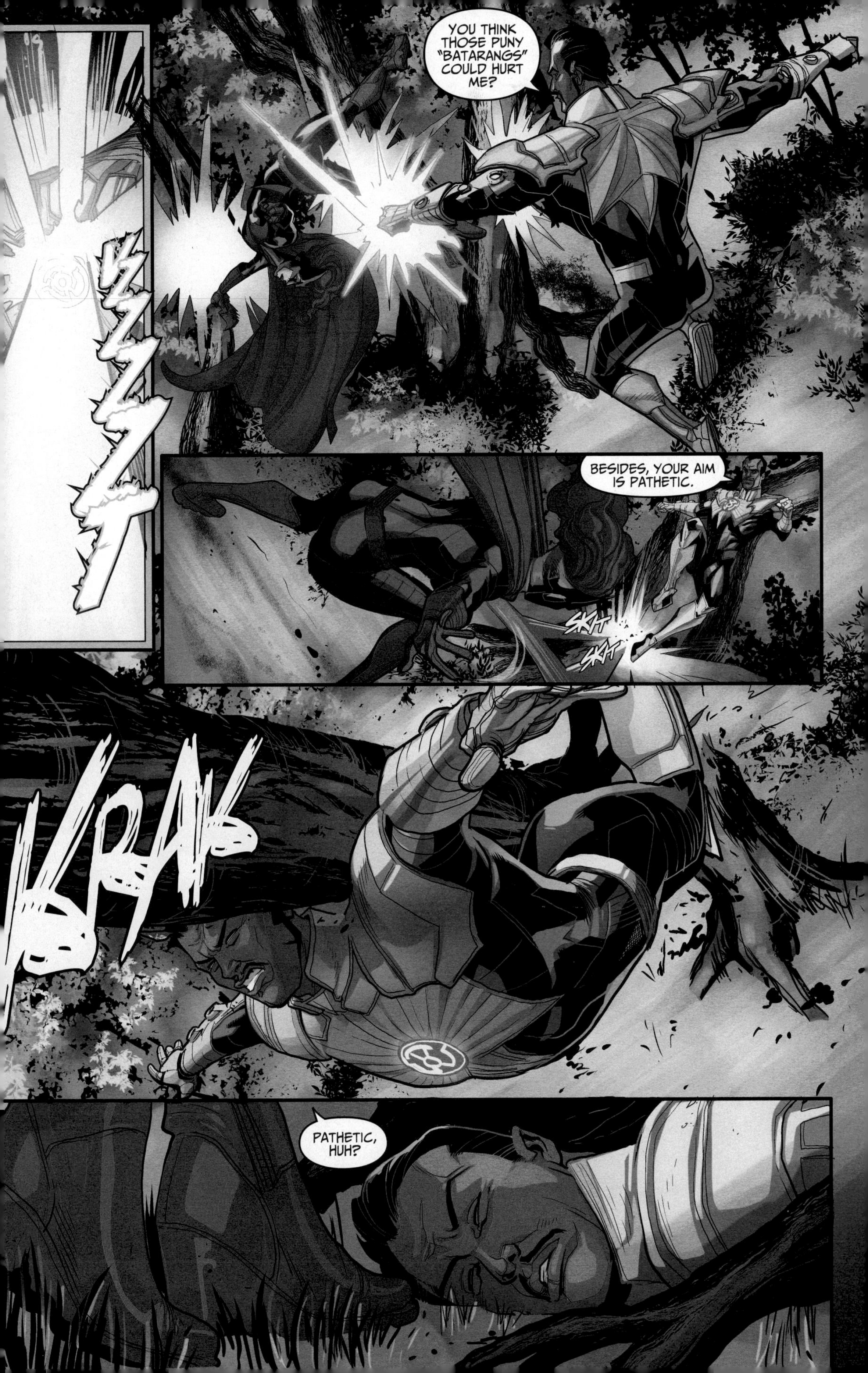
YOU THINK THOSE PUNY "BATARANGS" COULD HURT ME?
BESIDES, YOUR AIM IS PATHETIC.
SKIT
SKIT
KRAK
PATHETIC, HUH?

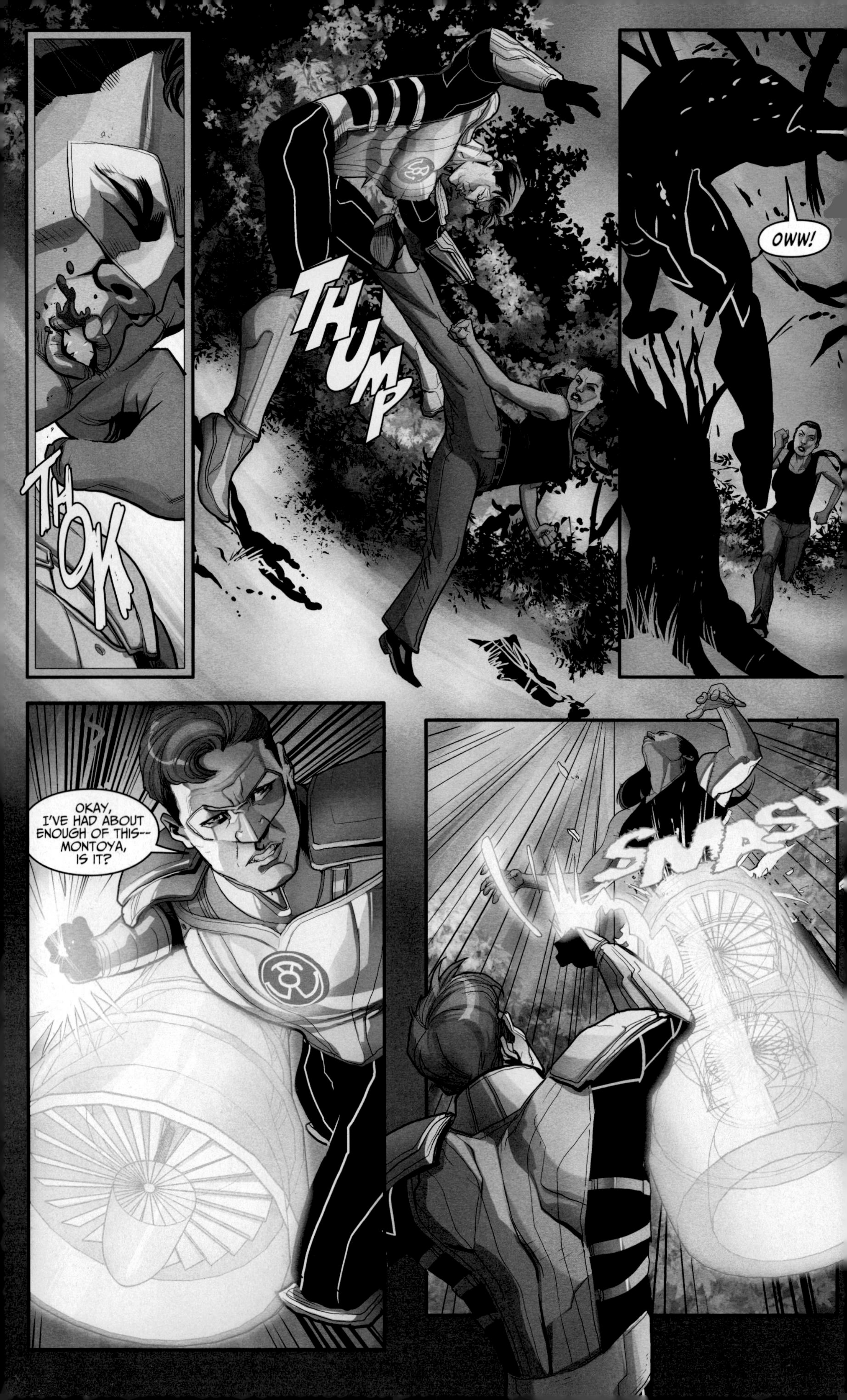
THOK
THUMP
OWW!
OKAY, I'VE HAD ABOUT ENOUGH OF THIS-- MONTOYA, IS IT?
SMASH

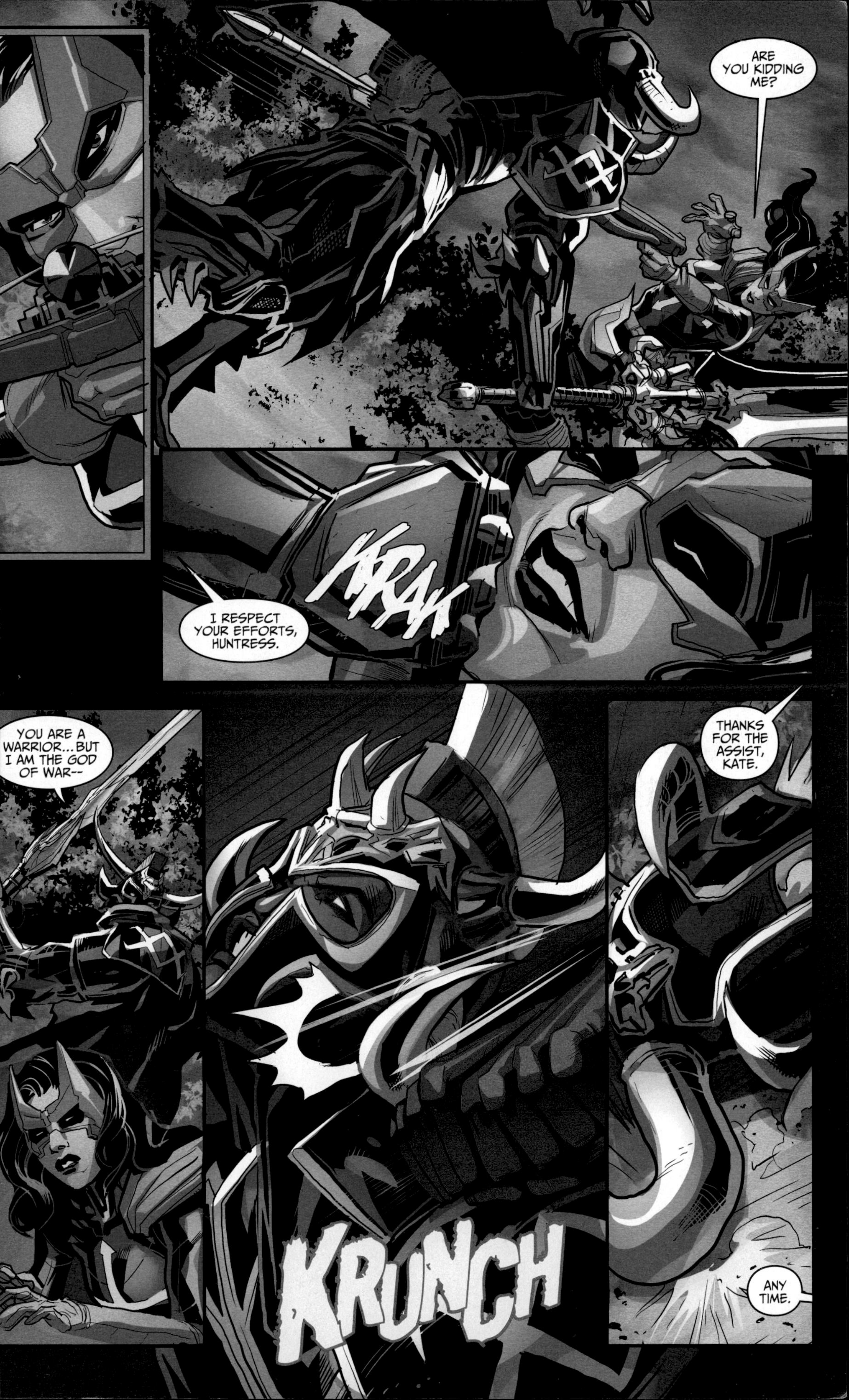
ARE YOU KIDDING ME?
KRAK
I RESPECT YOUR EFFORTS, HUNTRESS.
YOU ARE A WARRIOR...BUT I AM THE GOD OF WAR--
KRUNCH
THANKS FOR THE ASSIST, KATE.
ANY TIME.

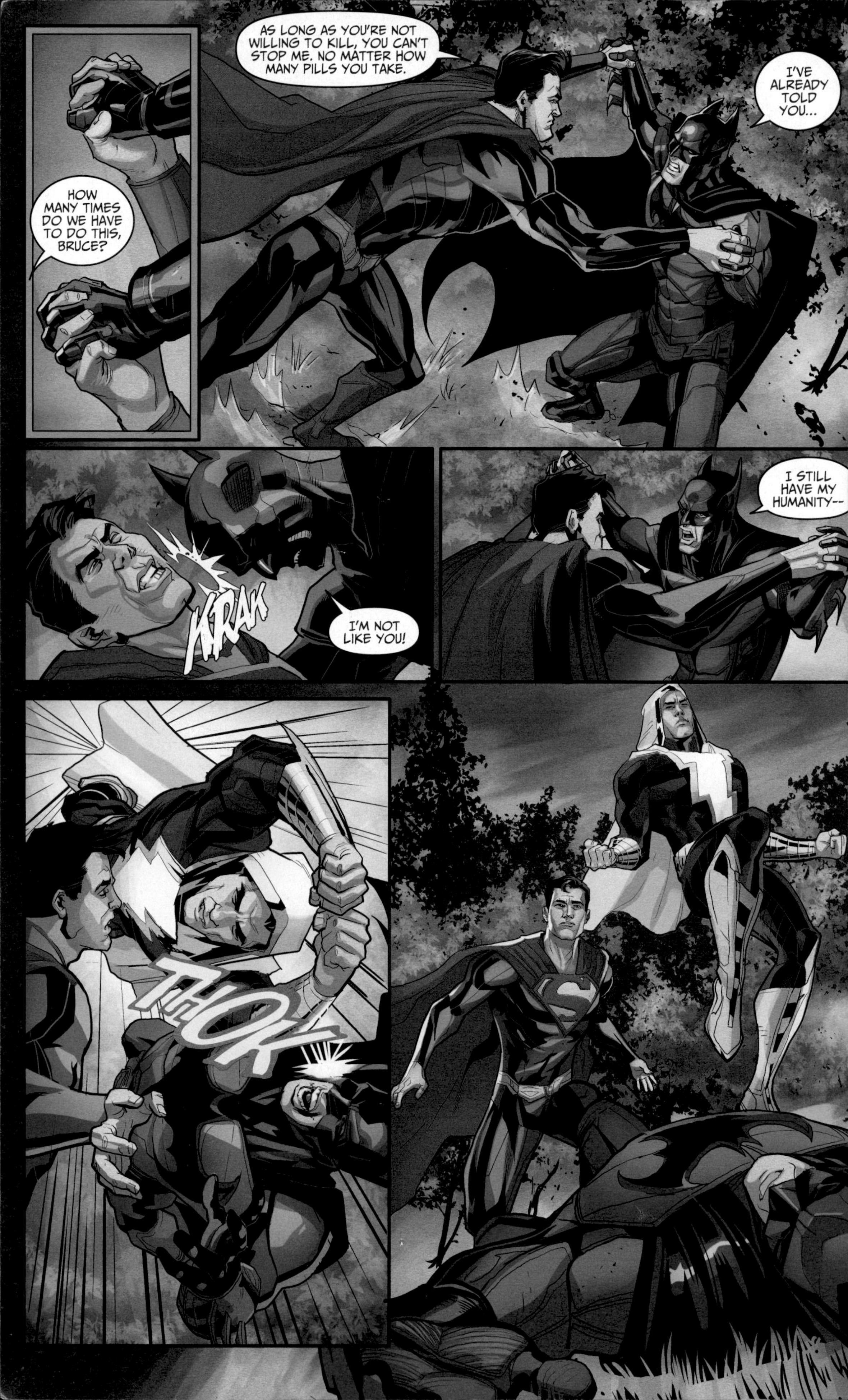
AS LONG AS YOU'RE NOT WILLING TO KILL, YOU CAN'T STOP ME. NO MATTER HOW MANY PILLS YOU TAKE.
I'VE ALREADY TOLD YOU...
HOW MANY TIMES DO WE HAVE TO DO THIS, BRUCE?
KRAK
I'M NOT LIKE YOU!
I STILL HAVE MY HUMANITY--
THOK

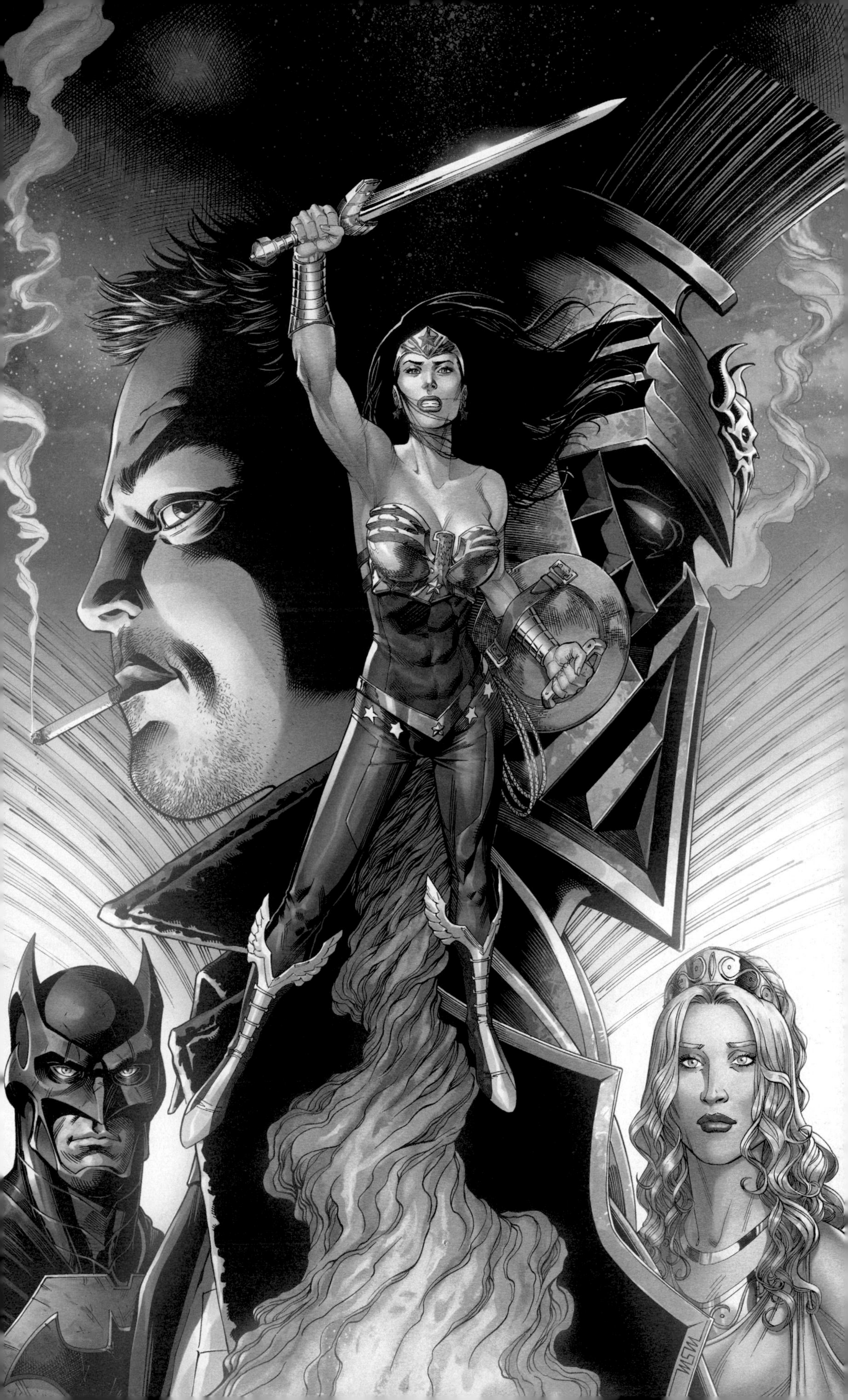

"Goodbyes and Farewells" Bruno Redondo and Juan Albarran - Artists Rex Lokus - Colorist
"Hellfire and Damnation" Mike S. Miller - Artist J. Nanjan - Colorist
Cover Art by Mike S. Miller and J. Nanjan

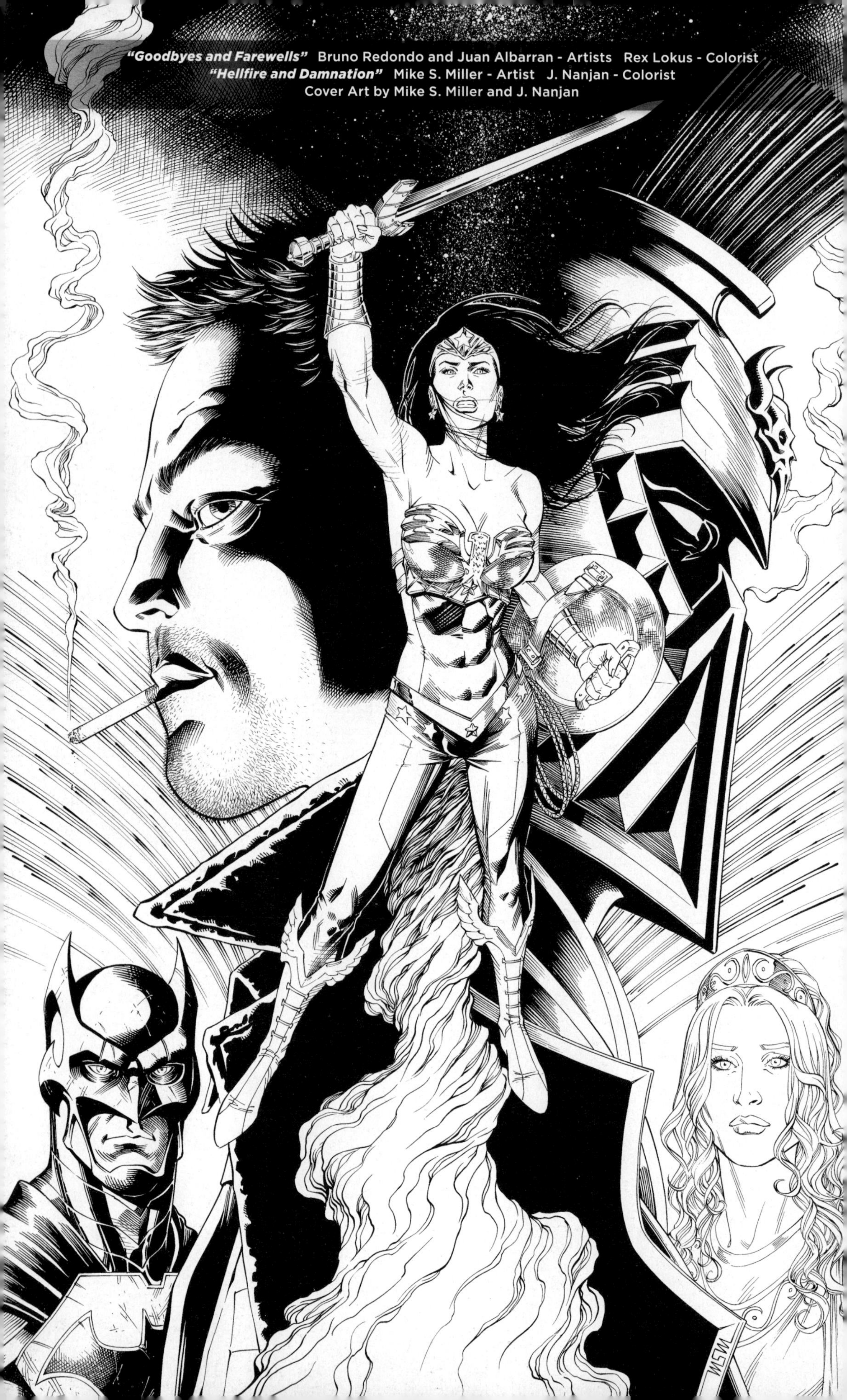

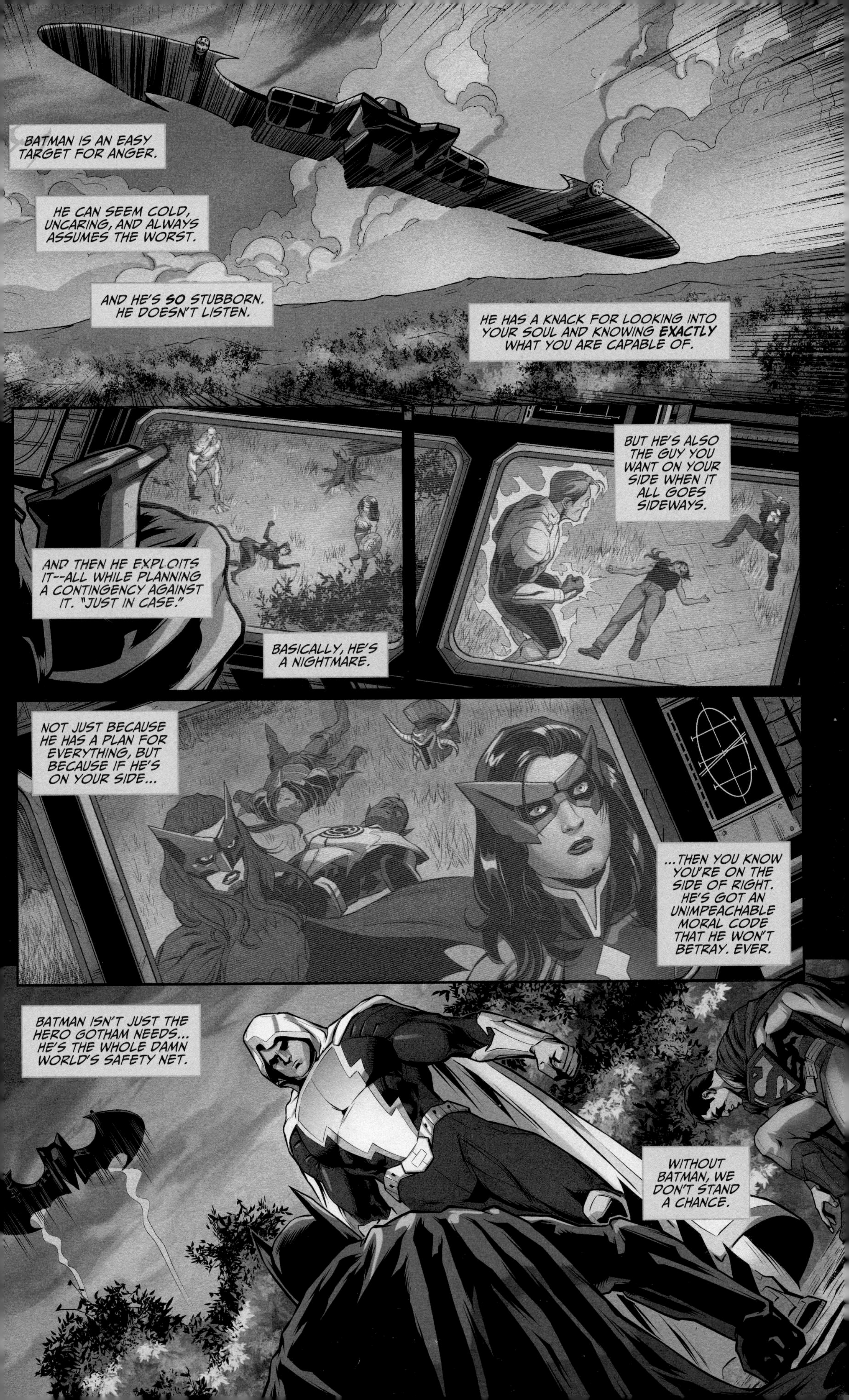
BATMAN IS AN EASY TARGET FOR ANGER.
HE CAN SEEM COLD, UNCARING, AND ALWAYS ASSUMES THE WORST.
AND HE'S SO STUBBORN. HE DOESN'T LISTEN.
HE HAS A KNACK FOR LOOKING INTO YOUR SOUL AND KNOWING EXACTLY WHAT YOU ARE CAPABLE OF.
AND THEN HE EXPLOITS IT--ALL WHILE PLANNING A CONTINGENCY AGAINST IT. "JUST IN CASE."
BASICALLY, HE'S A NIGHTMARE.
BUT HE'S ALSO THE GUY YOU WANT ON YOUR SIDE WHEN IT ALL GOES SIDEWAYS.
NOT JUST BECAUSE HE HAS A PLAN FOR EVERYTHING, BUT BECAUSE IF HE'S ON YOUR SIDE...
...THEN YOU KNOW YOU'RE ON THE SIDE OF RIGHT. HE'S GOT AN UNIMPEACHABLE MORAL CODE THAT HE WON'T BETRAY. EVER.
BATMAN ISN'T JUST THE HERO GOTHAM NEEDS... HE'S THE WHOLE DAMN WORLD'S SAFETY NET.
WITHOUT BATMAN, WE DON'T STAND A CHANCE.

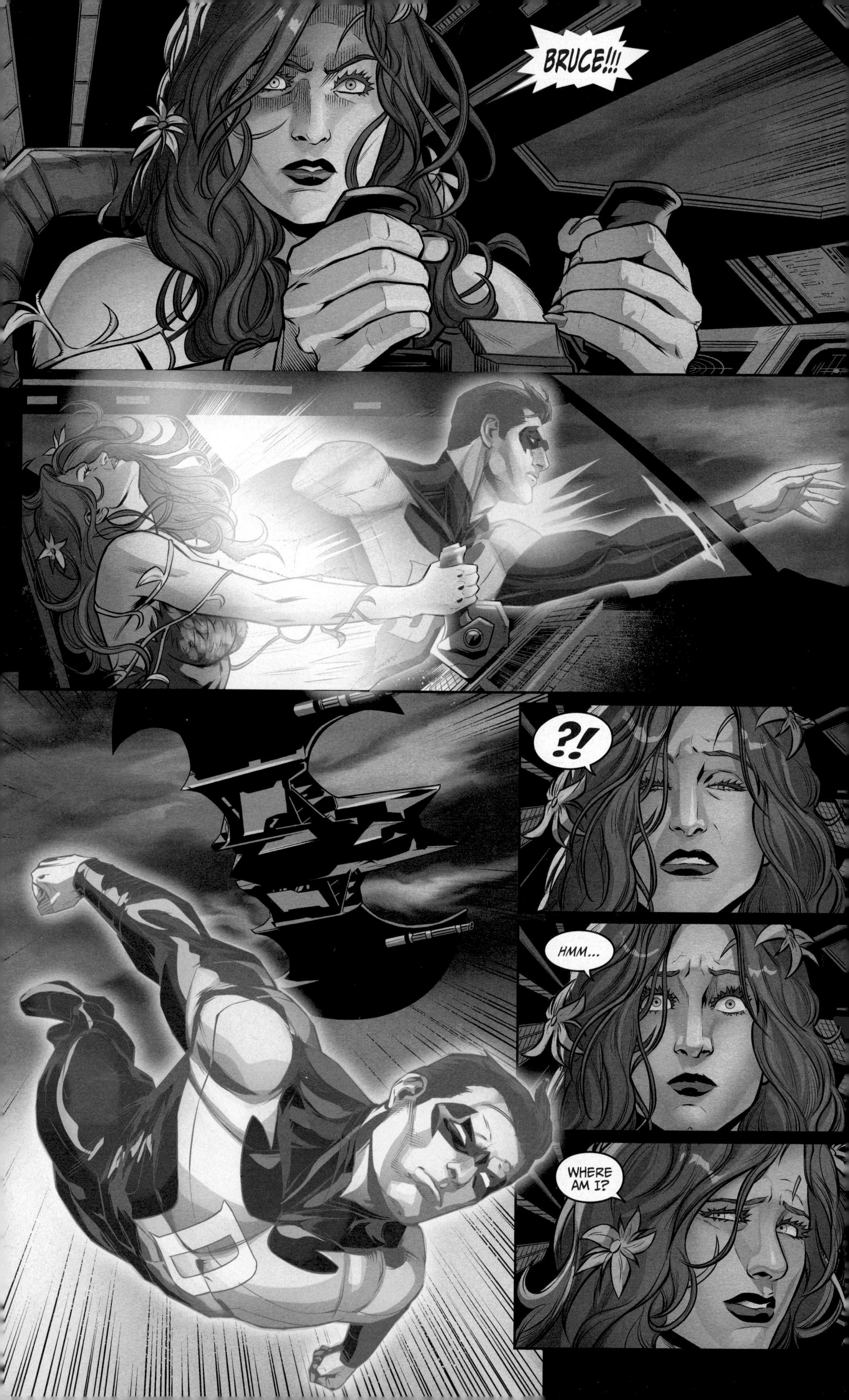
BRUCE!!!
?!
HMM...
WHERE AM I?

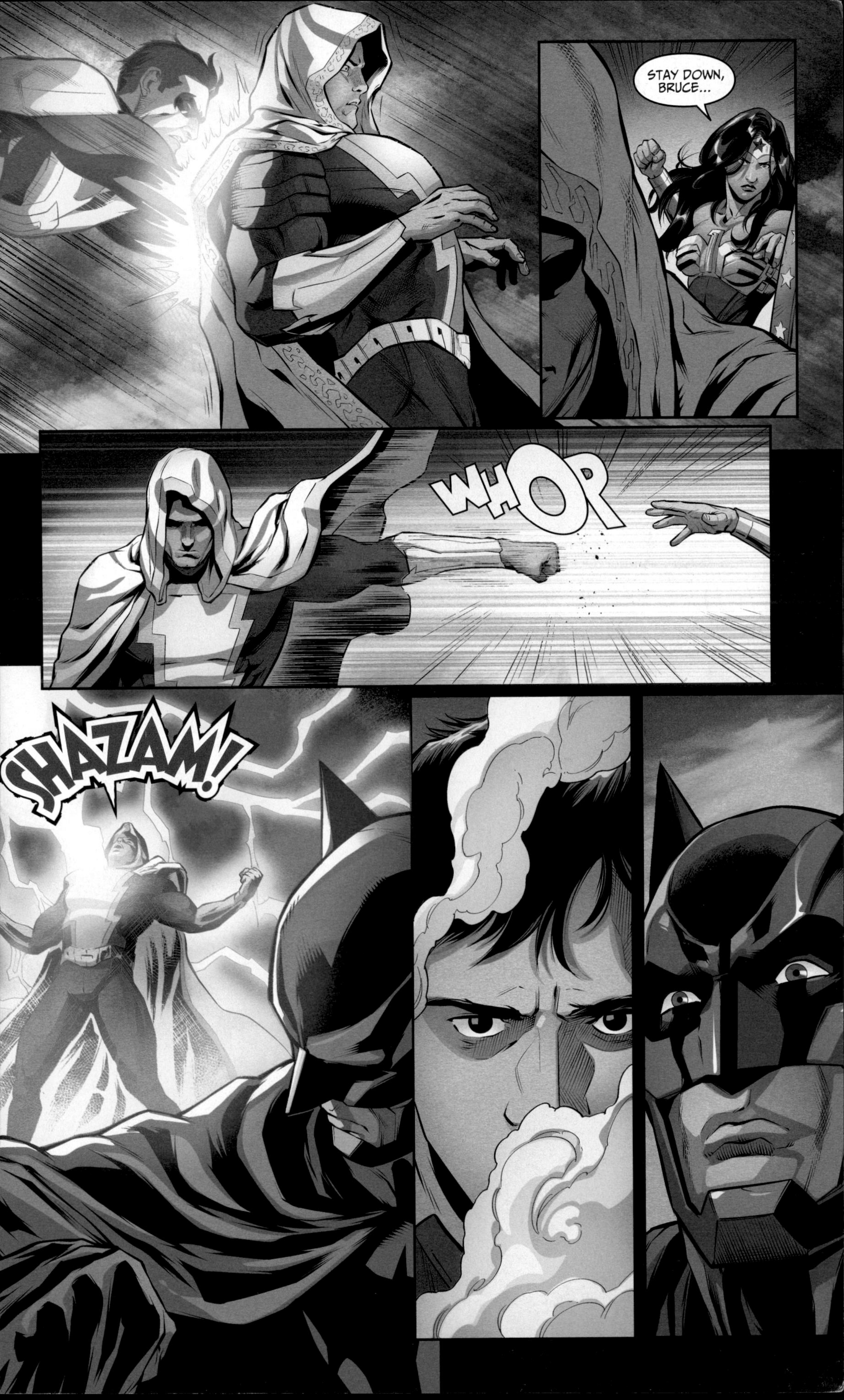
STAY DOWN, BRUCE...
WHOP
SHAZAM!

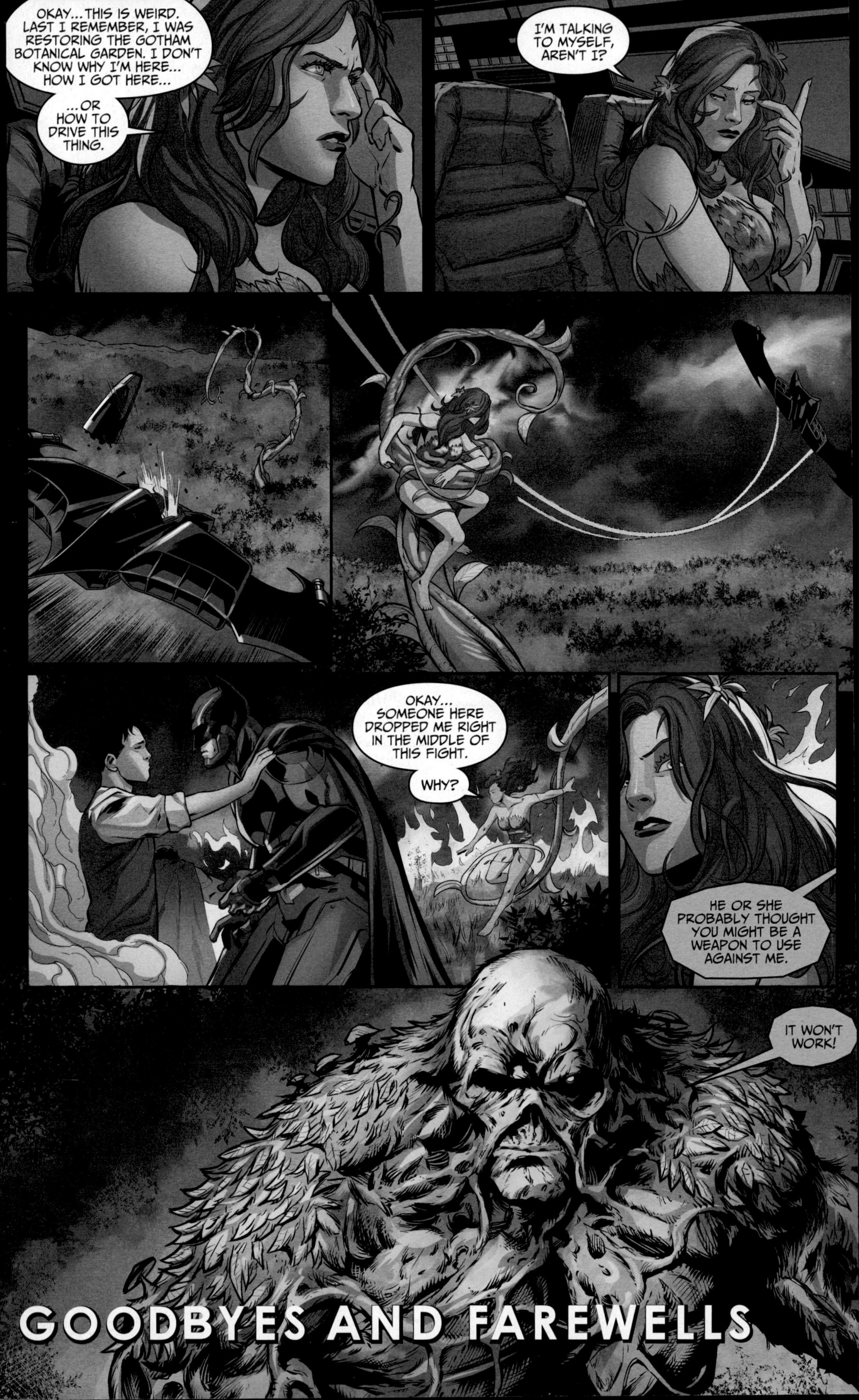

OKAY... THIS IS WEIRD. LAST I REMEMBER, I WAS RESTORING THE GOTHAM BOTANICAL GARDEN. I DON'T KNOW WHY I'M HERE... HOW I GOT HERE...
...OR HOW TO DRIVE THIS THING.
I'M TALKING TO MYSELF, AREN'T I?
OKAY... SOMEONE HERE DROPPED ME RIGHT IN THE MIDDLE OF THIS FIGHT.
WHY?
HE OR SHE PROBABLY THOUGHT YOU MIGHT BE A WEAPON TO USE AGAINST ME.
IT WON'T WORK!
GOODBYES AND FAREWELLS

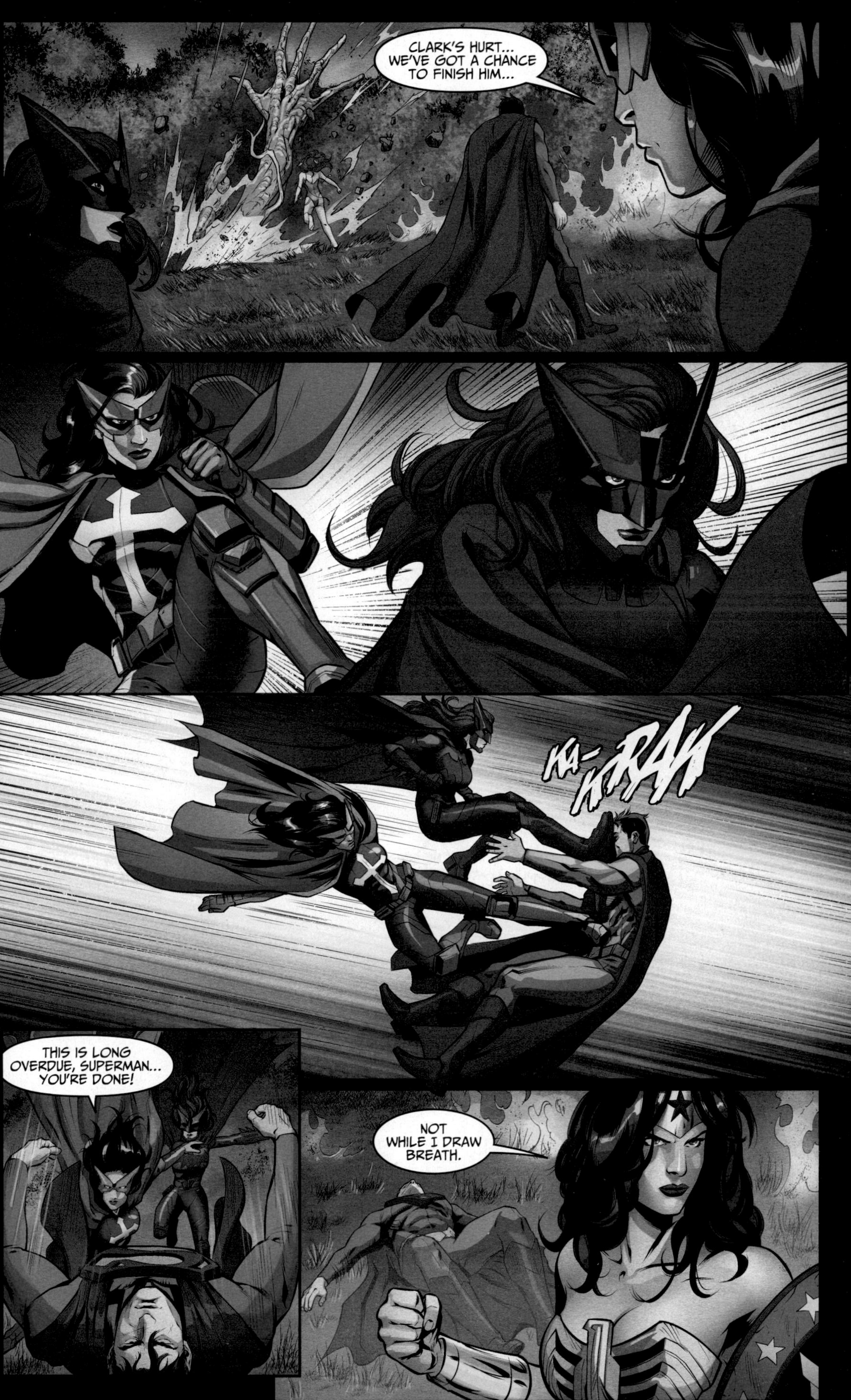
CLARK'S HURT... WE'VE GOT A CHANCE TO FINISH HIM...
KA-KRAK
THIS IS LONG OVERDUE, SUPERMAN... YOU'RE DONE!
NOT WHILE I DRAW BREATH.

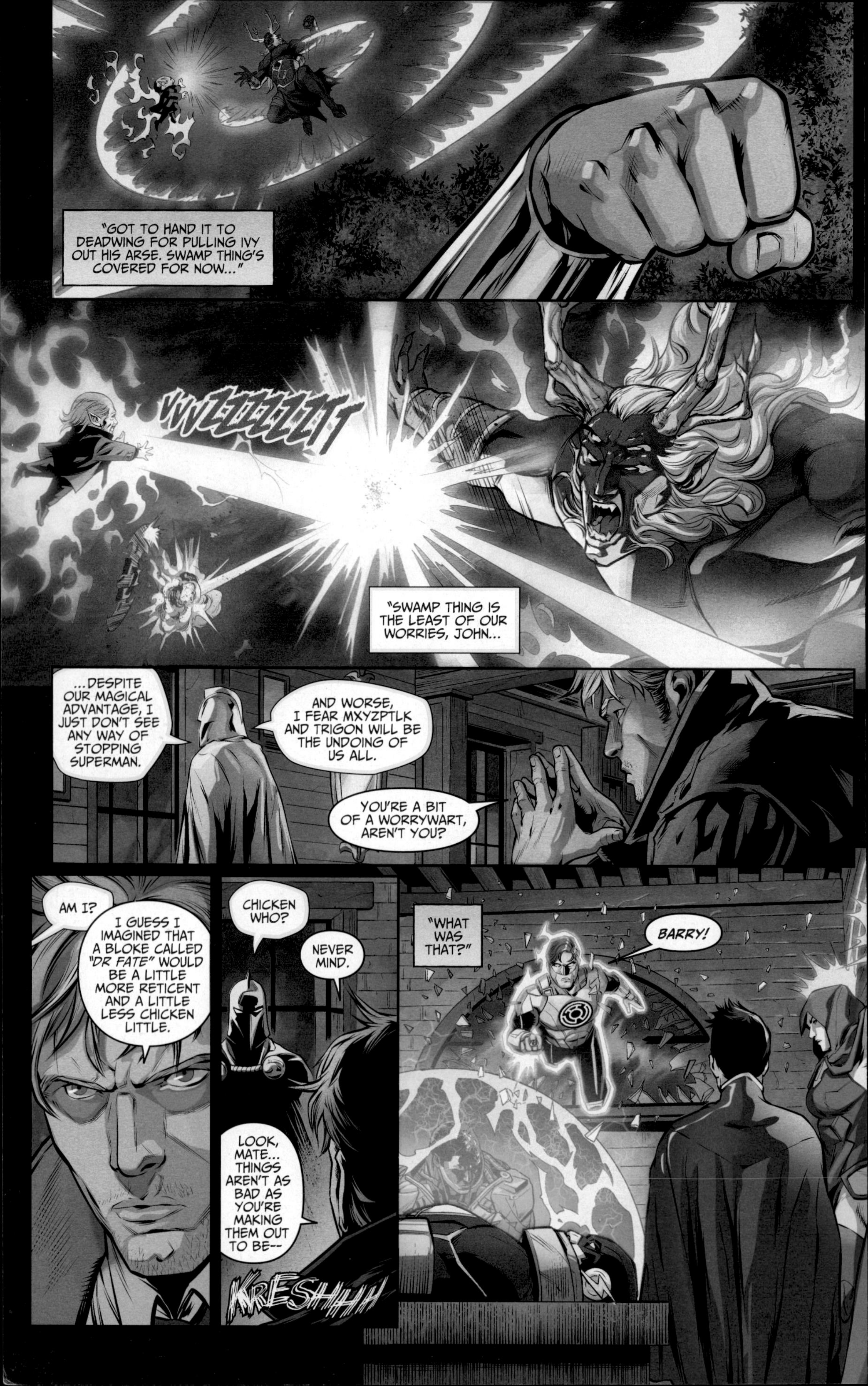
"GOT TO HAND IT TO DEADWING FOR PULLING IVY OUT HIS ARSE. SWAMP THING'S COVERED FOR NOW..."
VVVZZZZZZZT
"SWAMP THING IS THE LEAST OF OUR WORRIES, JOHN...
...DESPITE OUR MAGICAL ADVANTAGE, I JUST DON'T SEE ANY WAY OF STOPPING SUPERMAN.
AND WORSE, I FEAR MXYZPTLK AND TRIGON WILL BE THE UNDOING OF US ALL.
YOU'RE A BIT OF A WORRYWART, AREN'T YOU?
AM I?
I GUESS I IMAGINED THAT A BLOKE CALLED "DR FATE" WOULD BE A LITTLE MORE RETICENT AND A LITTLE LESS CHICKEN LITTLE.
CHICKEN WHO?
NEVER MIND.
LOOK, MATE... THINGS AREN'T AS BAD AS YOU'RE MAKING THEM OUT TO BE--
KRESHHH
"WHAT WAS THAT?"
BARRY!

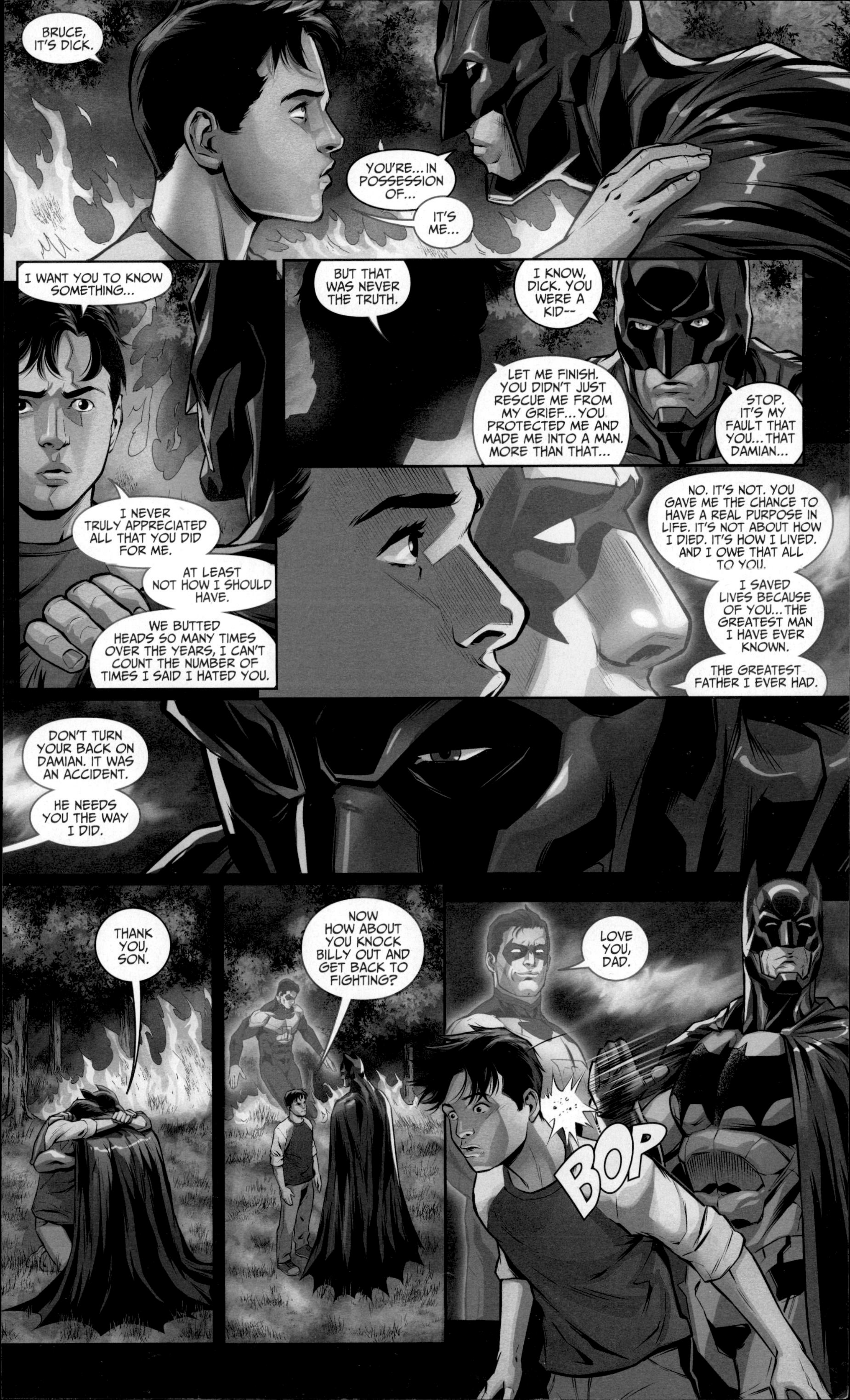
BRUCE, IT'S DICK.
YOU'RE... IN POSSESSION OF...
IT'S ME...
I WANT YOU TO KNOW SOMETHING...
BUT THAT WAS NEVER THE TRUTH.
I KNOW, DICK. YOU WERE A KID--
LET ME FINISH. YOU DIDN'T JUST RESCUE ME FROM MY GRIEF...YOU PROTECTED ME AND MADE ME INTO A MAN. MORE THAN THAT...
STOP. IT'S MY FAULT THAT YOU...THAT DAMIAN...
I NEVER TRULY APPRECIATED ALL THAT YOU DID FOR ME.
AT LEAST NOT HOW I SHOULD HAVE.
WE BUTTED HEADS SO MANY TIMES OVER THE YEARS, I CAN'T COUNT THE NUMBER OF TIMES I SAID I HATED YOU.
NO. IT'S NOT. YOU GAVE ME THE CHANCE TO HAVE A REAL PURPOSE IN LIFE. IT'S NOT ABOUT HOW I DIED. IT'S HOW I LIVED. AND I OWE THAT ALL TO YOU.
I SAVED LIVES BECAUSE OF YOU...THE GREATEST MAN I HAVE EVER KNOWN.
THE GREATEST FATHER I EVER HAD.
DON'T TURN YOUR BACK ON DAMIAN. IT WAS AN ACCIDENT.
HE NEEDS YOU THE WAY I DID.
THANK YOU, SON.
NOW HOW ABOUT YOU KNOCK BILLY OUT AND GET BACK TO FIGHTING?
LOVE YOU, DAD.
BOP

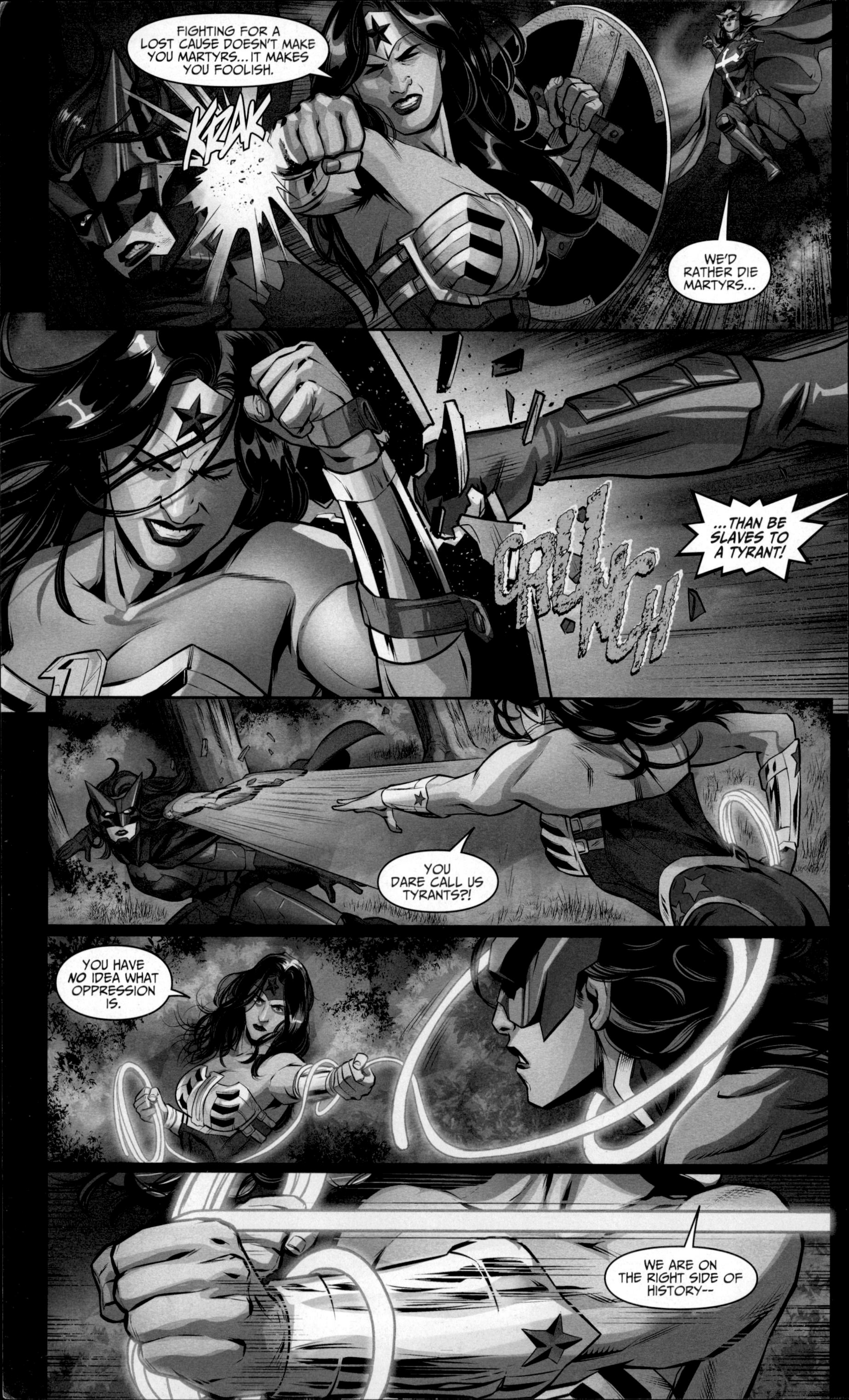
FIGHTING FOR A LOST CAUSE DOESN'T MAKE YOU MARTYRS... IT MAKES YOU FOOLISH.
KRAK
WE'D RATHER DIE MARTYRS...
...THAN BE SLAVES TO A TYRANT!
CRUNCH
YOU DARE CALL US TYRANTS?!
YOU HAVE NO IDEA WHAT OPPRESSION IS.
WE ARE ON THE RIGHT SIDE OF HISTORY--

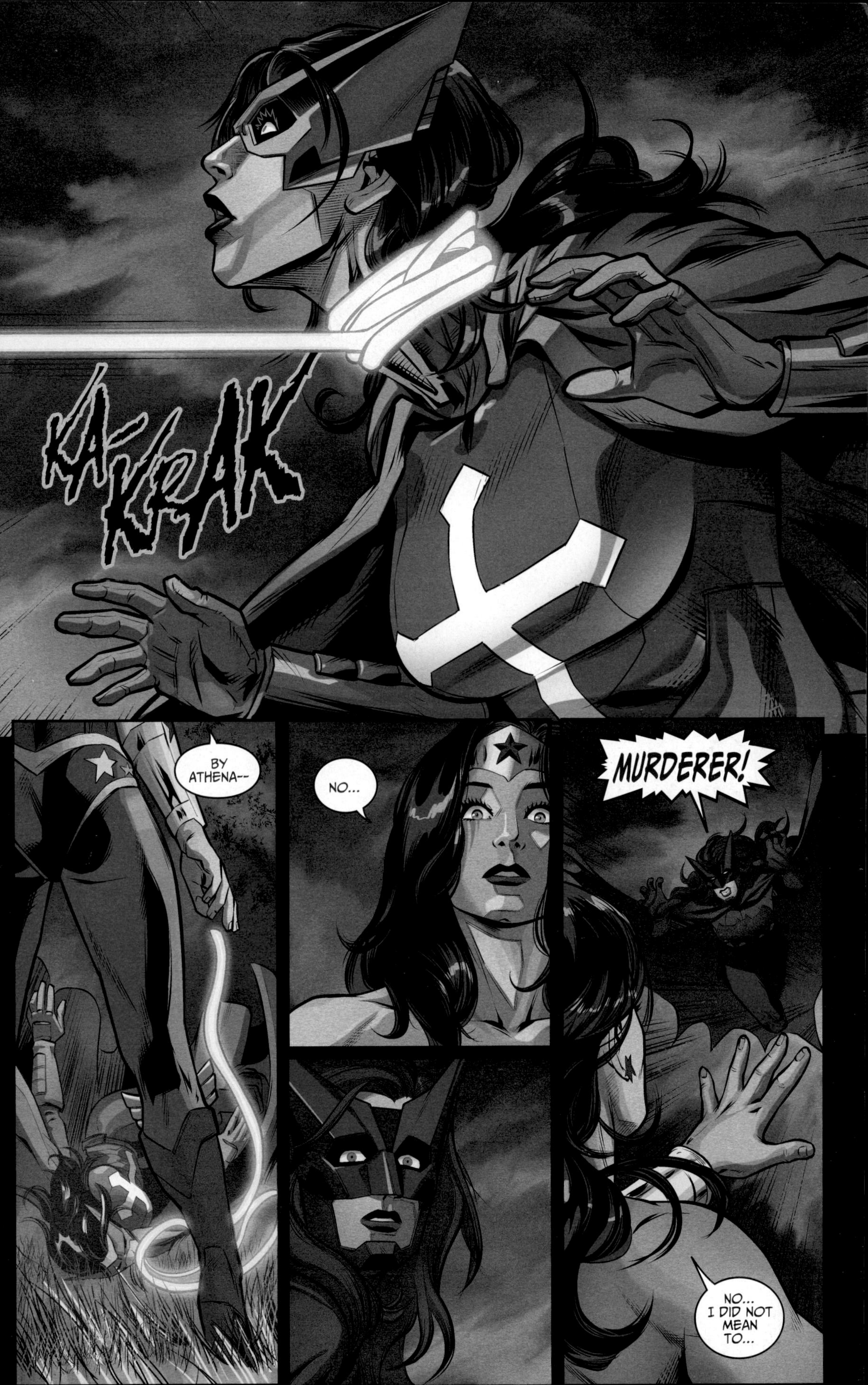
KA-KRAK
BY ATHENA--
NO...
MURDERER!
NO... I DID NOT MEAN TO...

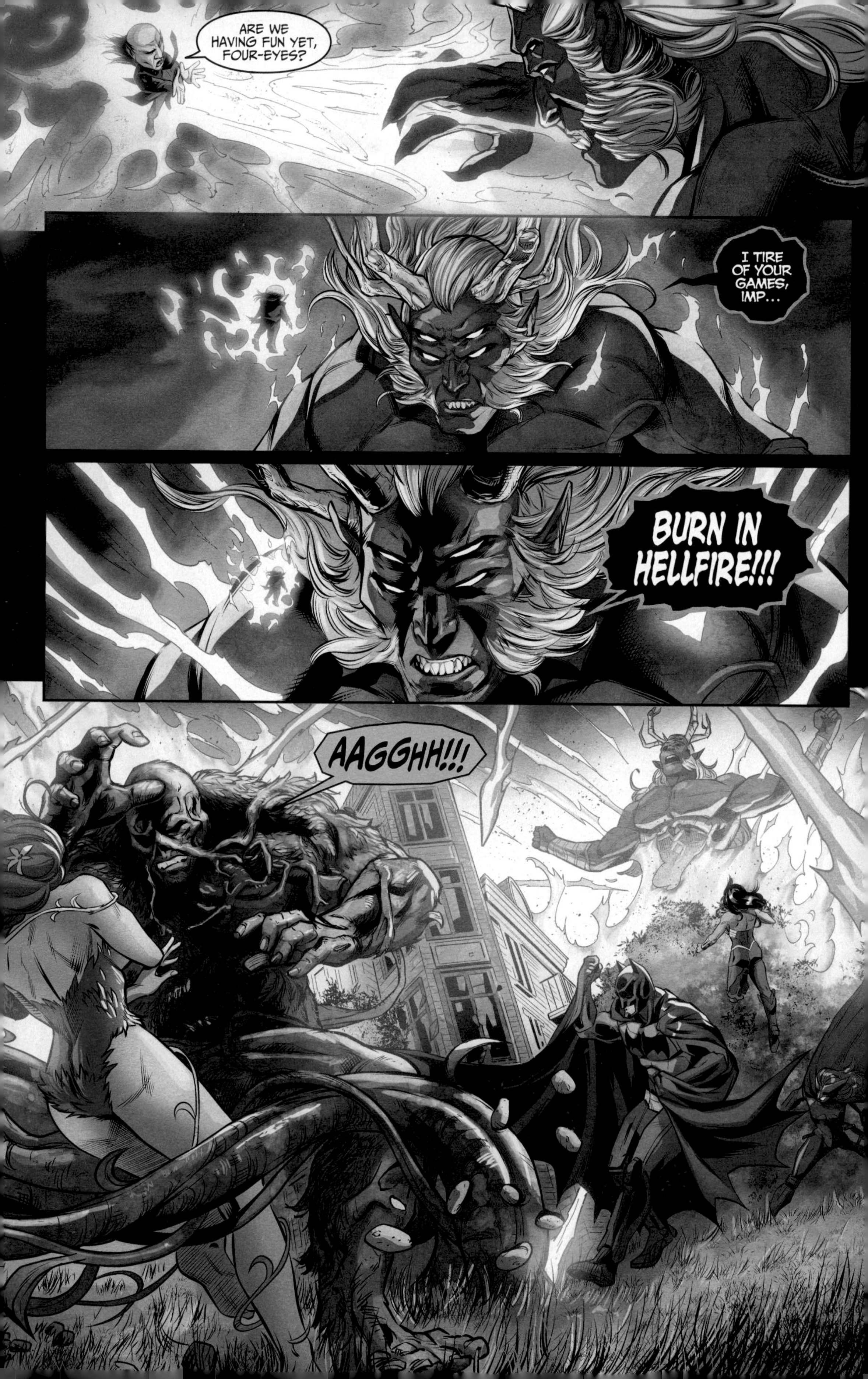
ARE WE HAVING FUN YET, FOUR-EYES?
I TIRE OF YOUR GAMES, IMP...
BURN IN HELLFIRE!!!
AAGGHH!!!

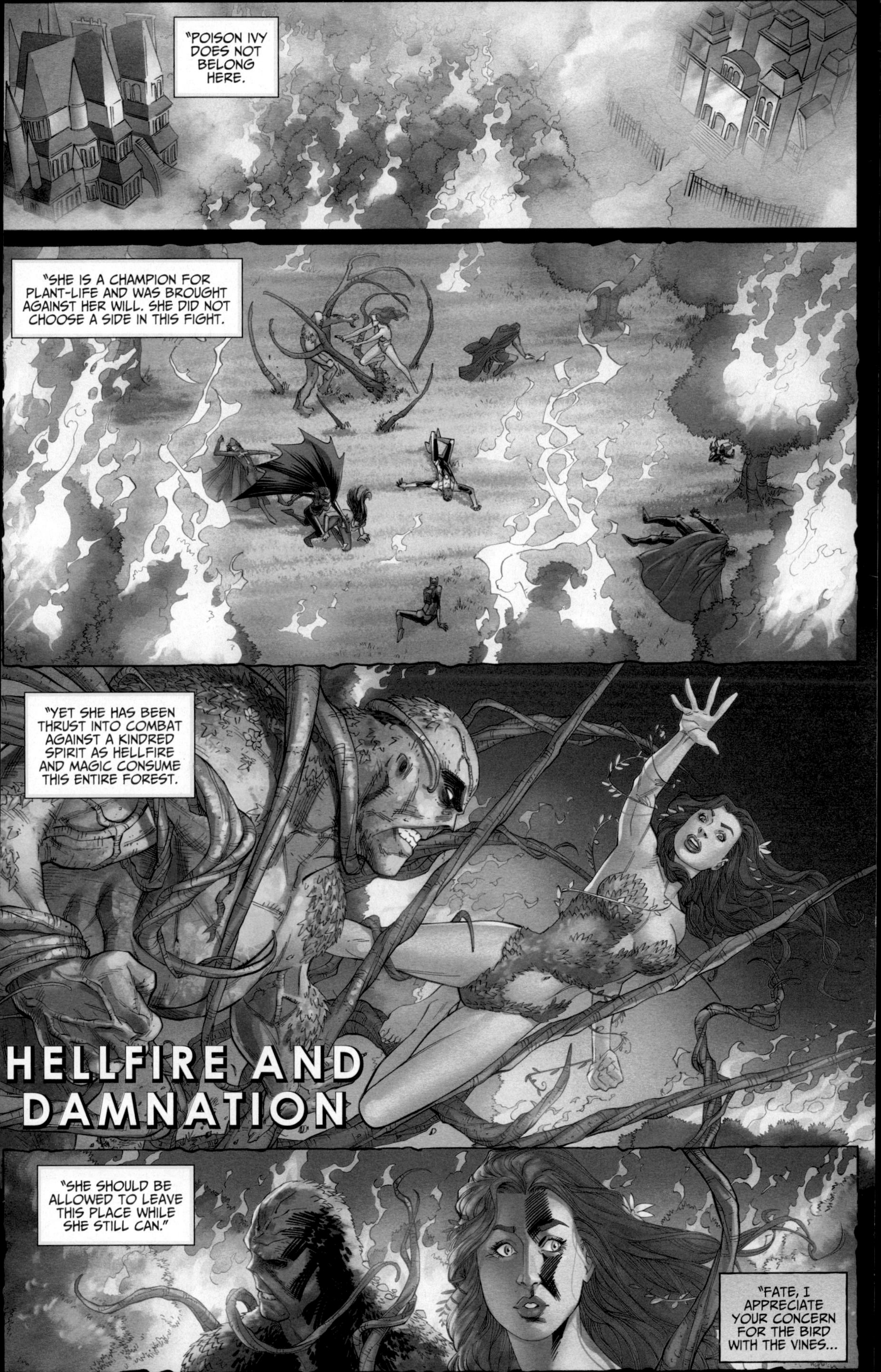
"POISON IVY DOES NOT BELONG HERE.
"SHE IS A CHAMPION FOR PLANT-LIFE AND WAS BROUGHT AGAINST HER WILL. SHE DID NOT CHOOSE A SIDE IN THIS FIGHT.
"YET SHE HAS BEEN THRUST INTO COMBAT AGAINST A KINDRED SPIRIT AS HELLFIRE AND MAGIC CONSUME THIS ENTIRE FOREST.
HELLFIRE AND DAMNATION
"SHE SHOULD BE ALLOWED TO LEAVE THIS PLACE WHILE SHE STILL CAN."
"FATE, I APPRECIATE YOUR CONCERN FOR THE BIRD WITH THE VINES...

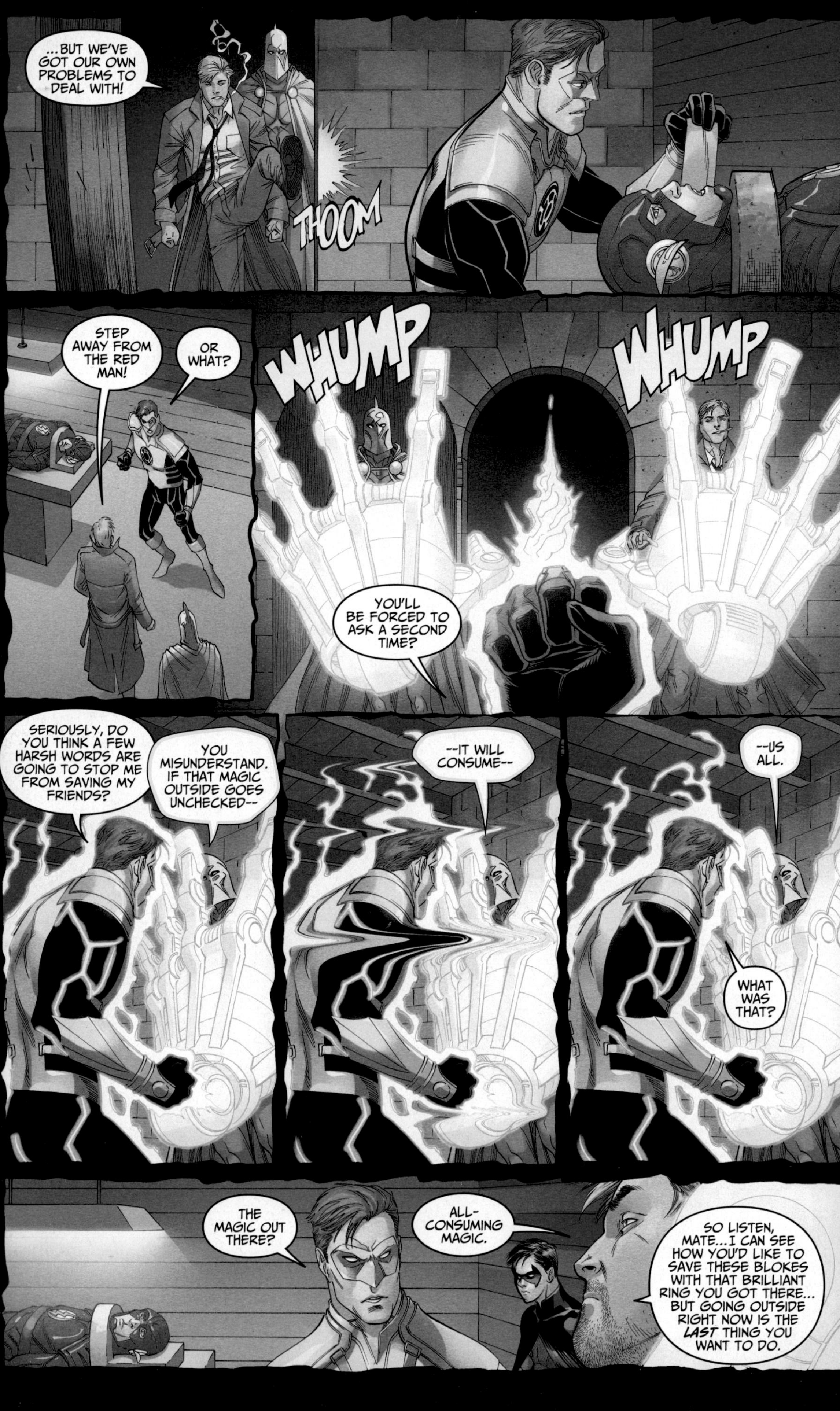
...BUT WE'VE GOT OUR OWN PROBLEMS TO DEAL WITH!
THOOM
STEP AWAY FROM THE RED MAN!
OR WHAT?
WHUMP
WHUMP
YOU'LL BE FORCED TO ASK A SECOND TIME?
SERIOUSLY, DO YOU THINK A FEW HARSH WORDS ARE GOING TO STOP ME FROM SAVING MY FRIENDS?
YOU MISUNDERSTAND. IF THAT MAGIC OUTSIDE GOES UNCHECKED--
--IT WILL CONSUME--
--US ALL.
WHAT WAS THAT?
THE MAGIC OUT THERE?
ALL-CONSUMING MAGIC.
SO LISTEN, MATE...I CAN SEE HOW YOU'D LIKE TO SAVE THESE BLOKES WITH THAT BRILLIANT RING YOU GOT THERE... BUT GOING OUTSIDE RIGHT NOW IS THE *LAST* THING YOU WANT TO DO.

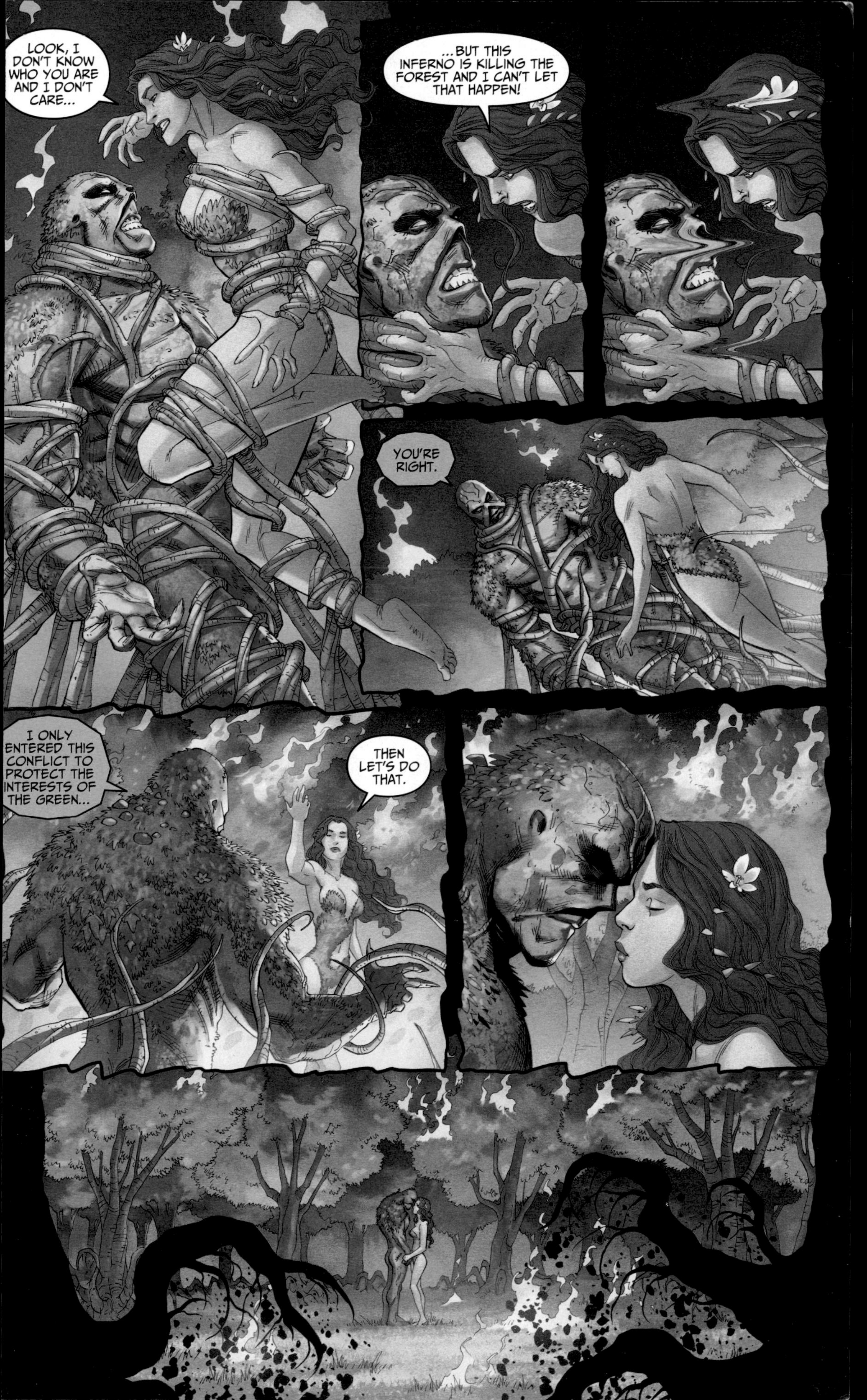
LOOK, I DON'T KNOW WHO YOU ARE AND I DON'T CARE...
...BUT THIS INFERNO IS KILLING THE FOREST AND I CAN'T LET THAT HAPPEN!
YOU'RE RIGHT.
I ONLY ENTERED THIS CONFLICT TO PROTECT THE INTERESTS OF THE GREEN...
THEN LET'S DO THAT.

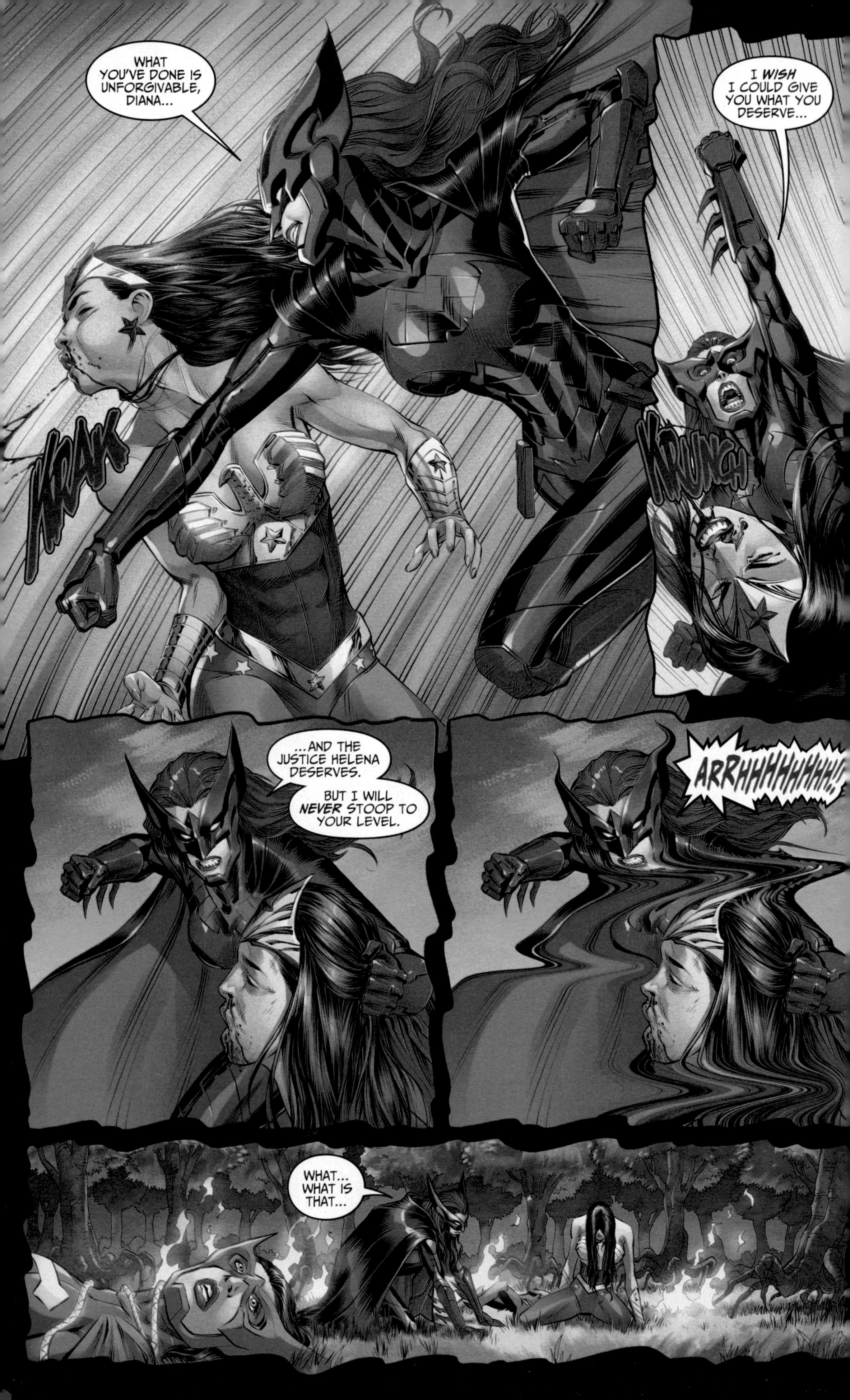
WHAT YOU'VE DONE IS UNFORGIVABLE, DIANA...
KRAK
I WISH I COULD GIVE YOU WHAT YOU DESERVE...
KRUNCH
...AND THE JUSTICE HELENA DESERVES.
BUT I WILL NEVER STOOP TO YOUR LEVEL.
ARRHHHHHHH!!
WHAT... WHAT IS THAT...

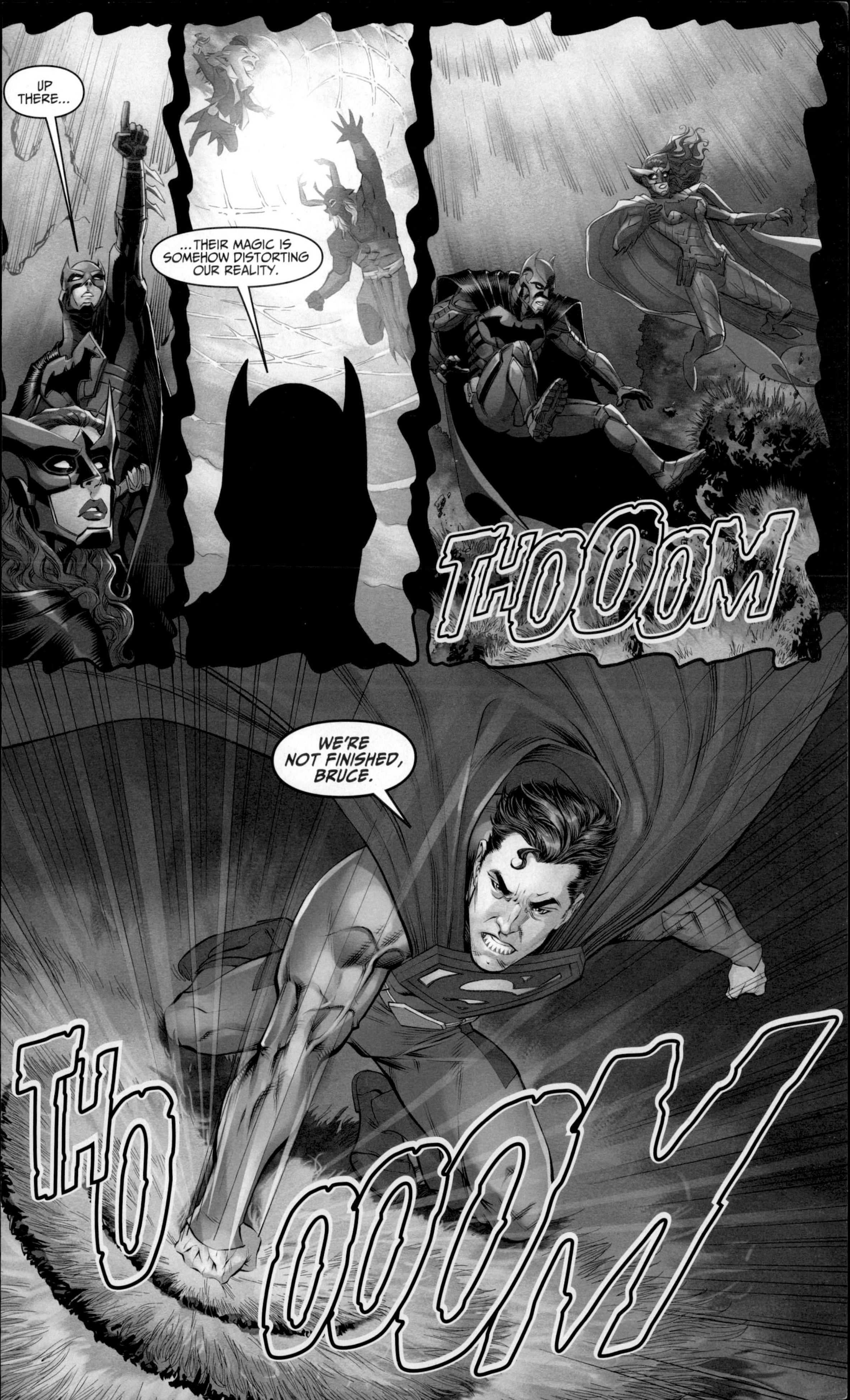
UP THERE...
...THEIR MAGIC IS SOMEHOW DISTORTING OUR REALITY.
THOOOM
WE'RE NOT FINISHED, BRUCE.
THOOOOM

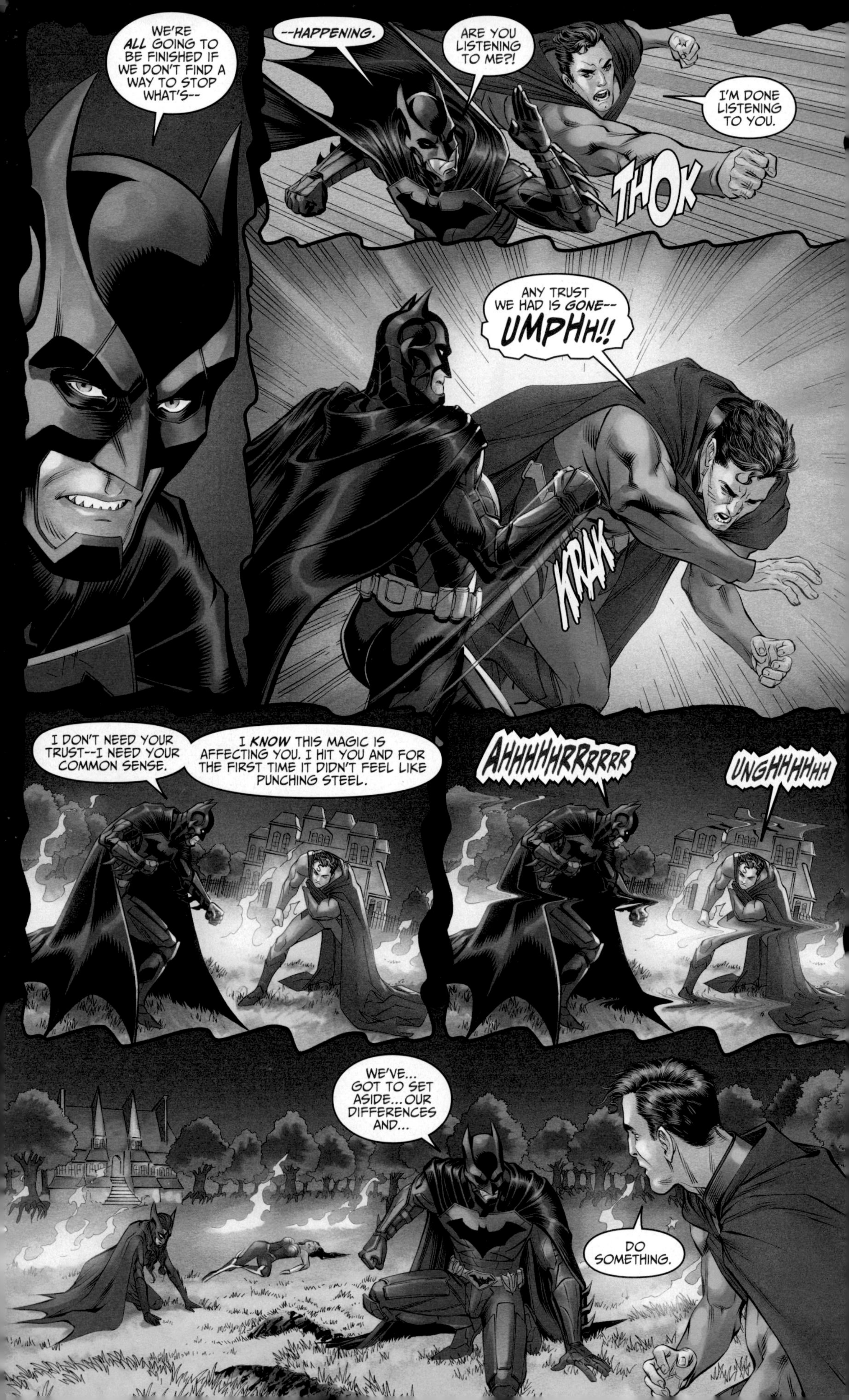
WE'RE ALL GOING TO BE FINISHED IF WE DON'T FIND A WAY TO STOP WHAT'S--
--HAPPENING.
ARE YOU LISTENING TO ME?!
I'M DONE LISTENING TO YOU.
THOK
ANY TRUST WE HAD IS GONE-- UMPHH!!
KRAK
I DON'T NEED YOUR TRUST--I NEED YOUR COMMON SENSE.
I KNOW THIS MAGIC IS AFFECTING YOU. I HIT YOU AND FOR THE FIRST TIME IT DIDN'T FEEL LIKE PUNCHING STEEL.
AHHHHHRRRRRR
UNGHHHHHH
WE'VE... GOT TO SET ASIDE...OUR DIFFERENCES AND...
DO SOMETHING.

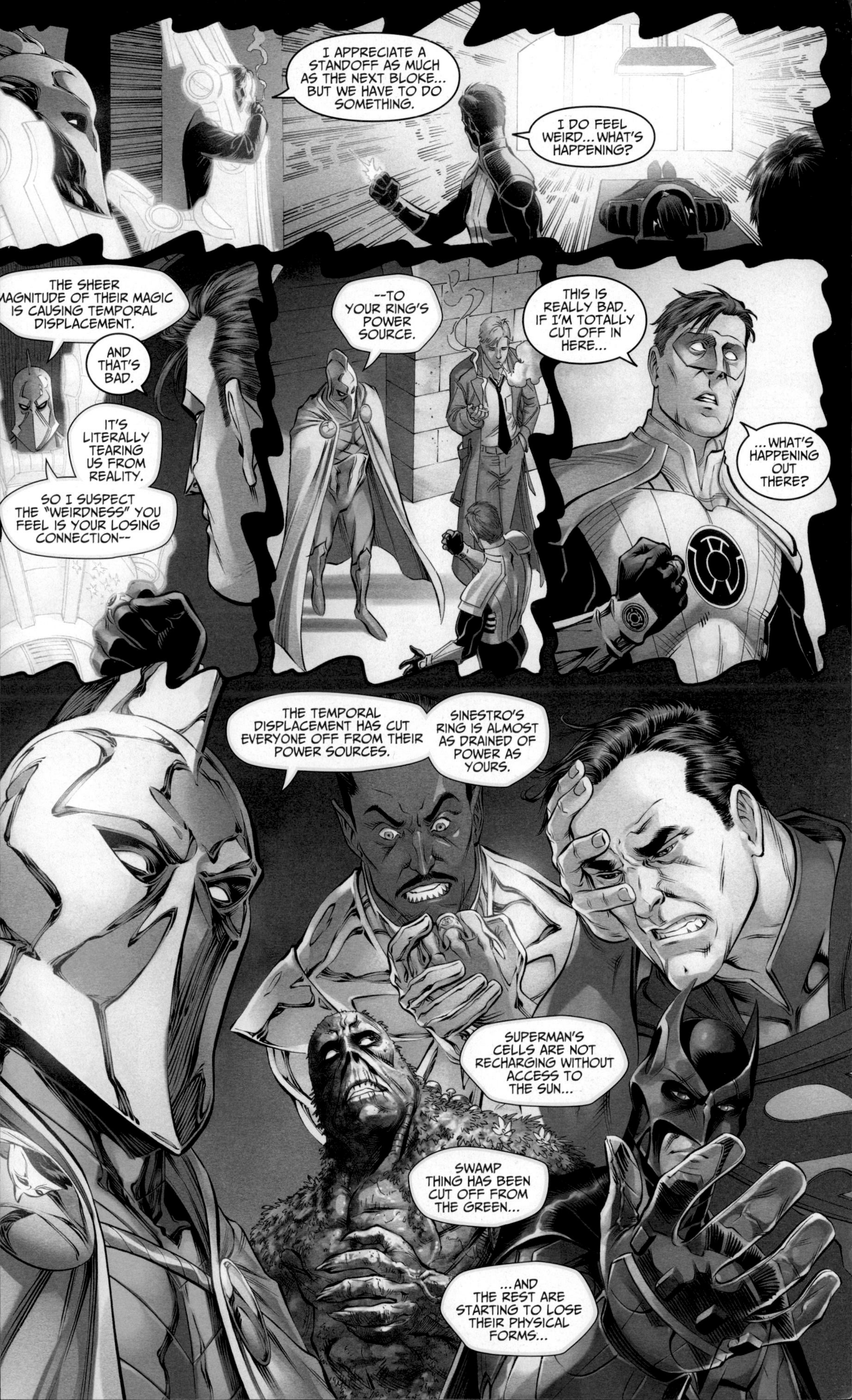
I APPRECIATE A STANDOFF AS MUCH AS THE NEXT BLOKE... BUT WE HAVE TO DO SOMETHING.
I DO FEEL WEIRD... WHAT'S HAPPENING?
THE SHEER MAGNITUDE OF THEIR MAGIC IS CAUSING TEMPORAL DISPLACEMENT.
AND THAT'S BAD.
IT'S LITERALLY TEARING US FROM REALITY.
SO I SUSPECT THE "WEIRDNESS" YOU FEEL IS YOUR LOSING CONNECTION--
--TO YOUR RING'S POWER SOURCE.
THIS IS REALLY BAD. IF I'M TOTALLY CUT OFF IN HERE...
...WHAT'S HAPPENING OUT THERE?
THE TEMPORAL DISPLACEMENT HAS CUT EVERYONE OFF FROM THEIR POWER SOURCES.
SINESTRO'S RING IS ALMOST AS DRAINED OF POWER AS YOURS.
SUPERMAN'S CELLS ARE NOT RECHARGING WITHOUT ACCESS TO THE SUN...
SWAMP THING HAS BEEN CUT OFF FROM THE GREEN...
...AND THE REST ARE STARTING TO LOSE THEIR PHYSICAL FORMS...

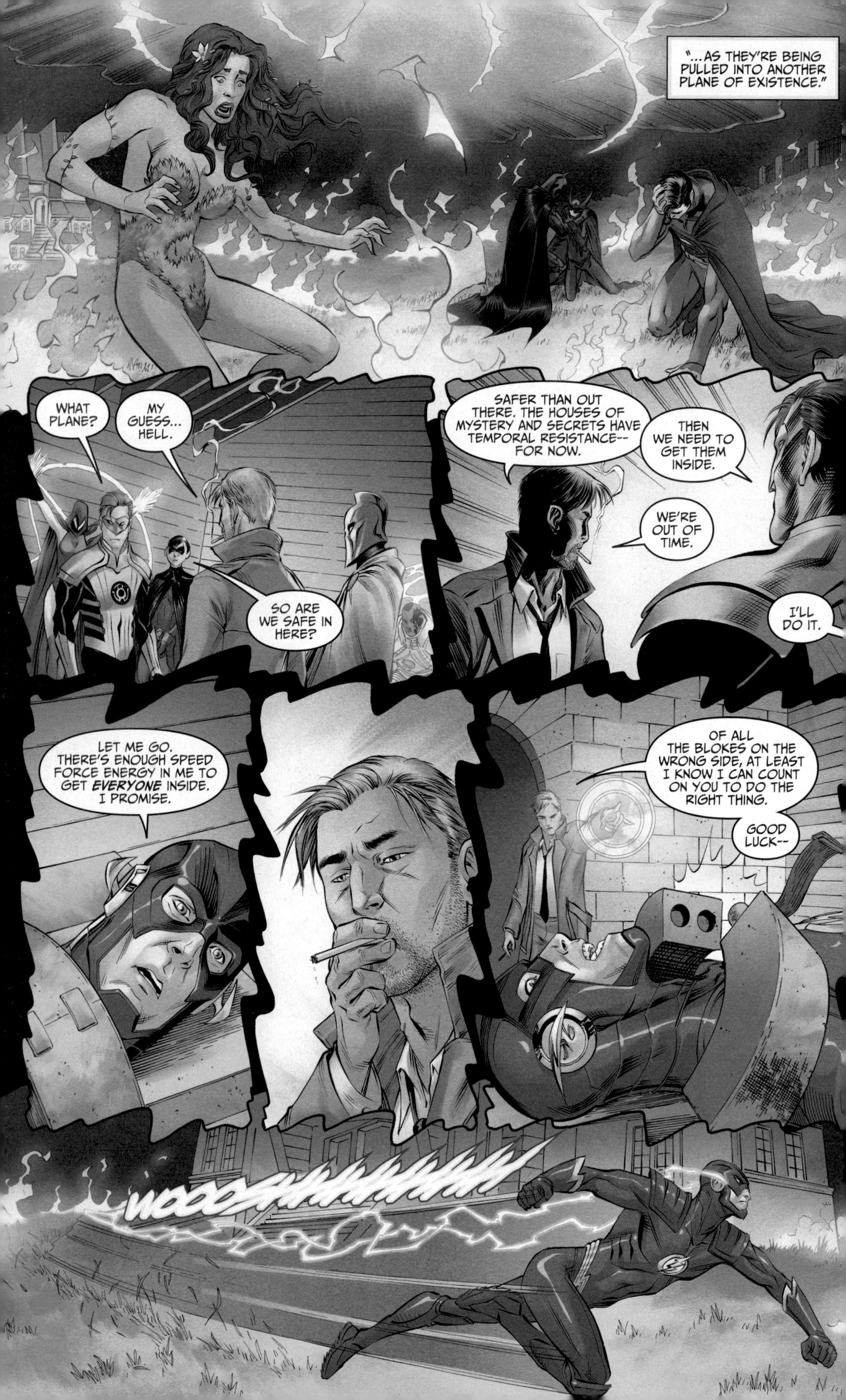
"...AS THEY'RE BEING PULLED INTO ANOTHER PLANE OF EXISTENCE."
WHAT PLANE?
MY GUESS... HELL.
SO ARE WE SAFE IN HERE?
SAFER THAN OUT THERE. THE HOUSES OF MYSTERY AND SECRETS HAVE TEMPORAL RESISTANCE-- FOR NOW.
THEN WE NEED TO GET THEM INSIDE.
WE'RE OUT OF TIME.
I'LL DO IT.
LET ME GO. THERE'S ENOUGH SPEED FORCE ENERGY IN ME TO GET EVERYONE INSIDE. I PROMISE.
OF ALL THE BLOKES ON THE WRONG SIDE, AT LEAST I KNOW I CAN COUNT ON YOU TO DO THE RIGHT THING.
GOOD LUCK--
WOOOSHHHHHHHH

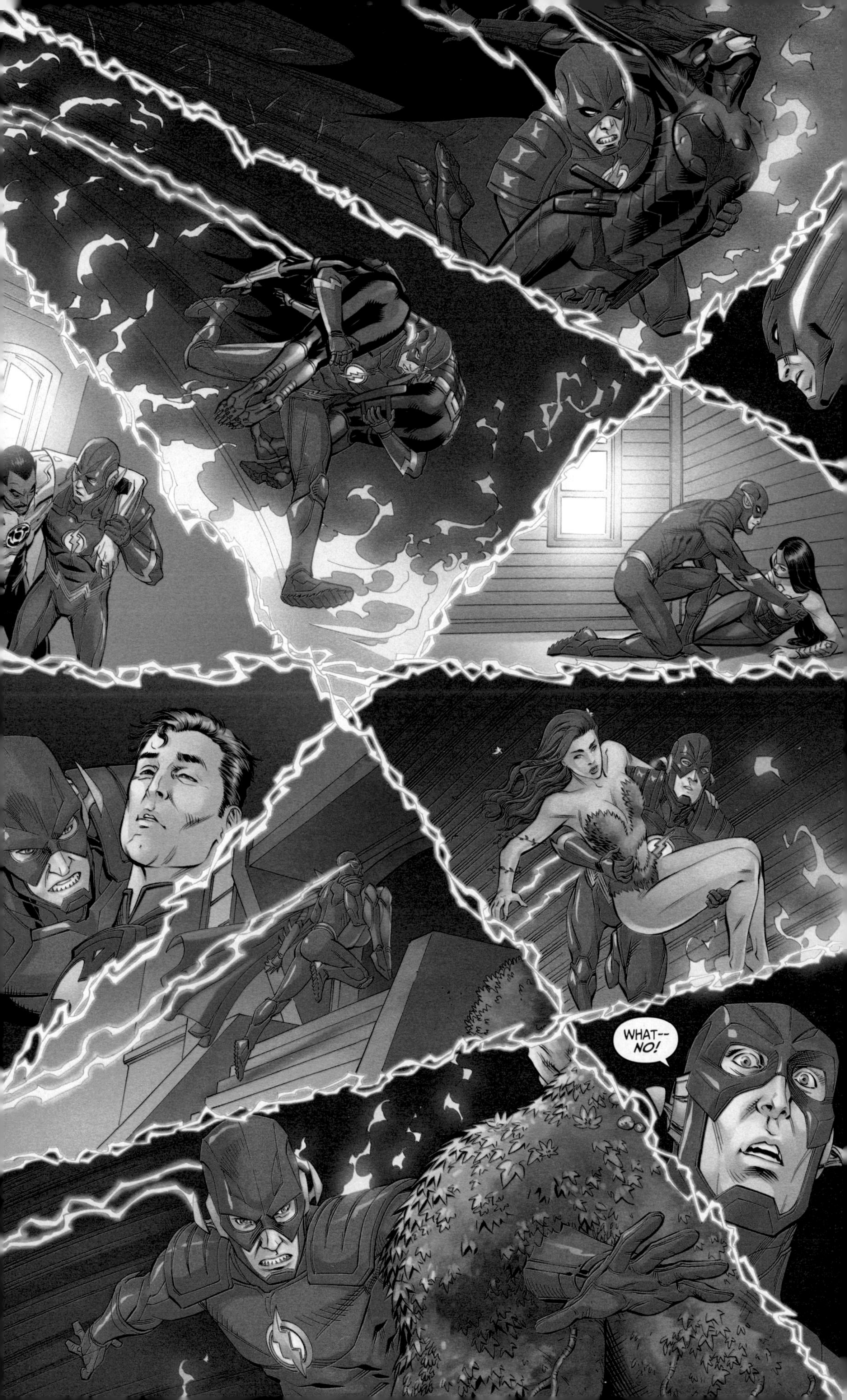
WHAT--
NO!

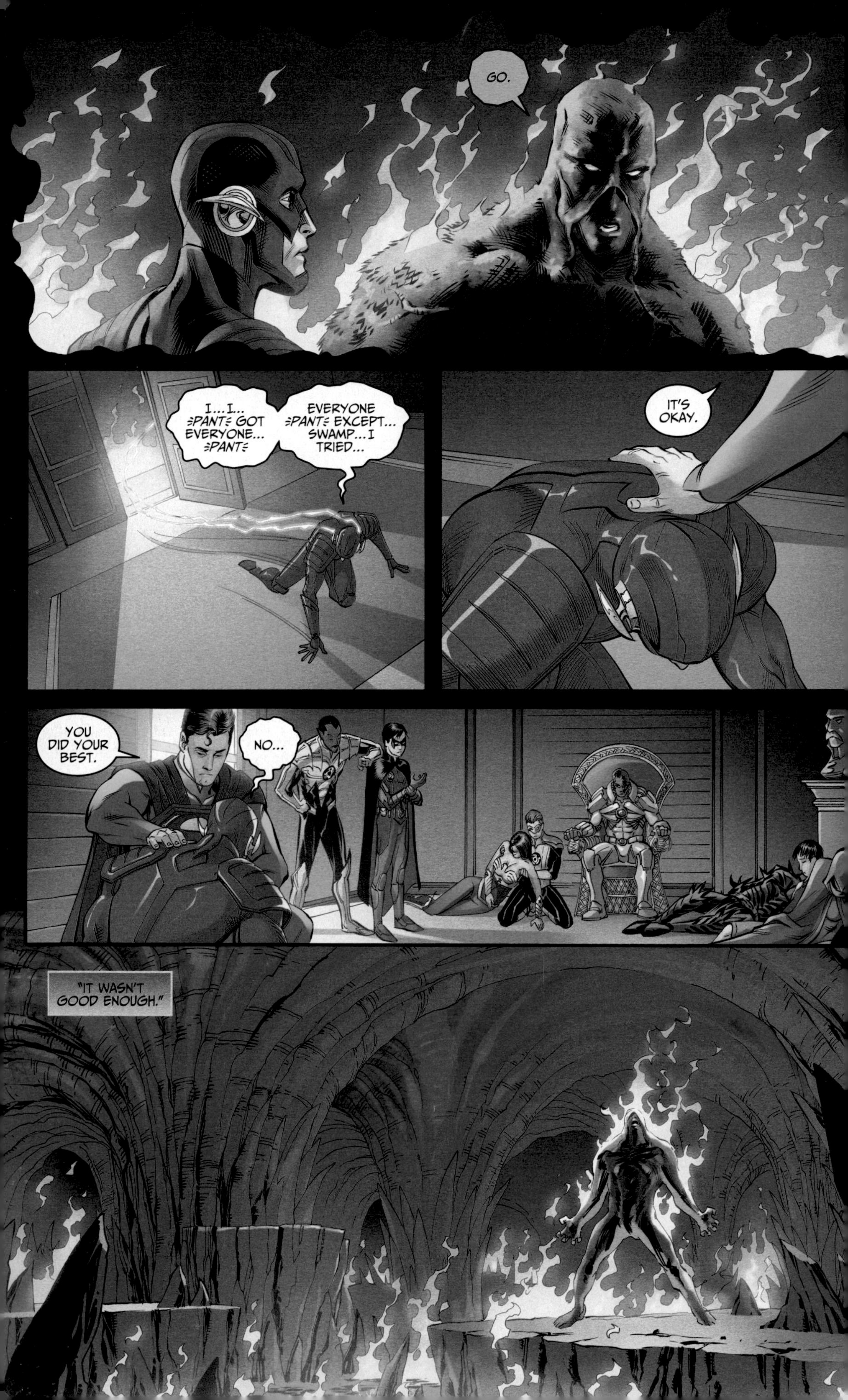
GO.
I... I... =PANT= GOT EVERYONE... =PANT=
EVERYONE =PANT= EXCEPT... SWAMP... I TRIED...
IT'S OKAY.
YOU DID YOUR BEST.
NO...
"IT WASN'T GOOD ENOUGH."

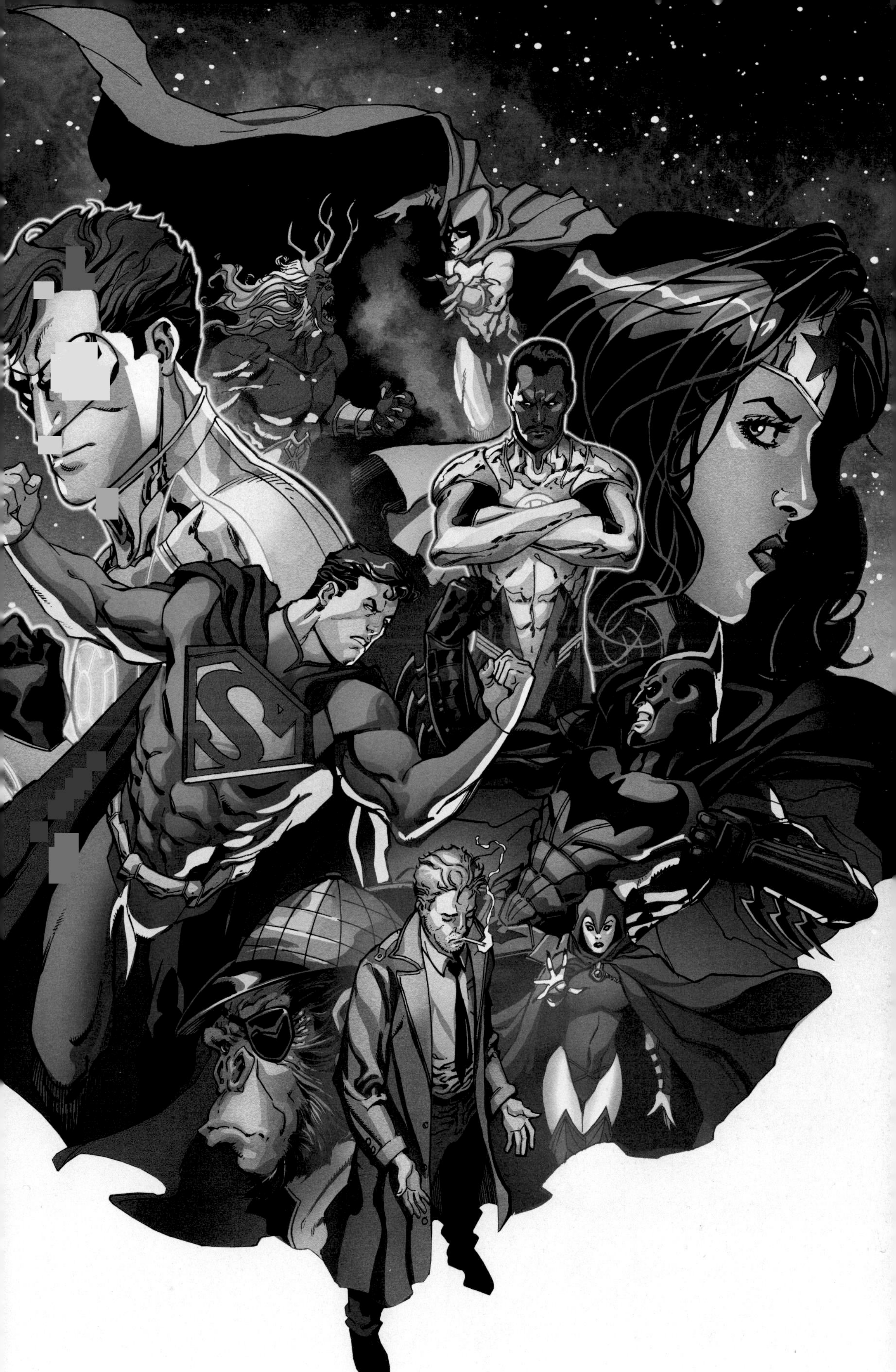

"Maelstrom" Mike S. Miller - Artists J. Nanjan - Colorist
"Endgame" Bruno Redondo and Juan Albarran - Artists Rex Lokus - Colorist
Cover Art by Aaron Lopresti and Rex Lokus

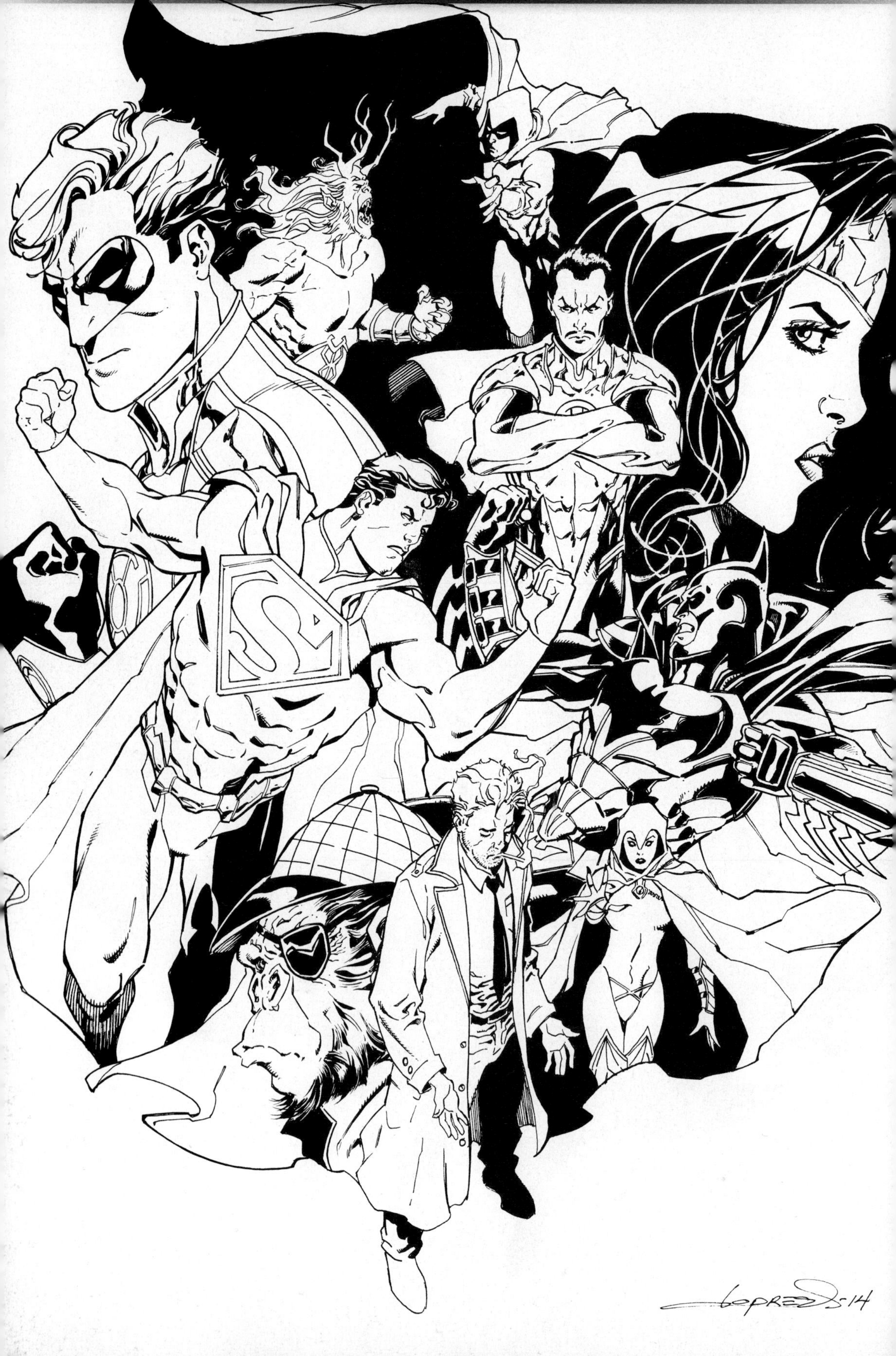

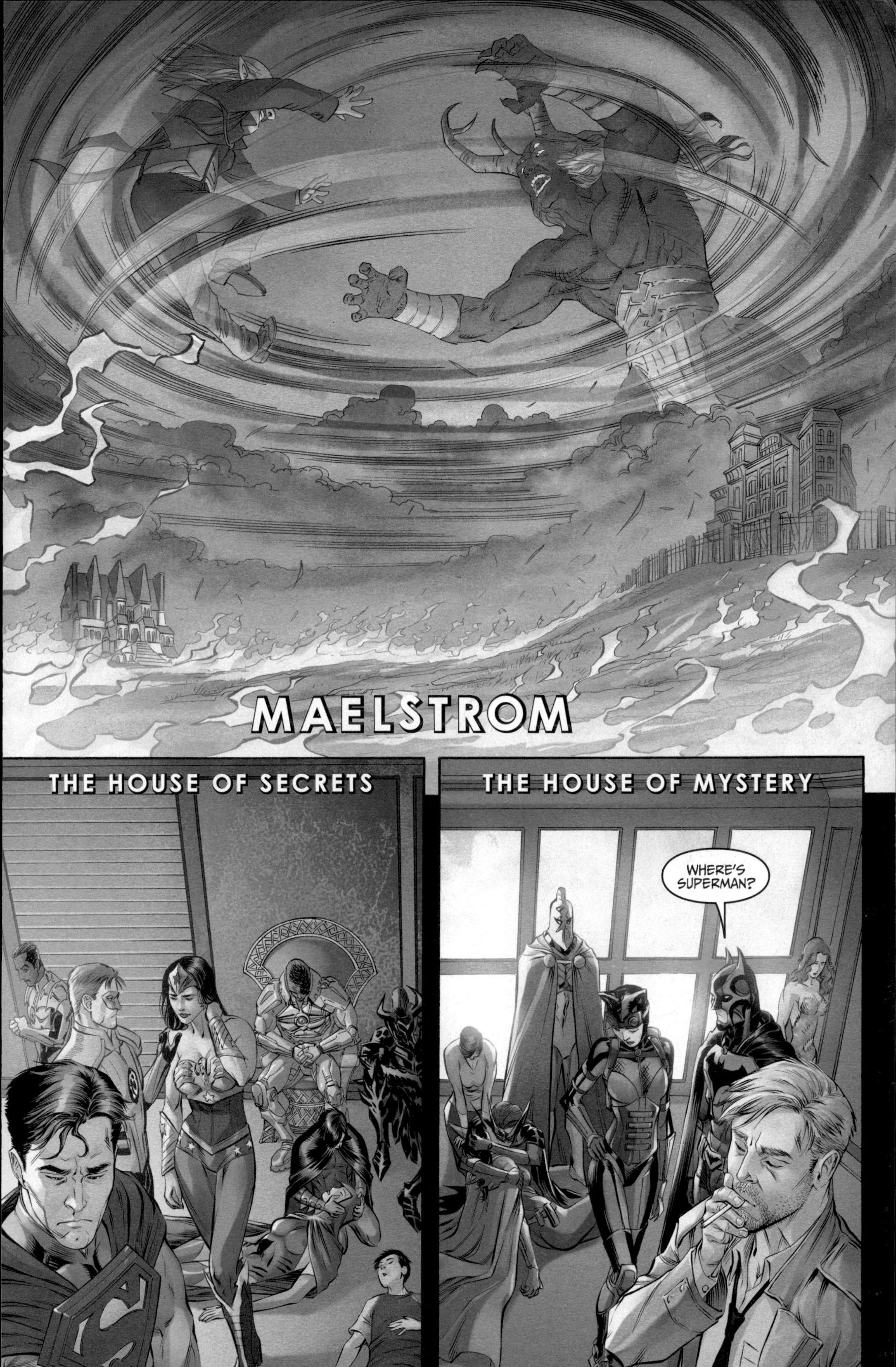
MAELSTROM
THE HOUSE OF SECRETS
THE HOUSE OF MYSTERY
WHERE'S SUPERMAN?

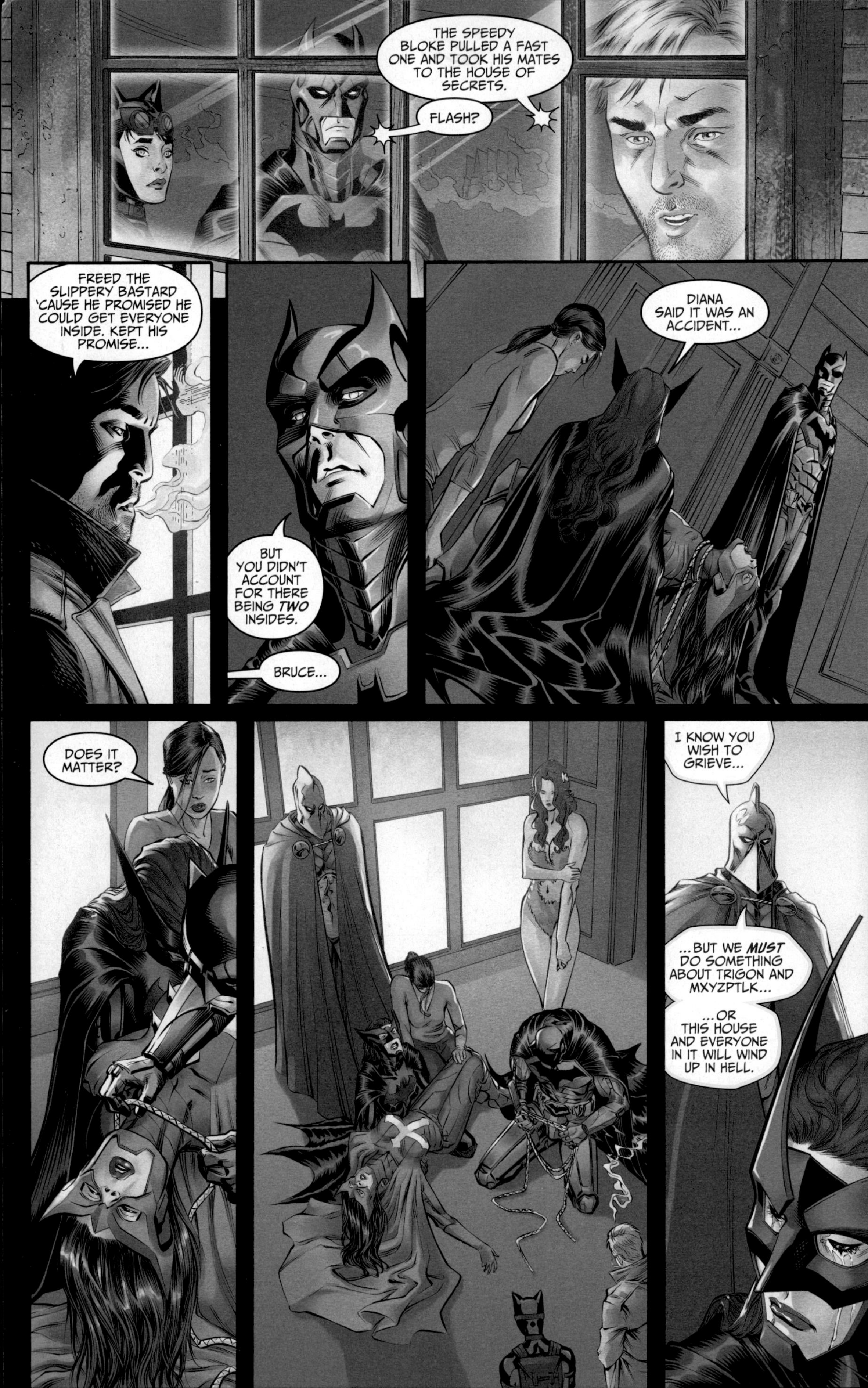
THE SPEEDY BLOKE PULLED A FAST ONE AND TOOK HIS MATES TO THE HOUSE OF SECRETS.
FLASH?
FREED THE SLIPPERY BASTARD 'CAUSE HE PROMISED HE COULD GET EVERYONE INSIDE. KEPT HIS PROMISE...
BUT YOU DIDN'T ACCOUNT FOR THERE BEING *TWO* INSIDES.
BRUCE...
DIANA SAID IT WAS AN ACCIDENT...
DOES IT MATTER?
I KNOW YOU WISH TO GRIEVE...
...BUT WE *MUST* DO SOMETHING ABOUT TRIGON AND MXYZPTLK...
...OR THIS HOUSE AND EVERYONE IN IT WILL WIND UP IN HELL.

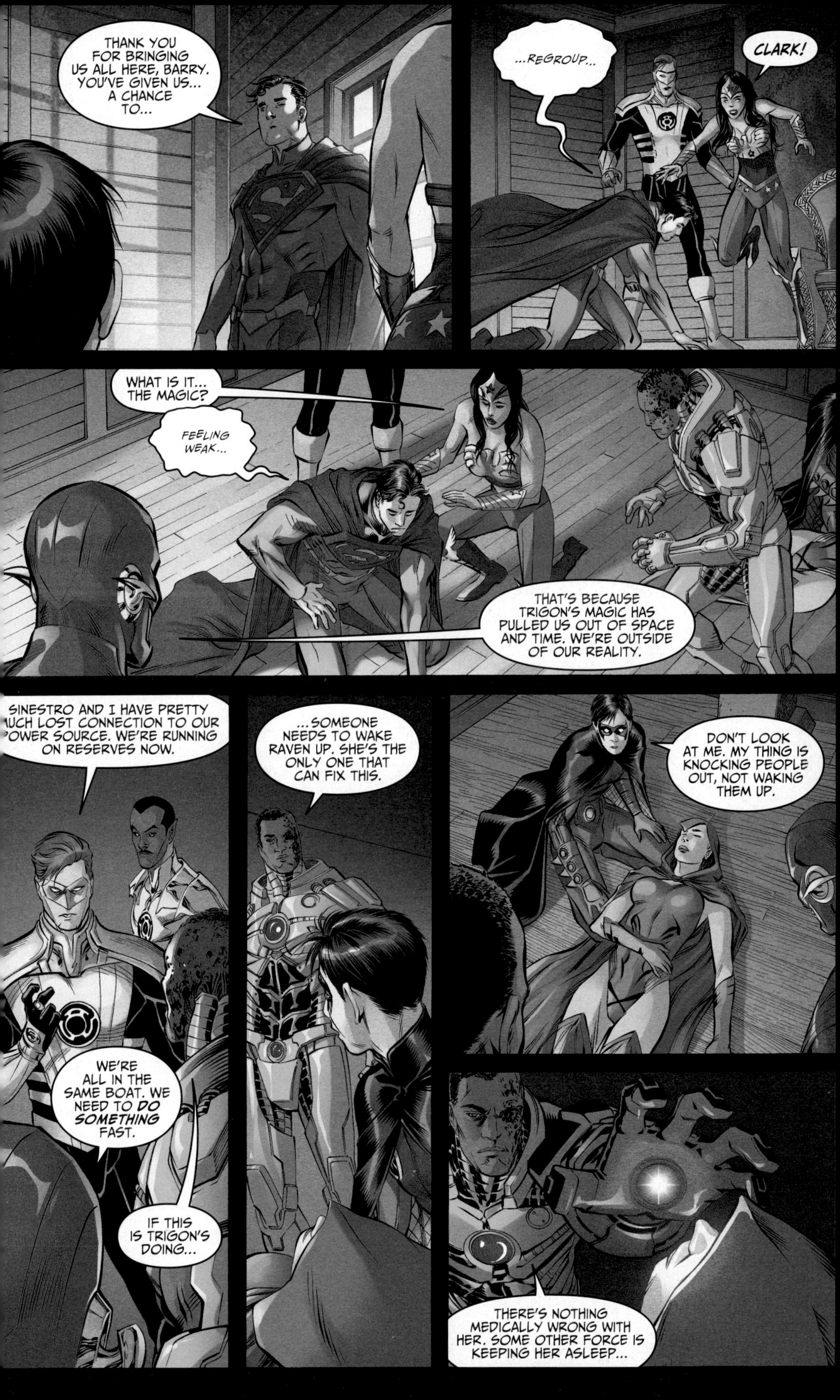
THANK YOU FOR BRINGING US ALL HERE, BARRY. YOU'VE GIVEN US... A CHANCE TO...
...REGROUP...
CLARK!
WHAT IS IT... THE MAGIC?
FEELING WEAK...
THAT'S BECAUSE TRIGON'S MAGIC HAS PULLED US OUT OF SPACE AND TIME. WE'RE OUTSIDE OF OUR REALITY.
SINESTRO AND I HAVE PRETTY MUCH LOST CONNECTION TO OUR POWER SOURCE. WE'RE RUNNING ON RESERVES NOW.
WE'RE ALL IN THE SAME BOAT. WE NEED TO DO SOMETHING FAST.
IF THIS IS TRIGON'S DOING...
...SOMEONE NEEDS TO WAKE RAVEN UP. SHE'S THE ONLY ONE THAT CAN FIX THIS.
DON'T LOOK AT ME. MY THING IS KNOCKING PEOPLE OUT, NOT WAKING THEM UP.
THERE'S NOTHING MEDICALLY WRONG WITH HER. SOME OTHER FORCE IS KEEPING HER ASLEEP...

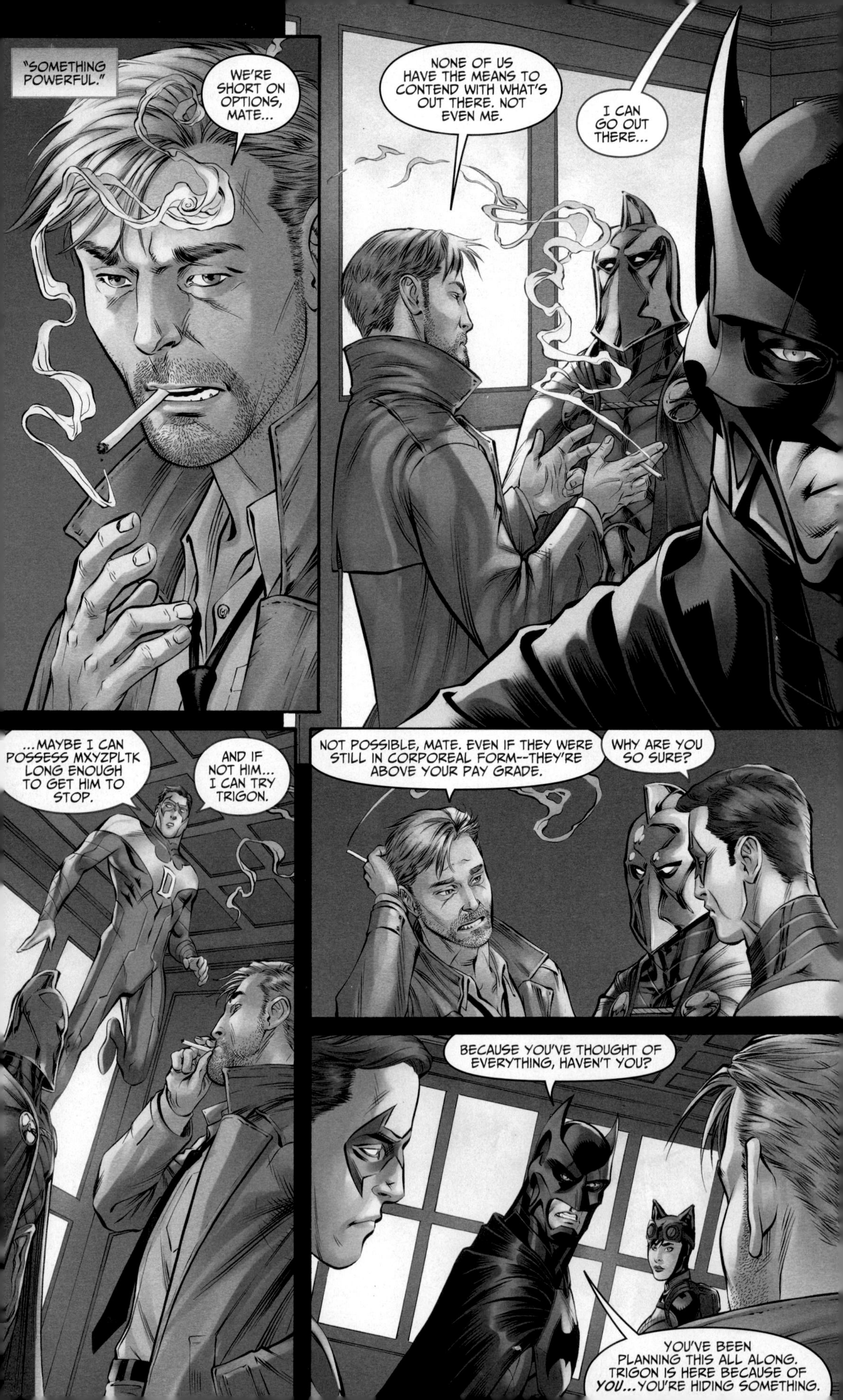
"SOMETHING POWERFUL."
WE'RE SHORT ON OPTIONS, MATE...
NONE OF US HAVE THE MEANS TO CONTEND WITH WHAT'S OUT THERE. NOT EVEN ME.
I CAN GO OUT THERE...
...MAYBE I CAN POSSESS MXYZPLTK LONG ENOUGH TO GET HIM TO STOP.
AND IF NOT HIM... I CAN TRY TRIGON.
NOT POSSIBLE, MATE. EVEN IF THEY WERE STILL IN CORPOREAL FORM--THEY'RE ABOVE YOUR PAY GRADE.
WHY ARE YOU SO SURE?
BECAUSE YOU'VE THOUGHT OF EVERYTHING, HAVEN'T YOU?
YOU'VE BEEN PLANNING THIS ALL ALONG. TRIGON IS HERE BECAUSE OF *YOU*...YOU'RE HIDING SOMETHING.

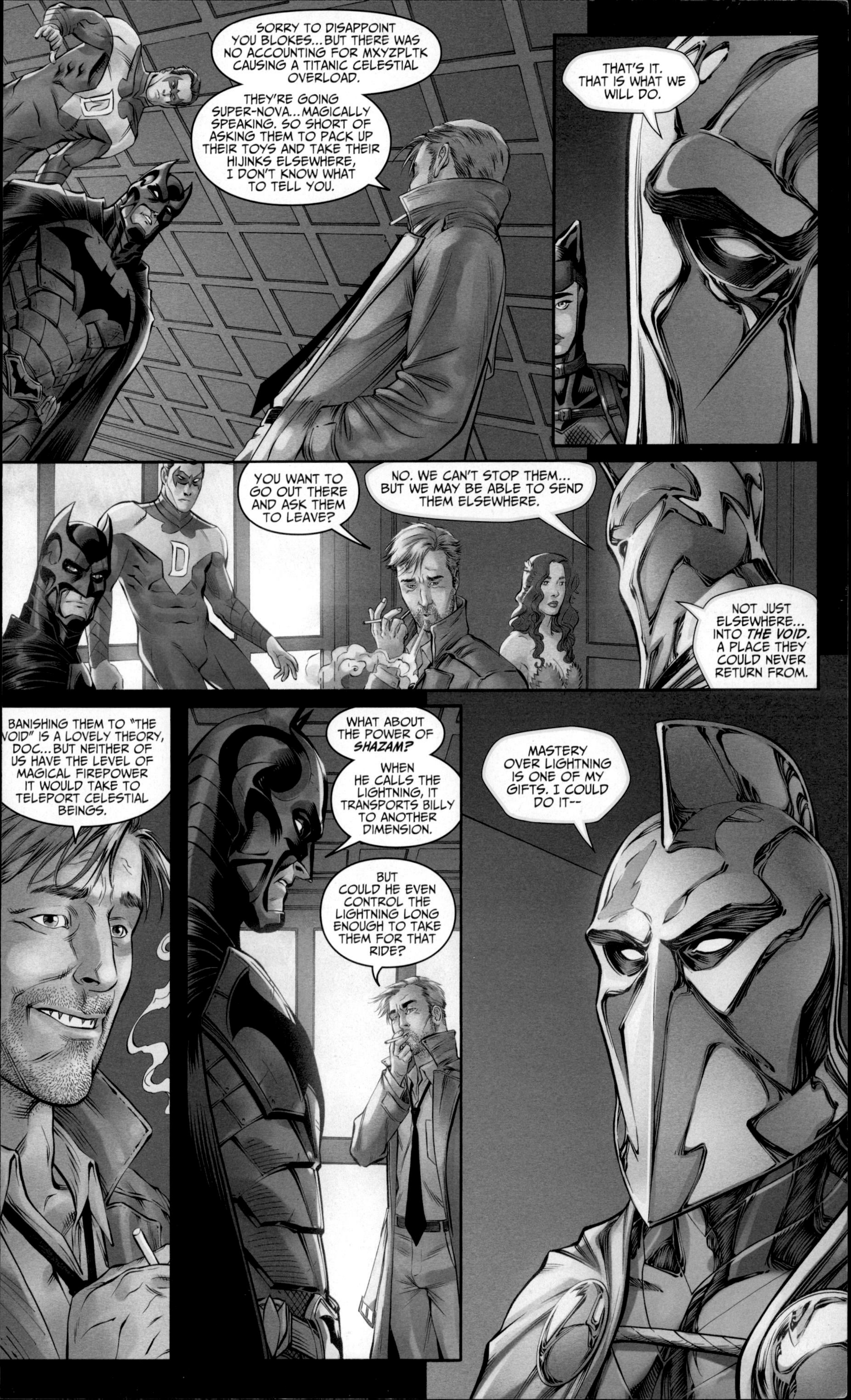
SORRY TO DISAPPOINT YOU BLOKES...BUT THERE WAS NO ACCOUNTING FOR MXYZPLTK CAUSING A TITANIC CELESTIAL OVERLOAD.
THEY'RE GOING SUPER-NOVA...MAGICALLY SPEAKING. SO SHORT OF ASKING THEM TO PACK UP THEIR TOYS AND TAKE THEIR HIJINKS ELSEWHERE, I DON'T KNOW WHAT TO TELL YOU.
THAT'S IT. THAT IS WHAT WE WILL DO.
YOU WANT TO GO OUT THERE AND ASK THEM TO LEAVE?
NO. WE CAN'T STOP THEM... BUT WE MAY BE ABLE TO SEND THEM ELSEWHERE.
NOT JUST ELSEWHERE... INTO *THE VOID.* A PLACE THEY COULD NEVER RETURN FROM.
BANISHING THEM TO "THE VOID" IS A LOVELY THEORY, DOC...BUT NEITHER OF US HAVE THE LEVEL OF MAGICAL FIREPOWER IT WOULD TAKE TO TELEPORT CELESTIAL BEINGS.
WHAT ABOUT THE POWER OF *SHAZAM?*
WHEN HE CALLS THE LIGHTNING, IT TRANSPORTS BILLY TO ANOTHER DIMENSION.
BUT COULD HE EVEN CONTROL THE LIGHTNING LONG ENOUGH TO TAKE THEM FOR THAT RIDE?
MASTERY OVER LIGHTNING IS ONE OF MY GIFTS. I COULD DO IT--

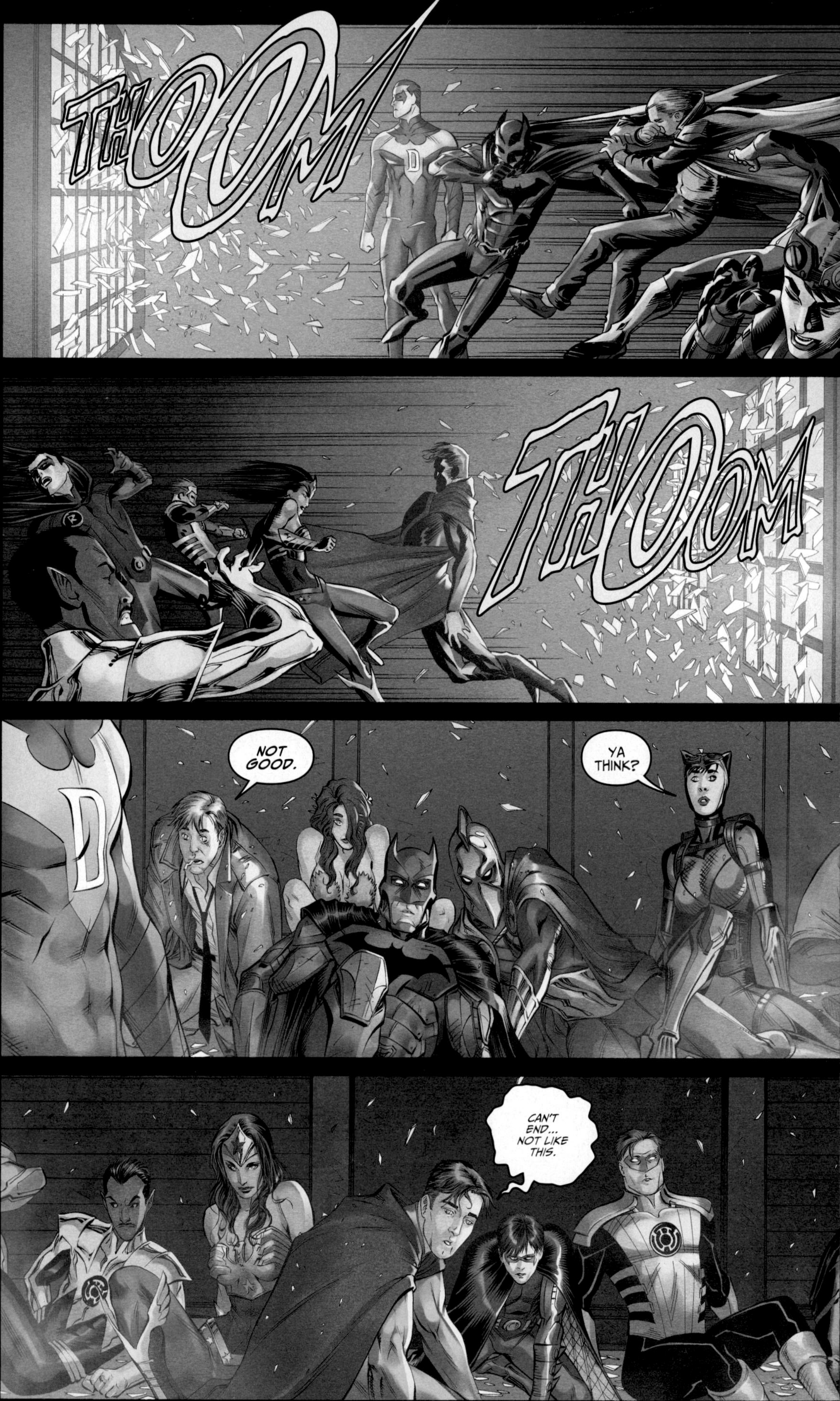
THOOM
THOOM
NOT GOOD.
YA THINK?
CAN'T END... NOT LIKE THIS.

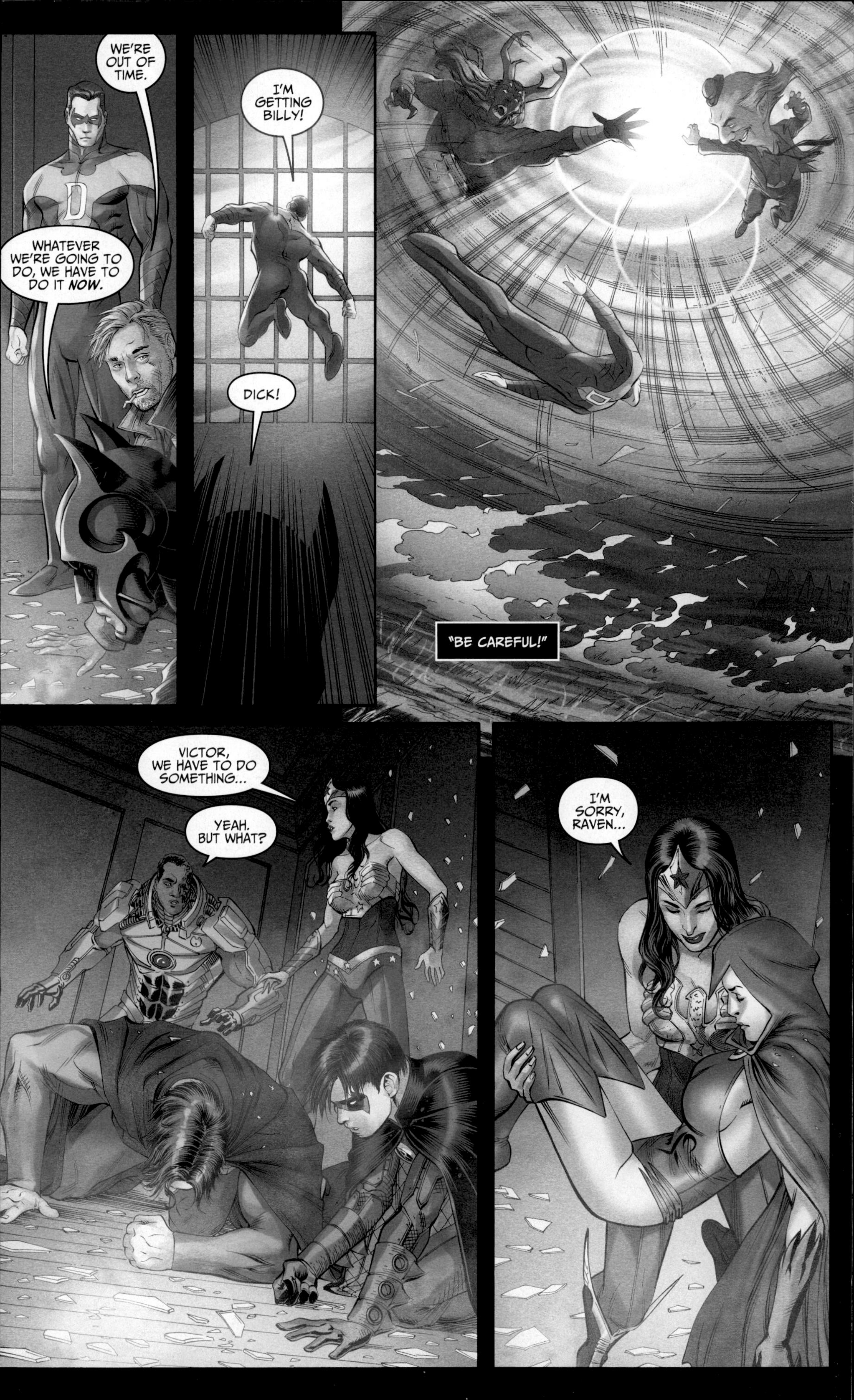
WE'RE OUT OF TIME.
WHATEVER WE'RE GOING TO DO, WE HAVE TO DO IT NOW.
I'M GETTING BILLY!
DICK!
"BE CAREFUL!"
VICTOR, WE HAVE TO DO SOMETHING...
YEAH. BUT WHAT?
I'M SORRY, RAVEN...

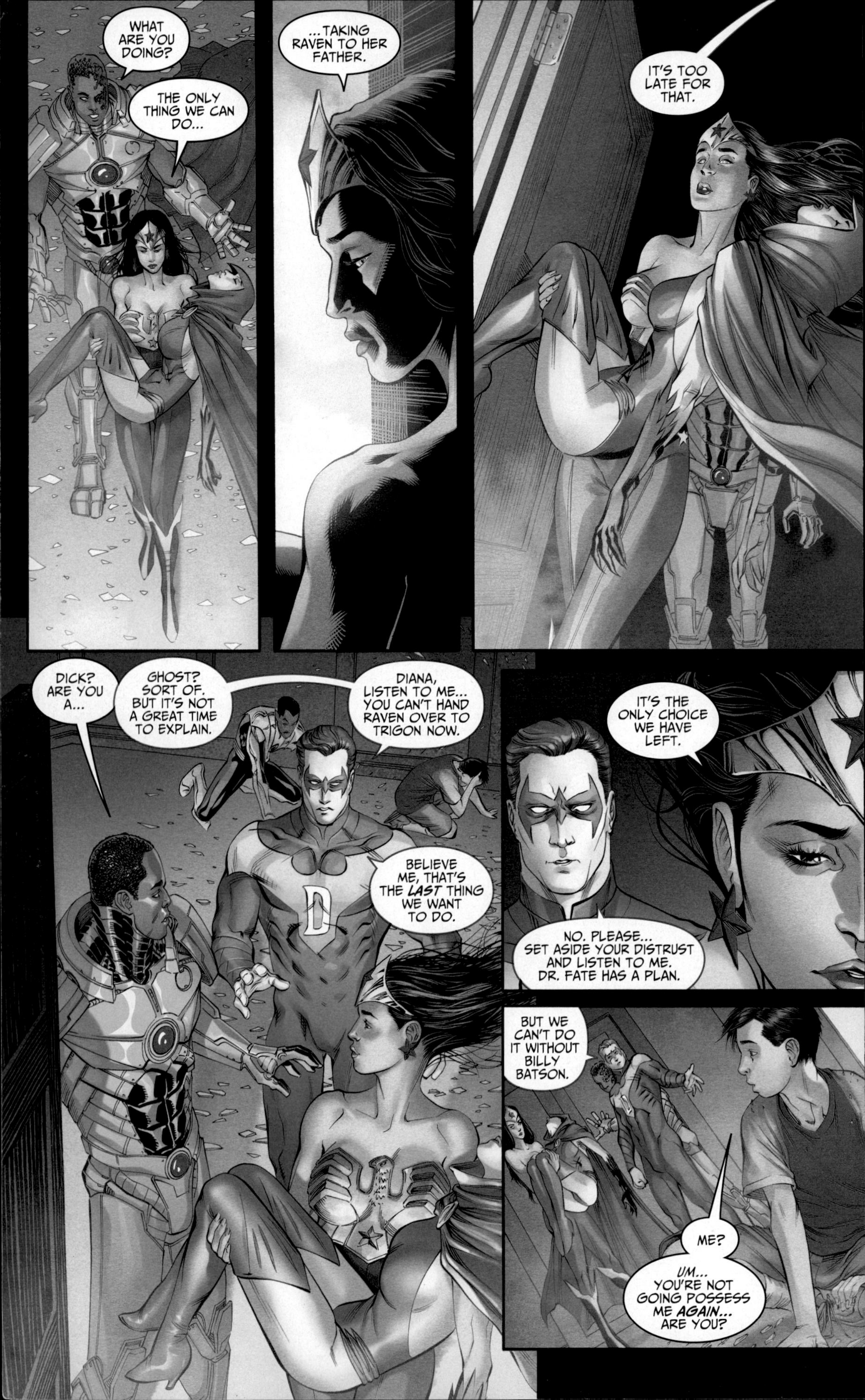
WHAT ARE YOU DOING?
THE ONLY THING WE CAN DO...
...TAKING RAVEN TO HER FATHER.
IT'S TOO LATE FOR THAT.
DICK? ARE YOU A...
GHOST? SORT OF. BUT IT'S NOT A GREAT TIME TO EXPLAIN.
DIANA, LISTEN TO ME... YOU CAN'T HAND RAVEN OVER TO TRIGON NOW.
BELIEVE ME, THAT'S THE *LAST* THING WE WANT TO DO.
IT'S THE ONLY CHOICE WE HAVE LEFT.
NO. PLEASE... SET ASIDE YOUR DISTRUST AND LISTEN TO ME. DR. FATE HAS A PLAN.
BUT WE CAN'T DO IT WITHOUT BILLY BATSON.
ME?
UM... YOU'RE NOT GOING POSSESS ME *AGAIN...* ARE YOU?

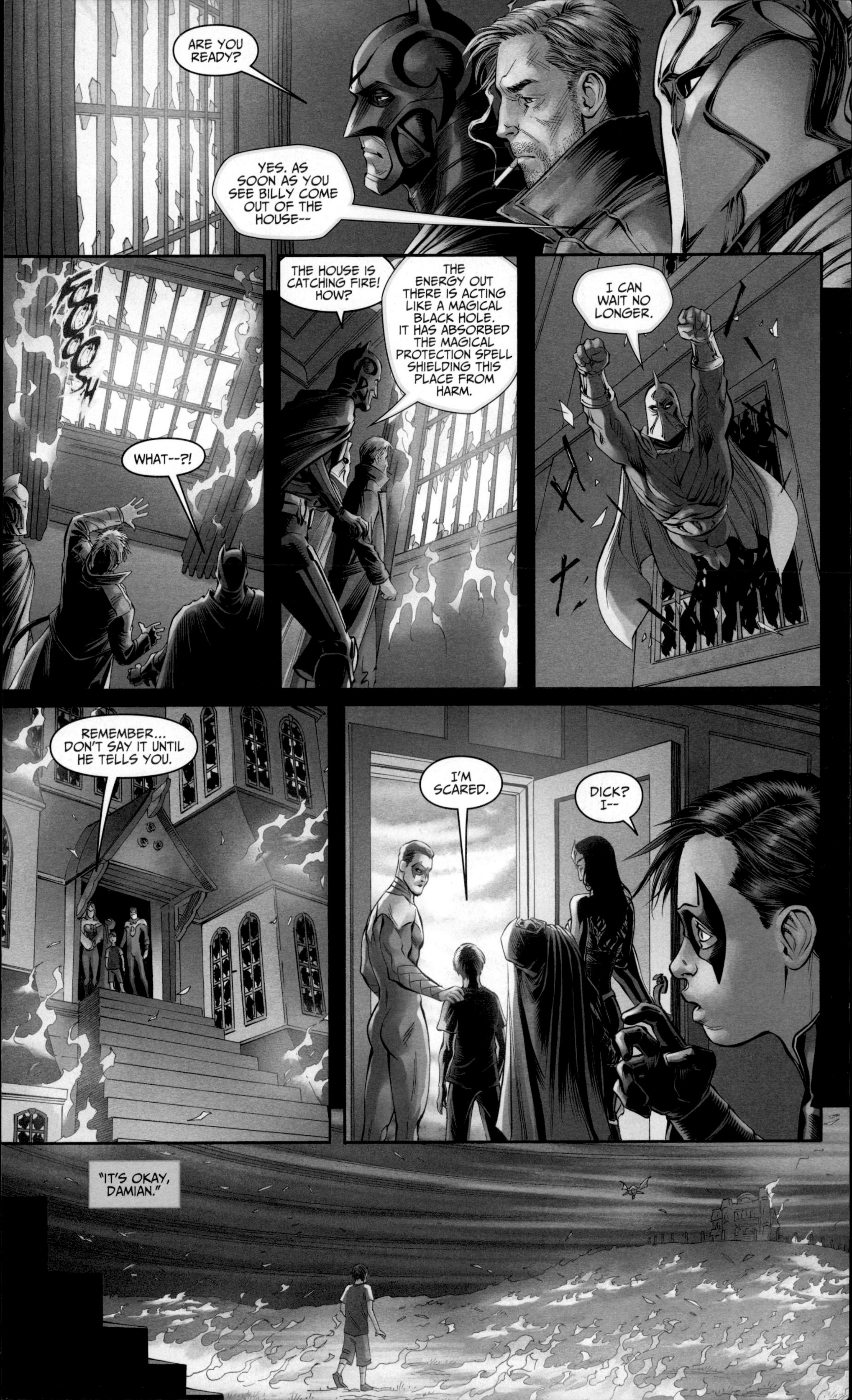
ARE YOU READY?
YES. AS SOON AS YOU SEE BILLY COME OUT OF THE HOUSE--
FOOOOSH
WHAT--?!
THE HOUSE IS CATCHING FIRE! HOW?
THE ENERGY OUT THERE IS ACTING LIKE A MAGICAL BLACK HOLE. IT HAS ABSORBED THE MAGICAL PROTECTION SPELL SHIELDING THIS PLACE FROM HARM.
I CAN WAIT NO LONGER.
REMEMBER... DON'T SAY IT UNTIL HE TELLS YOU.
I'M SCARED.
DICK? I--
"IT'S OKAY, DAMIAN."

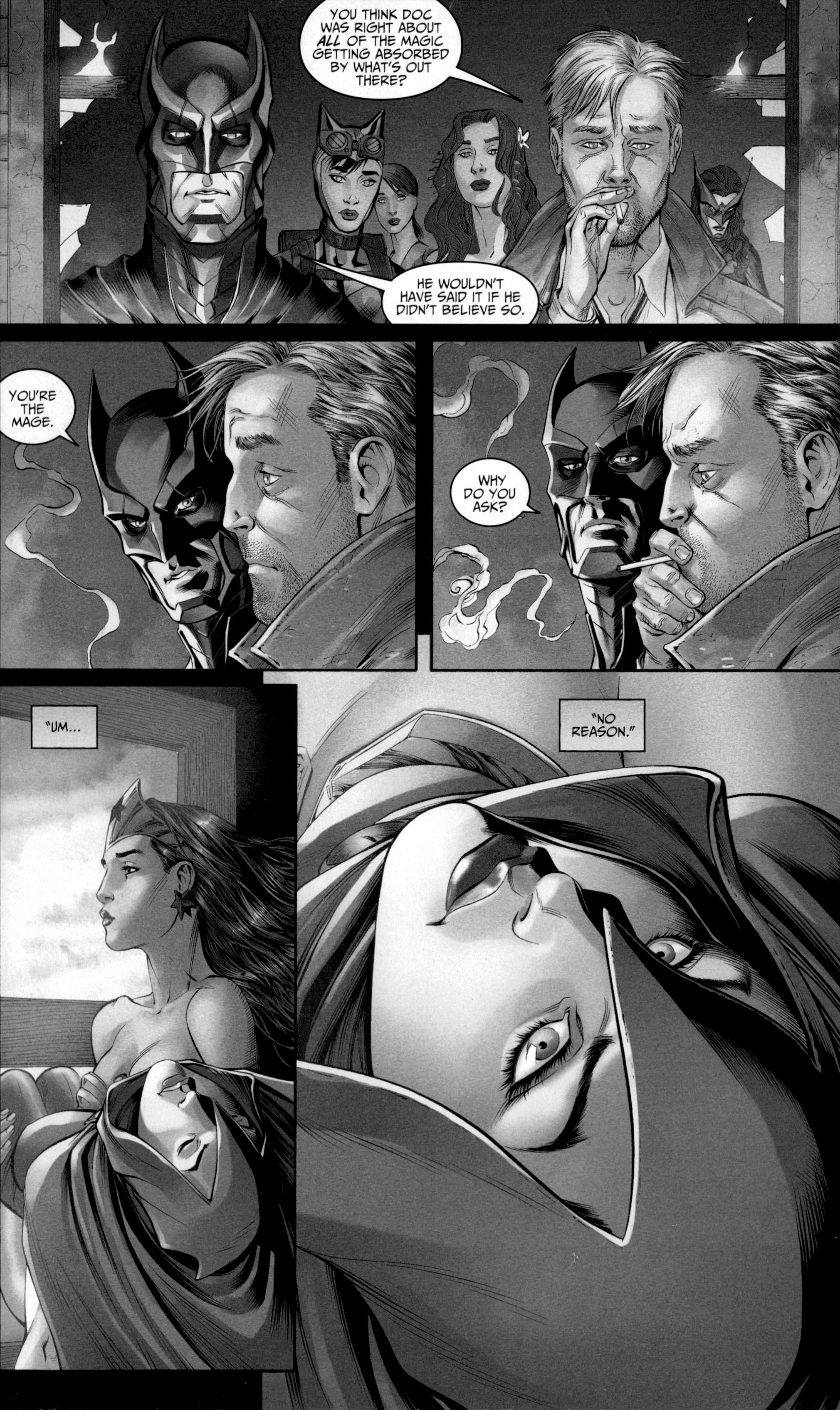
YOU THINK DOC WAS RIGHT ABOUT ALL OF THE MAGIC GETTING ABSORBED BY WHAT'S OUT THERE?
HE WOULDN'T HAVE SAID IT IF HE DIDN'T BELIEVE SO.
YOU'RE THE MAGE.
WHY DO YOU ASK?
"UM...
"NO REASON."

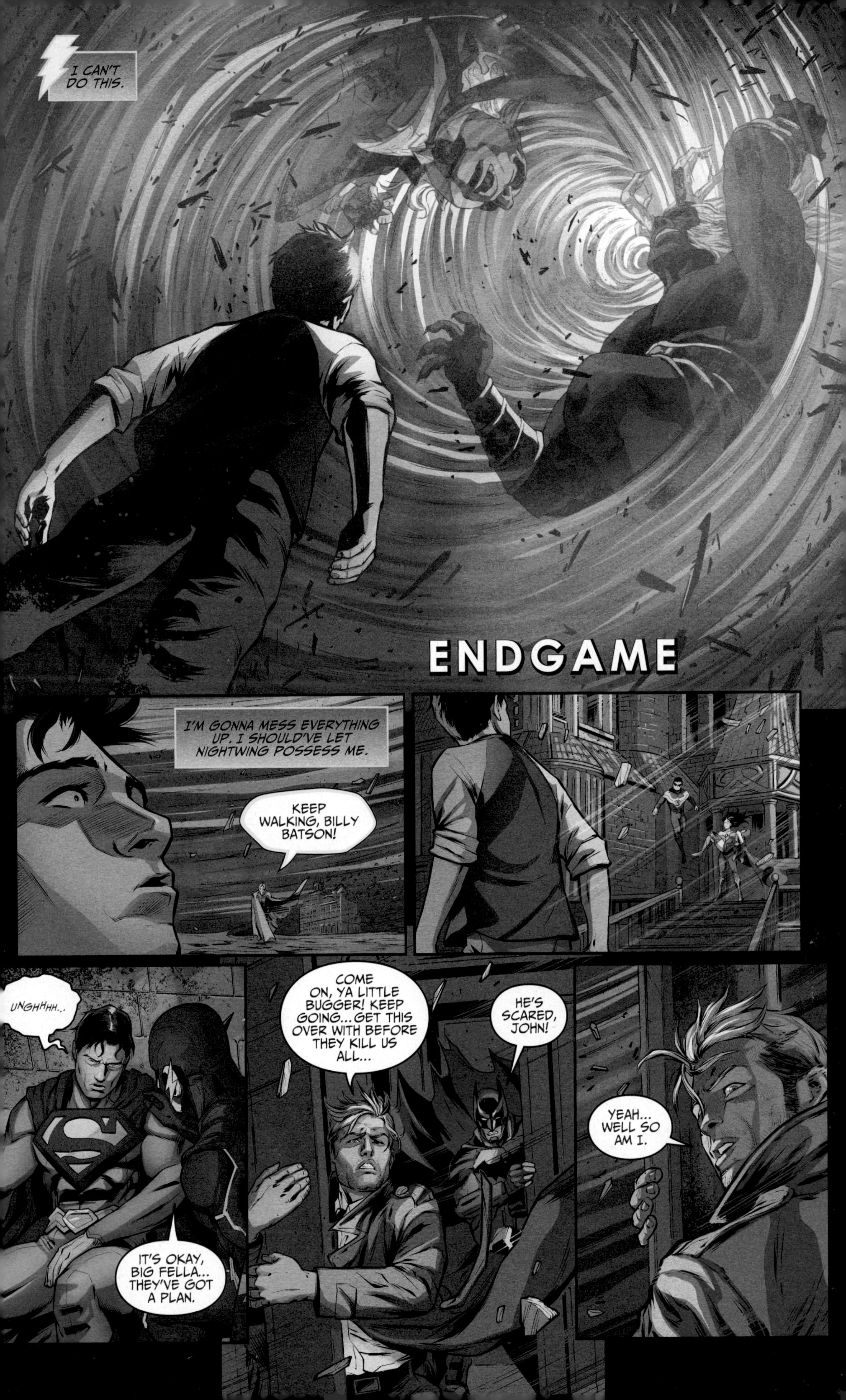
I CAN'T DO THIS.
ENDGAME
I'M GONNA MESS EVERYTHING UP. I SHOULD'VE LET NIGHTWING POSSESS ME.
KEEP WALKING, BILLY BATSON!
UNGHHHH...
IT'S OKAY, BIG FELLA... THEY'VE GOT A PLAN.
COME ON, YA LITTLE BUGGER! KEEP GOING...GET THIS OVER WITH BEFORE THEY KILL US ALL...
HE'S SCARED, JOHN!
YEAH... WELL SO AM I.

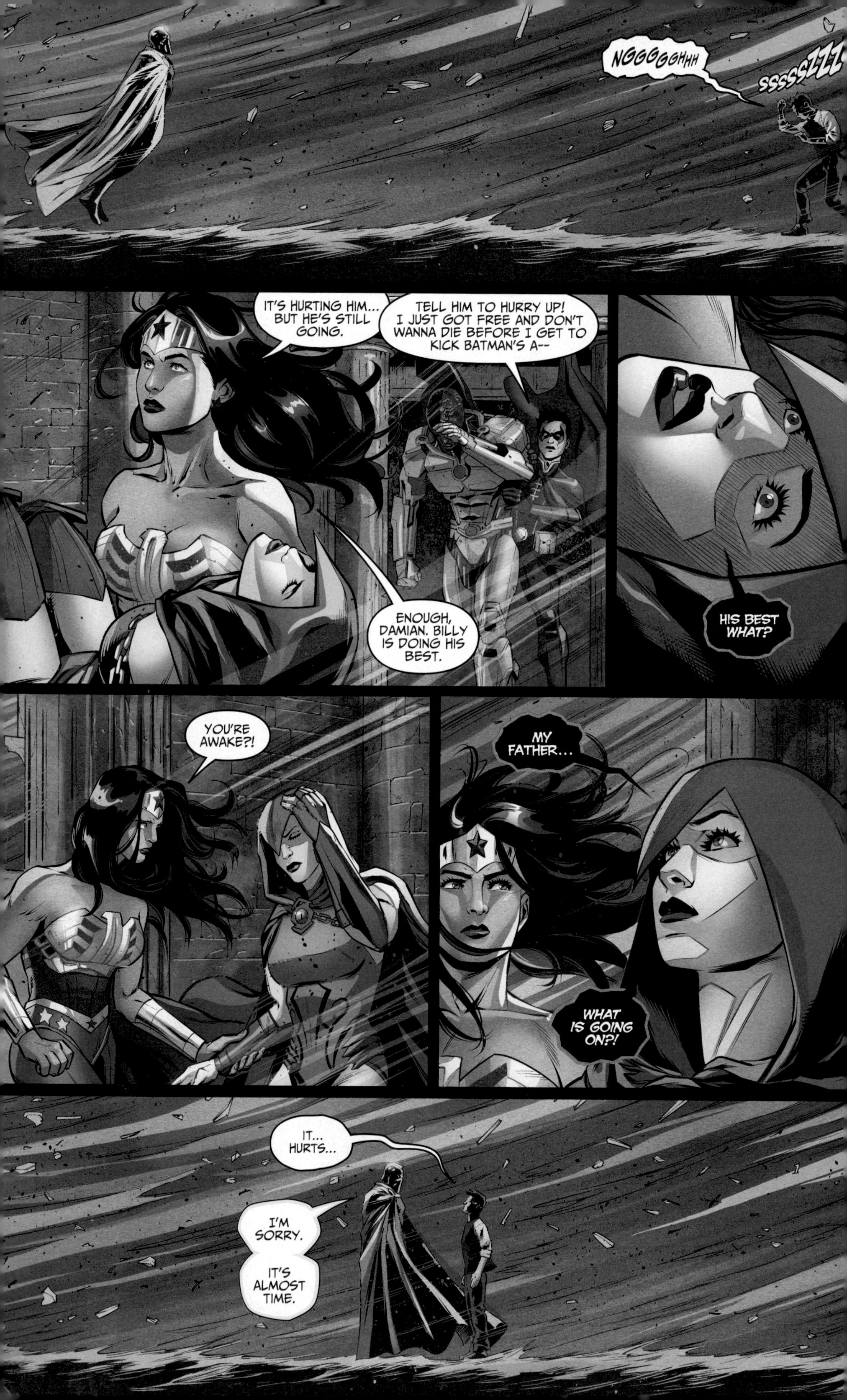
NGGGGGHHH
SSSSSZZZ
IT'S HURTING HIM... BUT HE'S STILL GOING.
TELL HIM TO HURRY UP! I JUST GOT FREE AND DON'T WANNA DIE BEFORE I GET TO KICK BATMAN'S A--
ENOUGH, DAMIAN. BILLY IS DOING HIS BEST.
HIS BEST WHAT?
YOU'RE AWAKE?!
MY FATHER...
WHAT IS GOING ON?!
IT... HURTS...
I'M SORRY.
IT'S ALMOST TIME.

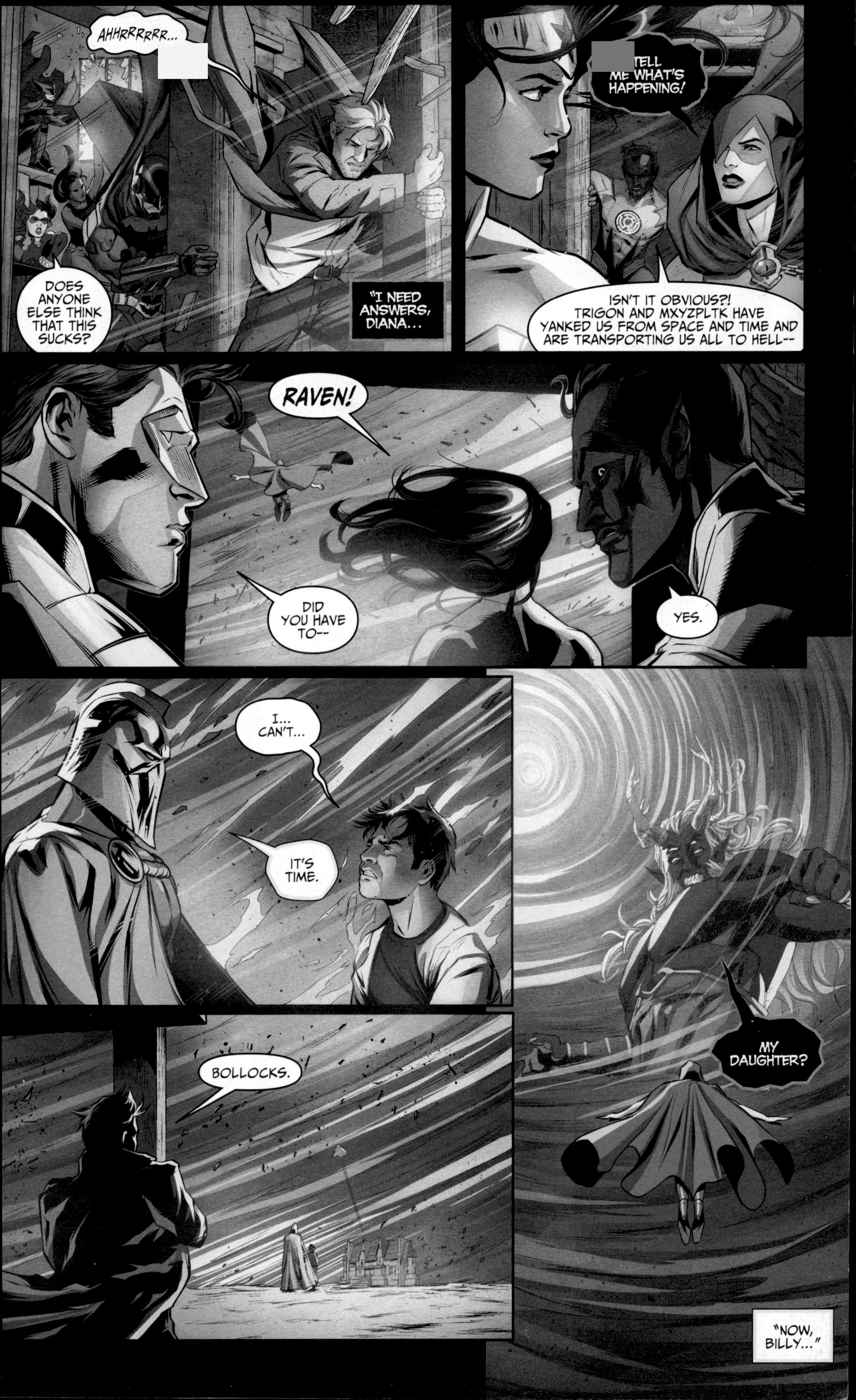

AHHRRRRRR...
DOES ANYONE ELSE THINK THAT THIS SUCKS?
"I NEED ANSWERS, DIANA...
TELL ME WHAT'S HAPPENING!
ISN'T IT OBVIOUS?! TRIGON AND MXYZPLTK HAVE YANKED US FROM SPACE AND TIME AND ARE TRANSPORTING US ALL TO HELL--
RAVEN!
DID YOU HAVE TO--
YES.
I... CAN'T...
IT'S TIME.
BOLLOCKS.
MY DAUGHTER?
"NOW, BILLY..."

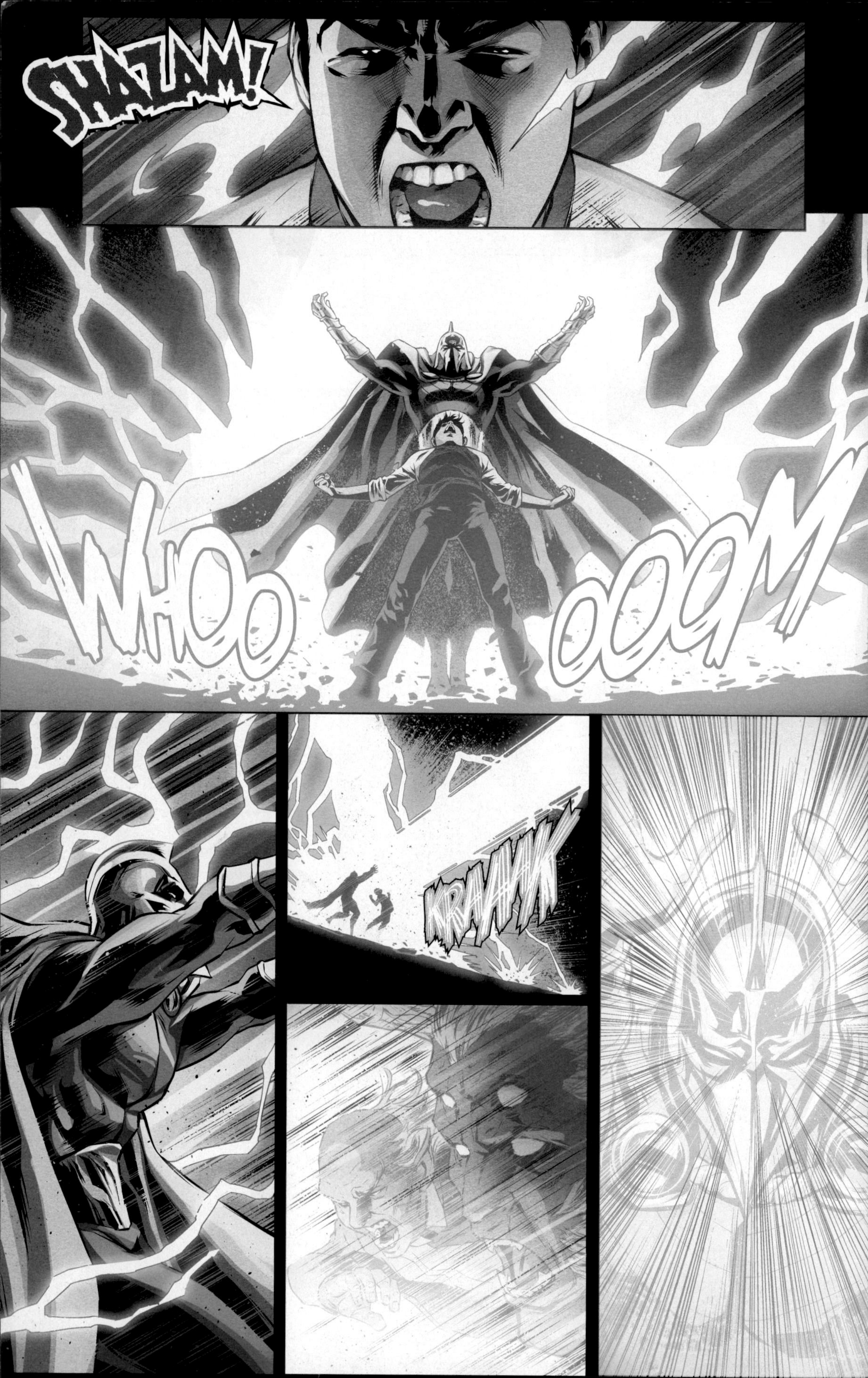
SHAZAM!
WHOOOOOM
KRAAAKK

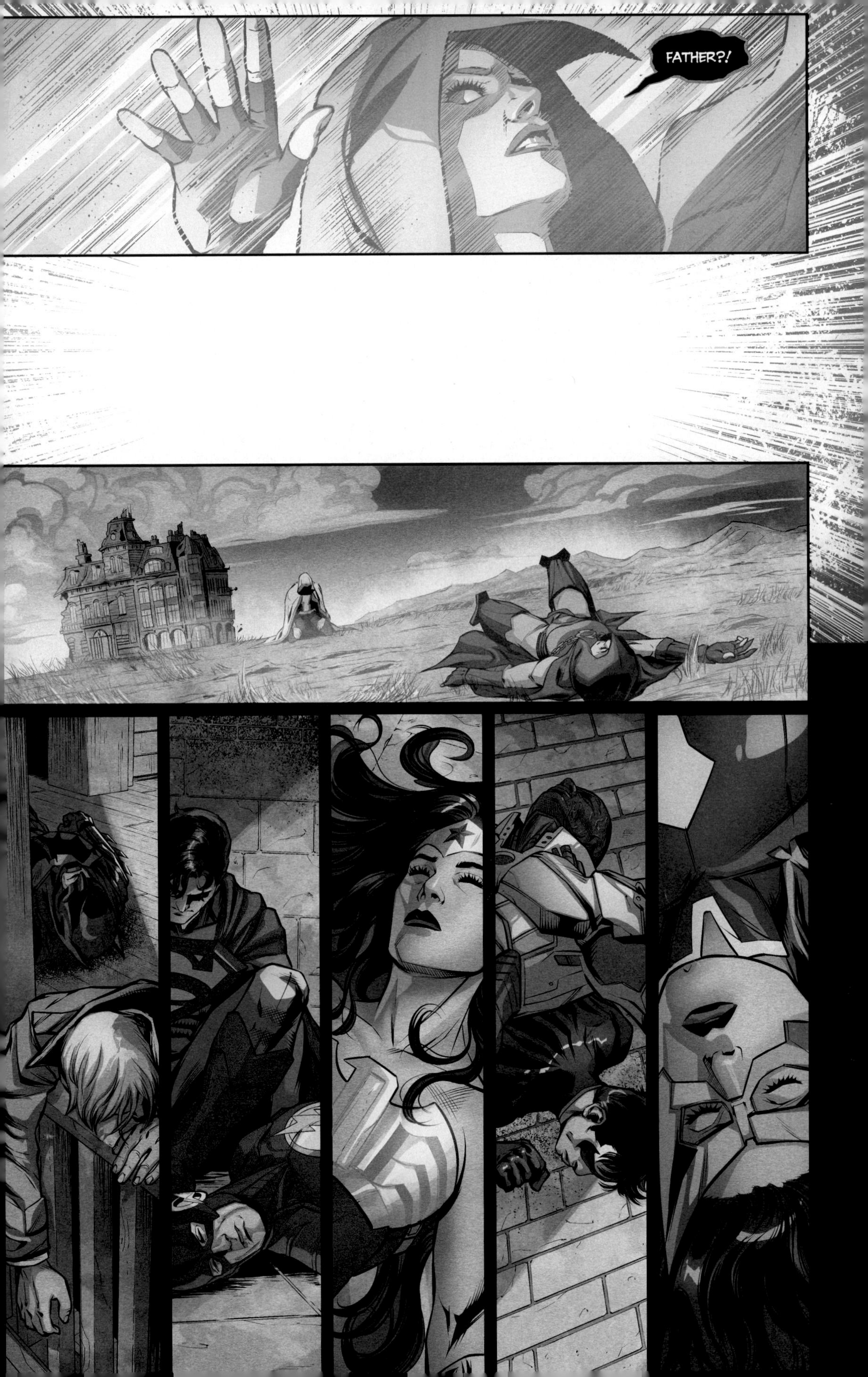
FATHER?!

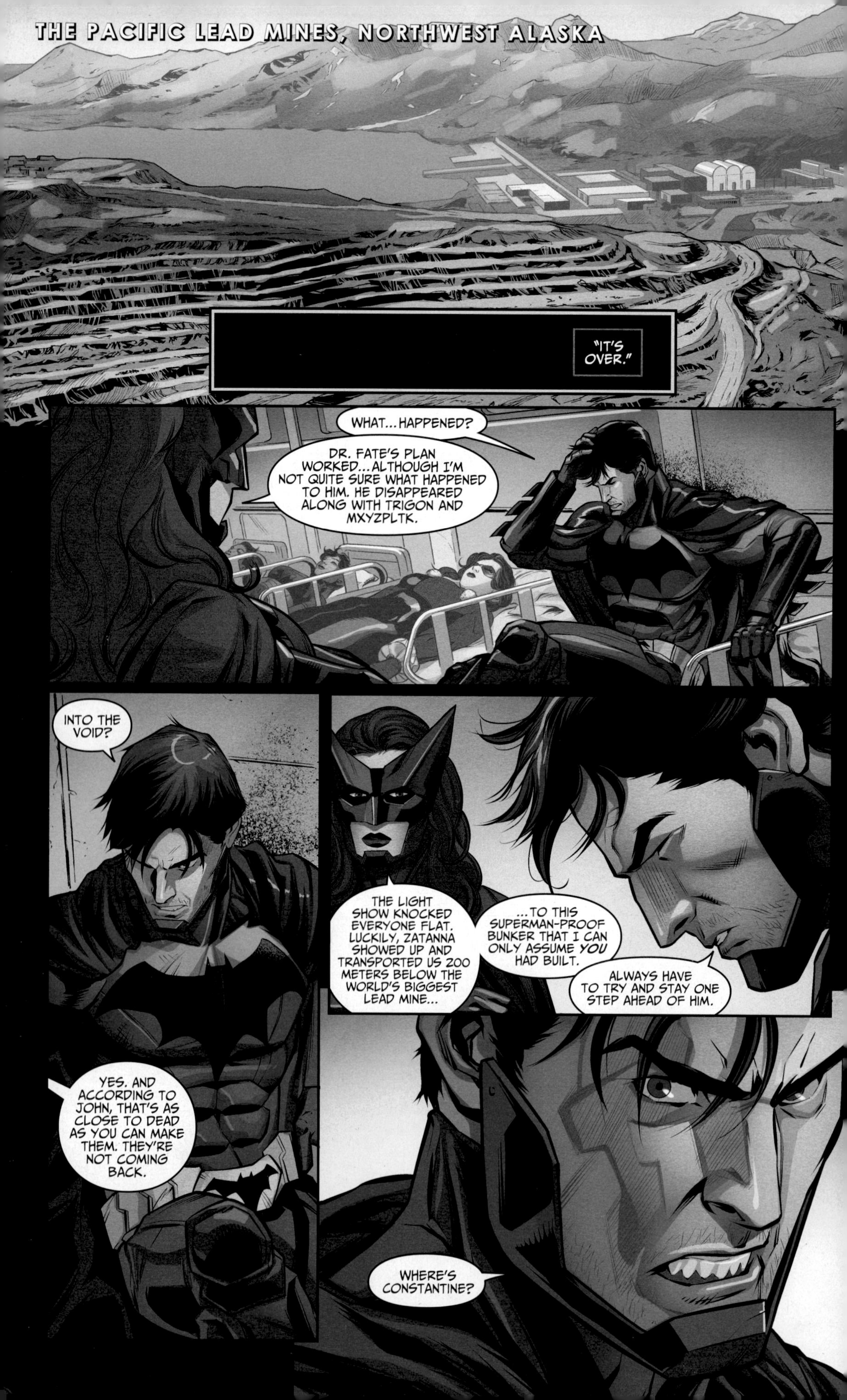
THE PACIFIC LEAD MINES, NORTHWEST ALASKA
"IT'S OVER."
WHAT...HAPPENED?
DR. FATE'S PLAN WORKED...ALTHOUGH I'M NOT QUITE SURE WHAT HAPPENED TO HIM. HE DISAPPEARED ALONG WITH TRIGON AND MXYZPLTK.
THE LIGHT SHOW KNOCKED EVERYONE FLAT. LUCKILY, ZATANNA SHOWED UP AND TRANSPORTED US 200 METERS BELOW THE WORLD'S BIGGEST LEAD MINE...
...TO THIS SUPERMAN-PROOF BUNKER THAT I CAN ONLY ASSUME YOU HAD BUILT.
ALWAYS HAVE TO TRY AND STAY ONE STEP AHEAD OF HIM.
WHERE'S CONSTANTINE?
INTO THE VOID?
YES. AND ACCORDING TO JOHN, THAT'S AS CLOSE TO DEAD AS YOU CAN MAKE THEM. THEY'RE NOT COMING BACK.

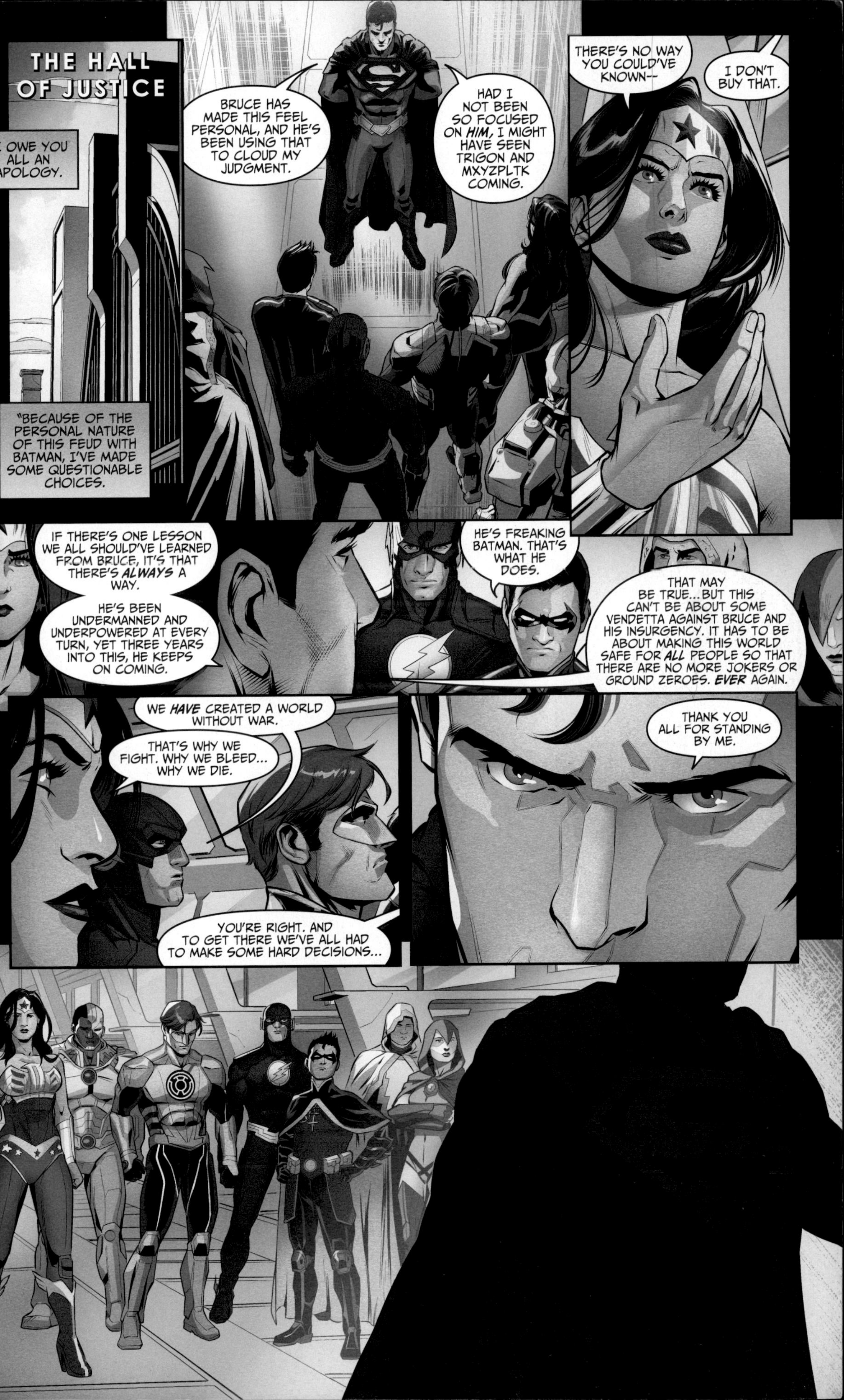
THE HALL OF JUSTICE
...E OWE YOU ALL AN ...APOLOGY.
"BECAUSE OF THE PERSONAL NATURE OF THIS FEUD WITH BATMAN, I'VE MADE SOME QUESTIONABLE CHOICES.
BRUCE HAS MADE THIS FEEL PERSONAL, AND HE'S BEEN USING THAT TO CLOUD MY JUDGMENT.
HAD I NOT BEEN SO FOCUSED ON HIM, I MIGHT HAVE SEEN TRIGON AND MXYZPLTK COMING.
THERE'S NO WAY YOU COULD'VE KNOWN--
I DON'T BUY THAT.
IF THERE'S ONE LESSON WE ALL SHOULD'VE LEARNED FROM BRUCE, IT'S THAT THERE'S ALWAYS A WAY.
HE'S BEEN UNDERMANNED AND UNDERPOWERED AT EVERY TURN, YET THREE YEARS INTO THIS, HE KEEPS ON COMING.
HE'S FREAKING BATMAN. THAT'S WHAT HE DOES.
THAT MAY BE TRUE... BUT THIS CAN'T BE ABOUT SOME VENDETTA AGAINST BRUCE AND HIS INSURGENCY. IT HAS TO BE ABOUT MAKING THIS WORLD SAFE FOR ALL PEOPLE SO THAT THERE ARE NO MORE JOKERS OR GROUND ZEROES. EVER AGAIN.
WE HAVE CREATED A WORLD WITHOUT WAR.
THAT'S WHY WE FIGHT. WHY WE BLEED... WHY WE DIE.
YOU'RE RIGHT. AND TO GET THERE WE'VE ALL HAD TO MAKE SOME HARD DECISIONS...
THANK YOU ALL FOR STANDING BY ME.

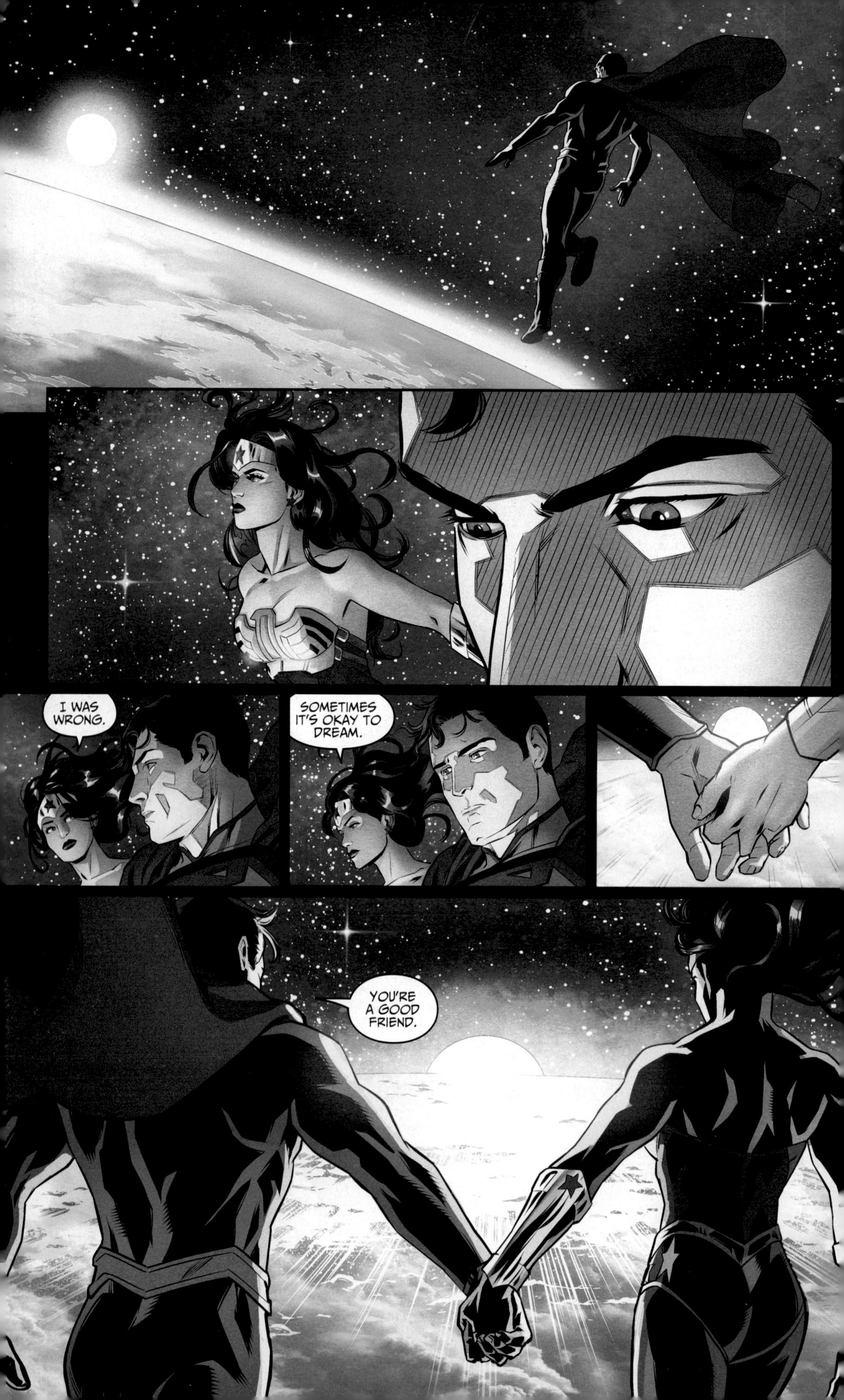
I WAS WRONG.
SOMETIMES IT'S OKAY TO DREAM.
YOU'RE A GOOD FRIEND.

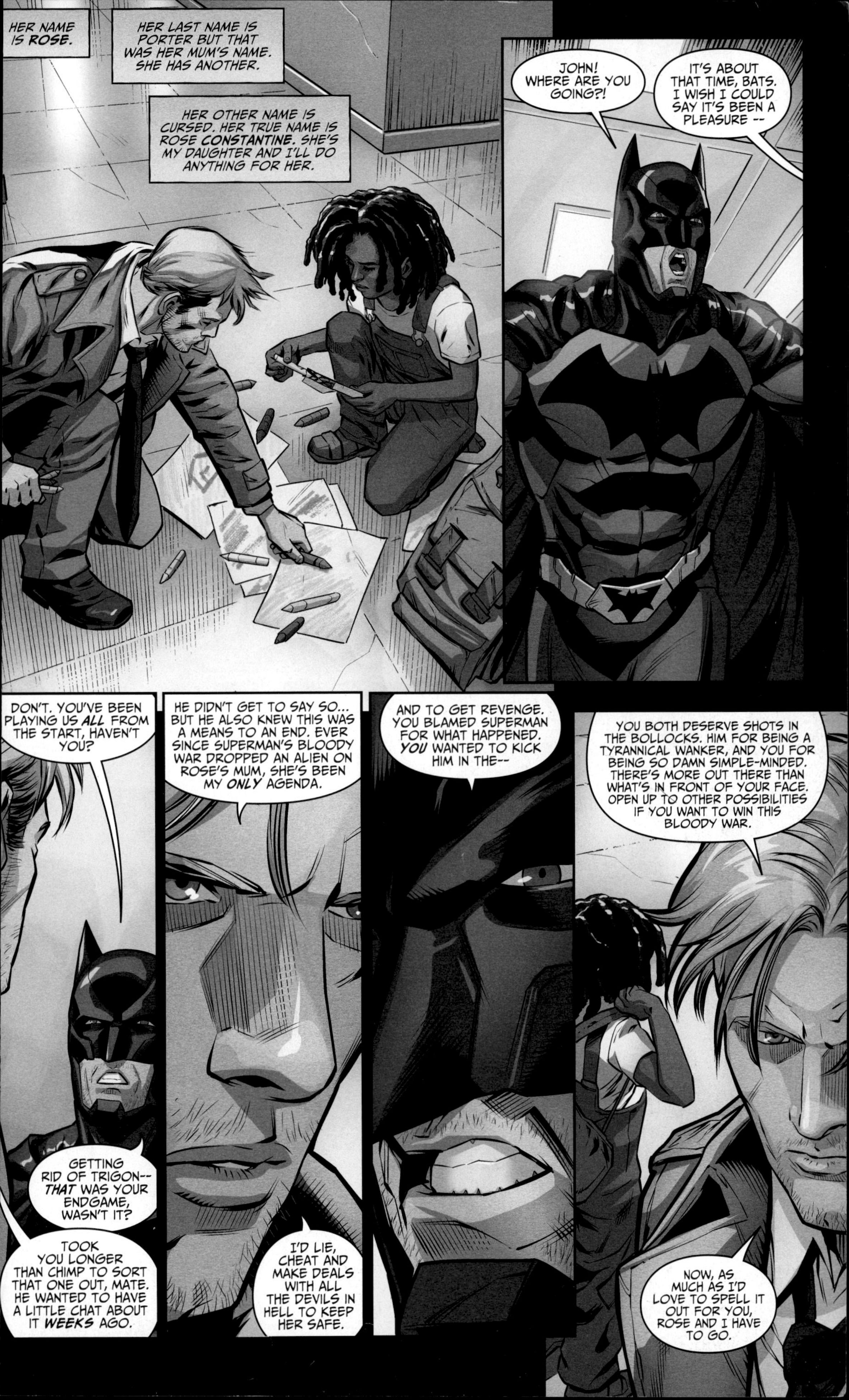
HER NAME IS ROSE.
HER LAST NAME IS PORTER BUT THAT WAS HER MUM'S NAME. SHE HAS ANOTHER.
HER OTHER NAME IS CURSED. HER TRUE NAME IS ROSE CONSTANTINE. SHE'S MY DAUGHTER AND I'LL DO ANYTHING FOR HER.
JOHN! WHERE ARE YOU GOING?!
IT'S ABOUT THAT TIME, BATS. I WISH I COULD SAY IT'S BEEN A PLEASURE --
DON'T. YOU'VE BEEN PLAYING US ALL FROM THE START, HAVEN'T YOU?
GETTING RID OF TRIGON-- THAT WAS YOUR ENDGAME, WASN'T IT?
TOOK YOU LONGER THAN CHIMP TO SORT THAT ONE OUT, MATE. HE WANTED TO HAVE A LITTLE CHAT ABOUT IT WEEKS AGO.
HE DIDN'T GET TO SAY SO... BUT HE ALSO KNEW THIS WAS A MEANS TO AN END. EVER SINCE SUPERMAN'S BLOODY WAR DROPPED AN ALIEN ON ROSE'S MUM, SHE'S BEEN MY ONLY AGENDA.
I'D LIE, CHEAT AND MAKE DEALS WITH ALL THE DEVILS IN HELL TO KEEP HER SAFE.
AND TO GET REVENGE. YOU BLAMED SUPERMAN FOR WHAT HAPPENED. YOU WANTED TO KICK HIM IN THE--
YOU BOTH DESERVE SHOTS IN THE BOLLOCKS. HIM FOR BEING A TYRANNICAL WANKER, AND YOU FOR BEING SO DAMN SIMPLE-MINDED. THERE'S MORE OUT THERE THAN WHAT'S IN FRONT OF YOUR FACE. OPEN UP TO OTHER POSSIBILITIES IF YOU WANT TO WIN THIS BLOODY WAR.
NOW, AS MUCH AS I'D LOVE TO SPELL IT OUT FOR YOU, ROSE AND I HAVE TO GO.

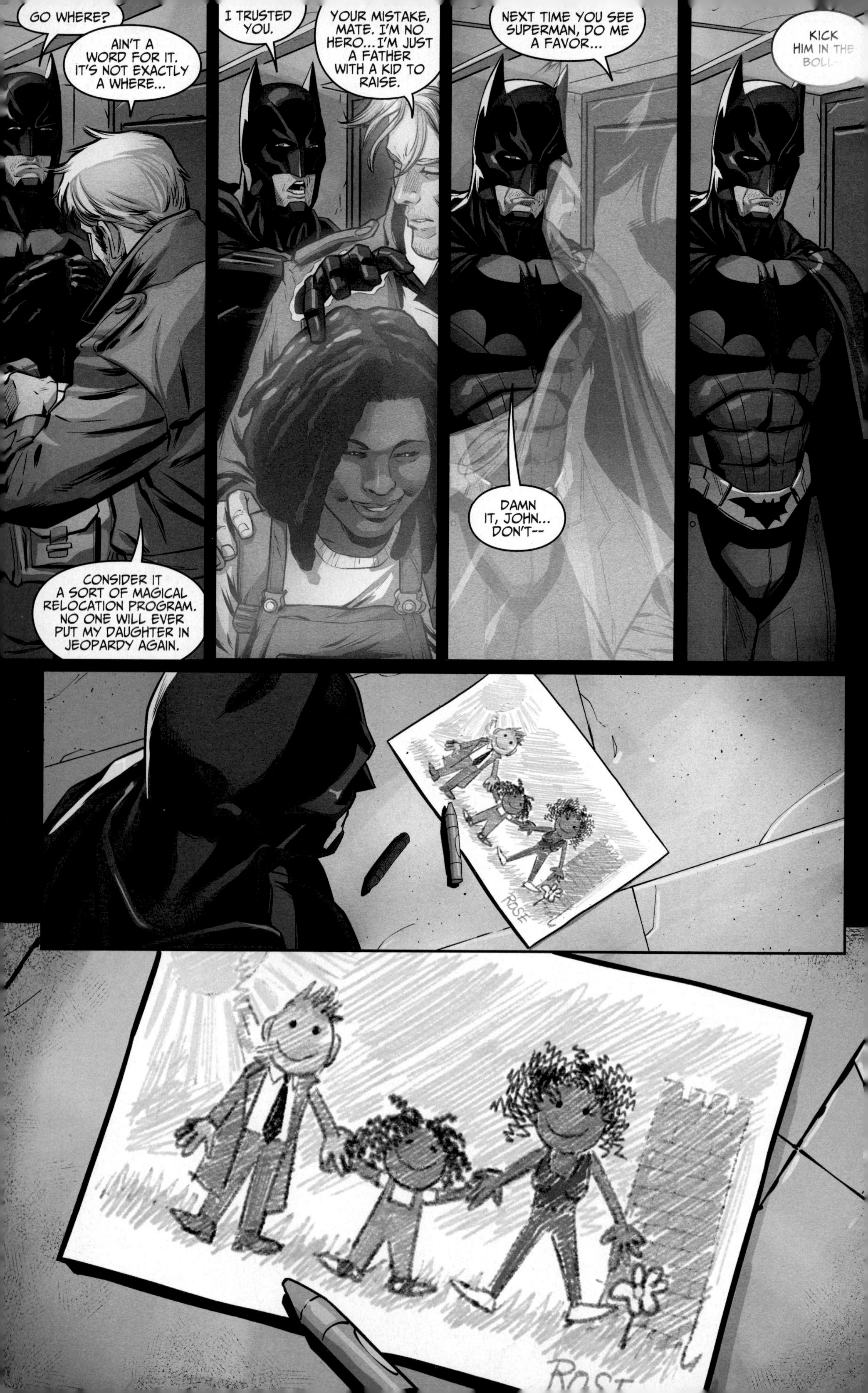
GO WHERE?
AIN'T A WORD FOR IT. IT'S NOT EXACTLY A WHERE...
CONSIDER IT A SORT OF MAGICAL RELOCATION PROGRAM. NO ONE WILL EVER PUT MY DAUGHTER IN JEOPARDY AGAIN.
I TRUSTED YOU.
YOUR MISTAKE, MATE. I'M NO HERO...I'M JUST A FATHER WITH A KID TO RAISE.
NEXT TIME YOU SEE SUPERMAN, DO ME A FAVOR...
DAMN IT, JOHN... DON'T--
KICK HIM IN THE BOLL--
ROSE
ROSE

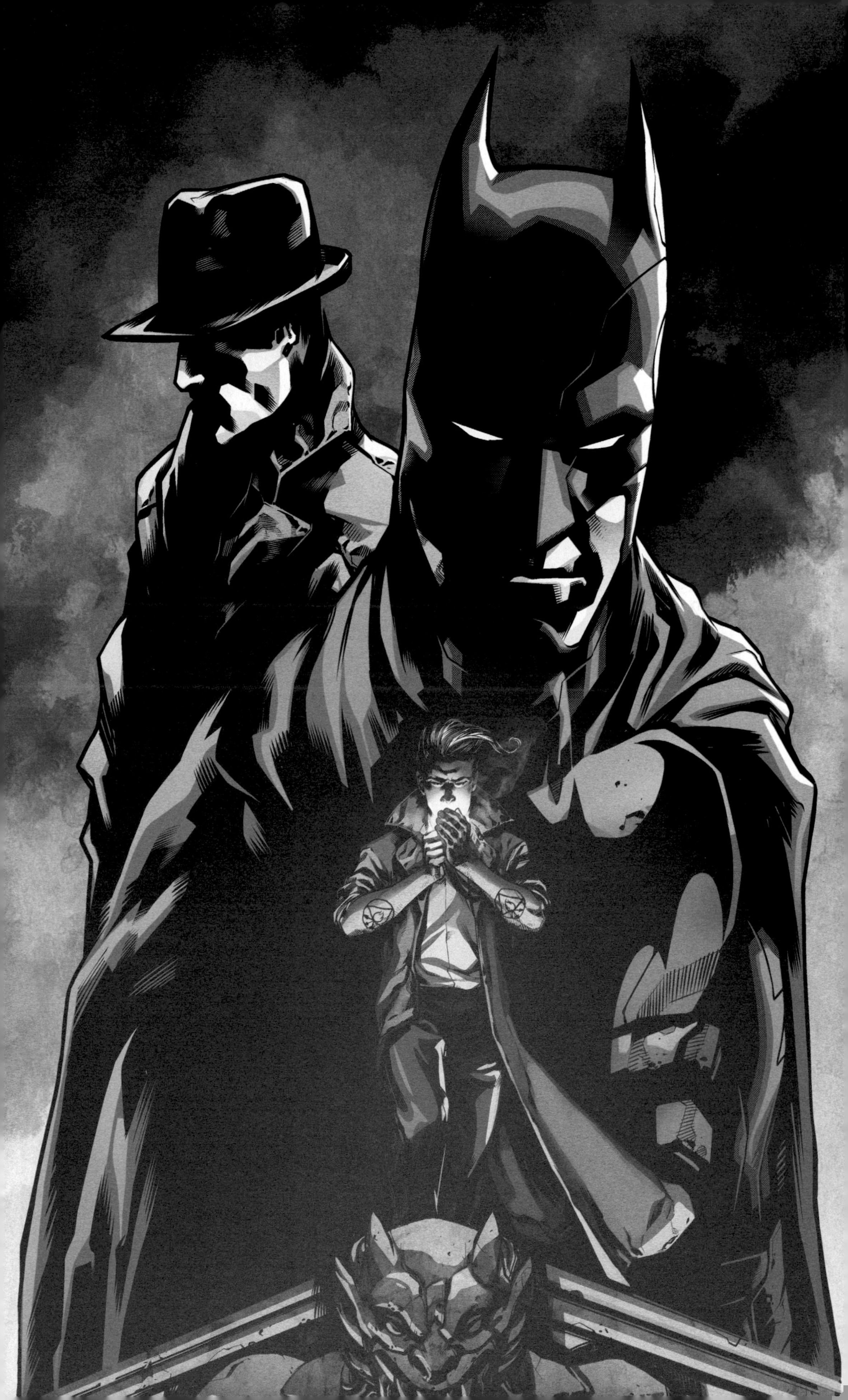

"A Proper Mage" Ray Fawkes - Writer Xermanico - Artist Alejandro Sanchez - Colorist
"Fall of the Titans" Sergio Davila and Juan Albarran - Artists Rex Lokus - Colorist
Cover Art by Neil Googe and Rex Lokus

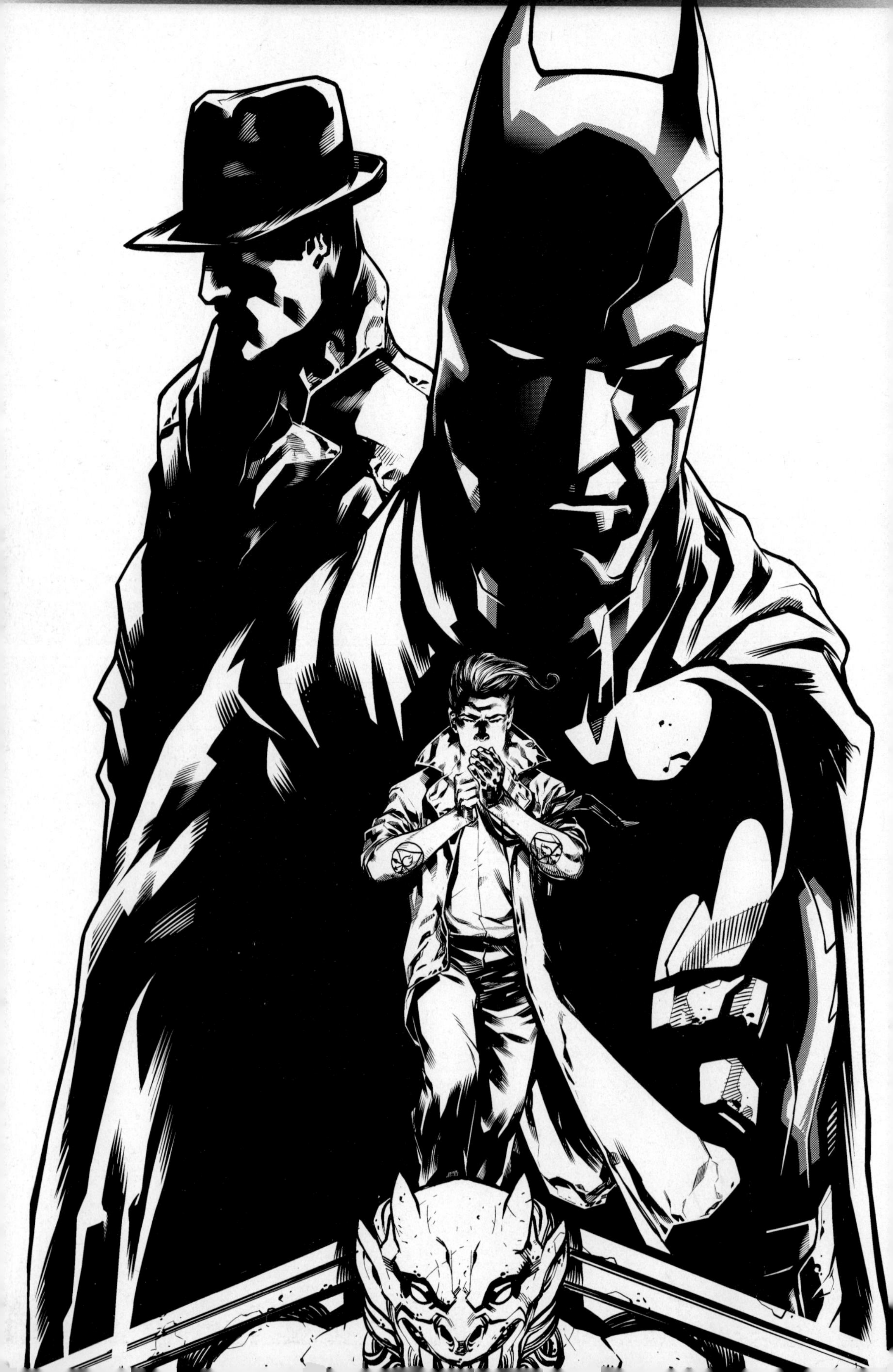

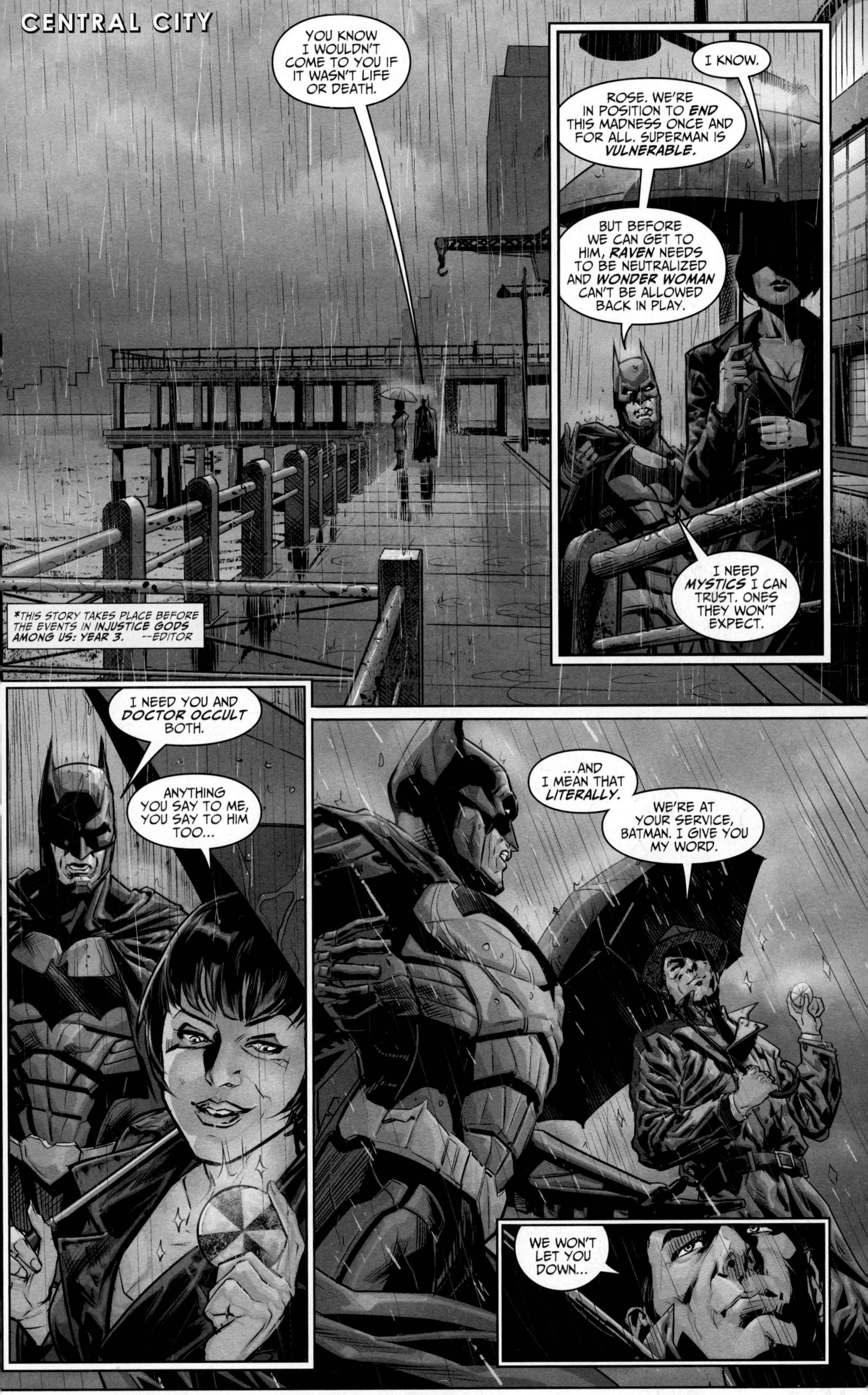
CENTRAL CITY
YOU KNOW I WOULDN'T COME TO YOU IF IT WASN'T LIFE OR DEATH.
I KNOW.
ROSE. WE'RE IN POSITION TO END THIS MADNESS ONCE AND FOR ALL. SUPERMAN IS VULNERABLE.
BUT BEFORE WE CAN GET TO HIM, RAVEN NEEDS TO BE NEUTRALIZED AND WONDER WOMAN CAN'T BE ALLOWED BACK IN PLAY.
I NEED MYSTICS I CAN TRUST. ONES THEY WON'T EXPECT.
*THIS STORY TAKES PLACE BEFORE THE EVENTS IN INJUSTICE GODS AMONG US: YEAR 3. --EDITOR
I NEED YOU AND DOCTOR OCCULT BOTH.
ANYTHING YOU SAY TO ME, YOU SAY TO HIM TOO...
...AND I MEAN THAT LITERALLY.
WE'RE AT YOUR SERVICE, BATMAN. I GIVE YOU MY WORD.
WE WON'T LET YOU DOWN...

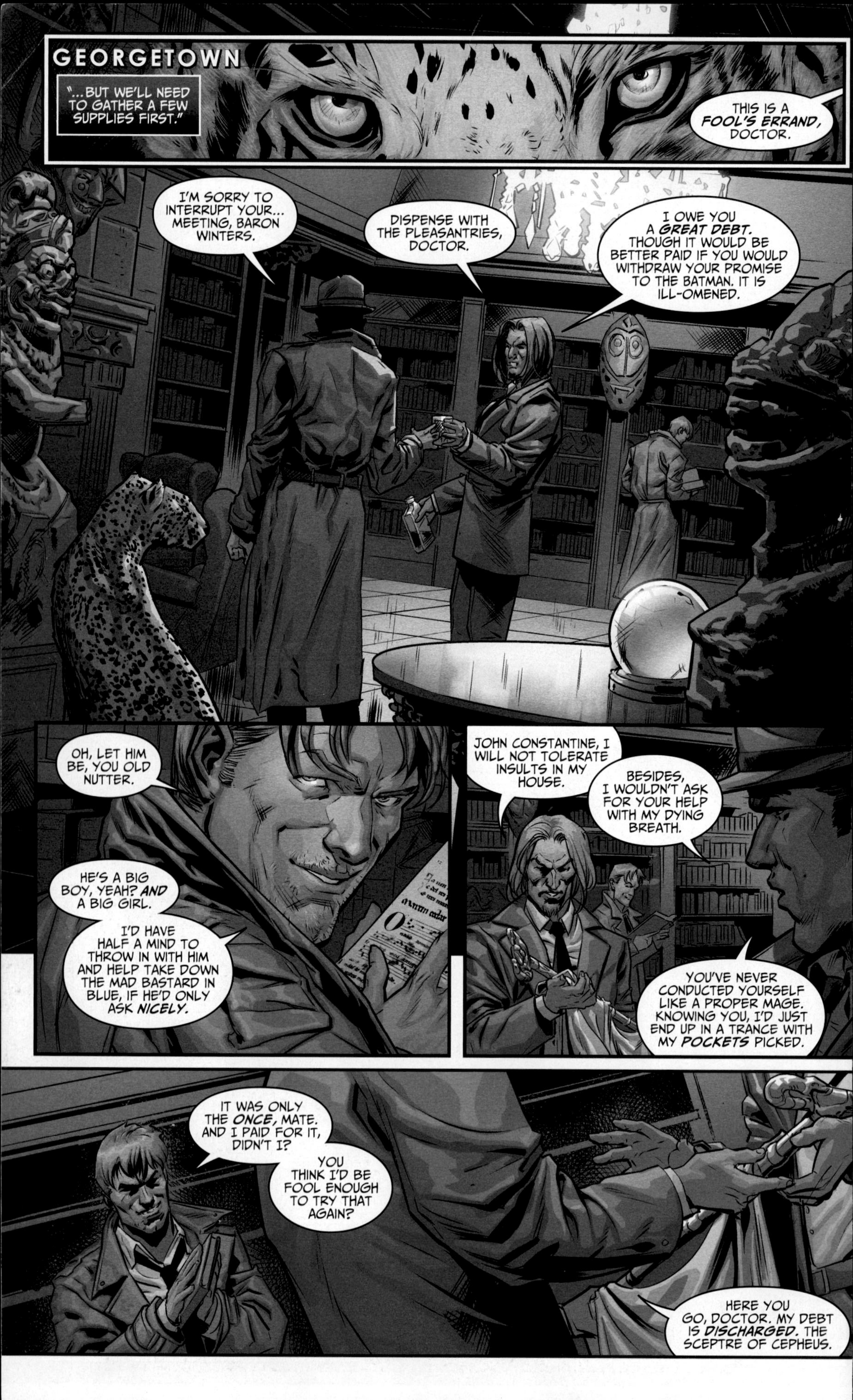
GEORGETOWN
"...BUT WE'LL NEED TO GATHER A FEW SUPPLIES FIRST."
THIS IS A *FOOL'S ERRAND,* DOCTOR.
I'M SORRY TO INTERRUPT YOUR... MEETING, BARON WINTERS.
DISPENSE WITH THE PLEASANTRIES, DOCTOR.
I OWE YOU A *GREAT DEBT.* THOUGH IT WOULD BE BETTER PAID IF YOU WOULD WITHDRAW YOUR PROMISE TO THE BATMAN. IT IS ILL-OMENED.
OH, LET HIM BE, YOU OLD NUTTER.
HE'S A BIG BOY, YEAH? *AND* A BIG GIRL.
I'D HAVE HALF A MIND TO THROW IN WITH HIM AND HELP TAKE DOWN THE MAD BASTARD IN BLUE, IF HE'D ONLY ASK *NICELY.*
JOHN CONSTANTINE, I WILL NOT TOLERATE INSULTS IN MY HOUSE.
BESIDES, I WOULDN'T ASK FOR YOUR HELP WITH MY DYING BREATH.
YOU'VE NEVER CONDUCTED YOURSELF LIKE A PROPER MAGE. KNOWING YOU, I'D JUST END UP IN A TRANCE WITH MY *POCKETS* PICKED.
IT WAS ONLY THE *ONCE,* MATE. AND I PAID FOR IT, DIDN'T I?
YOU THINK I'D BE FOOL ENOUGH TO TRY THAT AGAIN?
HERE YOU GO, DOCTOR. MY DEBT IS *DISCHARGED.* THE SCEPTRE OF CEPHEUS.

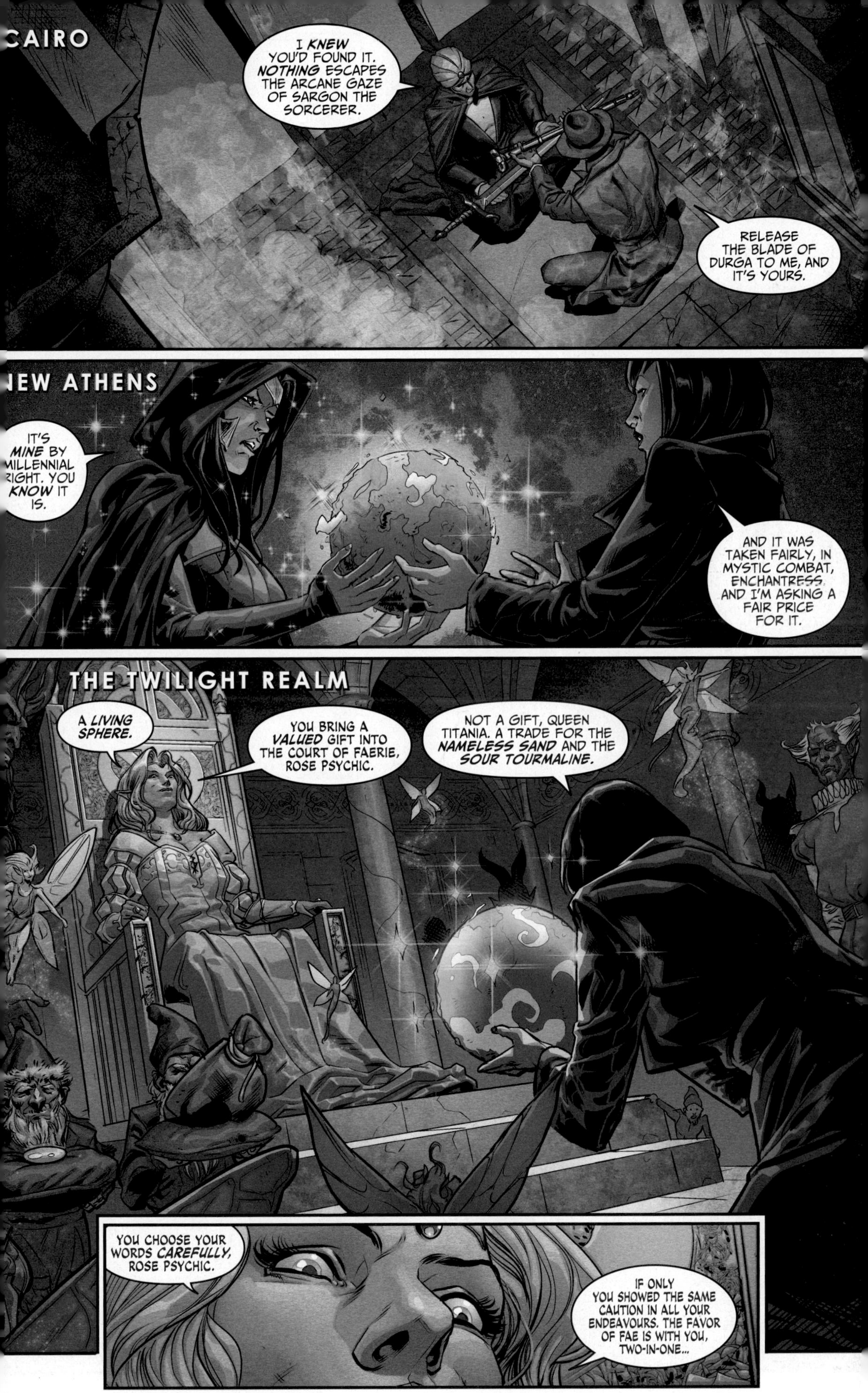
CAIRO
I KNEW YOU'D FOUND IT. NOTHING ESCAPES THE ARCANE GAZE OF SARGON THE SORCERER.
RELEASE THE BLADE OF DURGA TO ME, AND IT'S YOURS.
NEW ATHENS
IT'S MINE BY MILLENNIAL RIGHT. YOU KNOW IT IS.
AND IT WAS TAKEN FAIRLY, IN MYSTIC COMBAT, ENCHANTRESS. AND I'M ASKING A FAIR PRICE FOR IT.
THE TWILIGHT REALM
A LIVING SPHERE.
YOU BRING A VALUED GIFT INTO THE COURT OF FAERIE, ROSE PSYCHIC.
NOT A GIFT, QUEEN TITANIA. A TRADE FOR THE NAMELESS SAND AND THE SOUR TOURMALINE.
YOU CHOOSE YOUR WORDS CAREFULLY, ROSE PSYCHIC.
IF ONLY YOU SHOWED THE SAME CAUTION IN ALL YOUR ENDEAVOURS. THE FAVOR OF FAE IS WITH YOU, TWO-IN-ONE...

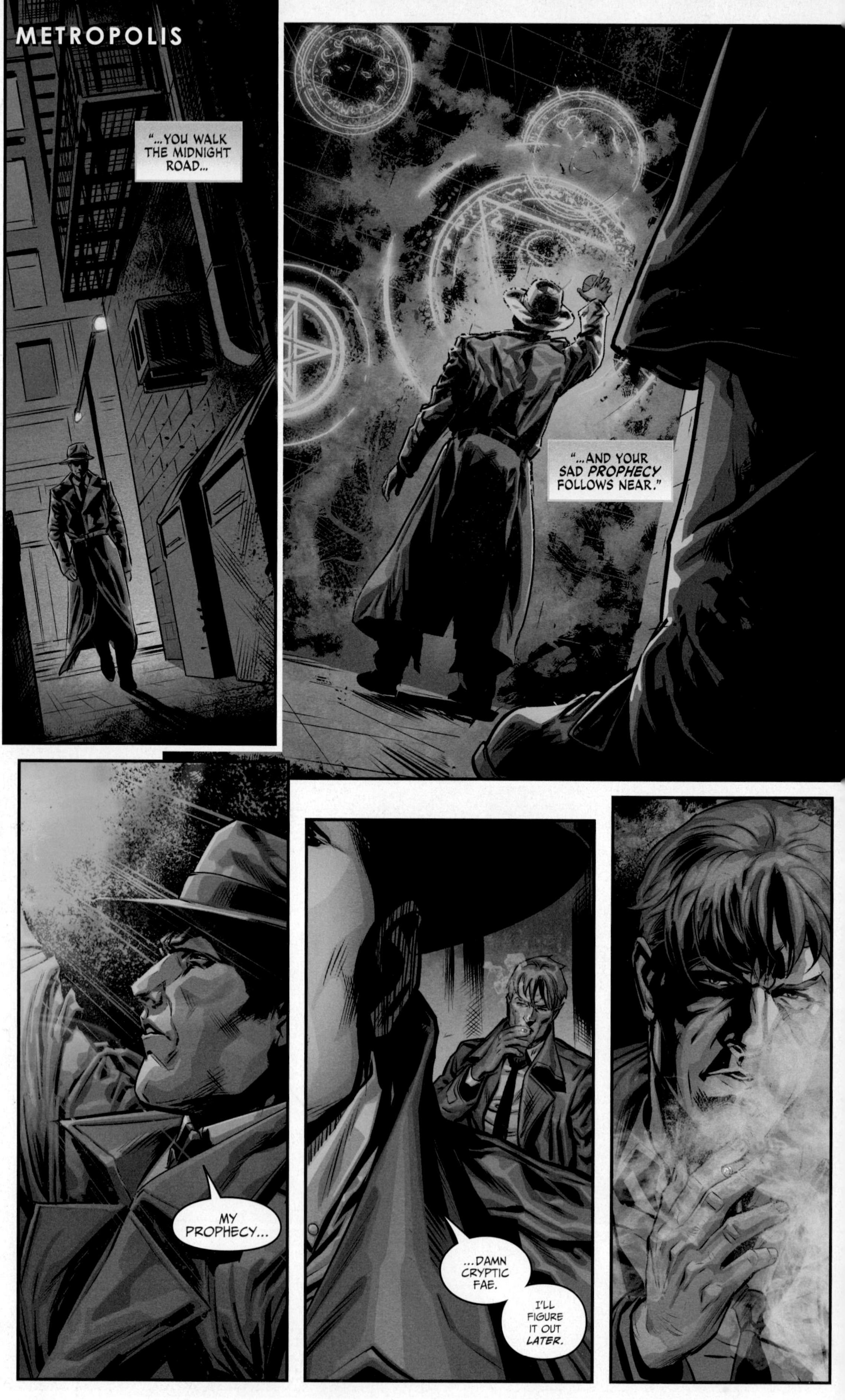
METROPOLIS
"...YOU WALK THE MIDNIGHT ROAD...
"...AND YOUR SAD PROPHECY FOLLOWS NEAR."
MY PROPHECY...
...DAMN CRYPTIC FAE.
I'LL FIGURE IT OUT LATER.

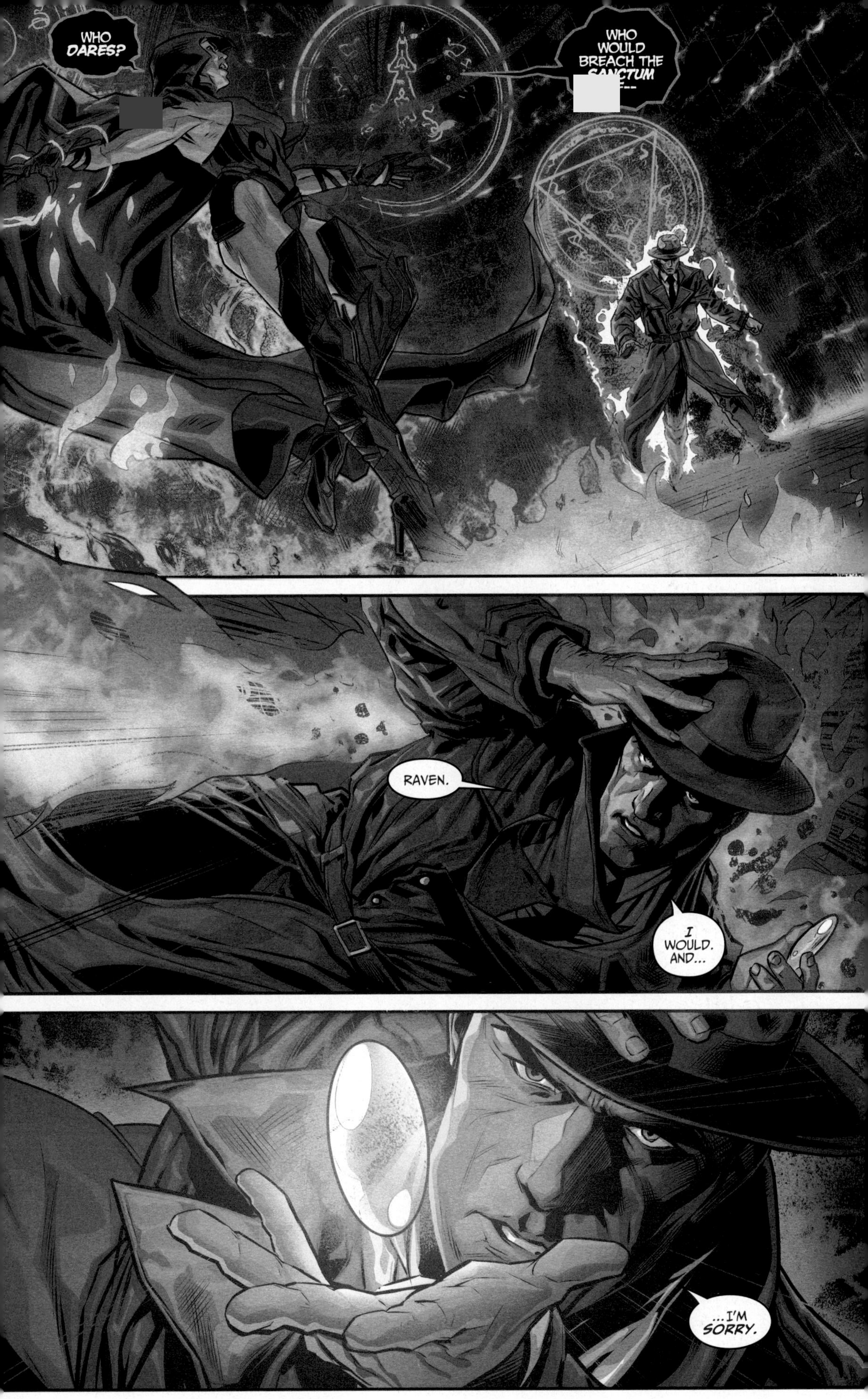
WHO DARES?
WHO WOULD BREACH THE SANCTUM
RAVEN.
I WOULD. AND...
...I'M SORRY.

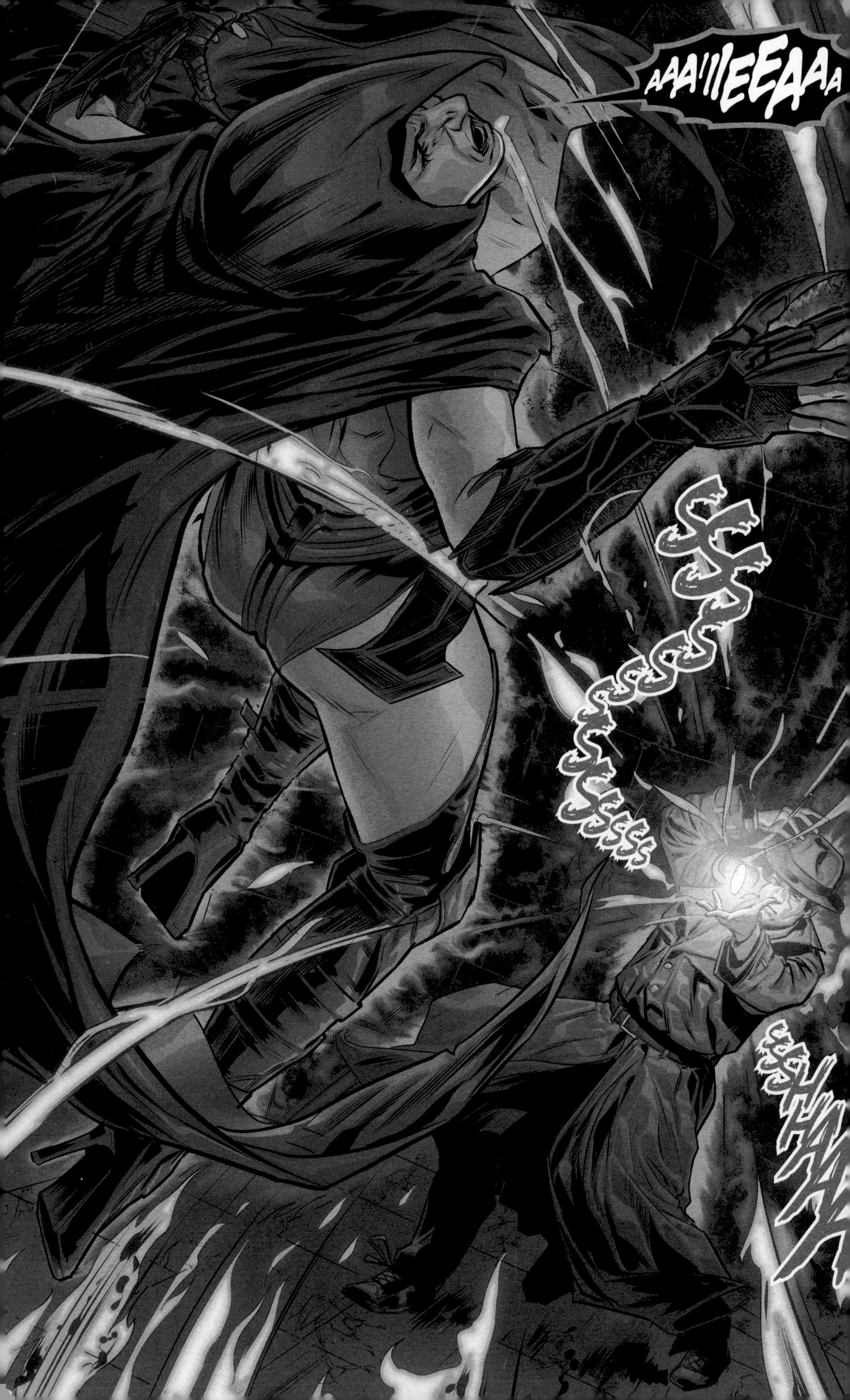
AAA'IIEEAAa
SSSSSSSSSSSSSSS

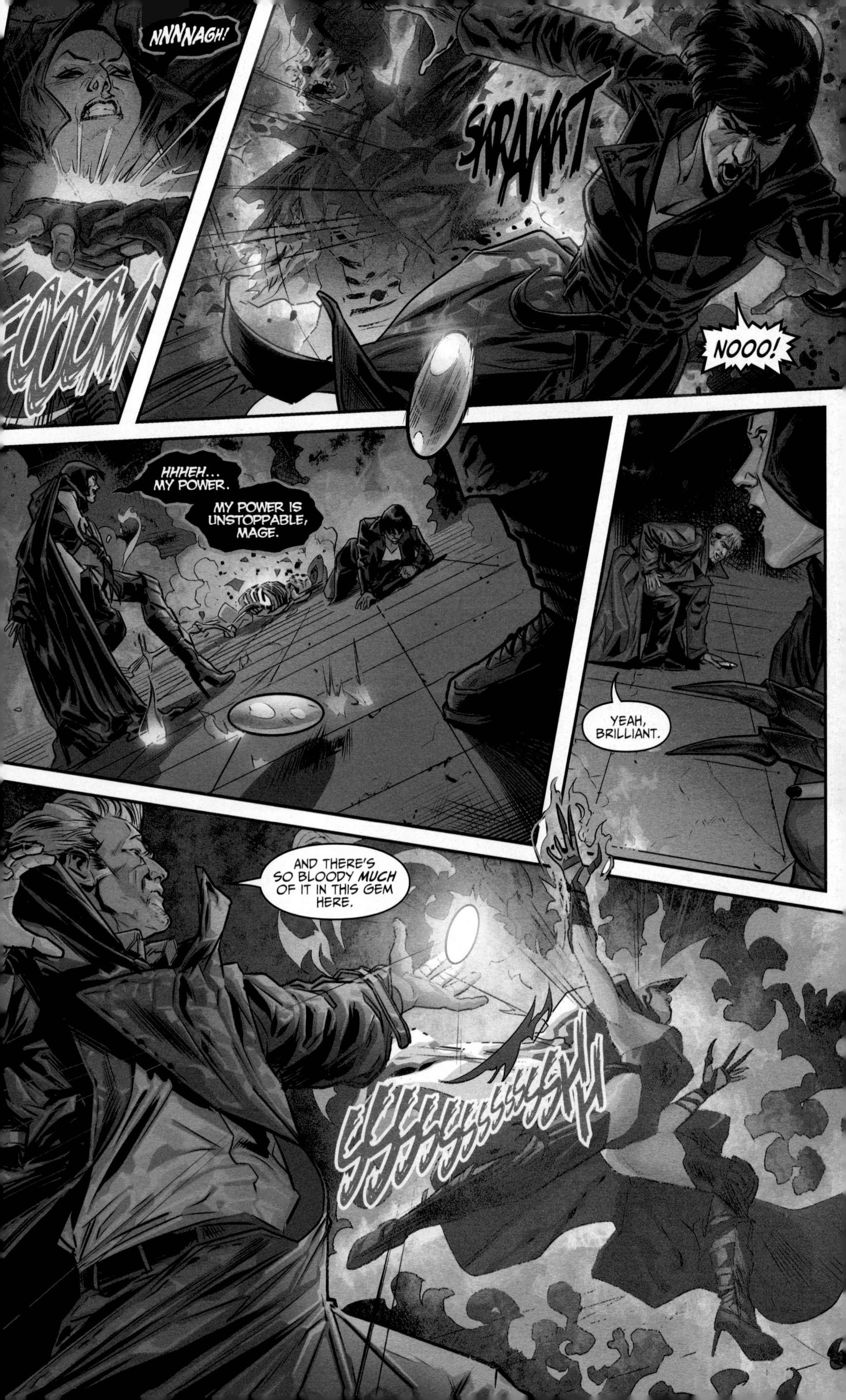
NNNNAGH!
FOOOM
SKRAKKT
NOOO!
HHHEH... MY POWER.
MY POWER IS UNSTOPPABLE, MAGE.
YEAH, BRILLIANT.
AND THERE'S SO BLOODY *MUCH* OF IT IN THIS GEM HERE.
SSSSSSSSSSHH

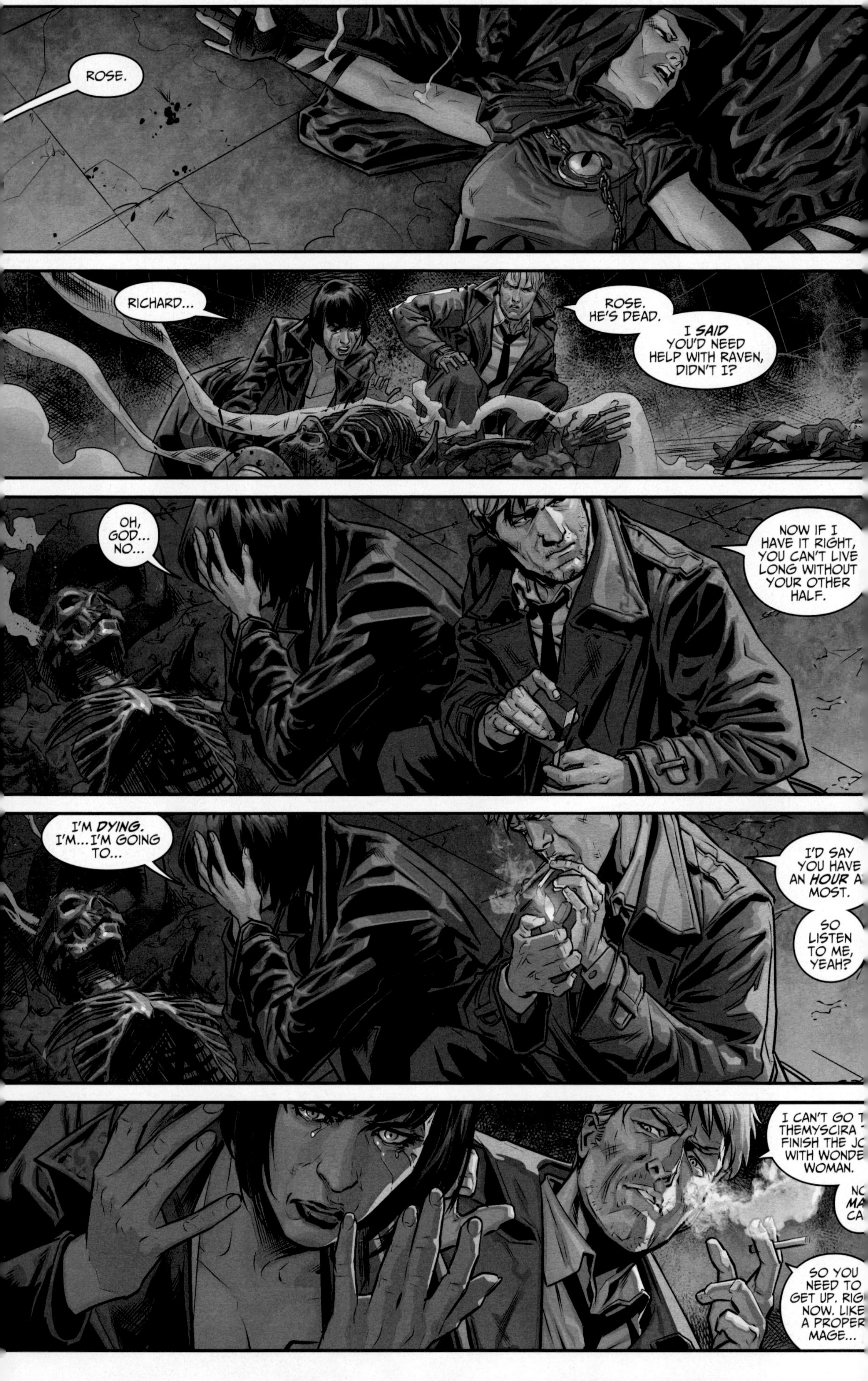
ROSE.
RICHARD...
ROSE. HE'S DEAD.
I SAID YOU'D NEED HELP WITH RAVEN, DIDN'T I?
OH, GOD... NO...
NOW IF I HAVE IT RIGHT, YOU CAN'T LIVE LONG WITHOUT YOUR OTHER HALF.
I'M DYING. I'M... I'M GOING TO...
I'D SAY YOU HAVE AN HOUR A MOST.
SO LISTEN TO ME, YEAH?
I CAN'T GO T THEMYSCIRA T FINISH THE JO WITH WONDE WOMAN.
NO MA CA
SO YOU NEED TO GET UP. RIG NOW. LIKE A PROPER MAGE...

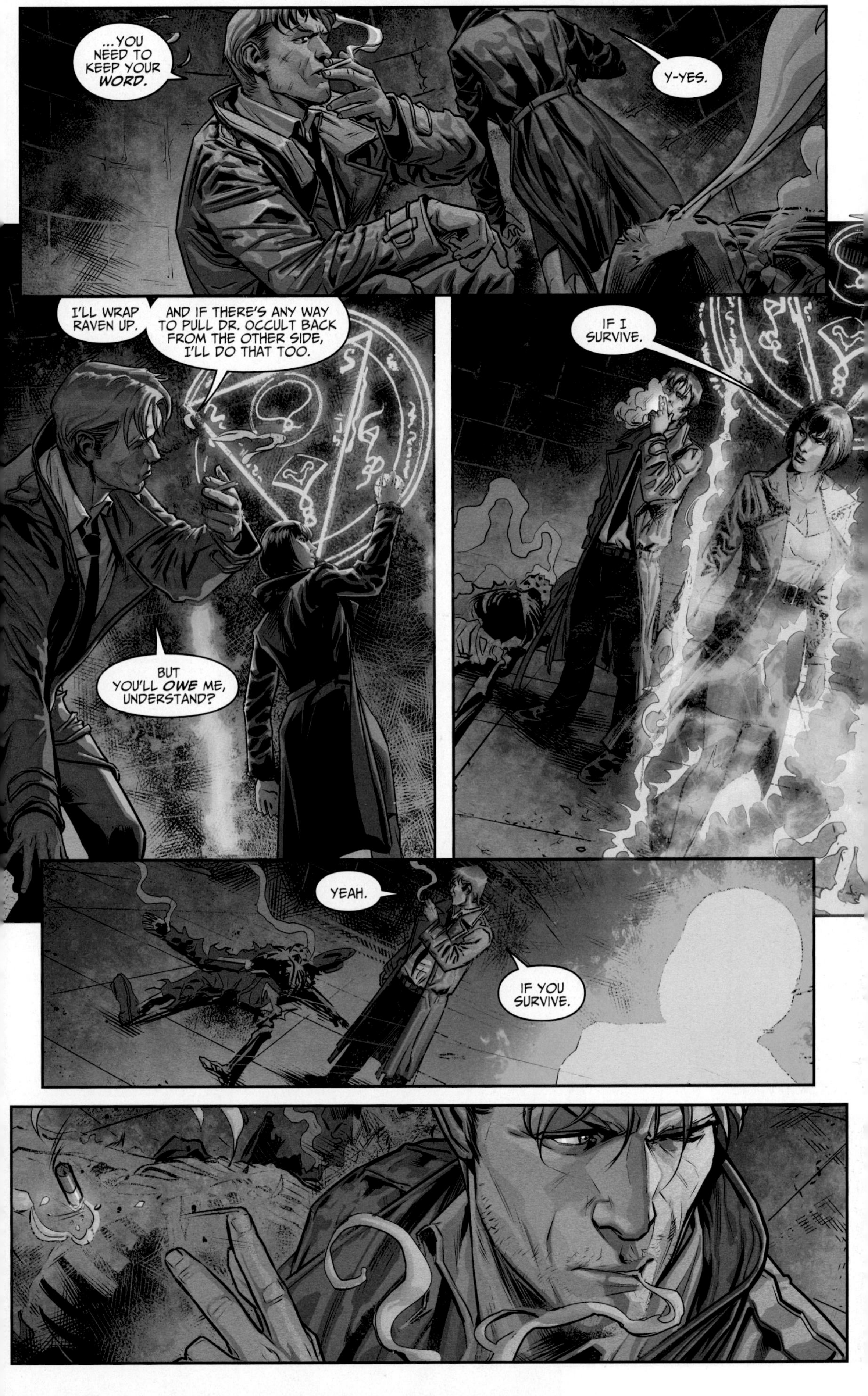
...YOU NEED TO KEEP YOUR WORD.
Y-YES.
I'LL WRAP RAVEN UP.
AND IF THERE'S ANY WAY TO PULL DR. OCCULT BACK FROM THE OTHER SIDE, I'LL DO THAT TOO.
BUT YOU'LL OWE ME, UNDERSTAND?
IF I SURVIVE.
YEAH.
IF YOU SURVIVE.

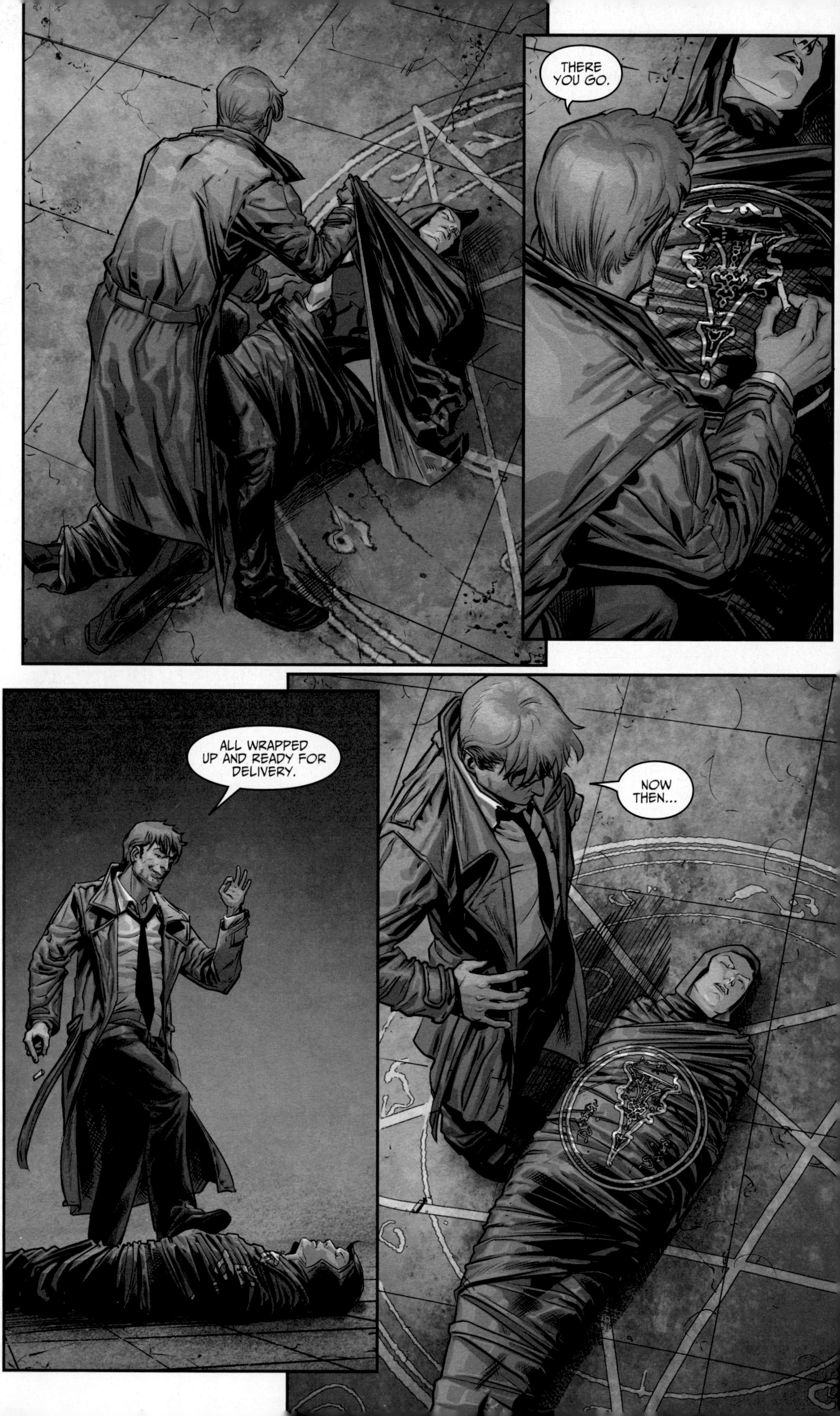
THERE YOU GO.
ALL WRAPPED UP AND READY FOR DELIVERY.
NOW THEN...

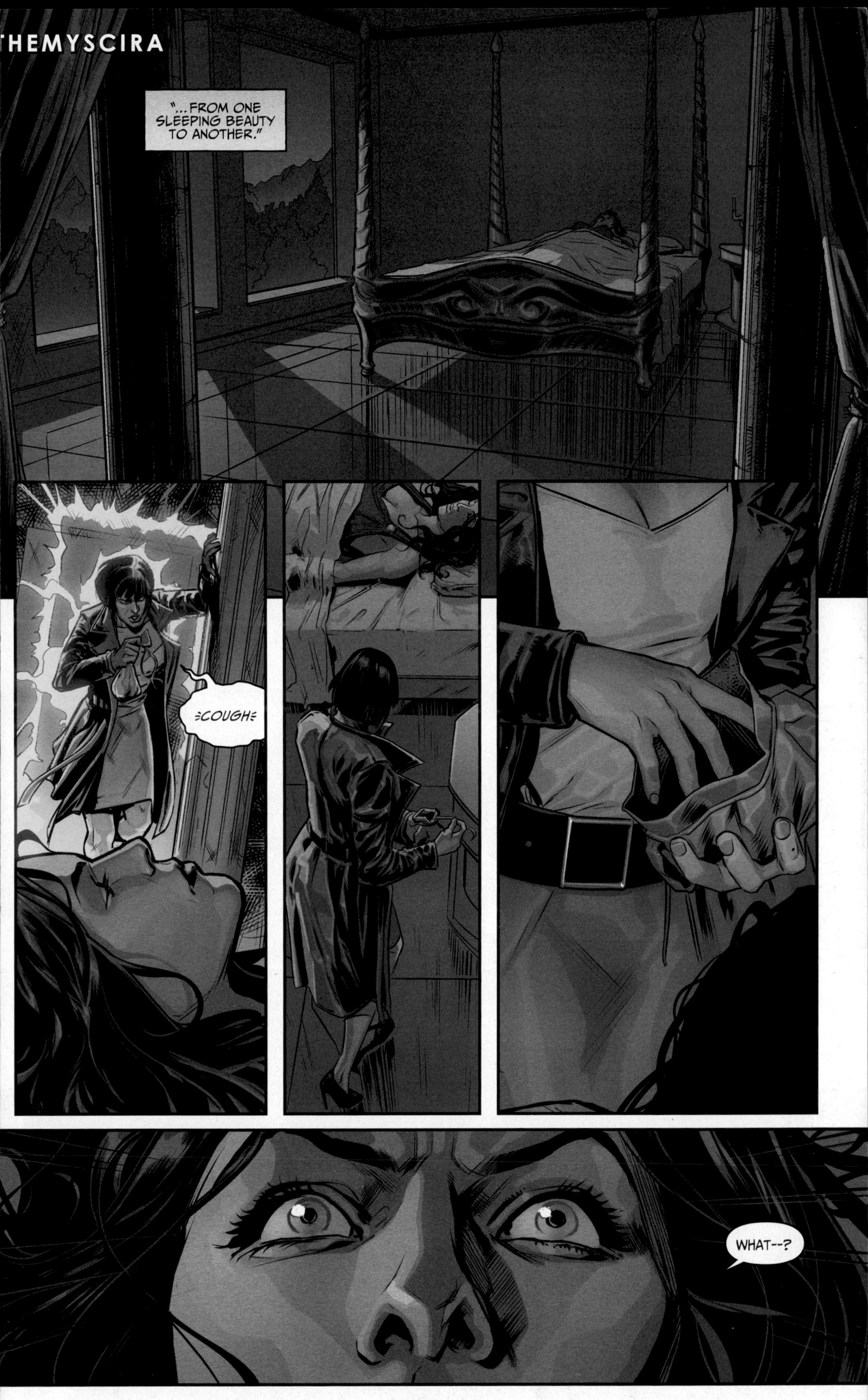
THEMYSCIRA
"...FROM ONE SLEEPING BEAUTY TO ANOTHER."
COUGH
WHAT--?

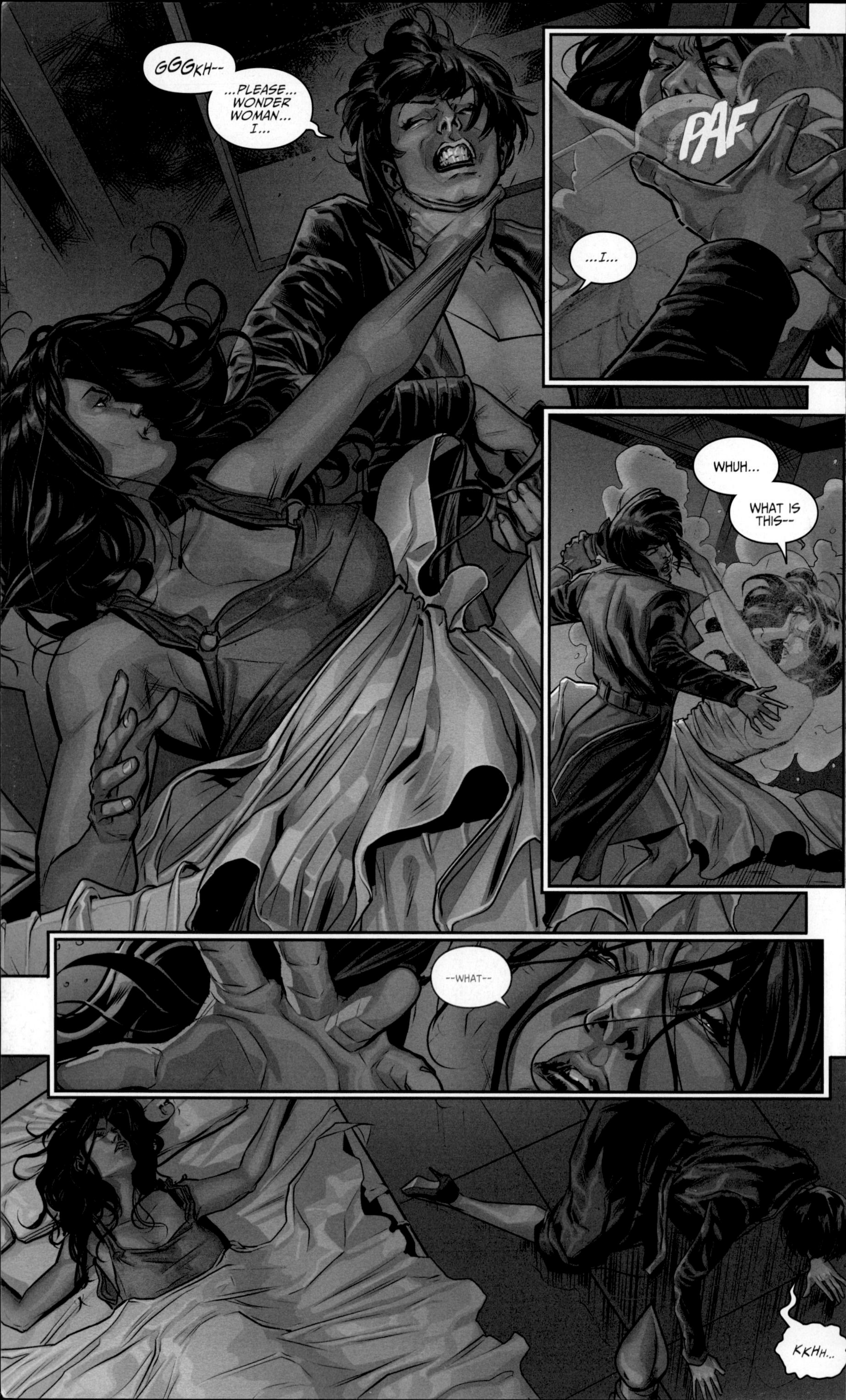
GGGKH--
...PLEASE... WONDER WOMAN... I...
PAF
...I...
WHUH...
WHAT IS THIS--
--WHAT--
KKHH...

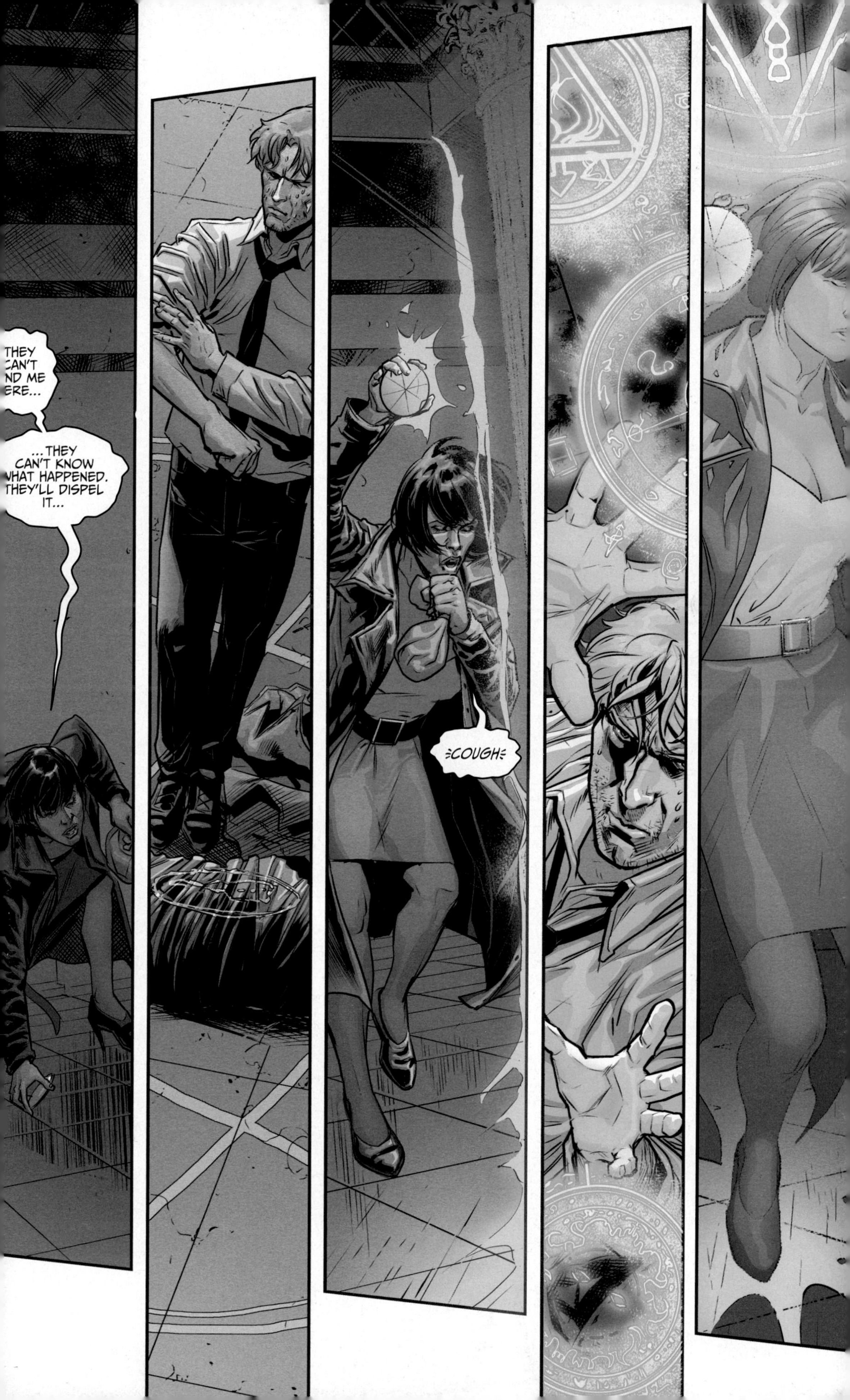
THEY CAN'T ND ME ERE...
...THEY CAN'T KNOW WHAT HAPPENED. THEY'LL DISPEL IT...
COUGH

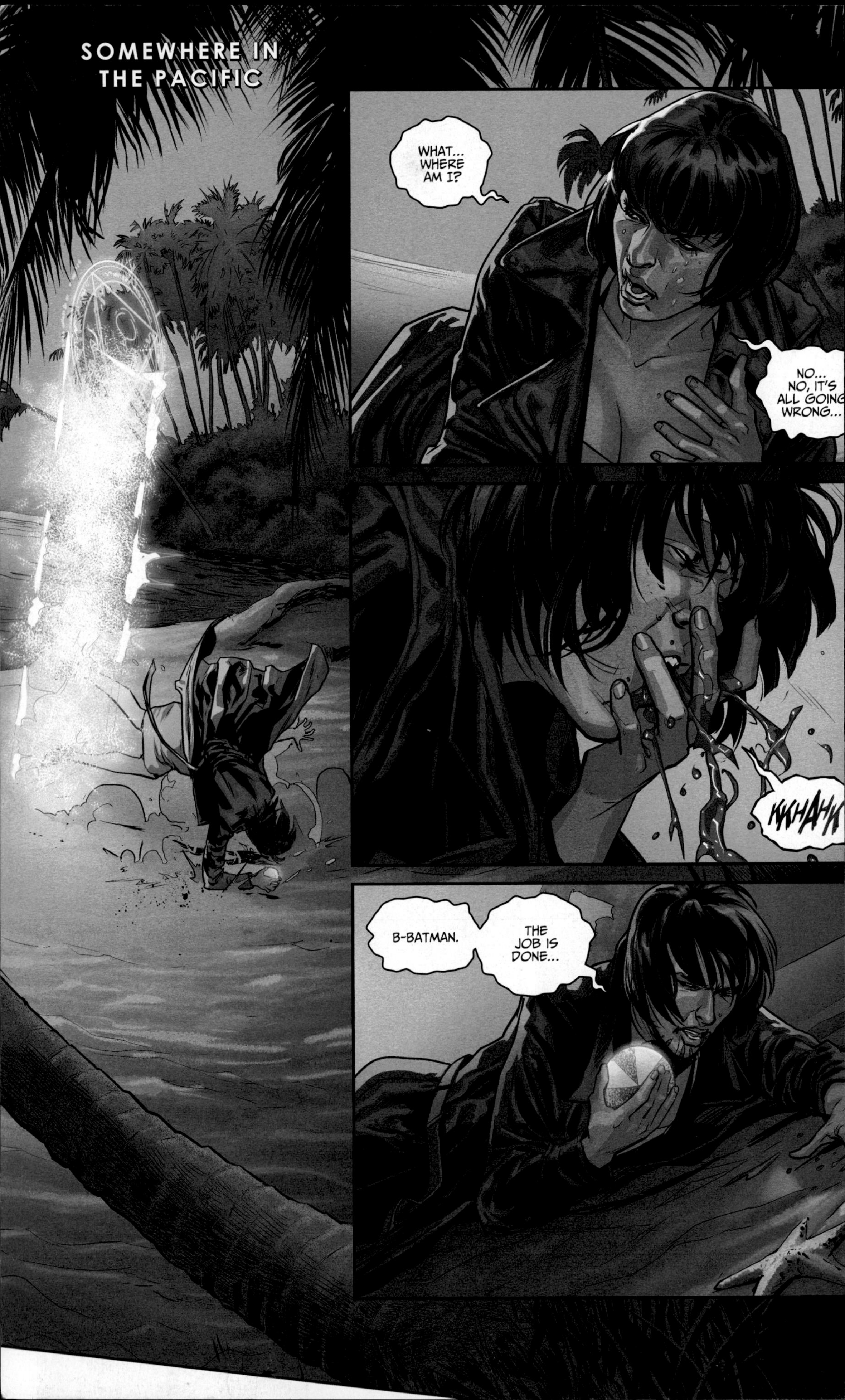
SOMEWHERE IN THE PACIFIC
WHAT... WHERE AM I?
NO... NO, IT'S ALL GOING WRONG...
KKHAHK
B-BATMAN.
THE JOB IS DONE...

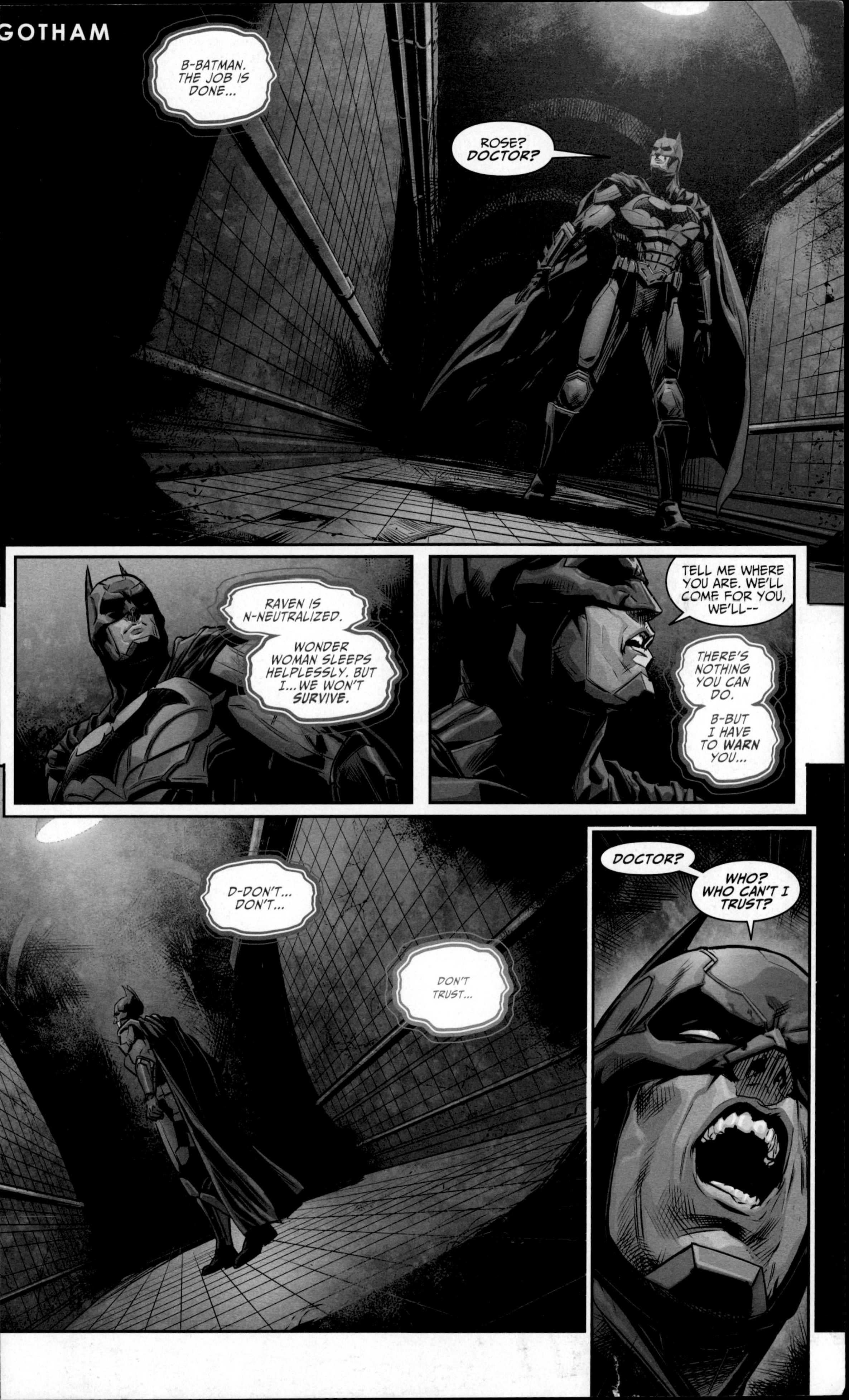
GOTHAM
B-BATMAN. THE JOB IS DONE...
ROSE? DOCTOR?
RAVEN IS N-NEUTRALIZED.
WONDER WOMAN SLEEPS HELPLESSLY. BUT I...WE WON'T SURVIVE.
TELL ME WHERE YOU ARE. WE'LL COME FOR YOU, WE'LL--
THERE'S NOTHING YOU CAN DO.
B-BUT I HAVE TO WARN YOU...
D-DON'T... DON'T...
DON'T TRUST...
DOCTOR?
WHO? WHO CAN'T I TRUST?

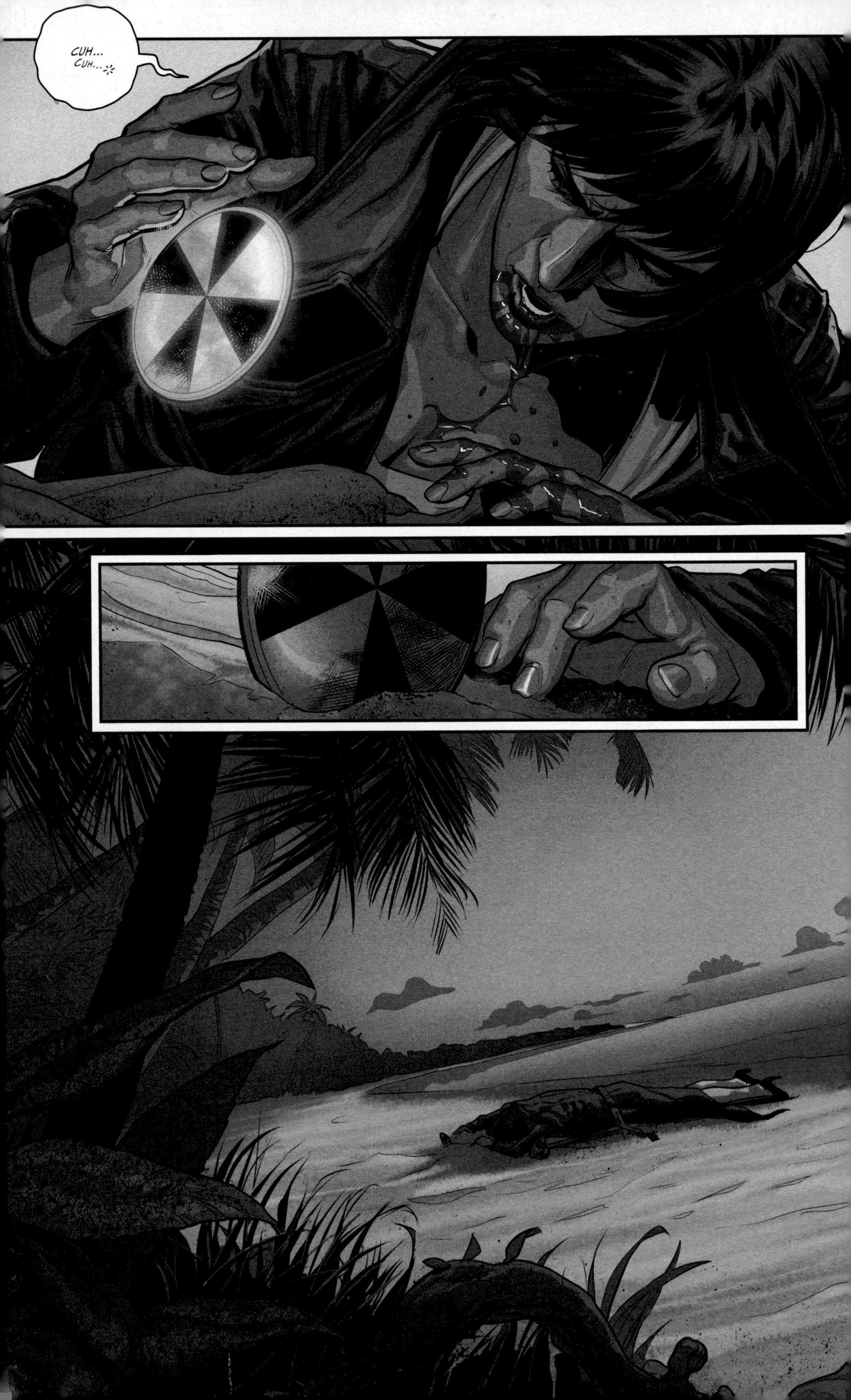
CUH... CUH...

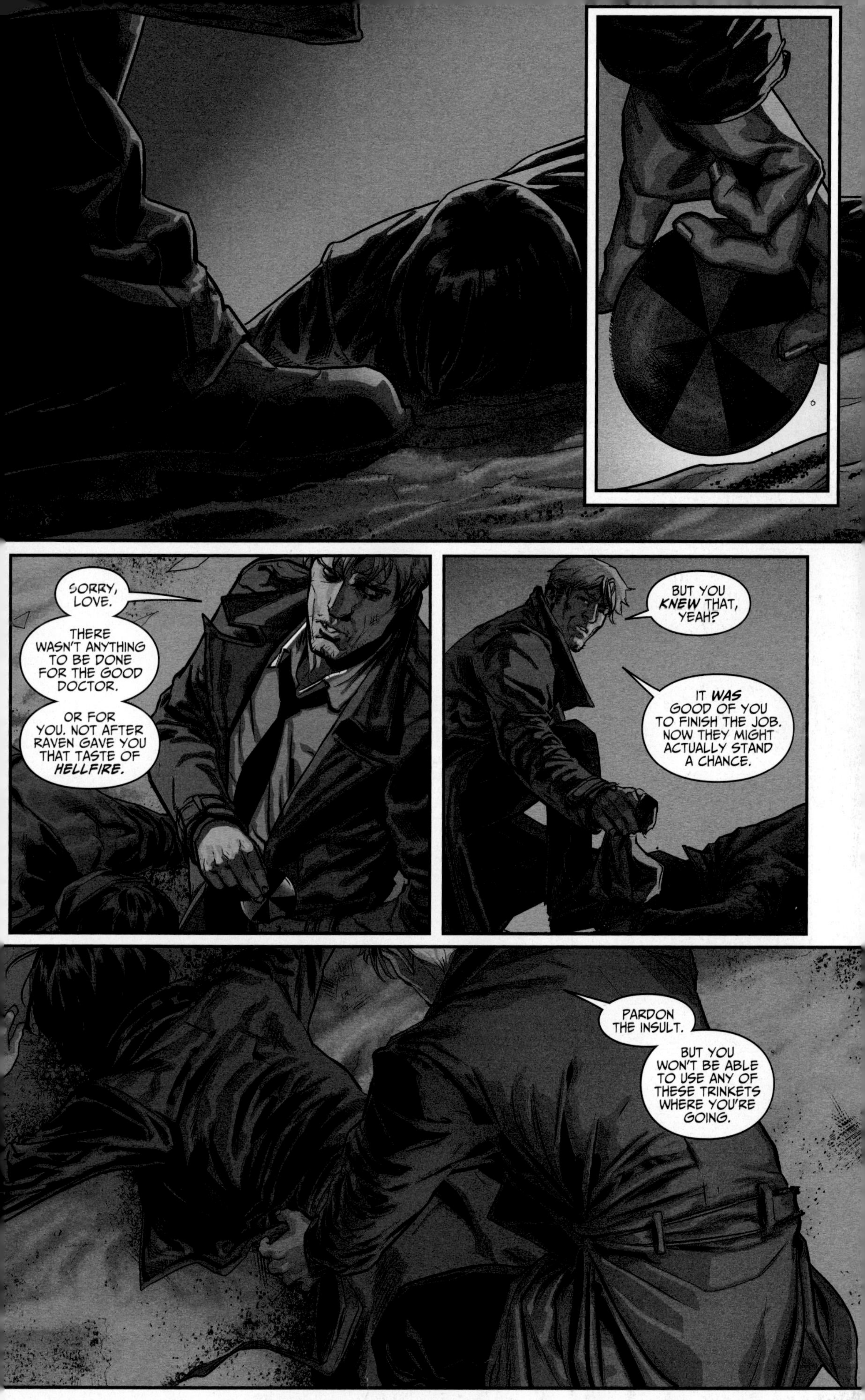
SORRY, LOVE.
THERE WASN'T ANYTHING TO BE DONE FOR THE GOOD DOCTOR.
OR FOR YOU. NOT AFTER RAVEN GAVE YOU THAT TASTE OF HELLFIRE.
BUT YOU KNEW THAT, YEAH?
IT WAS GOOD OF YOU TO FINISH THE JOB. NOW THEY MIGHT ACTUALLY STAND A CHANCE.
PARDON THE INSULT.
BUT YOU WON'T BE ABLE TO USE ANY OF THESE TRINKETS WHERE YOU'RE GOING.

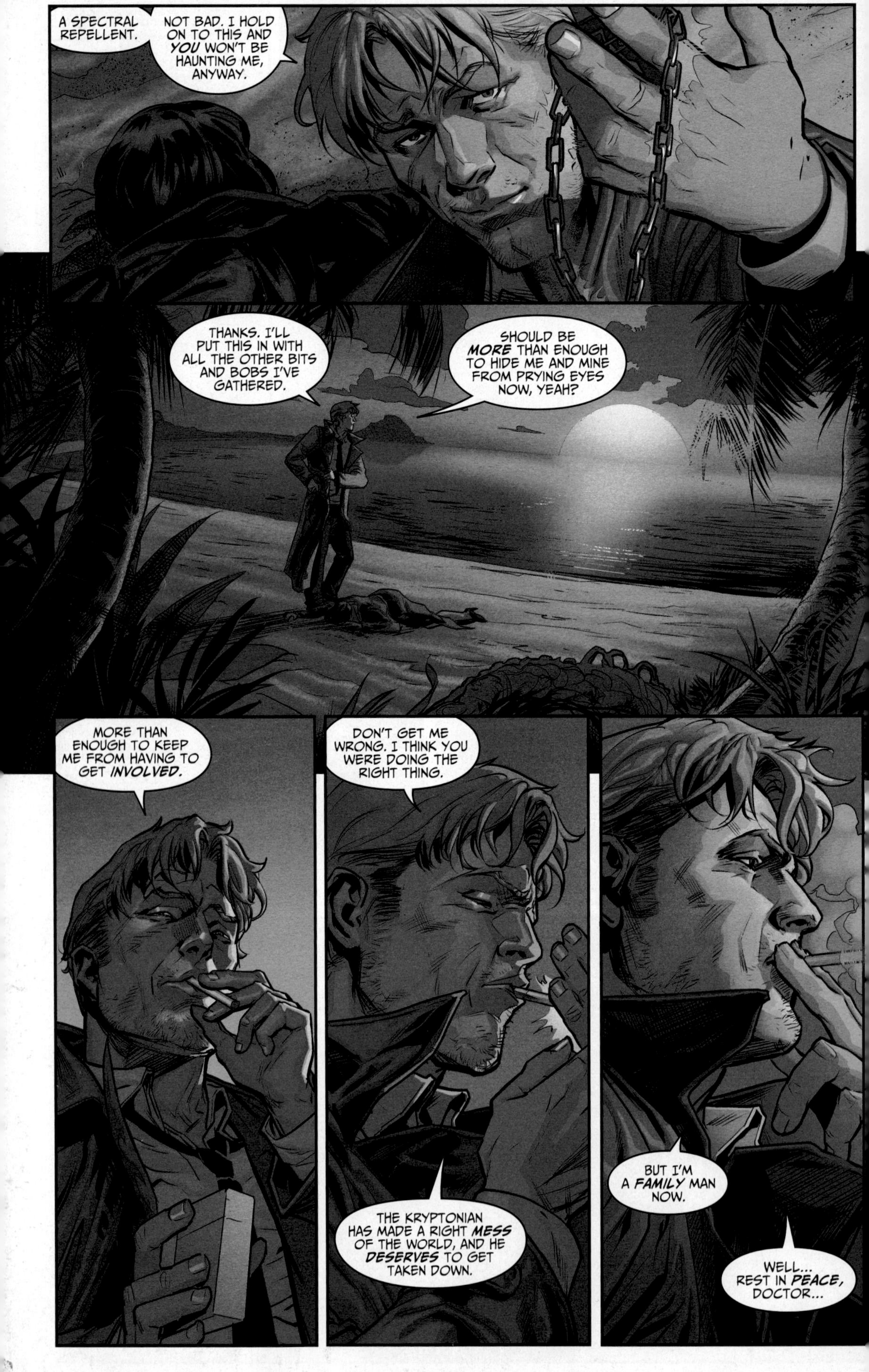
A SPECTRAL REPELLENT.
NOT BAD. I HOLD ON TO THIS AND YOU WON'T BE HAUNTING ME, ANYWAY.
THANKS. I'LL PUT THIS IN WITH ALL THE OTHER BITS AND BOBS I'VE GATHERED.
SHOULD BE MORE THAN ENOUGH TO HIDE ME AND MINE FROM PRYING EYES NOW, YEAH?
MORE THAN ENOUGH TO KEEP ME FROM HAVING TO GET INVOLVED.
DON'T GET ME WRONG. I THINK YOU WERE DOING THE RIGHT THING.
THE KRYPTONIAN HAS MADE A RIGHT MESS OF THE WORLD, AND HE DESERVES TO GET TAKEN DOWN.
BUT I'M A FAMILY MAN NOW.
WELL... REST IN PEACE, DOCTOR...

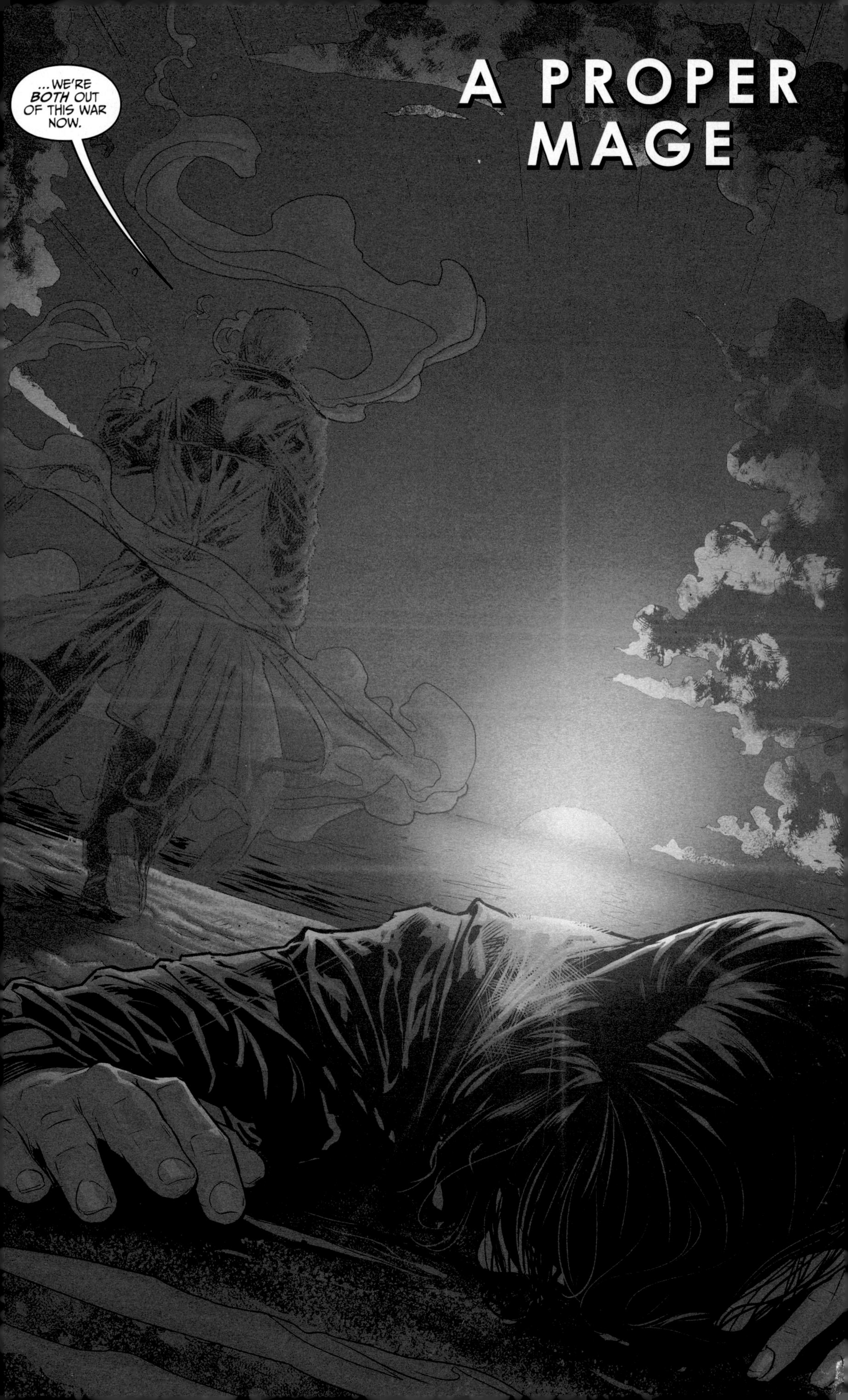
...WE'RE BOTH OUT OF THIS WAR NOW.
A PROPER MAGE

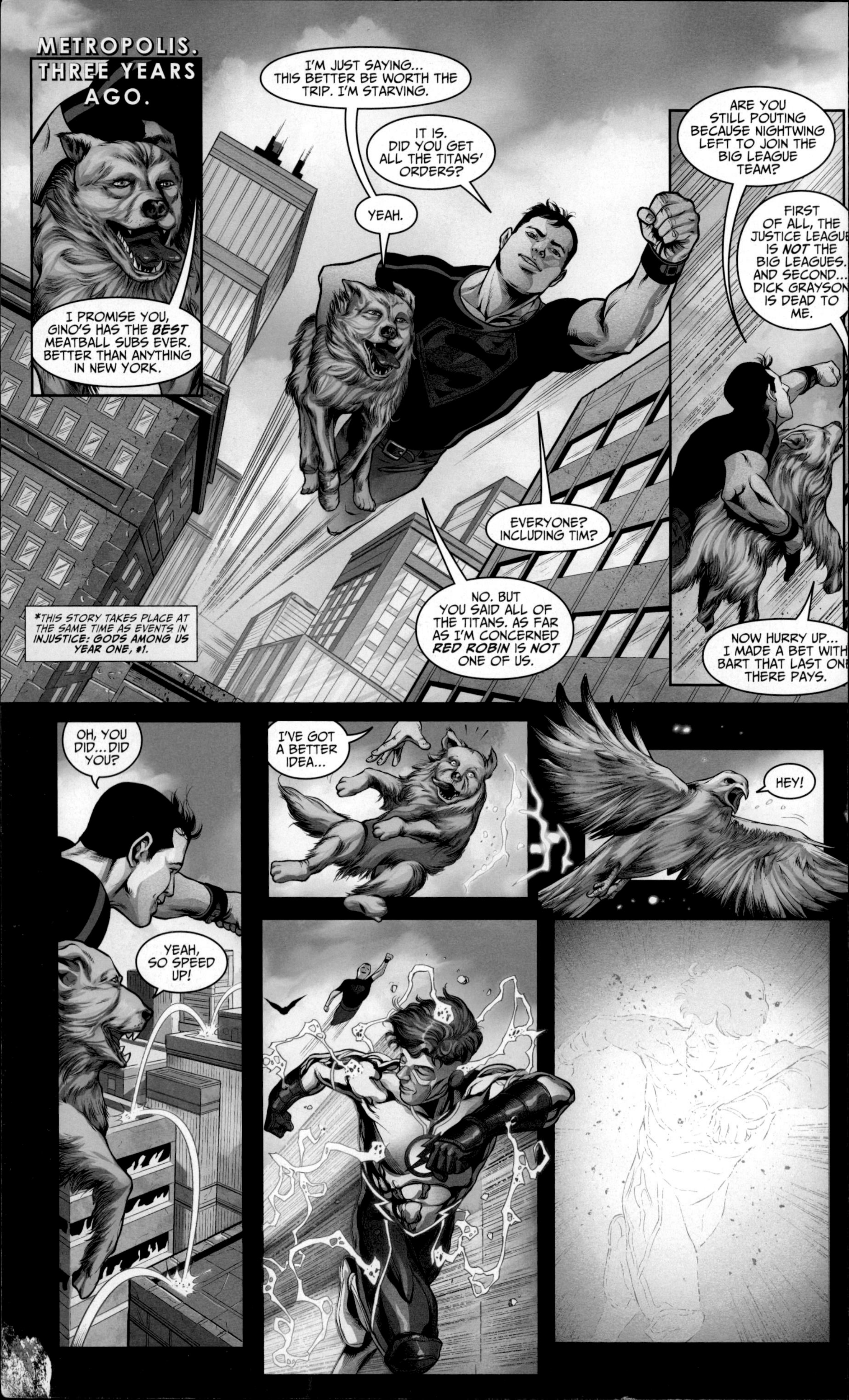
METROPOLIS. THREE YEARS AGO.
I PROMISE YOU, GINO'S HAS THE BEST MEATBALL SUBS EVER. BETTER THAN ANYTHING IN NEW YORK.
I'M JUST SAYING... THIS BETTER BE WORTH THE TRIP. I'M STARVING.
IT IS. DID YOU GET ALL THE TITANS' ORDERS?
YEAH.
EVERYONE? INCLUDING TIM?
NO. BUT YOU SAID ALL OF THE TITANS. AS FAR AS I'M CONCERNED RED ROBIN IS NOT ONE OF US.
*THIS STORY TAKES PLACE AT THE SAME TIME AS EVENTS IN INJUSTICE: GODS AMONG US YEAR ONE, #1.
ARE YOU STILL POUTING BECAUSE NIGHTWING LEFT TO JOIN THE BIG LEAGUE TEAM?
FIRST OF ALL, THE JUSTICE LEAGUE IS NOT THE BIG LEAGUES. AND SECOND... DICK GRAYSON IS DEAD TO ME.
NOW HURRY UP... I MADE A BET WITH BART THAT LAST ONE THERE PAYS.
OH, YOU DID...DID YOU?
YEAH, SO SPEED UP!
I'VE GOT A BETTER IDEA...
HEY!

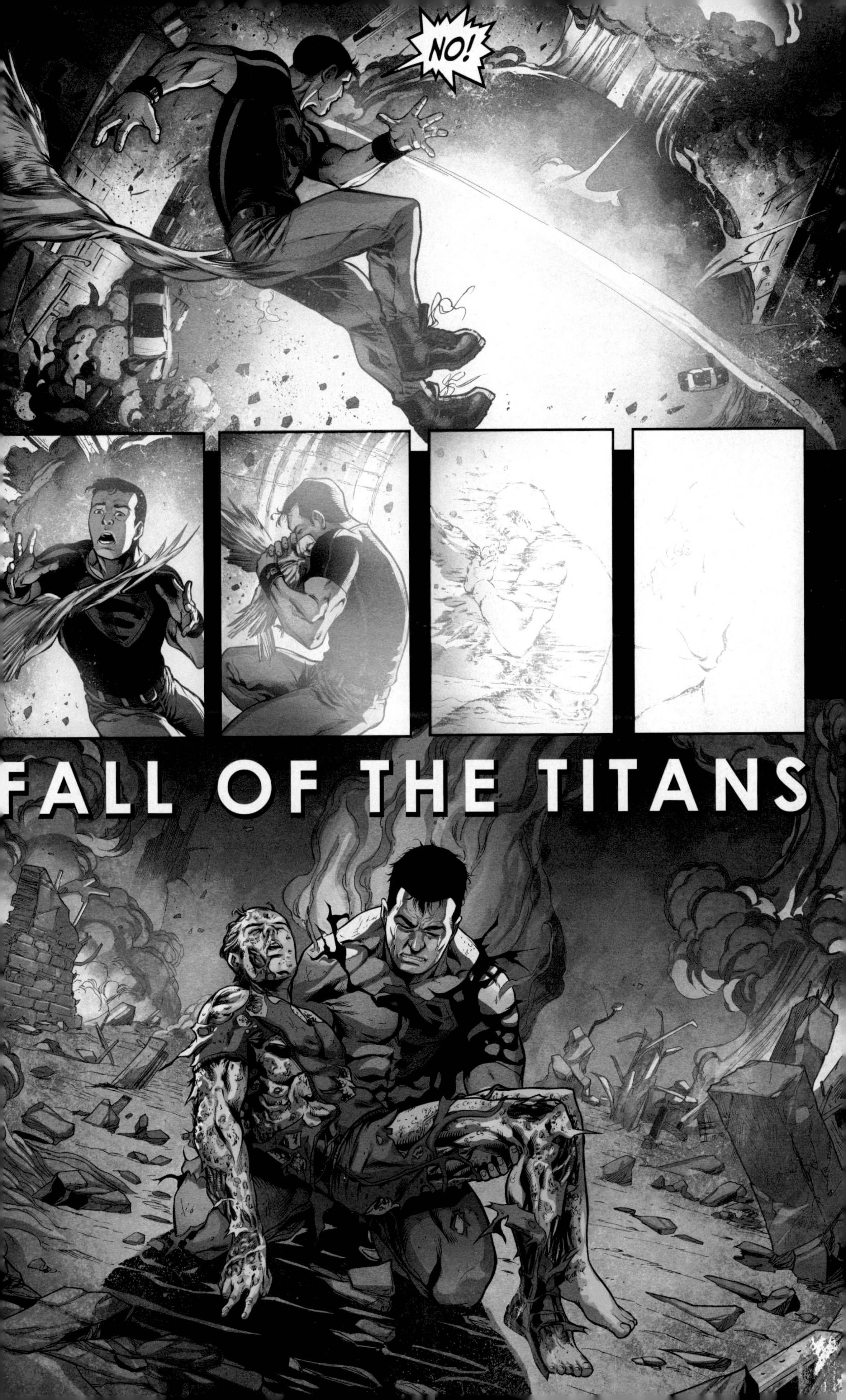
NO!
FALL OF THE TITANS

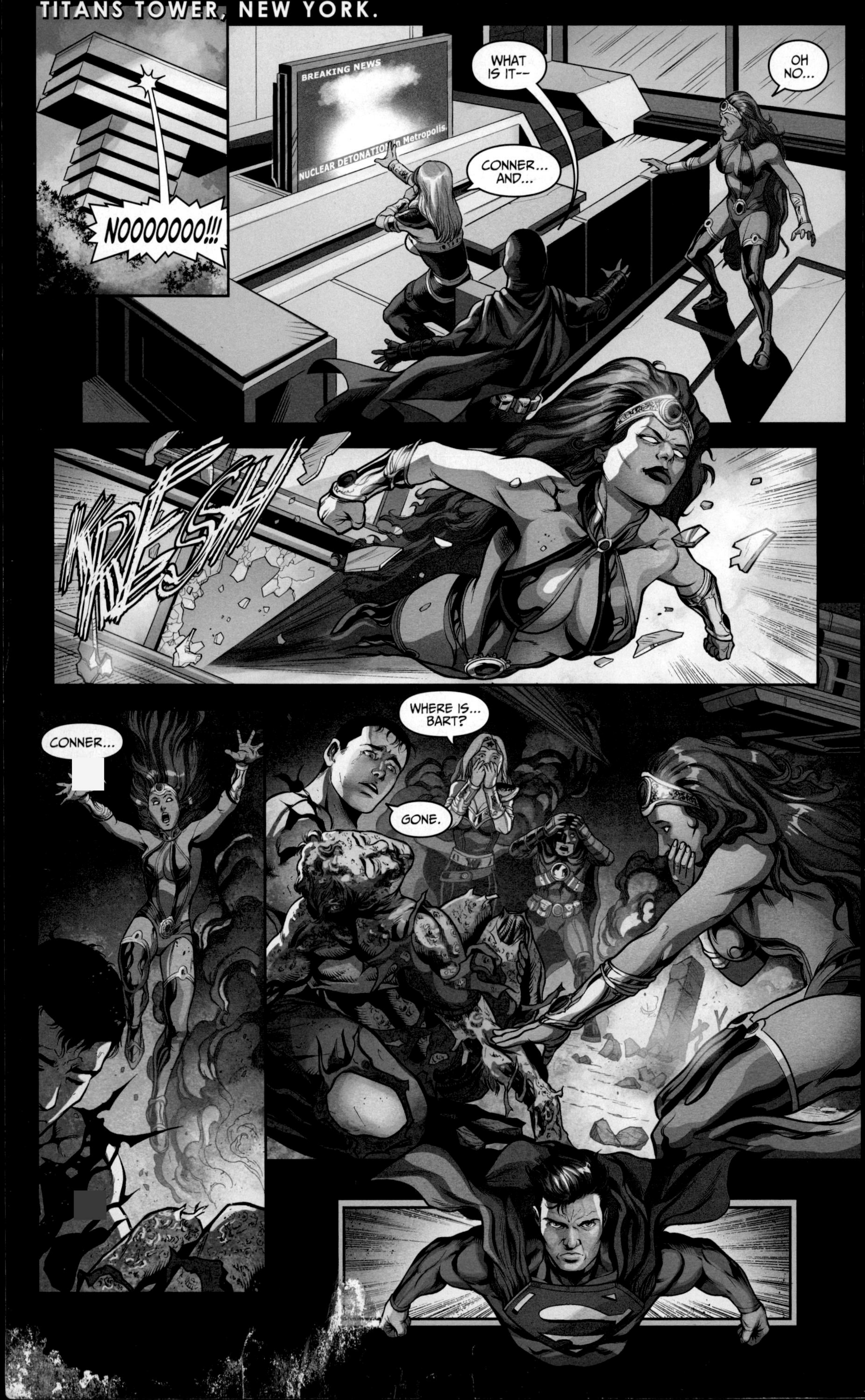
TITANS TOWER, NEW YORK.
NOOOOOOO!!!
BREAKING NEWS
NUCLEAR DETONATION in Metropolis
WHAT IS IT--
CONNER... AND...
OH NO...
KRESH
CONNER...
WHERE IS... BART?
GONE.

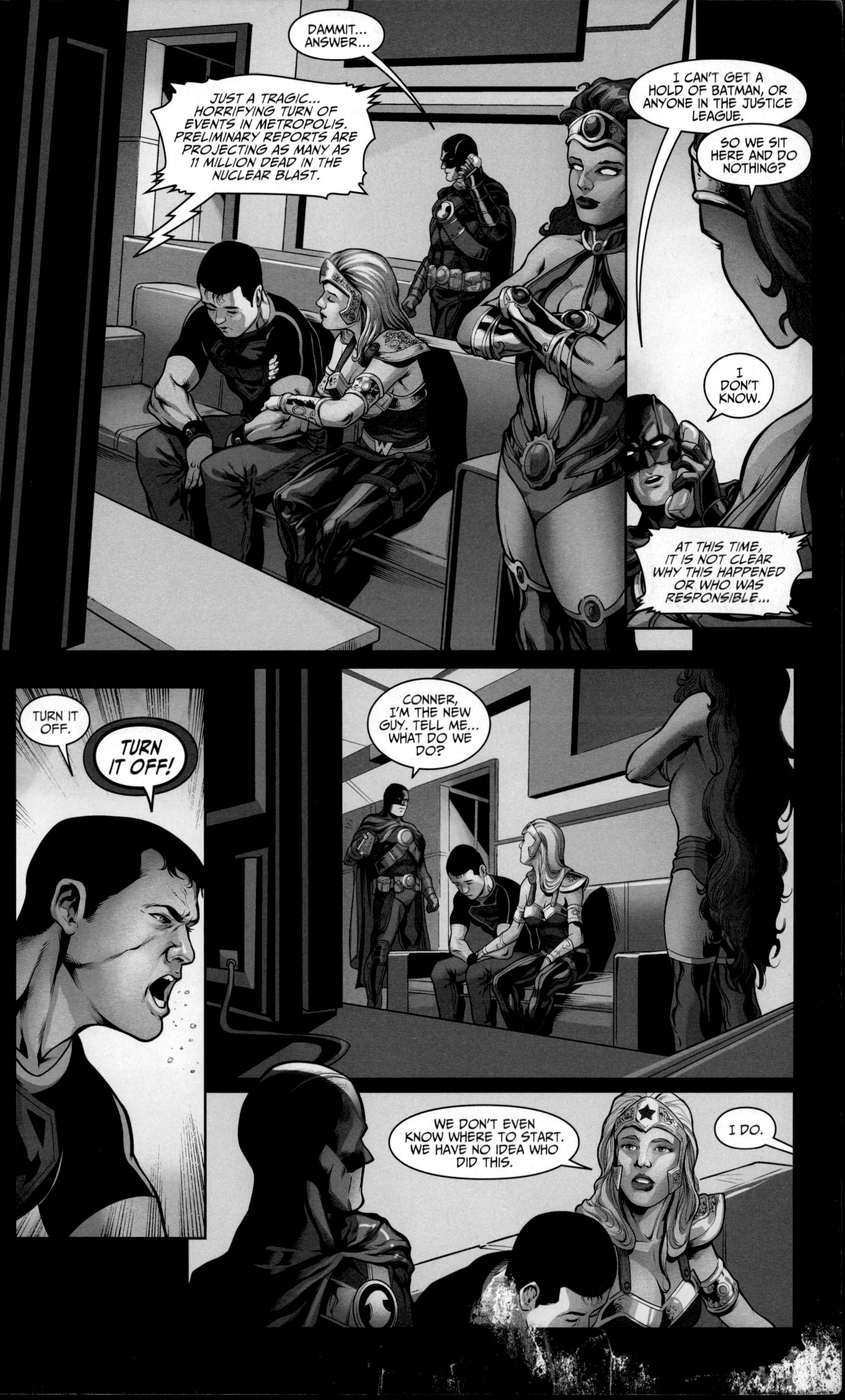

DAMMIT... ANSWER...
JUST A TRAGIC... HORRIFYING TURN OF EVENTS IN METROPOLIS. PRELIMINARY REPORTS ARE PROJECTING AS MANY AS 11 MILLION DEAD IN THE NUCLEAR BLAST.
I CAN'T GET A HOLD OF BATMAN, OR ANYONE IN THE JUSTICE LEAGUE.
SO WE SIT HERE AND DO NOTHING?
I DON'T KNOW.
AT THIS TIME, IT IS NOT CLEAR WHY THIS HAPPENED OR WHO WAS RESPONSIBLE...
TURN IT OFF.
TURN IT OFF!
CONNER, I'M THE NEW GUY. TELL ME... WHAT DO WE DO?
WE DON'T EVEN KNOW WHERE TO START. WE HAVE NO IDEA WHO DID THIS.
I DO.

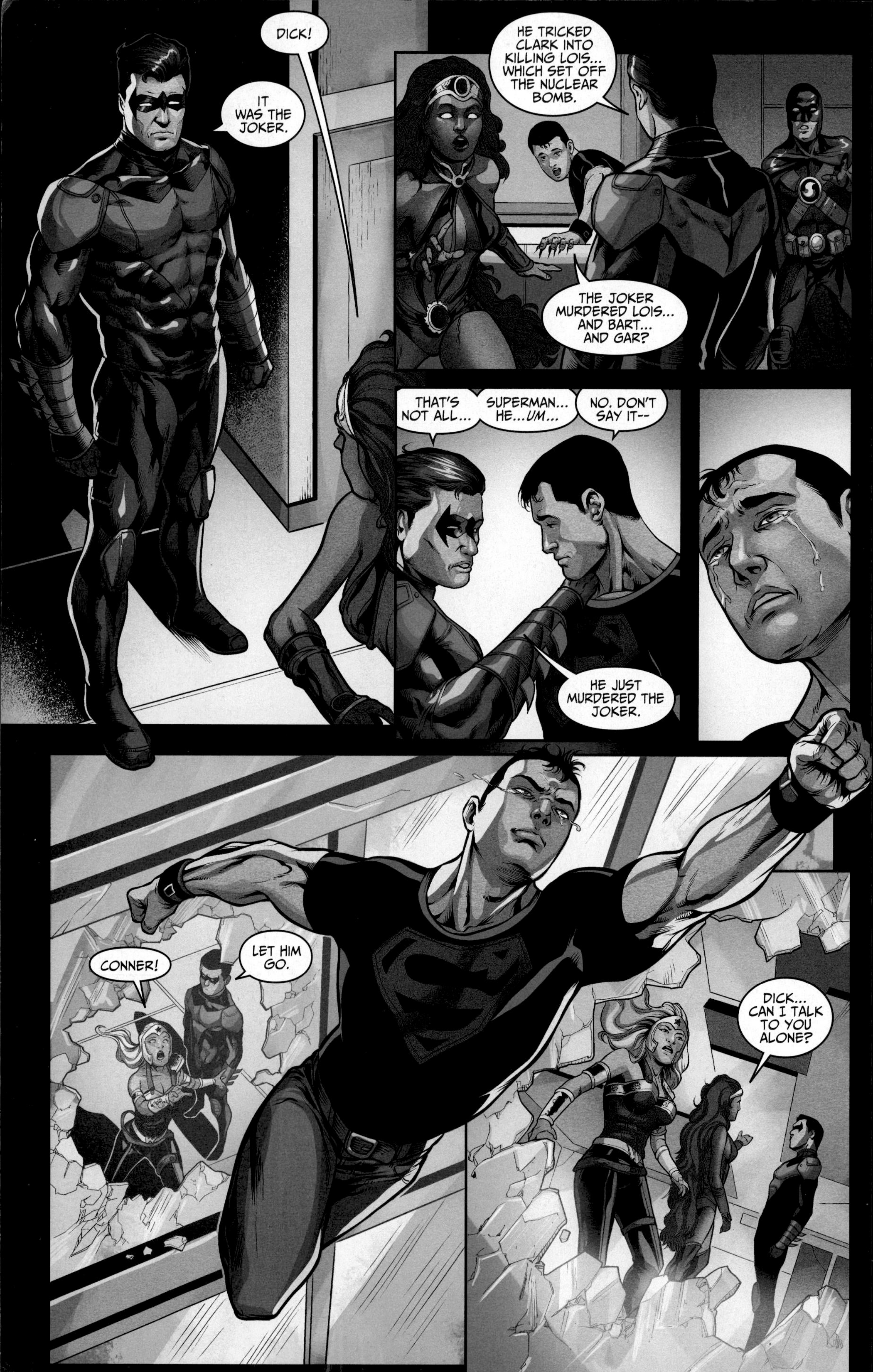
DICK!
IT WAS THE JOKER.
HE TRICKED CLARK INTO KILLING LOIS... WHICH SET OFF THE NUCLEAR BOMB.
THE JOKER MURDERED LOIS... AND BART... AND GAR?
THAT'S NOT ALL...
SUPERMAN... HE...UM...
NO. DON'T SAY IT--
HE JUST MURDERED THE JOKER.
CONNER!
LET HIM GO.
DICK... CAN I TALK TO YOU ALONE?

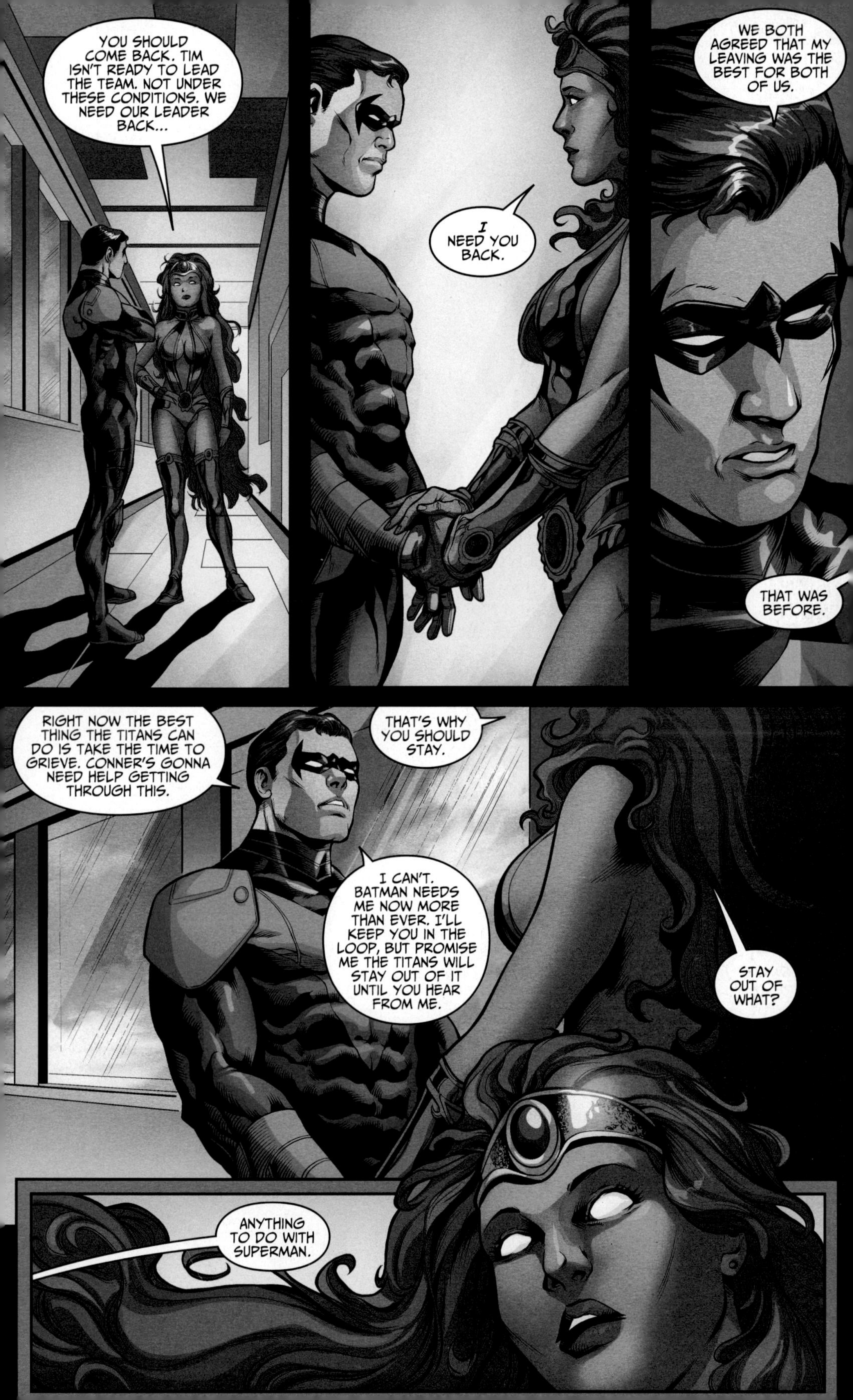
YOU SHOULD COME BACK. TIM ISN'T READY TO LEAD THE TEAM. NOT UNDER THESE CONDITIONS. WE NEED OUR LEADER BACK...
I NEED YOU BACK.
WE BOTH AGREED THAT MY LEAVING WAS THE BEST FOR BOTH OF US.
THAT WAS BEFORE.
RIGHT NOW THE BEST THING THE TITANS CAN DO IS TAKE THE TIME TO GRIEVE. CONNER'S GONNA NEED HELP GETTING THROUGH THIS.
THAT'S WHY YOU SHOULD STAY.
I CAN'T. BATMAN NEEDS ME NOW MORE THAN EVER. I'LL KEEP YOU IN THE LOOP, BUT PROMISE ME THE TITANS WILL STAY OUT OF IT UNTIL YOU HEAR FROM ME.
STAY OUT OF WHAT?
ANYTHING TO DO WITH SUPERMAN.

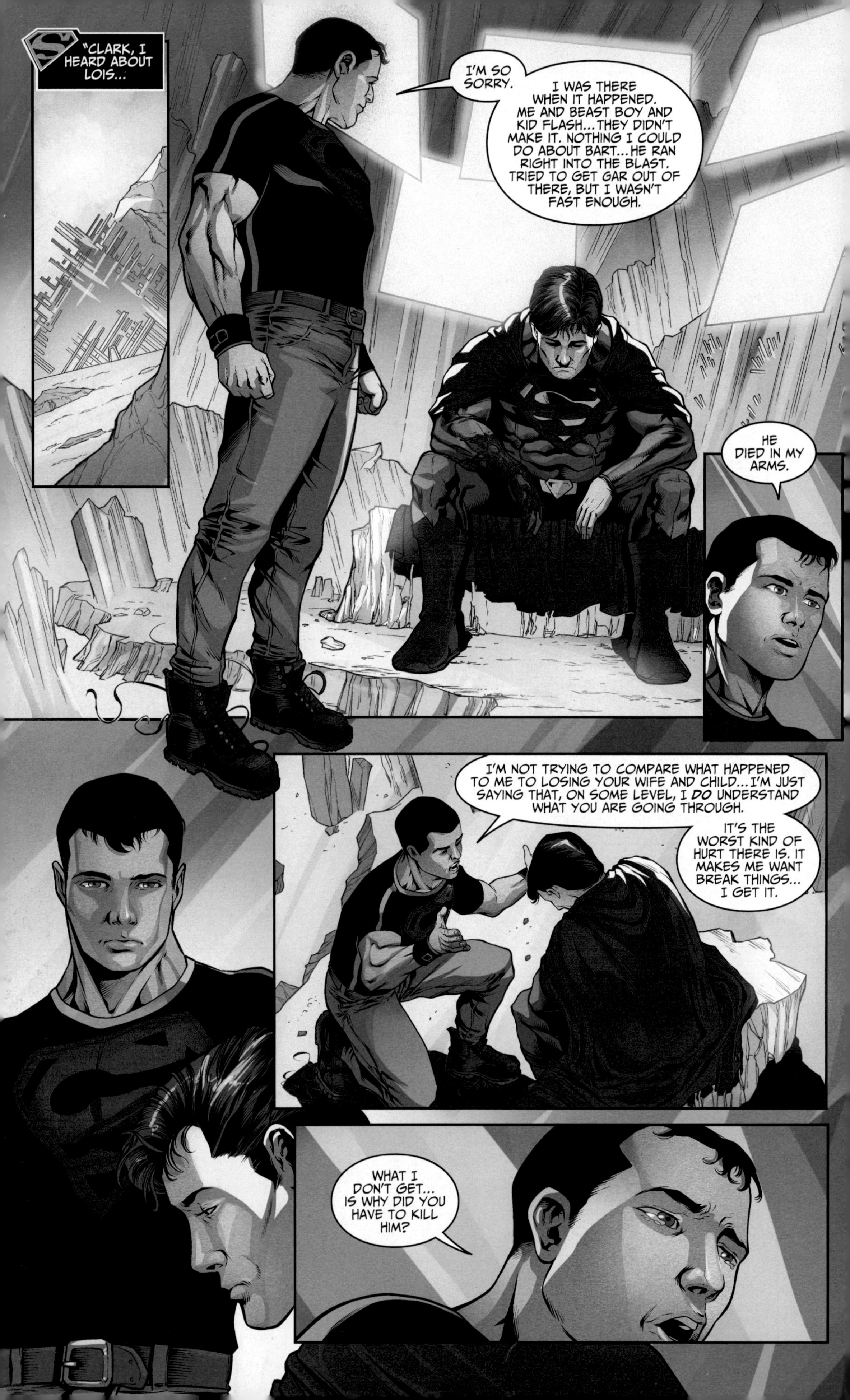
"CLARK, I HEARD ABOUT LOIS...
I'M SO SORRY.
I WAS THERE WHEN IT HAPPENED. ME AND BEAST BOY AND KID FLASH...THEY DIDN'T MAKE IT. NOTHING I COULD DO ABOUT BART...HE RAN RIGHT INTO THE BLAST. TRIED TO GET GAR OUT OF THERE, BUT I WASN'T FAST ENOUGH.
HE DIED IN MY ARMS.
I'M NOT TRYING TO COMPARE WHAT HAPPENED TO ME TO LOSING YOUR WIFE AND CHILD...I'M JUST SAYING THAT, ON SOME LEVEL, I DO UNDERSTAND WHAT YOU ARE GOING THROUGH.
IT'S THE WORST KIND OF HURT THERE IS. IT MAKES ME WANT BREAK THINGS... I GET IT.
WHAT I DON'T GET... IS WHY DID YOU HAVE TO KILL HIM?

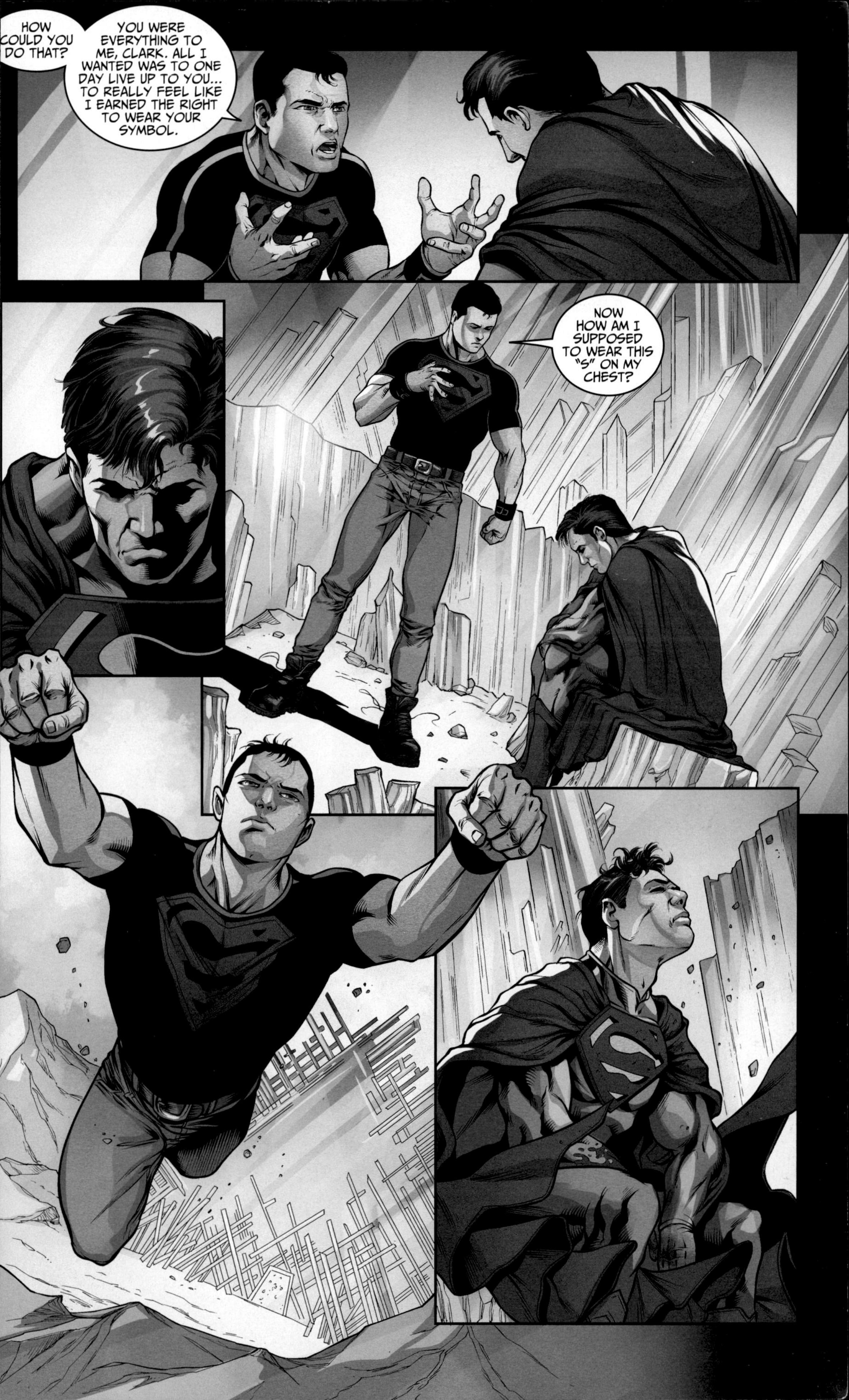
HOW COULD YOU DO THAT?
YOU WERE EVERYTHING TO ME, CLARK. ALL I WANTED WAS TO ONE DAY LIVE UP TO YOU... TO REALLY FEEL LIKE I EARNED THE RIGHT TO WEAR YOUR SYMBOL.
NOW HOW AM I SUPPOSED TO WEAR THIS "S" ON MY CHEST?

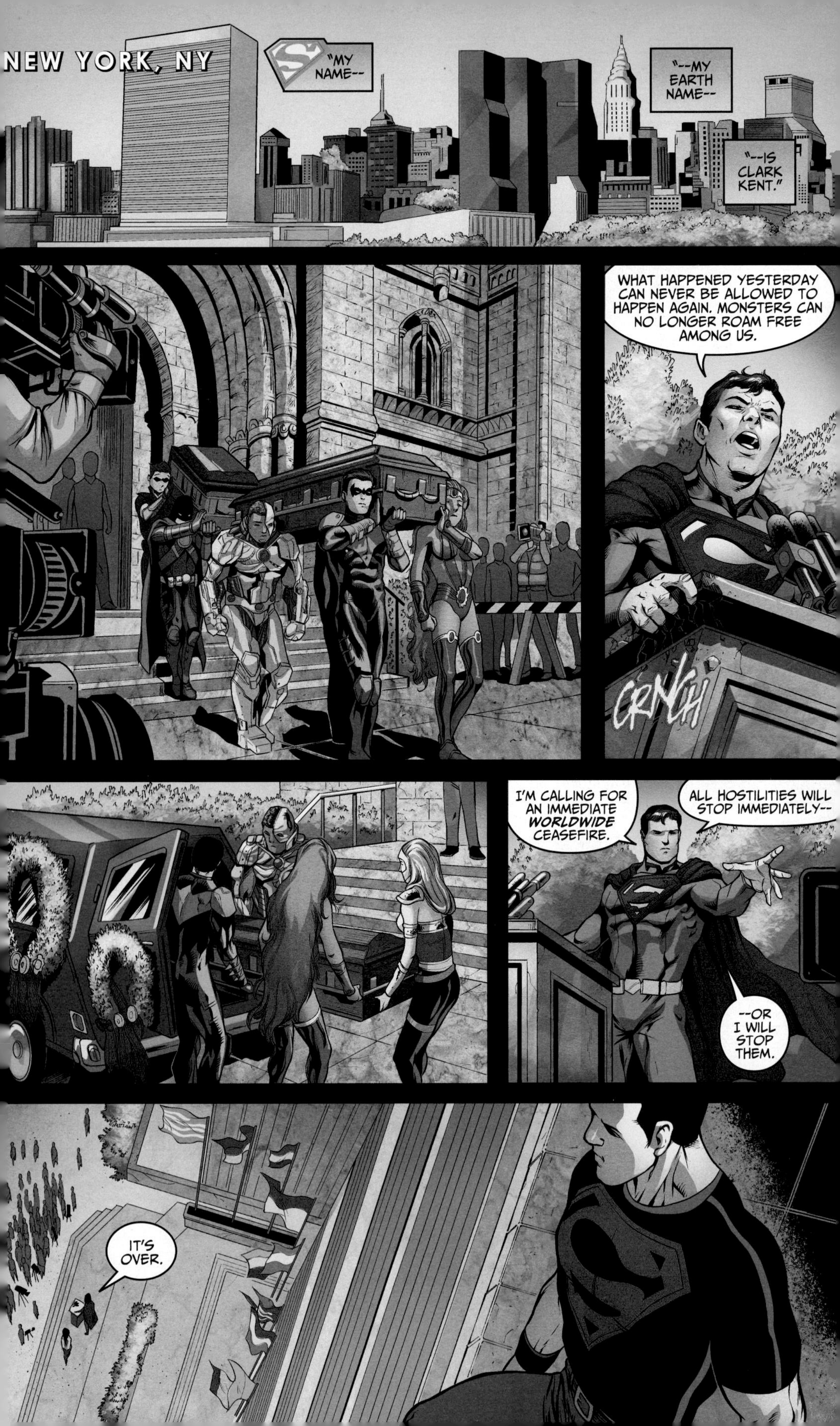

NEW YORK, NY
"MY NAME--
"--MY EARTH NAME--
"--IS CLARK KENT."
WHAT HAPPENED YESTERDAY CAN NEVER BE ALLOWED TO HAPPEN AGAIN. MONSTERS CAN NO LONGER ROAM FREE AMONG US.
CRNCH
I'M CALLING FOR AN IMMEDIATE *WORLDWIDE* CEASEFIRE.
ALL HOSTILITIES WILL STOP IMMEDIATELY--
--OR I WILL STOP THEM.
IT'S OVER.

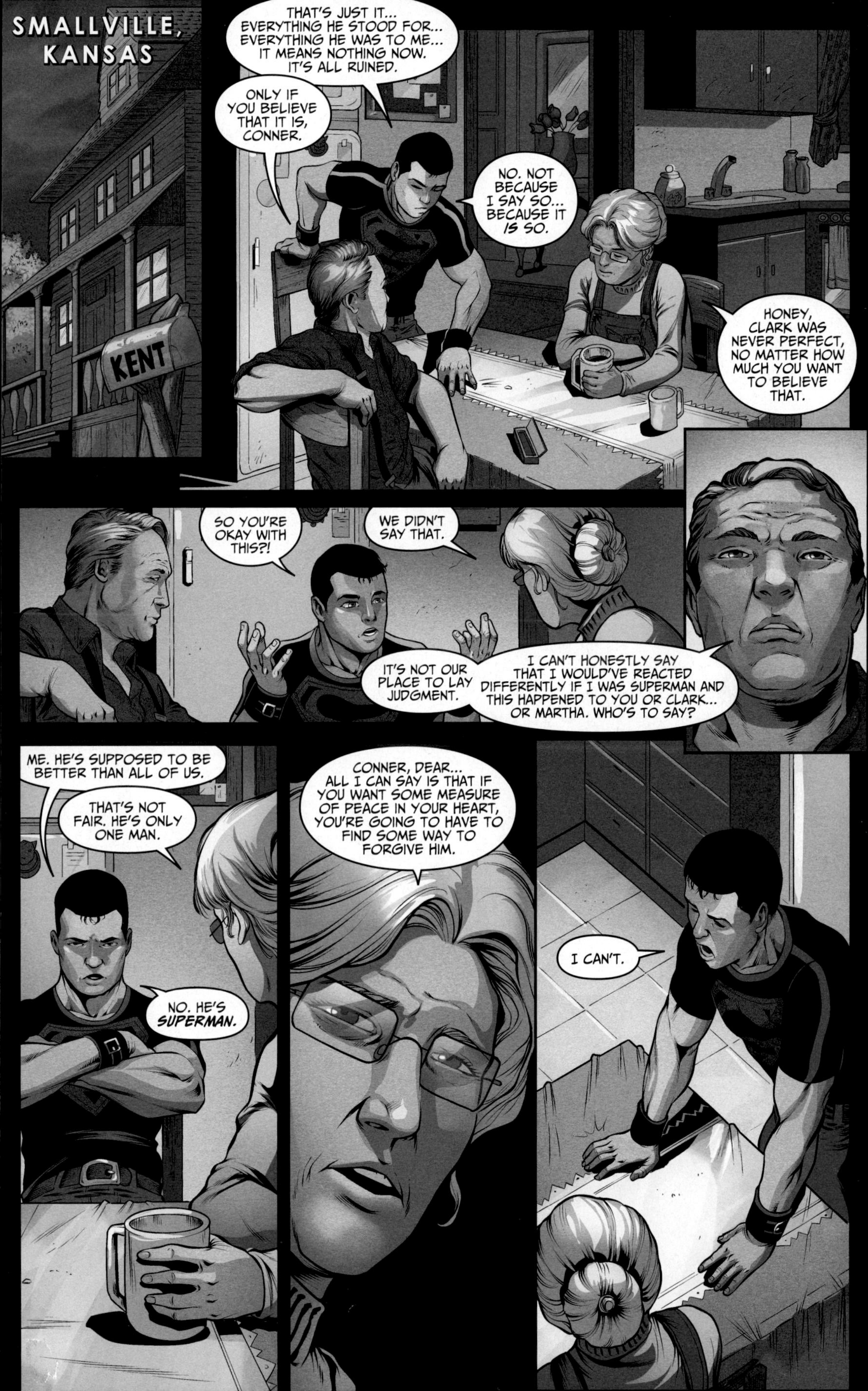
SMALLVILLE, KANSAS
KENT
THAT'S JUST IT... EVERYTHING HE STOOD FOR... EVERYTHING HE WAS TO ME... IT MEANS NOTHING NOW. IT'S ALL RUINED.
ONLY IF YOU BELIEVE THAT IT IS, CONNER.
NO. NOT BECAUSE I SAY SO... BECAUSE IT *IS* SO.
HONEY, CLARK WAS NEVER PERFECT, NO MATTER HOW MUCH YOU WANT TO BELIEVE THAT.
SO YOU'RE OKAY WITH THIS?!
WE DIDN'T SAY THAT.
IT'S NOT OUR PLACE TO LAY JUDGMENT.
I CAN'T HONESTLY SAY THAT I WOULD'VE REACTED DIFFERENTLY IF I WAS SUPERMAN AND THIS HAPPENED TO YOU OR CLARK... OR MARTHA. WHO'S TO SAY?
ME. HE'S SUPPOSED TO BE BETTER THAN ALL OF US.
THAT'S NOT FAIR. HE'S ONLY ONE MAN.
NO. HE'S *SUPERMAN.*
CONNER, DEAR... ALL I CAN SAY IS THAT IF YOU WANT SOME MEASURE OF PEACE IN YOUR HEART, YOU'RE GOING TO HAVE TO FIND SOME WAY TO FORGIVE HIM.
I CAN'T.

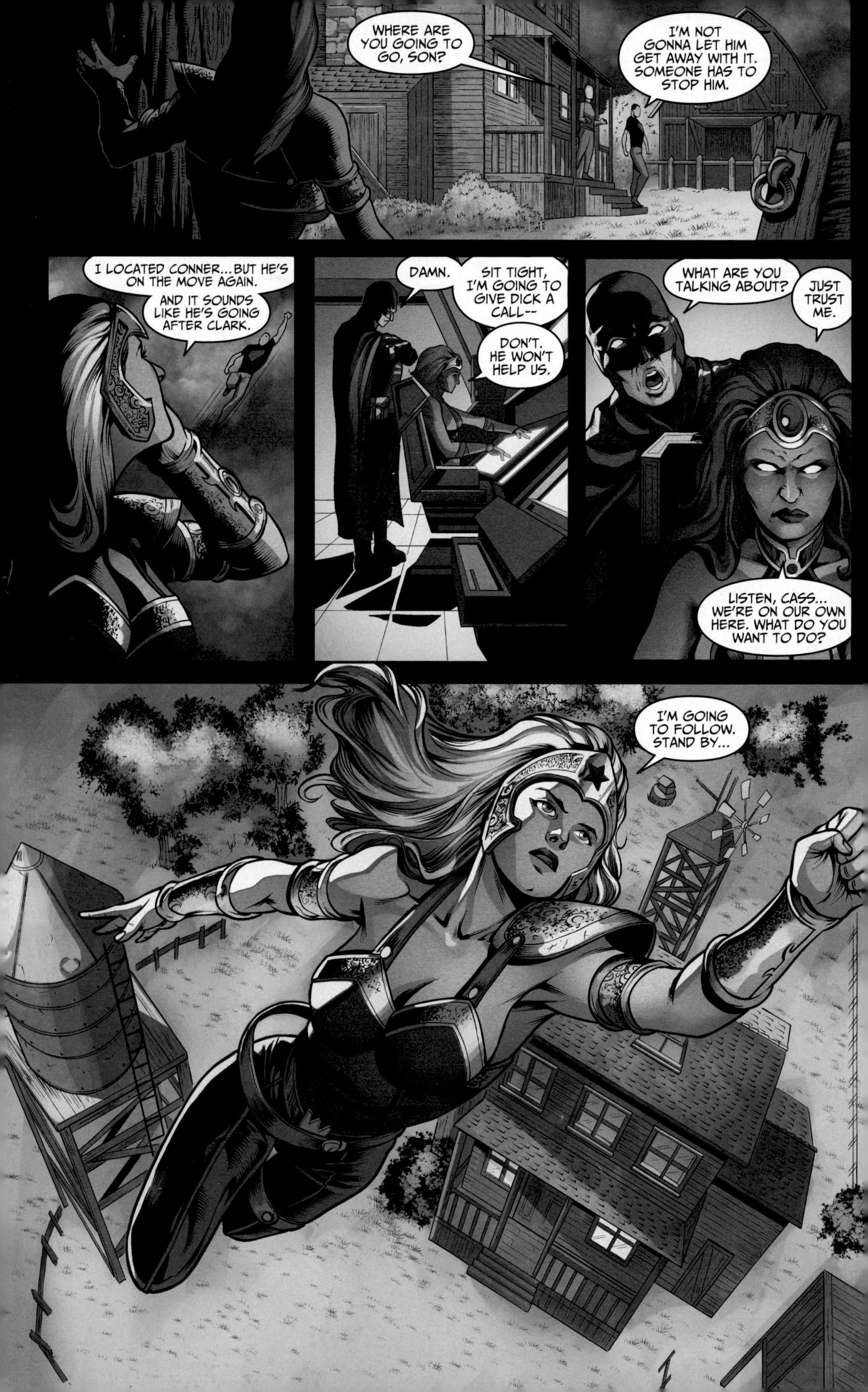
WHERE ARE YOU GOING TO GO, SON?
I'M NOT GONNA LET HIM GET AWAY WITH IT. SOMEONE HAS TO STOP HIM.
I LOCATED CONNER...BUT HE'S ON THE MOVE AGAIN.
AND IT SOUNDS LIKE HE'S GOING AFTER CLARK.
DAMN.
SIT TIGHT, I'M GOING TO GIVE DICK A CALL--
DON'T. HE WON'T HELP US.
WHAT ARE YOU TALKING ABOUT?
JUST TRUST ME.
LISTEN, CASS... WE'RE ON OUR OWN HERE. WHAT DO YOU WANT TO DO?
I'M GOING TO FOLLOW. STAND BY...

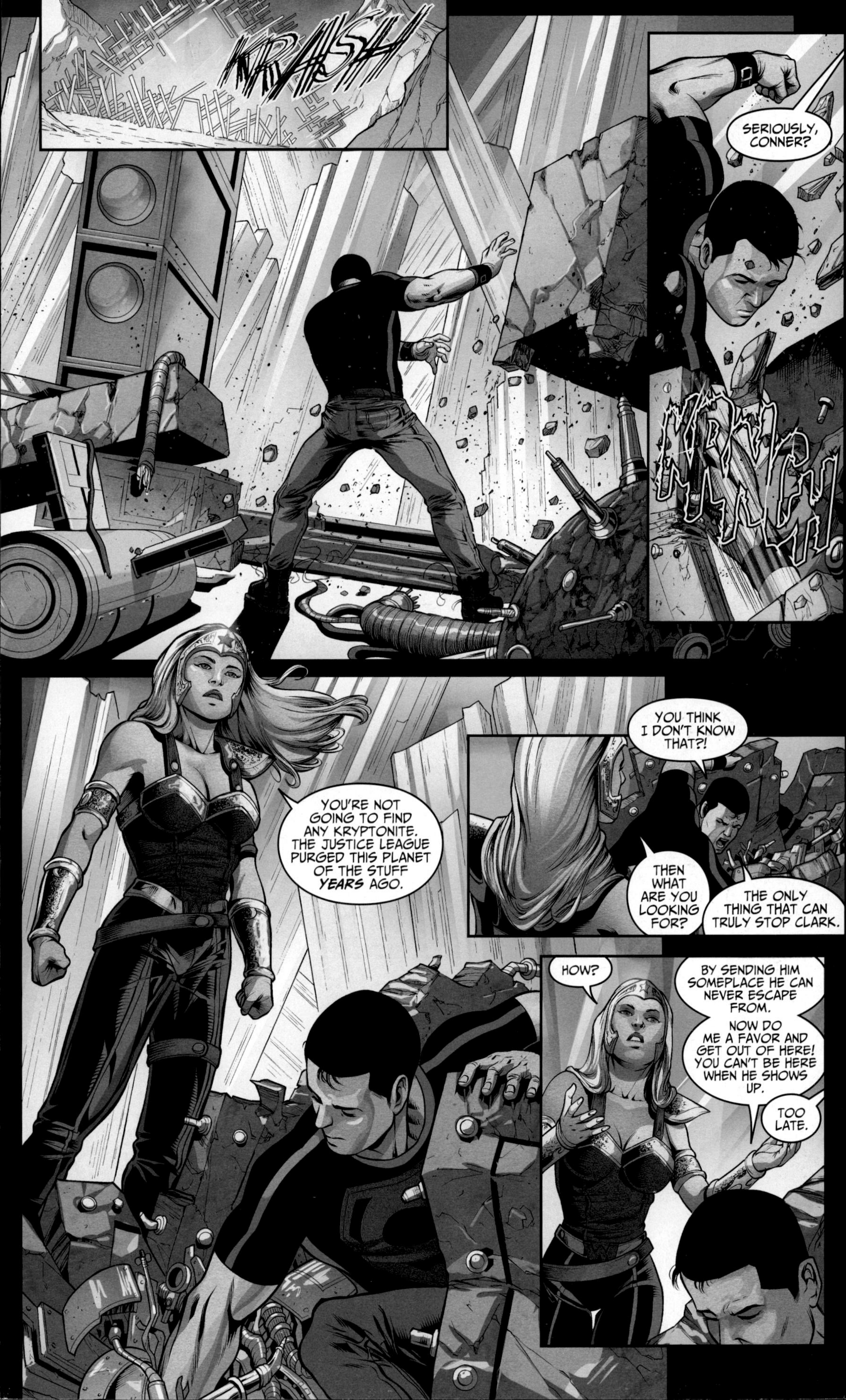
KRAASH
SERIOUSLY, CONNER?
KRRNCH
YOU'RE NOT GOING TO FIND ANY KRYPTONITE. THE JUSTICE LEAGUE PURGED THIS PLANET OF THE STUFF YEARS AGO.
YOU THINK I DON'T KNOW THAT?!
THEN WHAT ARE YOU LOOKING FOR?
THE ONLY THING THAT CAN TRULY STOP CLARK.
HOW?
BY SENDING HIM SOMEPLACE HE CAN NEVER ESCAPE FROM.
NOW DO ME A FAVOR AND GET OUT OF HERE! YOU CAN'T BE HERE WHEN HE SHOWS UP.
TOO LATE.

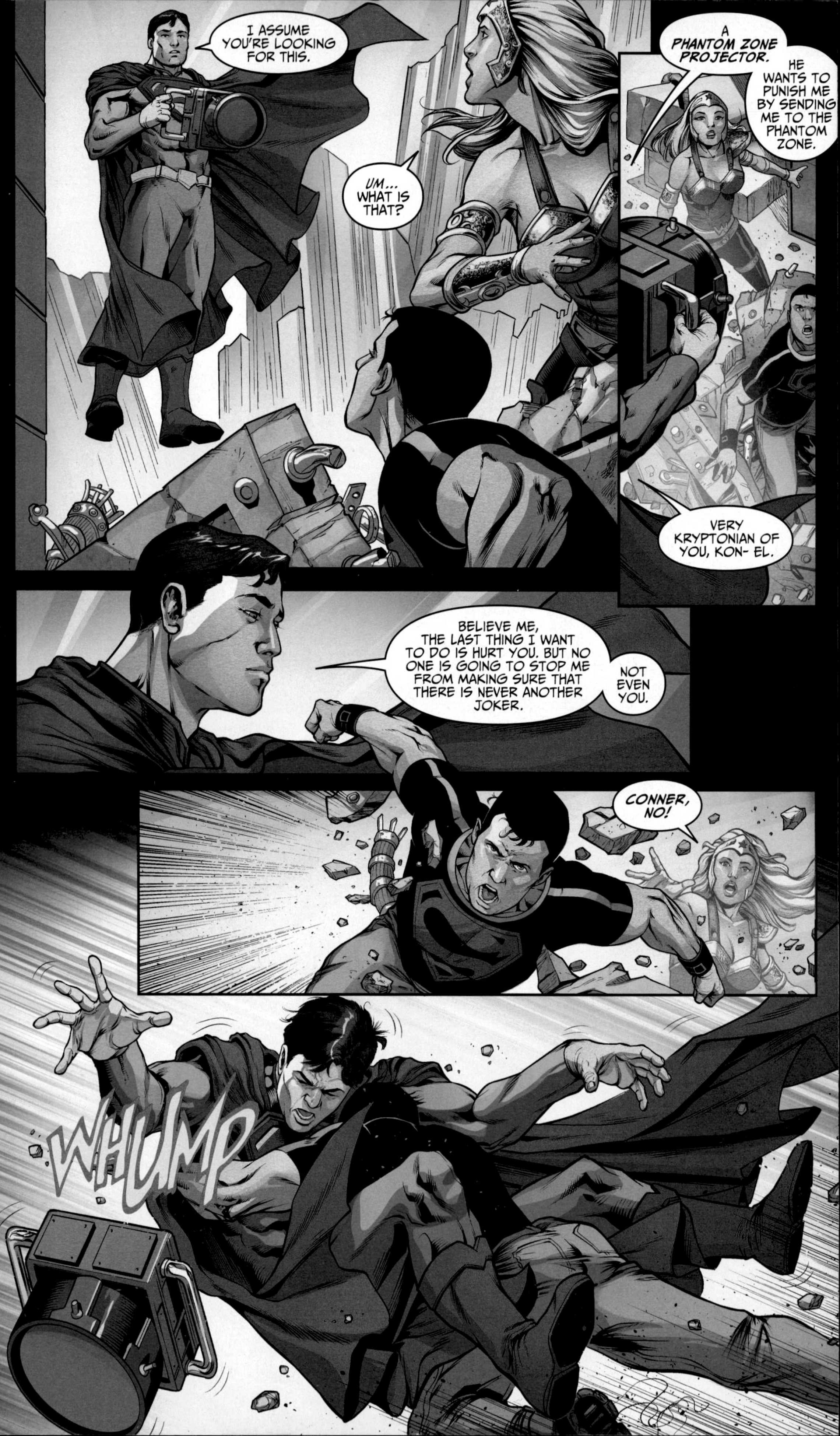
I ASSUME YOU'RE LOOKING FOR THIS.
UM... WHAT IS THAT?
A PHANTOM ZONE PROJECTOR.
HE WANTS TO PUNISH ME BY SENDING ME TO THE PHANTOM ZONE.
VERY KRYPTONIAN OF YOU, KON-EL.
BELIEVE ME, THE LAST THING I WANT TO DO IS HURT YOU. BUT NO ONE IS GOING TO STOP ME FROM MAKING SURE THAT THERE IS NEVER ANOTHER JOKER.
NOT EVEN YOU.
CONNER, NO!
WHUMP

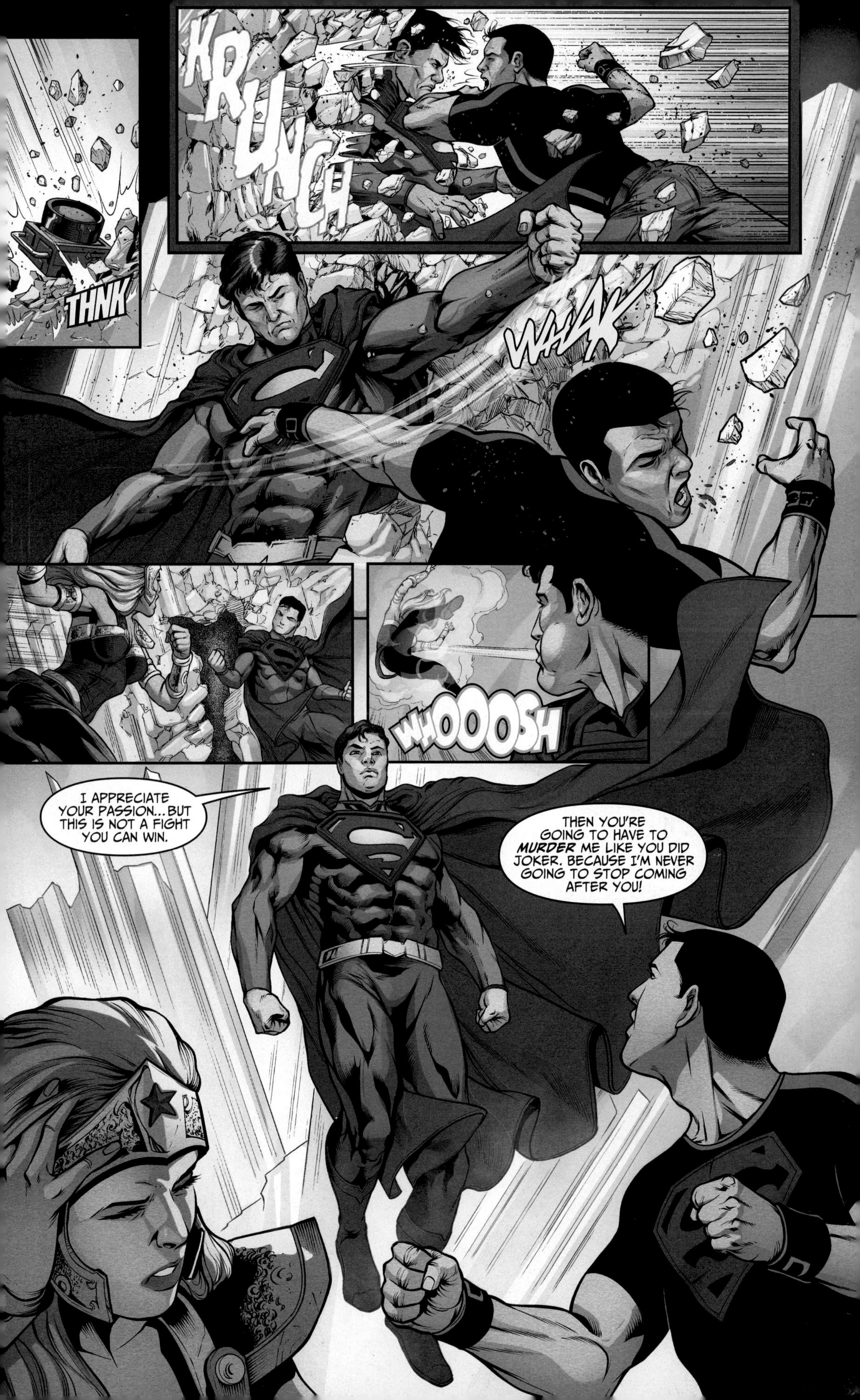
KRUNCH
THNK
WHAK
WHOOOSH
I APPRECIATE YOUR PASSION... BUT THIS IS NOT A FIGHT YOU CAN WIN.
THEN YOU'RE GOING TO HAVE TO *MURDER* ME LIKE YOU DID JOKER. BECAUSE I'M NEVER GOING TO STOP COMING AFTER YOU!

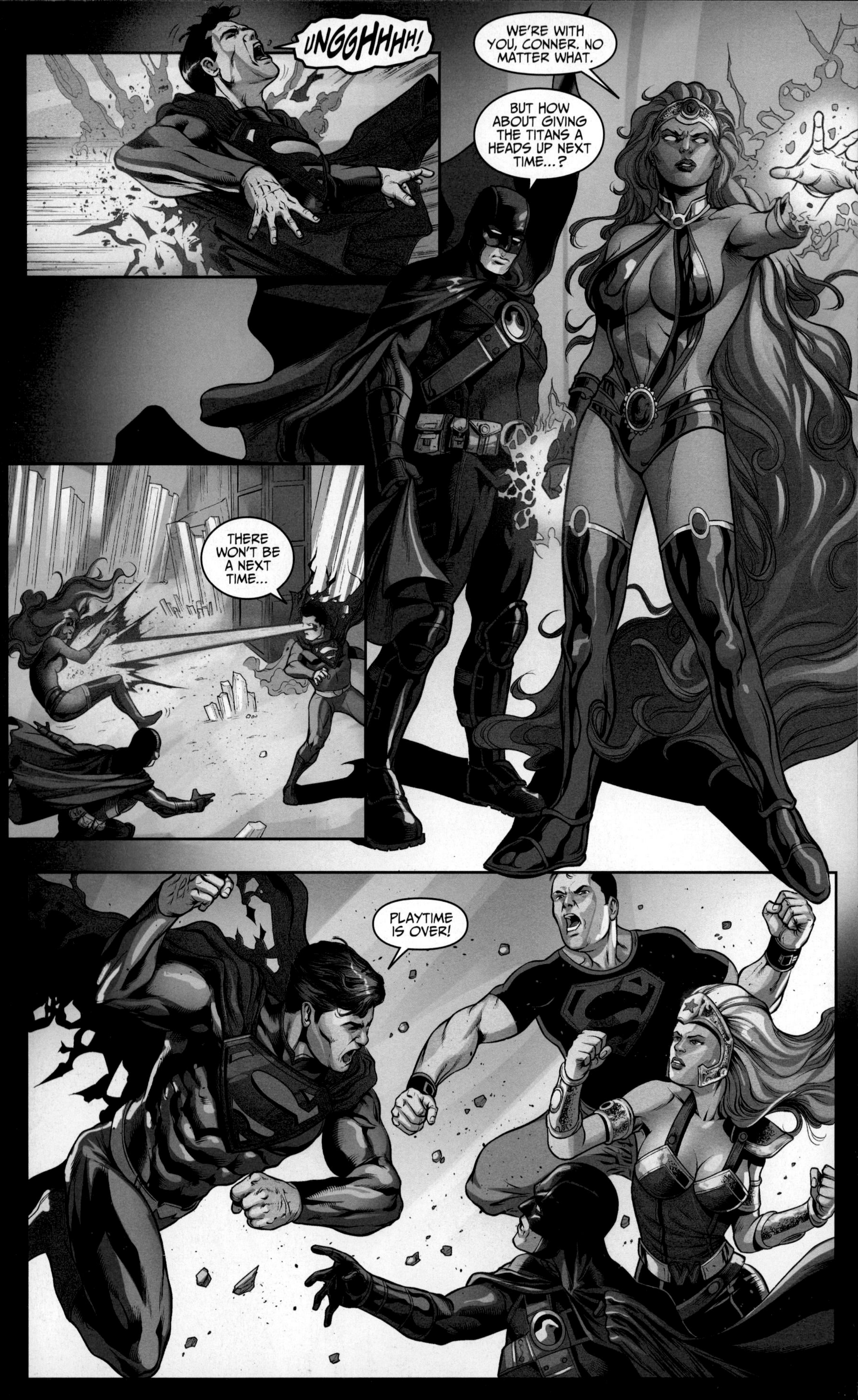
UNGGHHHH!
WE'RE WITH YOU, CONNER. NO MATTER WHAT.
BUT HOW ABOUT GIVING THE TITANS A HEADS UP NEXT TIME...?
THERE WON'T BE A NEXT TIME...
PLAYTIME IS OVER!

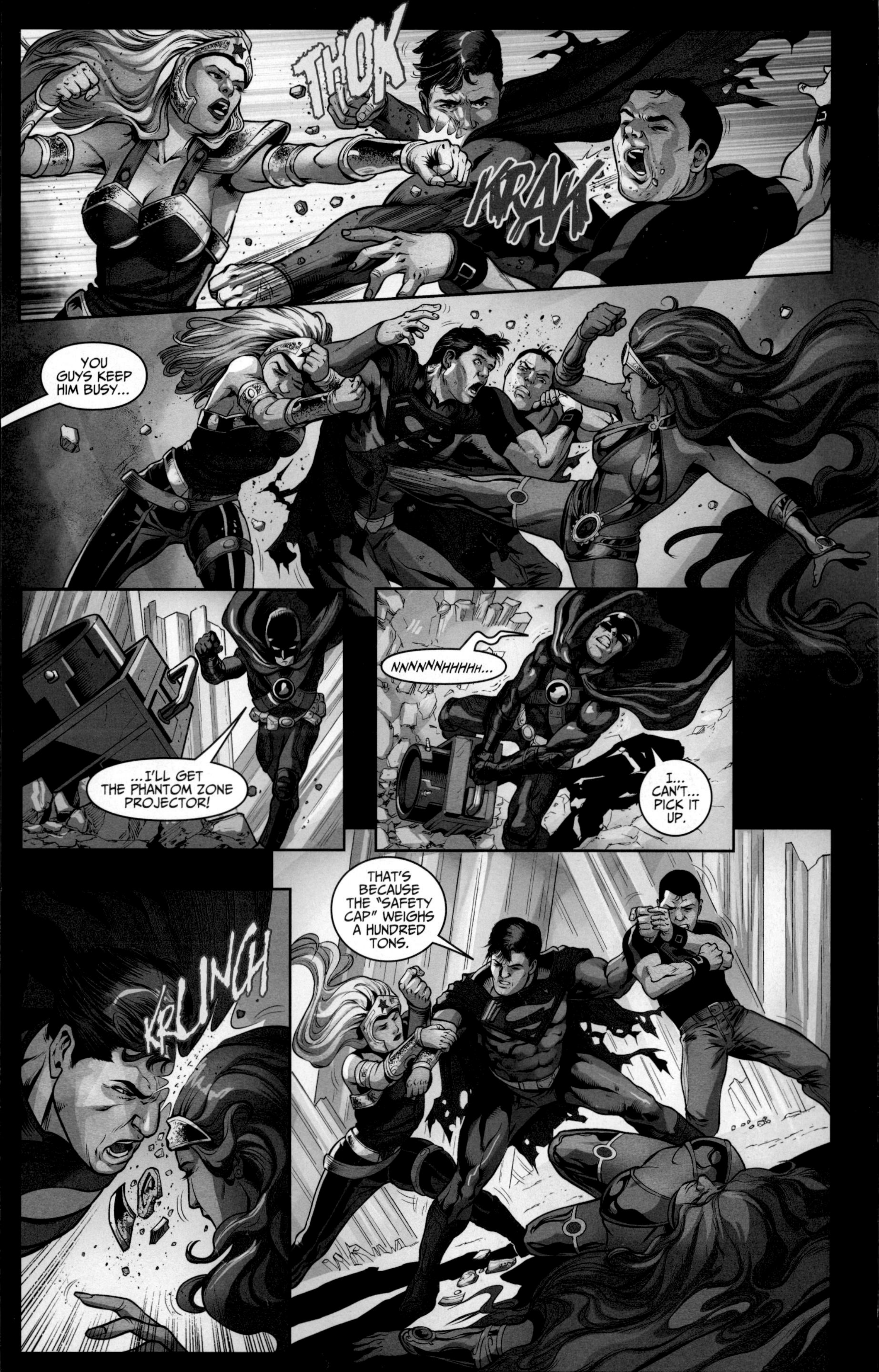
THOK
KRAK
YOU GUYS KEEP HIM BUSY...
...I'LL GET THE PHANTOM ZONE PROJECTOR!
NNNNNNHHHHH...
I... CAN'T... PICK IT UP.
KRUNCH
THAT'S BECAUSE THE "SAFETY CAP" WEIGHS A HUNDRED TONS.

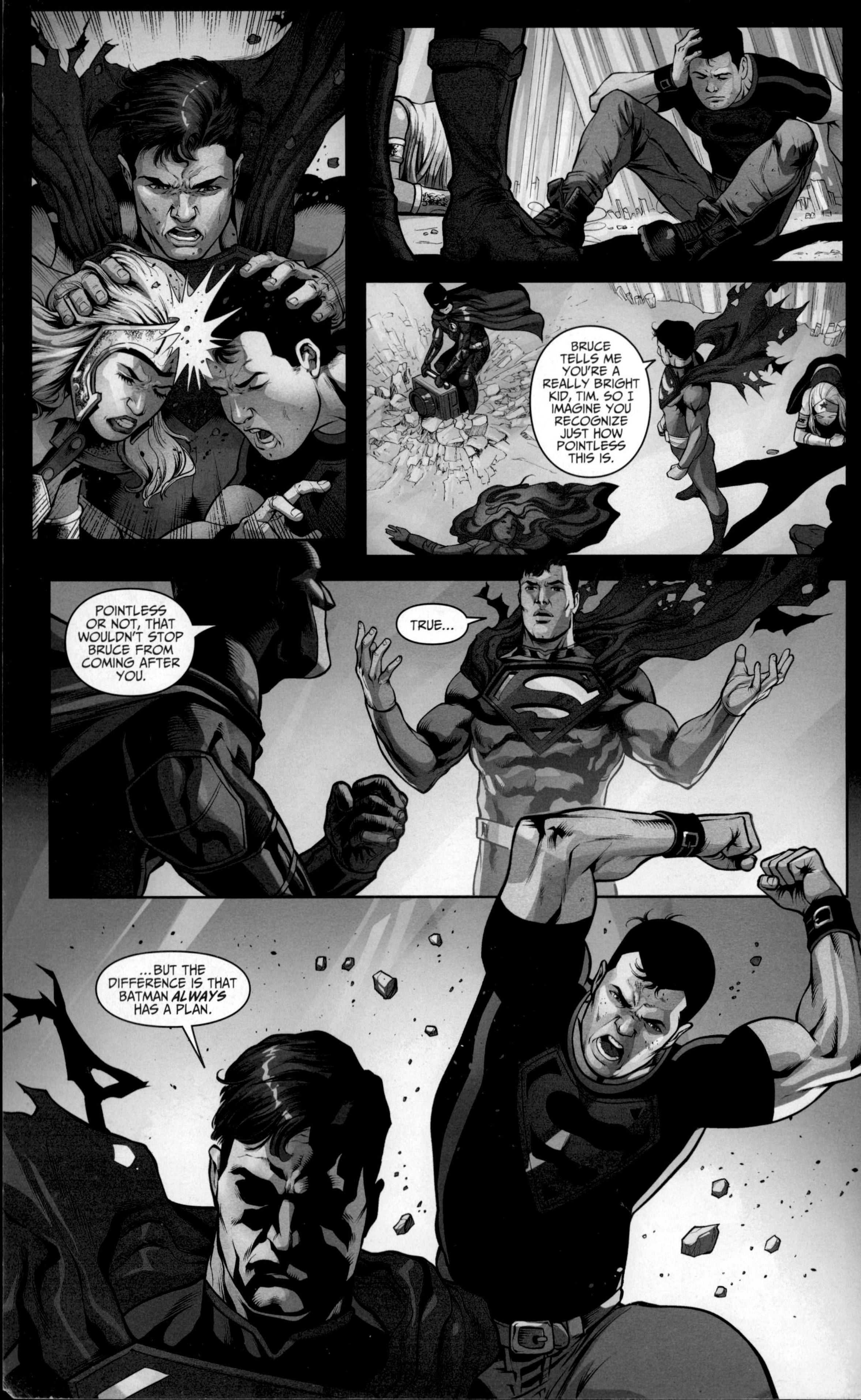
BRUCE TELLS ME YOU'RE A REALLY BRIGHT KID, TIM. SO I IMAGINE YOU RECOGNIZE JUST HOW POINTLESS THIS IS.
POINTLESS OR NOT, THAT WOULDN'T STOP BRUCE FROM COMING AFTER YOU.
TRUE...
...BUT THE DIFFERENCE IS THAT BATMAN *ALWAYS* HAS A PLAN.

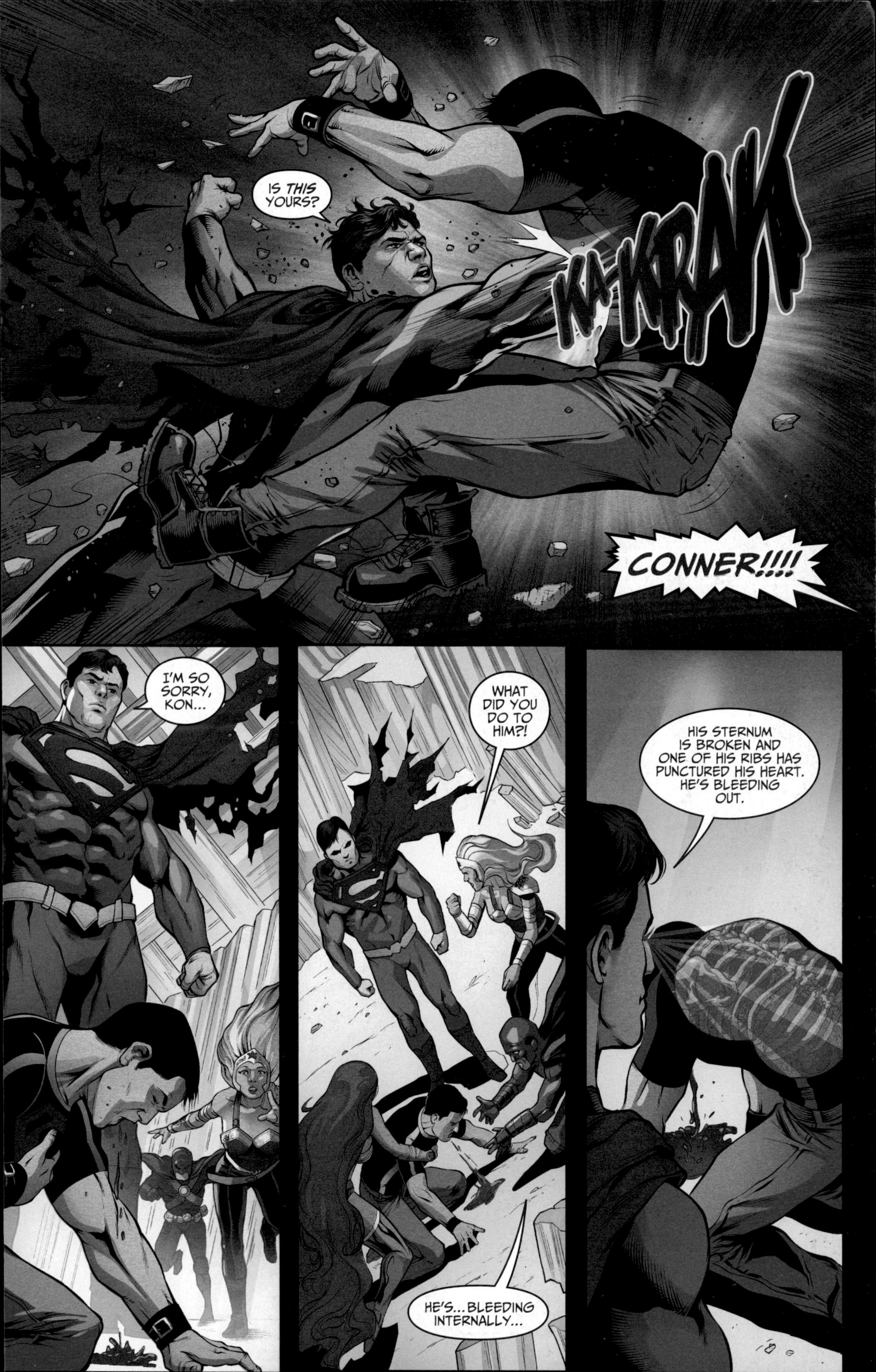
IS THIS YOURS?
KA-KRAK
CONNER!!!!
I'M SO SORRY, KON...
WHAT DID YOU DO TO HIM?!
HE'S...BLEEDING INTERNALLY...
HIS STERNUM IS BROKEN AND ONE OF HIS RIBS HAS PUNCTURED HIS HEART. HE'S BLEEDING OUT.

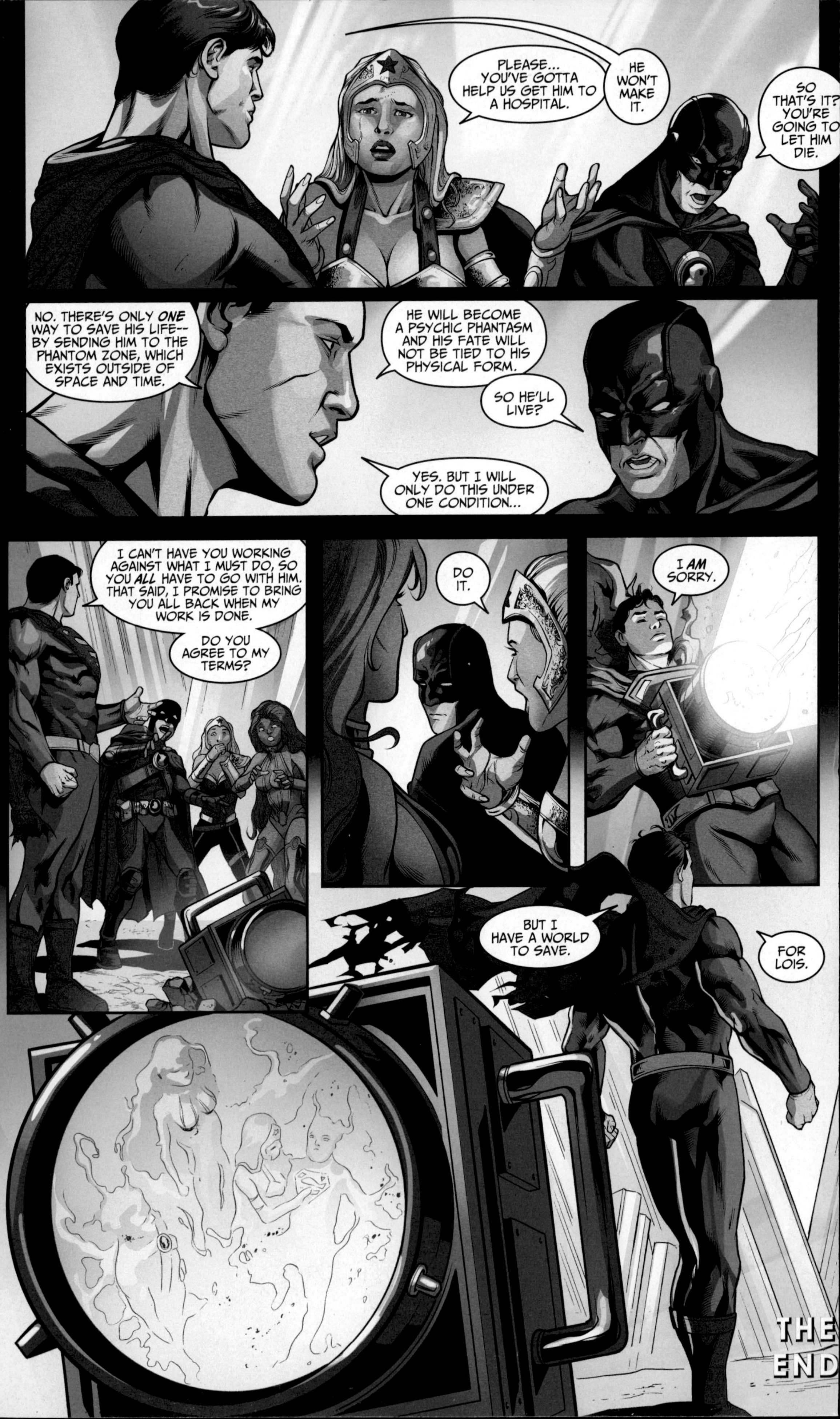
PLEASE... YOU'VE GOTTA HELP US GET HIM TO A HOSPITAL.
HE WON'T MAKE IT.
SO THAT'S IT? YOU'RE GOING TO LET HIM DIE.
NO. THERE'S ONLY ONE WAY TO SAVE HIS LIFE-- BY SENDING HIM TO THE PHANTOM ZONE, WHICH EXISTS OUTSIDE OF SPACE AND TIME.
HE WILL BECOME A PSYCHIC PHANTASM AND HIS FATE WILL NOT BE TIED TO HIS PHYSICAL FORM.
SO HE'LL LIVE?
YES. BUT I WILL ONLY DO THIS UNDER ONE CONDITION...
I CAN'T HAVE YOU WORKING AGAINST WHAT I MUST DO, SO YOU ALL HAVE TO GO WITH HIM. THAT SAID, I PROMISE TO BRING YOU ALL BACK WHEN MY WORK IS DONE.
DO YOU AGREE TO MY TERMS?
DO IT.
I AM SORRY.
BUT I HAVE A WORLD TO SAVE.
FOR LOIS.
THE END

INJUSTICE YEAR THREE Sketchbook.

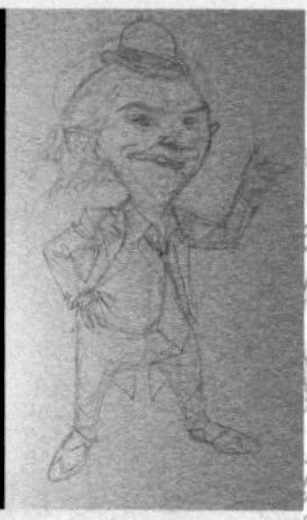

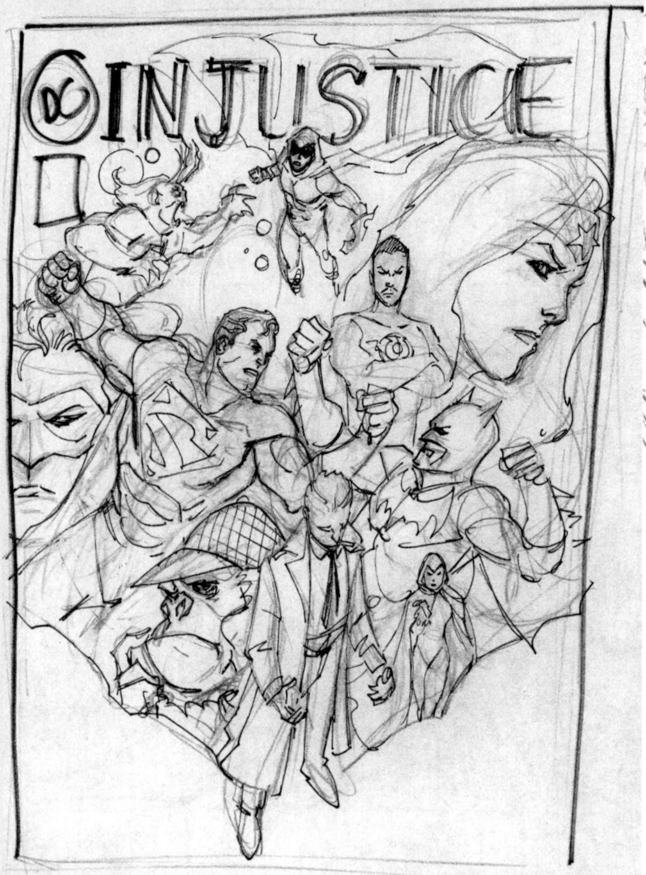
INJUSTICE

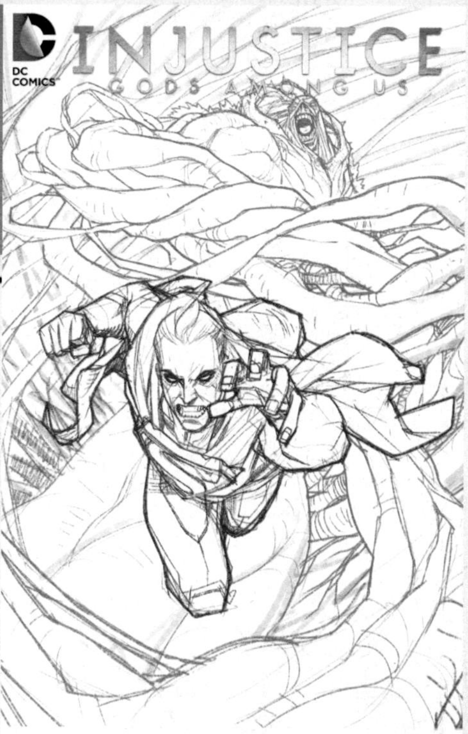
DC COMICS
INJUSTICE
GODS AMONG US

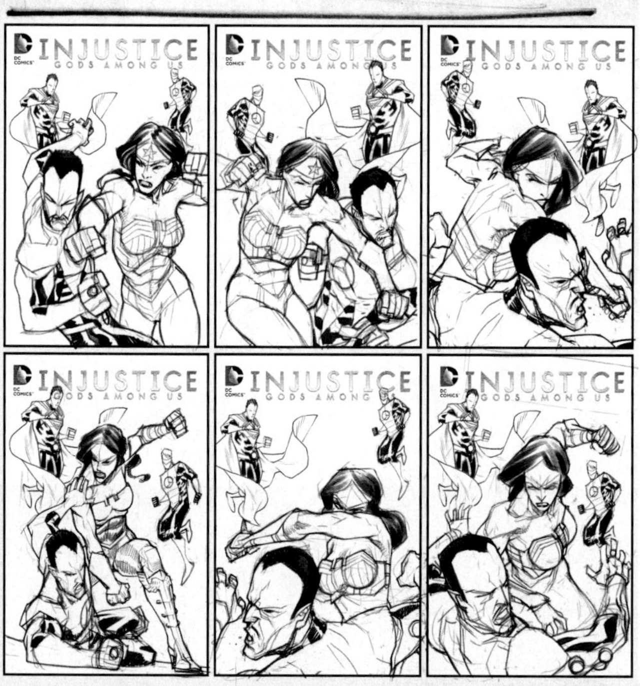
INJUSTICE
GODS AMONG US

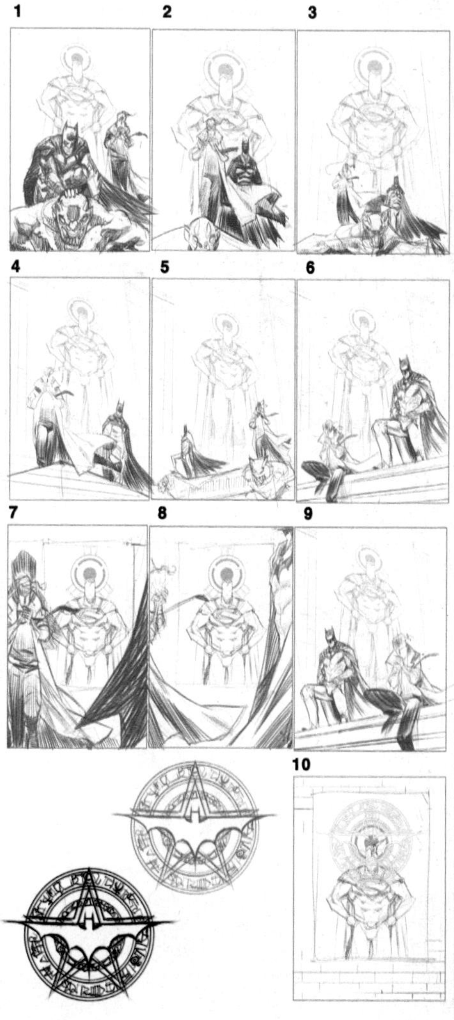
1
2
3
4
5
6
7
8
9
10

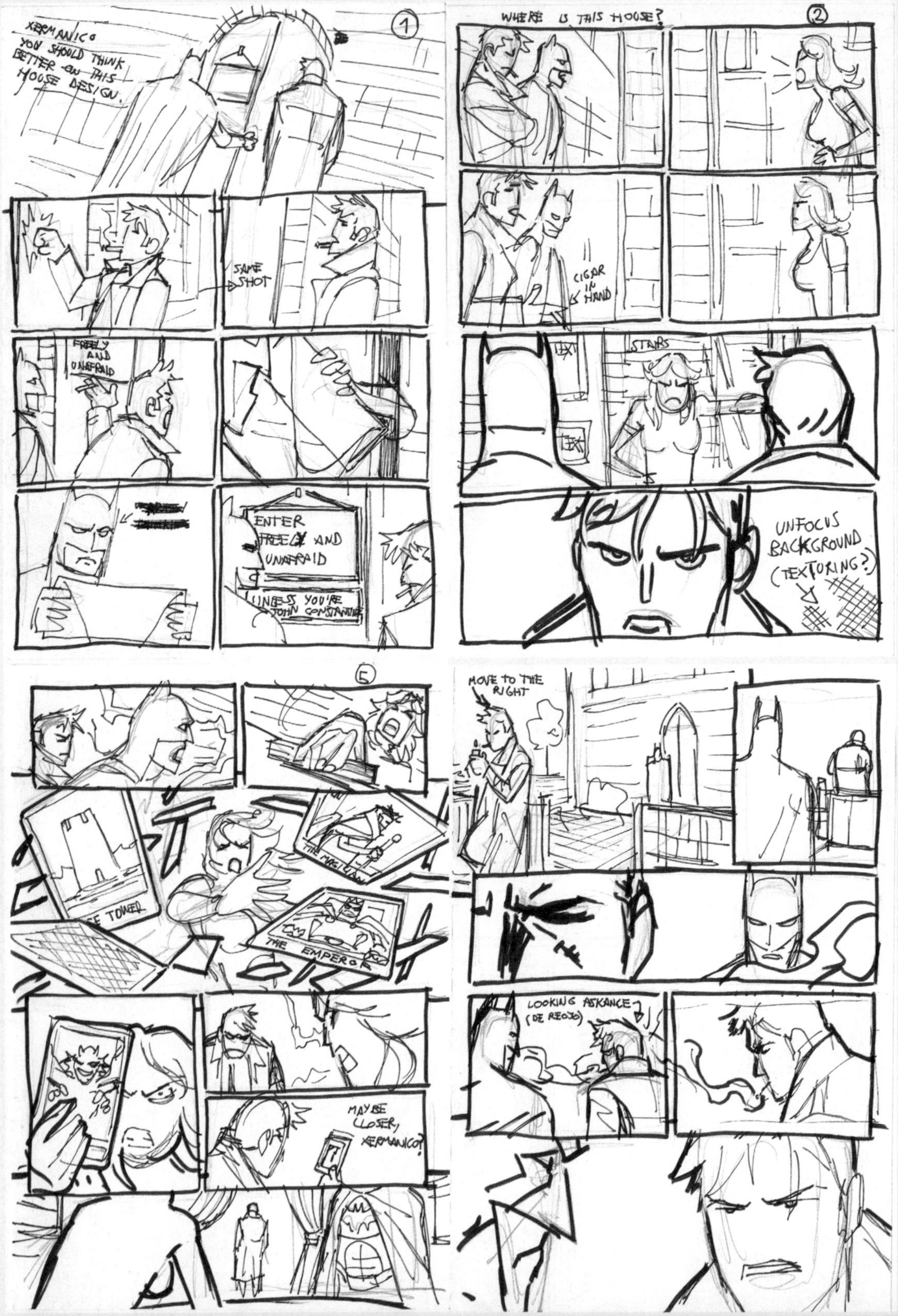
1
XERMANICO
YOU SHOULD THINK
BETTER ON THIS
HOUSE DESIGN.
SAME SHOT
FREELY AND UNAFRAID
ENTER FREELY AND UNAFRAID
UNLESS YOU'RE JOHN CONSTANTINE
WHERE IS THIS HOUSE?
2
CIGAR IN HAND
TEXT
STAIRS
TEXT
UNFOCUS BACKGROUND (TEXTURING?)
5
THE MAGICIAN
THE EMPEROR
MAYBE CLOSER, XERMANICO?
MOVE TO THE RIGHT
LOOKING ASKANCE
(DE REOJO)

[redacted]

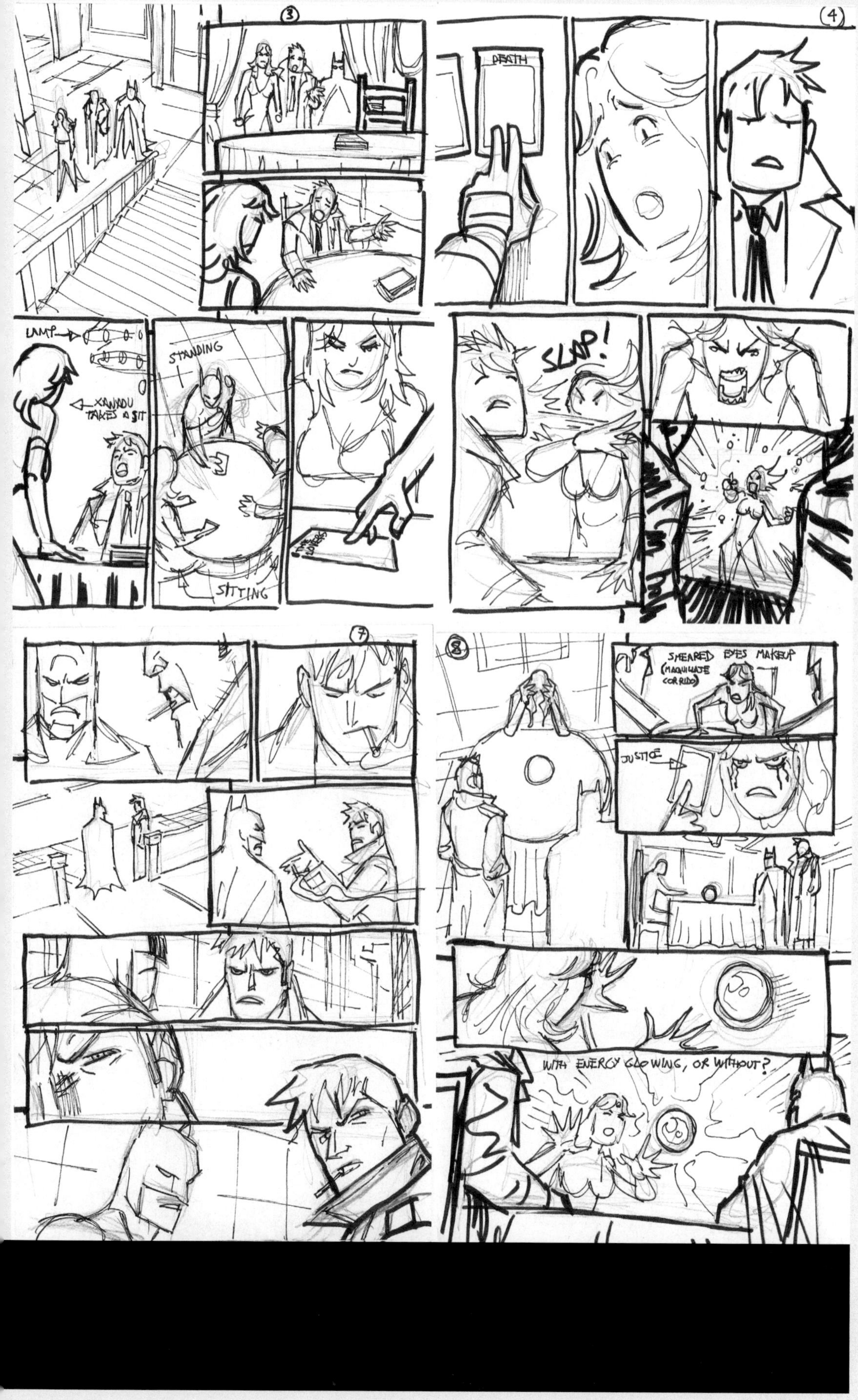
3
4
DEATH
LAMP
XANADU TAKES A SIT
STANDING
THE LOVERS
SITTING
SLAP!
7
8
SMEARED EYES MAKEUP
(MAQUILLAJE CORRIDO)
JUSTICE
WITH ENERGY GLOWING, OR WITHOUT?

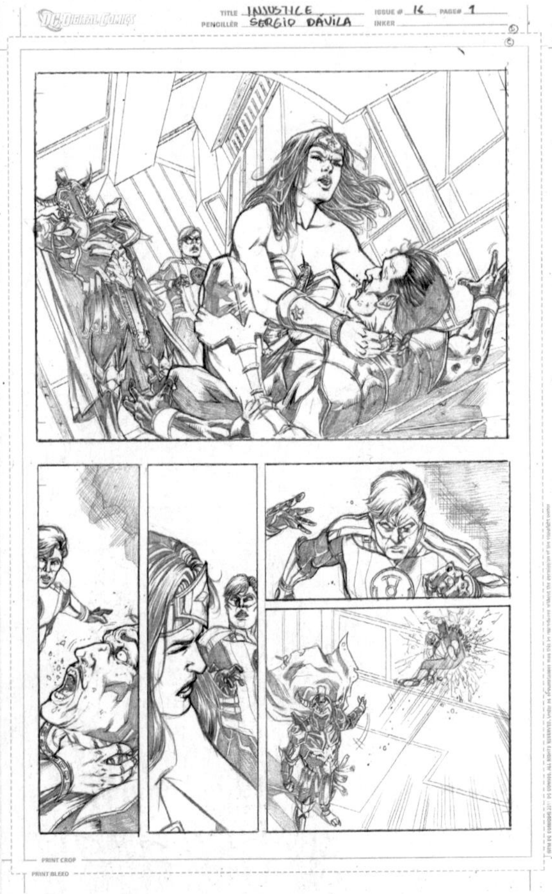
TITLE INJUSTICE
ISSUE # 16 PAGE# 1
PENCILLER SERGIO DÁVILA
INKER
PRINT CROP
PRINT BLEED
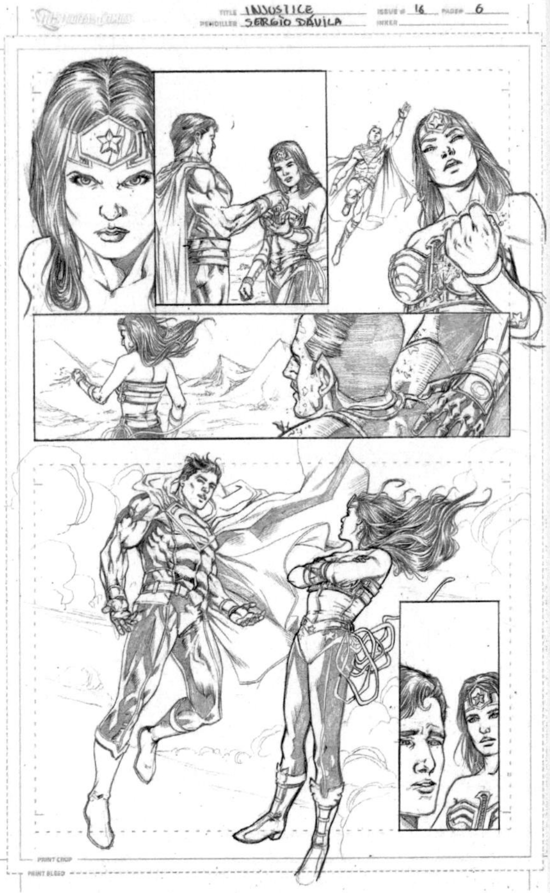
TITLE INJUSTICE
ISSUE # 16 PAGE# 6
PENCILLER SERGIO DÁVILA
INKER
PRINT CROP
PRINT BLEED
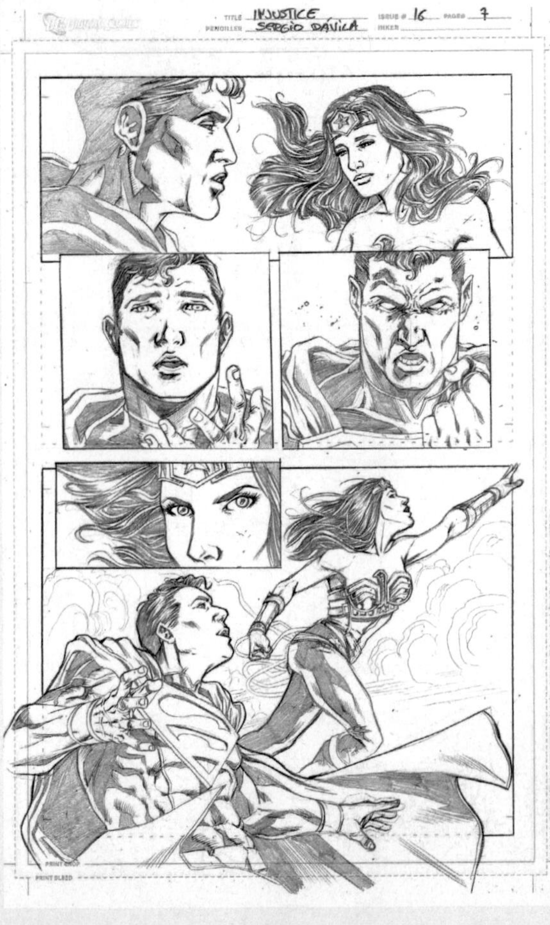
TITLE INJUSTICE
ISSUE # 16 PAGE# 7
PENCILLER SERGIO DÁVILA
INKER
PRINT CROP
PRINT BLEED
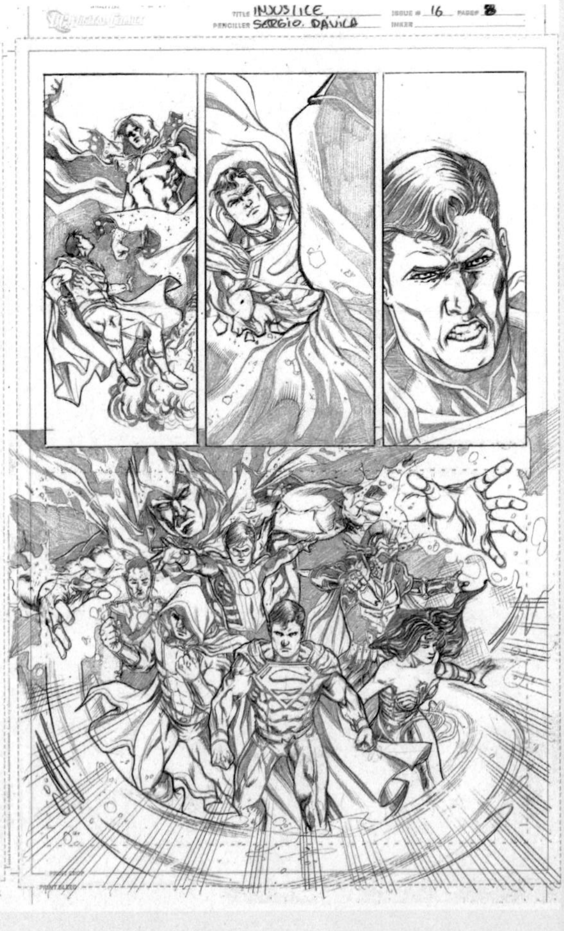
TITLE INJUSTICE
ISSUE # 16 PAGE# 8
PENCILLER SERGIO DÁVILA
INKER
PRINT BLEED

TITLE INJUSTICE
PENCILLER SERGIO DÁVILA
ISSUE # 16 PAGE# 9
INKER

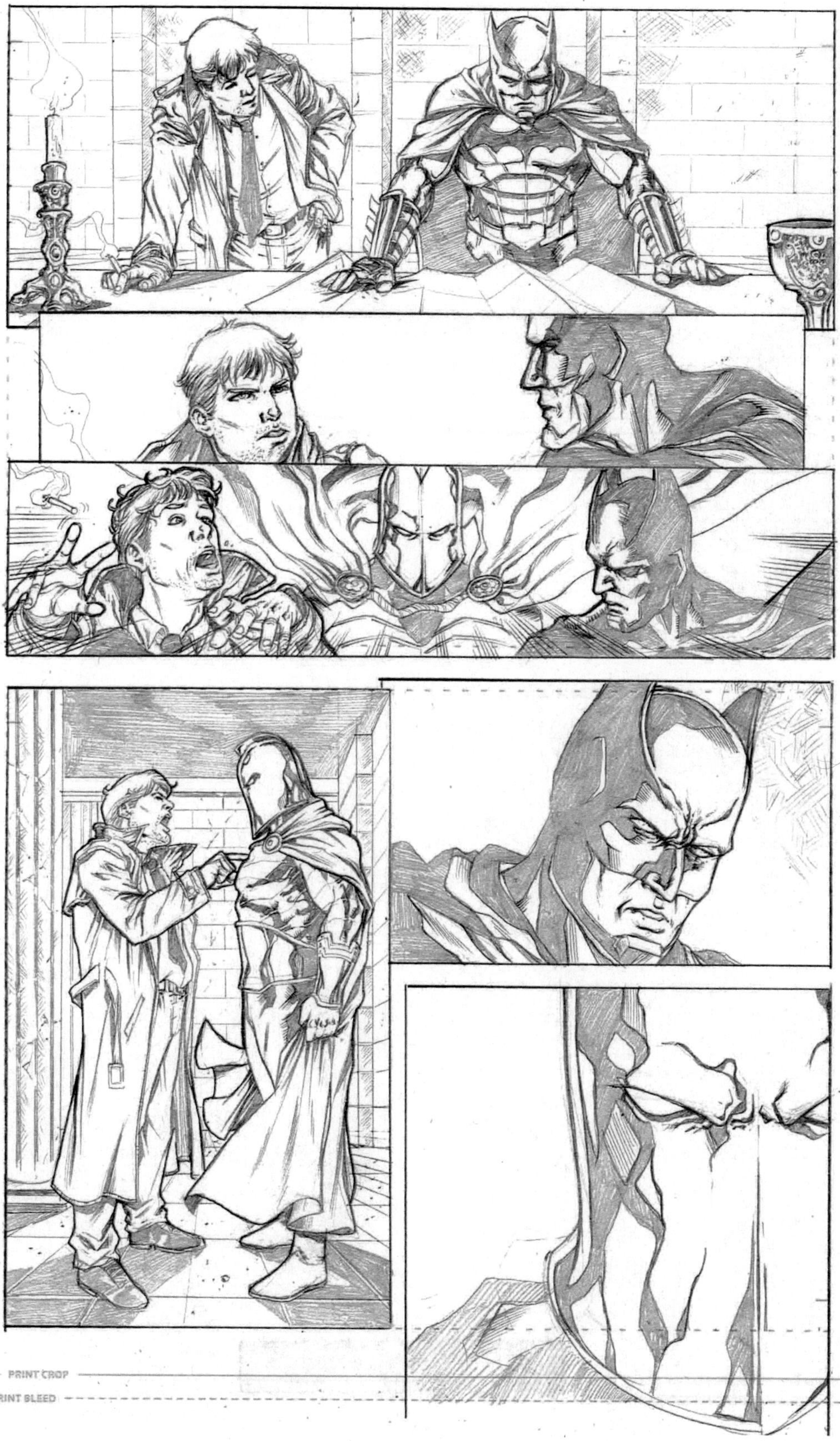

PRINT CROP
PRINT BLEED

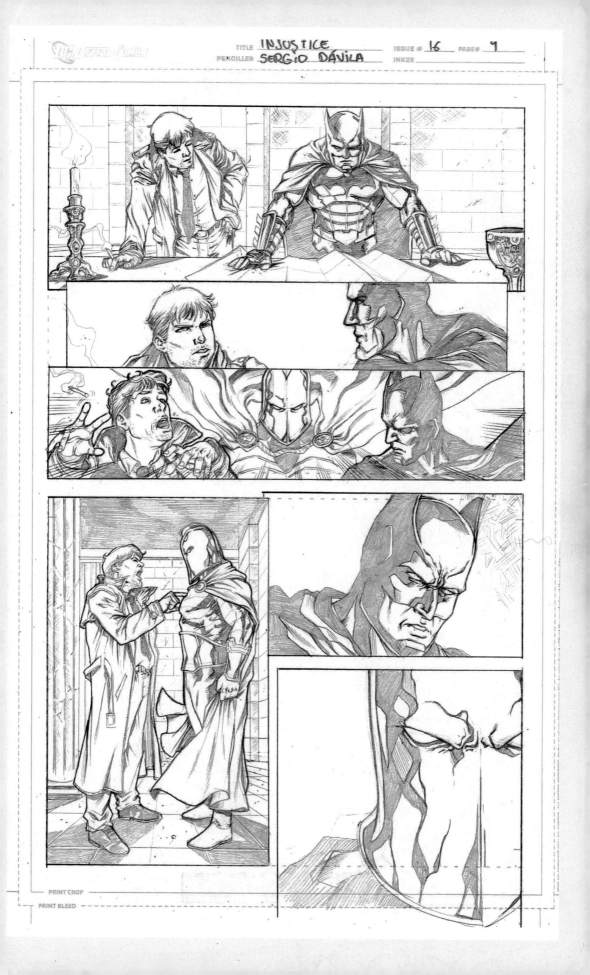